Social History of Africa

THE AFRICAN
RANK-AND-FILE

THE AFRICAN RANK-AND-FILE

SOCIAL IMPLICATIONS OF COLONIAL MILITARY SERVICE IN THE KING'S AFRICAN RIFLES, 1902–1964

Timothy H. Parsons

HEINEMANN   JAMES CURREY   DAVID PHILIP   EAEP   FOUNTAIN
Portsmouth, NH   Oxford   Cape Town   Nairobi   Kampala

Heinemann	James Currey Ltd.	David Philip Publishers (Pty) Ltd.	EAEP	Fountain Publishers
A division of Reed Elsevier Inc.	73 Botley Road	208 Werdmuller Centre	PO Box 45314	PO Box 488
361 Hanover Street	Oxford OX2 0BS	Claremont 7708	Nairobi	Kampala
Portsmouth, NH 03801-3912	United Kingdom	South Africa	Kenya	Uganda
USA				

www.heinemann.com

Offices and agents throughout the world

ISBN 0–325–00141–3 (Heinemann cloth)
ISBN 0–325–00140–5 (Heinemann paper)
ISBN 0–85255–687–X (James Currey cloth)
ISBN 0–85255–637–3 (James Currey paper)

British Library Cataloguing in Publication Data
Parsons, Timothy H.
The African rank-and-file : social implications of colonial military service in the King's African Rifles, 1902–1964.—(Social history of Africa series)
1. Great Britain. Army. King's African Rifles   2. Soldiers—Africa, East—Social conditions—20th century   3. Africa, East—Social conditions—20th century
I. Title
355.3'1'09676
ISBN 0–85255–637–3 (James Currey paper)   0–85255–687–X (James Currey cloth)

Library of Congress Cataloging-in-Publication Data

Parsons, Timothy, 1962–
The African rank-and-file : social implications of colonial military service in the King's African Rifles, 1902–1964 / Timothy H. Parsons.
p. cm. — (Social history of Africa, 1099–8098)
Includes bibliographical references and index.
ISBN 0–325–00141–3 (alk. paper)
ISBN 0–325–00140–5 (pbk. : alk. paper)
1. Great Britain. Army. King's African Rifles—History.   2. Soldiers—Africa, East—Social conditions.   3. Africa, East—Social conditions—20th century. I. Title.   II. Series.
UA855.5 .P38   1999
355.3'51'09676—dc21   99–25009

Paperback cover photo: Askaris embarking for Madagascar, August 1942. Courtesy of the Trustees of the Imperial War Museum, London (K2613). Reprinted with permission.

Printed in the United States of America on acid-free paper.

03 02 01 00 99 SB 1 2 3 4 5 6 7 8 9

To
George Parsons, Frances Marx, and Ann Parsons

CONTENTS

ILLUSTRATIONS

MAP

TABLES

FIGURES

ACKNOWLEDGMENTS

This project was funded by a Fulbright Grant and a Social Science Research Council–MacArthur Foundation Fellowship in International Peace and Security. The research began under the supervision of Sara Berry and Philip Curtin. John Lonsdale merits a special word of thanks for providing me with warm encouragement and most of the initial contacts that set the study in motion.

Friends and colleagues who helped me with my research in Kenya include Henry Mutoro, David Sperling, B. K. ole Kantai, H. K. Nyongesa, Richard Ambani, Peterson Kithuka Nthiwa, Jeremiah Kitunda, Derek Peterson, and Tom Gensheimer. In Malawi, I owe a special debt of gratitude to Kings and Jean Phiri and to, Diana, Tim, Jeff, and Chris Cammack. While working in Great Britain, I received advice and encouragement from Lawrence Freedman, David Anderson, David Killingray, and Douglas Johnson. I am also particularly grateful to John Nunneley, Brigadier Michael Biggs, and George Shepperson of the King's African Rifles Dinner Club. Citations from the Dimoline Papers are made with the permission of the Liddell Hart Centre for Military Archives.

While writing the manuscript, I was a Visiting Fellow at the University of Rochester's Frederick Douglass Institute, where I benefited from the advice and guidance of Cary Fraser, Elias Mandala, and especially the late Sam Nolutshungu. Finally, I must thank my friends and colleagues Richard Davis and Priscilla Stone of Washington University in St. Louis for their support and encouragement.

ABBREVIATIONS

AAG	Assistant Adjutant General
AAPC	African Auxiliary Pioneer Corps
AHR	Annual Historical Report
AIM	African Inland Mission
AR	Annual Report
ASBL	African Section of the British Legion, Kenya
BESL	British Empire Ex-Services League
BNCO	British Non-Commissioned Officer
CAC	Central Africa Command
CAF	Central African Federation
CAR	Central African Rifles
CCK	Christian Council of Kenya
CEB	Central Employment Bureau
CIGS	Chief of the Imperial General Staff
CMS	Church Missionary Society
CNC	Chief Native Commissioner, Kenya
CnC	Commander-in-Chief
CO	Colonial Office
CPK	Church of the Province of Kenya
CPL	Corporal
CRB	Civil Reabsorption Board
CRO	Civil Reabsorption Officer
CSEAG	Chief Secretary, East African Governor's Conference
CSK	Chief Secretary, Kenya
CSM	Church of Scotland Mission
CSNY	Chief Secretary, Nyasaland
CST	Chief Secretary, Tanganyika

CSU	Chief Secretary, Uganda
DA & QMG	Deputy Adjutant and Quartermaster-General
DACG	Deputy Assistant Chaplain General
DC	District Commissioner
DO	District Officer
DWO	District Welfare Officer
EA	East Africa
EAA	East Africa Artillery
EAAC	East Africa Armoured Corps
EAAChD	East Africa Army Chaplains Department
EAAEC	East Africa Army Education Corps
EAAMC	East Africa Army Medical Corps
EAAOC	East Africa Army Ordnance Corps
EAASC	East Africa Army Service Corps
EAC	East Africa Command
EACF	East African Construction Force
EACMP	East Africa Corps of Military Police
EAE	East Africa Engineers
EAEME	East Africa Electrical and Mechanical Engineers
EAHC	East Africa High Commission
EALFO	East African Land Forces Organization
EAMLS	East African Military Labour Service
EAPLO	East Africa Political Liaison Officer
EAR	East Africa Rifles
FSS	Field Security Section
GOC	General Officer Commanding
GRO	General Routine Order
HoR	Handing-Over Report
HoW	History of the War
IBEAC	Imperial British East Africa Company
IGR	Inspector General's Report
IR	Intelligence Report
IWM	Imperial War Museum, London
JLC	Junior Leader Company
KANU	Kenya African National Union
KAR	King's African Rifles
KAR OCA	King's African Rifles Old Comrades Association, Kenya
KAU	Kenya African Union
KCA	Kikuyu Central Association
KIO	Kenya Information Officer
KNA	Kenyan National Archives, Nairobi
LCK	Labour Commissioner, Kenya

LCN	Labour Commissioner, Nyasaland
LCPL	Lance Corporal
LHC	Liddell Hart Centre
LPC	Last Pay Certificate
MCP	Malawi Congress Party
ME	Middle East
MNA	Malawi National Archives, Zomba
NAM	National Army Museum, London
NCO	non-commissioned officer
NESUK	National Ex-Servicemen's Union of Kenya
NFP	Northern Frontier Province, Kenya
NRR	Northern Rhodesia Regiment
NY	Nyasaland
NZA	Nyanza Province, Kenya
O/C	Officer Commanding
ODC	Overseas Defence Committee
ODRP	Oxford Development Records Project
PC	Provincial Commissioner
PCRO	Principal Civil Reabsorption Officer
POSB	Post Office Savings Bank
POW	prisoner of war
PRO	Public Record Office, London
PTE	Private
QHR	Quarterly Historical Report
QR	Quarterly Report
RAEC	Royal Army Education Corps
RAR	Rhodesian African Rifles
RC	Roman Catholic
RHL	Rhodes House Library, Oxford
RVP	Rift Valley Province, Kenya
S & T	Supply and Transport
SBIS	Special Branch Intelligence Summary
SCC	Somaliland Camel Corps
SEAC	Southeast Asia Command
SGT	Sergeant
TANU	Tanganyika African National Union
VD	Venereal Disease
UMA	Ukamba Members Association
WNLA	Witwatersrand Native Labour Association
WO	War Office
WOPC	Warrant Officer Platoon Commander

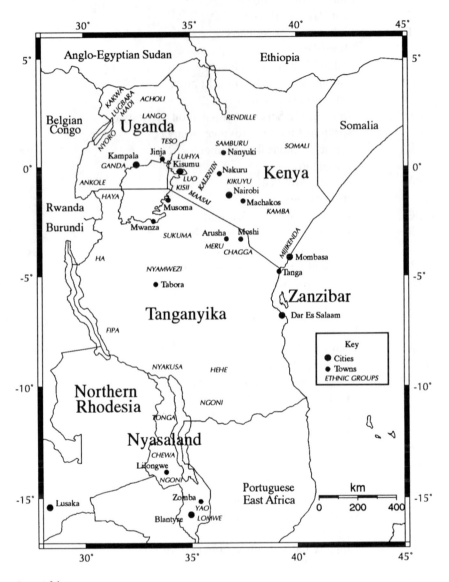

East Africa

1

INTRODUCTION

Colonial military service must be examined in its social context to understand the full complexity of African experiences in the King's African Rifles (KAR). Britain needed African soldiers to maintain its authority in East Africa and endeavored to secure their cooperation through a variety of coercive and remunerative measures, which in turn set them apart from the general population. The willingness of Africans to serve in the colonial army was determined by a variety of social and economic factors that changed over time. Aside from the absolute necessity that askaris[1] (East African soldiers) be politically reliable, the nature and character of their service were determined largely by a process of conflict and accommodation between colonial governments, British officers, and rank-and-file African soldiers. Contested areas included labor, pay, food and shelter, ethnic identity, physical appearance, health, religious belief, gender, sexual relations, family life, and social status. These issues were never decided solely on the basis of military utility; ultimately the inferior position of Africans in colonial society influenced every aspect of service in the King's African Rifles. Thus, the social history of military service in East Africa offers significant insights into the tensions and contradictions of British colonial rule.

THE NECESSITY OF A COLONIAL ARMY

From 1902 to 1964, the King's African Rifles comprised the armed forces of Kenya, Uganda, Tanganyika (modern Tanzania), and Nyasaland (modern Malawi). Malawi is tied economically to southern Africa, but colonial Nyasaland was part of East Africa for military and strategic purposes. At various times, East African military authorities also administered the Somaliland Camel Corps, the Northern Rhodesia Regiment, and the Rhodesian African Rifles, but these were never formally part of the King's African Rifles. The European armed forces of Southern Rhodesia and South Africa had no connection with the KAR, and the Royal West

African Frontier Force, Britain's West African colonial army, was also an entirely separate entity.

The King's African Rifles was an infantry regiment that linked lightly armed infantry battalions raised in various territories of British East Africa.[2] In peacetime, the KAR was small, generally consisting of five to seven battalions of 400 to 600 askaris each. Before the Second World War, each battalion was paid for and administered by the territory in which it was recruited and was therefore under the jurisdiction of the Colonial Office. The War Office only assumed direct responsibility for the colonial forces in wartime.

As this book is organized thematically, it is important to pay close attention to the main chronological divisions that marked the development of the King's African Rifles. From roughly 1880 until 1914, these territorial forces consisted of improvised units that amounted to little more than lightly armed African militias. During World War I, the KAR grew to almost 32,000 infantrymen and was supported by an estimated half a million African non-combatants, conscripted as carriers to transport supplies and ammunition. The colonial army shrank to its original size during the inter-war era but underwent a massive expansion during World War II, when over 320,000 askaris were in uniform.[3] Motorized transport eliminated the need for carriers, but military authorities recruited large numbers of uniformed African laborers to support the vast East African forces. The necessities of modern warfare also spawned a host of African support and technical units, including artillery, engineers, and signals, medical, and education corps. The King's African Rifles returned officially to local control after the war, but the British government continued to borrow individual battalions for imperial missions.

While East African soldiers served occasionally as imperial troops and provided frontier defense for Kenya and Uganda, the colonial army's primary mission was internal security. Yet the Regiment was not a police force; its paramount peacetime function was to intimidate potential African opponents of the colonial regime. Ultimately, the King's African Rifles provided the coercive force that made British rule in East Africa possible. European colonialism subjugated or destroyed indigenous political institutions, restructured African economic systems, and introduced Western cultural values. As Mahmood Mamdani has observed:

> Beyond the market, there was only one way of driving land and labor out of the world of the customary: force. The day-to-day violence of the colonial system was embedded in customary Native Authorities in the local state, not in civil power at the center. Yet we must not forget that customary local authority was reinforced and backed up by central civil power.[4]

While the colonial system created new opportunities, it more often brought considerable hardship to a significant segment of the subject population. The primary function of the KAR as an agent of the central civil power was to ensure Africans did not use force to resist these changes.

THE KING'S AFRICAN RIFLES IN HISTORICAL PERSPECTIVE

All modern governments endeavor to monopolize the instruments of lethal force, but the colonial African case is significant because the armed forces that supported foreign rule were almost exclusively composed of Africans. British officers and non-commissioned officers (NCOs) rarely constituted more than six percent of a 600-man KAR battalion. Moreover, no regular British infantry unit was deployed in Kenya between 1916 and 1952 (the advent of the Mau Mau Emergency), and the British Army was never stationed in Uganda, Tanganyika, or Nyasaland. A British battalion cost four times as much as a KAR battalion, and the East African colonies were not valuable or strategically important enough to justify the expense of a European garrison.[5] Therefore, the stability and security of British rule in East Africa depended largely upon African soldiers. European settlers raised doubts about the wisdom of enlisting subject peoples, but since individual territories paid for their own local defense, KAR askaris were the only soldiers they could afford.

While the idea of an authoritarian state relying on an army of disenfranchised subjects as its primary means of defense may appear to be a unique adaptation of the British Empire, in reality the King's African Rifles was one of the last incarnations of a military system common to many pre-industrial multiethnic societies. The national citizen armies taken as the norm today are relatively recent innovations that sprang from nineteenth-century western Europe. Military service is an arduous and dangerous occupation, and pre-industrial empires often recruited politically marginal groups for their armed forces. These soldiers were either drawn from the lower classes or subject ethnic groups or, in the most extreme cases, were actually enslaved. Generally considered disposable, they relieved dominant classes (who usually served as officers) of the onerous task of combat. As Maury Feld has noted:

> In its most naked sense, the simple existence of an armed force answers the question of how much an individual is worth to society and how much society is worth to him. The decisions—about who is to serve, in what capacity, and for what sort of compensation—describe the social policies of a political system. . . . Military service is one area of social activity that continually calls into question the costs of commonly shared goals and that deliberately sets a price on human life.[6]

The lives of politically marginal soldiers were cheap and could be sacrificed in large numbers without incurring condemnation from society as a whole.

It is therefore worthwhile to question African motives for serving in colonial armies. Over the past thirty years, historians of Africa have paid little attention to rank-and-file colonial soldiers. Myron Echenberg and Nancy Lawler have explored the nature of African service in France's *Tirailleurs Sénégalais*, but the French colonial army relied primarily on wholesale conscription and as such offers limited insights into why most of the Africans in the King's African Rifles were nominal volunteers. Kenneth Grundy's characterization of black Africans in the apartheid-era South African Defense Force as "soldiers without politics" provides a more useful comparative model vis-à-vis British East Africa: "The readiness of some blacks to join the armed forces clearly grows out of a perception of their economic prospects offset by their sense of political and social alienation."[7] Yet with the exception of Anthony Clayton and David Killingray's *Khaki and Blue*, and a few short articles by African historians, the only detailed works on Britain's East African colonial army are a handful of semi-official military histories published over forty years ago.[8] Official histories of the KAR portray askaris as loyal servants of "Kingi Georgi" (King George) and the British Empire, whereas African historians depict African servicemen either as men "awed" by European prestige, and thus duped by "intensive propaganda," or as collaborators and self-interested mercenaries.[9]

Most institutional histories of the King's African Rifles were written from the top down and tend to mistake the discipline of African troops for either loyalty or collaboration. Much of the research dealing with British colonial Africa has been unconsciously influenced by these biases. Historians have tended to treat African soldiers as an undifferentiated unit of analysis, when in fact they were divided by ethnicity, education, military specialization, and territorial origin. To understand the motives and aspirations of African soldiers, one must study the social and economic factors that influenced their recruitment and service. In an insightful study of African labor in the port of Mombasa, Frederick Cooper argued that "dockworkers" were an unworkable unit of research. He found it more effective to "explore the place of dockwork in the lives of people who at times did other things, and in the wider context of family, village, and regional life. To do urban labor history, in other words, is also to do rural history."[10]

The same could be said for African soldiers. Although askaris served throughout East Africa, their origins were overwhelmingly rural. It is therefore most productive to consider them a class of unskilled, but privileged, labor migrants. As was the case for African miners in central and southern Africa, most askaris returned to their rural homes after retirement. They received no pensions until the 1950s and depended on relatives for food and shelter in their old age. KAR battalions were cheaper than comparable European units because British officials transferred the social costs of reproducing askaris to the African countryside.[11] The link between the colonial army and civilian migrant labor was not merely academic; most African servicemen viewed their enlistment in the KAR as a long-term labor contract. As a Malawian veteran explained to Melvin Page: "[Military service] is just like the way people go to the mines in South Africa."[12]

In one sense, the colonial African soldiery was a kind of labor aristocracy. Historians of Africa usually define labor aristocrats as a class of skilled and educated African workers whose expertise was needed to run the colonial economy. They served as artisans, technicians, and clerks in return for superior pay and benefits.[13] Most KAR askaris, however, were unskilled illiterates; their special "talent" was their willingness to accept military discipline. It did not take much expertise to follow orders or use a gun, but the colonial regime needed men willing to use lethal force against the civil population. Thus, it sought to co-opt African soldiers by treating them as a privileged class; military service was the most lucrative form of wage labor for young unskilled African males. Yet uncertainty over the extent of these privileges also produced most of the tensions and contradictions of colonial military service. British officials worried that the African soldiery's wealth and prestige would upset the racial hierarchy of colonial society, and askaris had to weigh the rewards of military service against the colonial army's inherent physical risks and social alienation.

The army transformed Africans into disciplined askaris by weakening their ties to mainstream society. In addition to keeping soldiers physically segregated from civilians through formal regulations, the KAR exploited African ethnic divisions through "martial" recruiting policies borrowed from the Indian Army. British officers preferred soldiers from groups they judged to possess "natural" militaristic qualities, and in most cases, the value of a recruit was determined solely by his ethnic origins. This strategy was entirely in keeping with the doctrine of indirect rule, which treated Africans as members of a "tribe" rather than as individuals. British colonial doctrine held that African "tribes" were distinct cultural units, each with a common language, distinctive social system, and an established body of customary law. Indirect rule co-opted "traditional" rulers of these "tribes" into the lower levels of the colonial administration, where they served as brokers between merchant capital and African household labor.[14] Yet many African "tribal" identities were actually twentieth-century creations, and colonial officials invented "chiefs" and "headmen" for societies that lacked institutions of centralized political authority.[15]

KAR officers similarly celebrated, and sometimes fabricated, "martial traditions" for their soldiers. In reality "martial" reputations in East Africa were based largely on the disposition of large numbers of men from a particular ethnic group to accept military discipline. Their willingness to enlist was determined primarily by social and economic factors that changed over time, which meant "martial" status was fluid. Ethnic groups that derived considerable wealth and status from the KAR tended to make military service a defining feature of their communal identities, a process which Cynthia Enloe has termed the "Gurkha syndrome."[16] Most askaris considered themselves superior to better-educated "non-martial races," who often opposed the colonial regime through overtly political means. They had few reservations about using force against such groups. Yet the necessity of granting African soldiers special benefits and privileges also encouraged them to consider themselves superior to all civilians, including members of their own ethnic groups. While this built esprit de corps, it also raised the threat of Praetorianism. The development of an African military corporate identity undermined the very foundations of indirect rule by weakening "tribal" loyalties.

These inherent tensions in the King's African Rifles reflected the larger contradictions of British rule in East Africa. As Bruce Berman and John Lonsdale have shown, the Kenyan colonial state was in the difficult position of trying to balance the demands of metropolitan capital to restructure local systems of production while at the same time preventing economic change from undermining the "tribal notables" who played a vital role in the institutions of indirect rule.[17] Similarly, military officials sought to discipline African soldiers by offering them privileges and pay that set them apart from the greater civilian population. The colonial governments, on the other hand, worried that the army's generosity would create a privileged class of "detribalized" veterans that would challenge the preeminence of the "native authorities," thereby weakening indirect rule. British officials therefore followed a policy of "retribalization," which emphasized the communal obligations of askaris and often compelled them to return to rural life after they were discharged.

African servicemen both consciously and unconsciously exploited these contradictions to seek greater rights and status. Ann Laura Stoler and Frederick Cooper are absolutely correct when they remind us: "One of the most basic forms of colonial control . . . depended on soldiers who were simultaneously coerced and coercing, who enforced the will of the elite yet made demands themselves."[18] The struggles of the African rank-and-file with the colonial regime were part of an ongoing debate over the boundaries of military service in colonial society. This line of analysis follows Cooper's suggestion that historians of Africa should pay closer attention to "the ways in which movements among Africans and colonial interventions shaped each other."[19] The contradictory nature of African service in the King's African Rifles demonstrates that British colonialism was not the omnipotent monolithic force that many studies of colonial Africa have assumed it to be. The KAR was one of Cooper's points of "mutual intelligibility and interaction" where Africans dealt with the colonial ruling classes on an intimate and systematic basis. As a result, African soldiers had considerable influence in determining the form and content of colonial policy. To put it another way, the British may have set the rules of the colonial game, but it was their African intermediaries who determined how it was played.

METHOD

Most of the archival work and field interviews for this project were carried out in Kenya and Malawi.[20] While local conditions of service varied in each East African territory, these countries are the most logical places to study the experiences of rank-and-file askaris. Their national armies retain more of the organizational framework and traditions of their original KAR battalions than those of either Uganda or Tanzania. Moreover, Kenya and Nyasaland were the primary suppliers of manpower to the KAR. Kenya was the only territory to maintain three peacetime KAR battalions, and the headquarters of the East Africa Command was in Nairobi. In 1951, fifty-one percent of all African soldiers in the KAR were Kenyans. Nyasaland had minimal internal security needs but supported two KAR battalions, even though it had the smallest population of the four East African territories. By comparison, Uganda and Tanganyika each raised only a single battalion. Nyasaland's economic ties to southern Africa made it a leading exporter of African labor, and it had a higher per capita rate of enlistment than any other territory. In 1937, almost two percent of the Protectorate's adult male work force was in the army.[21]

A comparison of military service in Kenya and Nyasaland therefore provides a reasonably representative picture of African service in the KAR. Furthermore, since the KAR was an inter-territorial force, the national archives of Kenya and Malawi also contain a great deal of material dealing with military matters in Uganda, Tanganyika, British Somaliland, and the Rhodesias. Additional detailed information on East African colonial military policy in general is available in the British Public Record Office and various archives throughout Great Britain. These sources provide a wealth of corroborative data and support informed hypotheses about the nature of colonial military service in all of East Africa.

This book also relies heavily on the personal accounts of former British officers and African veterans and their families in Kenya, Malawi, and Great Britain. Locating and communicating with the approximately 130 African ex-servicemen interviewed for this project was a tremendous challenge. Since there are no detailed military personnel records from the colonial era, African veterans were found through word of mouth by undergraduate research assistants who searched their home areas for ex-servicemen. For reasons that will be made clear in this book, many former askaris are suspicious when asked about their military service by foreigners. The research assistants put them at ease and provided translation assistance for informants who were not fluent in English or Swahili. While this approach yielded a rich variety of material, it also had drawbacks. Translators invariably influence the material they help to collect. In some cases, veterans may have emphasized the most negative aspects of military service to establish their nationalist credentials in the eyes of their young countrymen.

Ideally, it would have been best to have conducted all of the interviews in the vernacular of each informant. Even if that were possible, however, it would still have been difficult to break through the barrier of distrust that comes from a foreigner asking pointed questions about the colonial military. Some former askaris continue to feel a sense of betrayal over their "abandonment" by the colonial army, whereas others still hope to collect unpaid pensions. In one exceptional but still illustrative case, a handful of elderly but hale Kenyan veterans described themselves as reservists and demanded to see a government research permit before discussing "sensitive" military information.[22] Such men were reluctant to have their interviews recorded. Therefore, informants are listed by random numbers rather than names, and many of the African accounts in this book are short and fragmentary.

While the testimonies of British officers and colonial officials presented few translation problems, most former officers were equally influenced by contemporary political issues. Acutely aware of current popular and academic criticism of the colonial enterprise, they are extremely sensitive to charges that they exploited the African rank-and-file. Many ex-officers, particularly veterans of the Second World War, remain sincerely concerned with the welfare of former askaris and disdain officers who did not appreciate their askaris. As a result, they tended to be as concerned with proving their benevolent paternalism as African veterans were with establishing themselves as anti-colonial nationalists. Furthermore, several retired officers also desired not to be identified by name when recounting negative aspects of the colonial military.

Former askaris can easily provide detailed personal accounts of their enlistment in the King's African Rifles, their experiences in the army, their perceptions of the colonial military, and their post-service careers. Their testimony offers a wealth of rich and diverse information on the day-to-day lives and aspirations of the African rank-and-file. Yet as former enlisted men, most ex-askaris have little understanding of the larger institution of the colonial army. It is also impossible to write from the point of view of the "typical" East African serviceman. The army's regional and ethnic recruiting base changed considerably over time, and as a class, askaris were divided by occupation, education, and experience.

In practice, the KAR itself was the only common point of reference for the tens of thousands of Africans who served in the colonial forces. The King's African Rifles was an African army where distinctions of rank between commissioned officers and enlisted men were sharpened by race and culture. For all intents and purposes, the KAR's British and African personnel inhabited different worlds, and only senior African NCOs who spoke both English and Swahili could bridge the two spheres. Serious disciplinary issues in the KAR were caused by conflicting perceptions of the nature of colonial military service. These differing viewpoints are still evident in the contradictory recollections of retired officers and former members of the African rank-and-file and are inflamed by the influence of modern political sensibilities on oral history.

ORGANIZATION

This book examines the inherent tensions in colonial military service by exploring the daily lives and aspirations of rank-and-file askaris in six thematic chapters. After the introduction, the second chapter lays out the history of the King's African Rifles from the perspective of the African soldiery and analyzes how the changing mission and organization of the Regiment set the parameters of military service. The inability of civil and military officials to agree on the role of African soldiers in colonial society created opportunities for the African rank-and-file to enhance their social status.

Chapter 3 examines the shifting social and economic stimuli that drew Africans into the colonial army and is concerned primarily with the political economy of recruiting and connections between stereotypes of "martial race," patterns of enlistment, and ethnic identity. While the colonial governments conscripted Africans for military labor (and sometimes indirectly for combat units) during the world wars, most askaris joined the army out of necessity, attracted by either relatively lucrative military wages or the security and privilege of government service. The martial stereotypes used in African recruiting were actually an index of the changing political economy of recruitment. British officers considered "martial race" an innate cultural attribute, but it was actually a descriptive label signifying an acceptance of military discipline. In reality, the willingness of Africans to serve in the King's African Rifles was based on the extent of their integration into the colonial economy. African societies were most "martial" when taxation and land shortages forced them to seek paid employment, and educational limitations and racial distinctions in hiring limited their options to unpaid wage labor.

Chapter 4 explores the unique culture of the KAR and its implications for colonial soldiers as a class. As the only group in colonial society with access to the instruments of lethal force, British officials sought to insulate the African soldiery from the greater civilian population. This significant degree of social isolation was accomplished through the evolution of a distinct military culture that encouraged askaris to see themselves as different from, and superior to, African civilians. Yet the ill-defined scope of military service in colonial East Africa created tensions between military officials, civil authorities, and African soldiers. KAR officers sought to reward askaris by granting them special privileges, but civil officials feared that the inflated status of the African soldiery would lead to social disruption and undermine the institutions of indirect rule. African soldiers often exploited these tensions by using their access to military patronage to improve conditions of service and challenge their subordinate position in colonial society.

The competition between the colonial army, askaris, and African women to define the nature of "family" within the context of military service is covered in Chapter 5. African women had considerable value in the colonial army. They provided domestic labor and sexual gratification and reproduced future generations of soldiers. Many British officers, however, viewed women as sources of medical and political contamination and strove to define the military family as monogamous and nuclear to better control the social relations of their soldiers. By comparison, African women who had conjugal relations with askaris sought access to the prestige and patronage of the colonial army but resisted the discipline and paternalism of military life. African servicemen considered access to women and the prerogative of keeping a family in the barracks a perquisite of military service, but they opposed official attempts to define their social relations. Furthermore, the army rewarded reliable service by providing young soldiers with a greater access to women they normally would not have enjoyed in most East African societies until they were much older. Through this, military service reordered domestic relations in martial societies and destabilized prevailing institutions of civil authority.

Chapter 6 addresses the ongoing debate over the loyalties of African soldiers by examining the circumstances under which they challenged their subordinate status. During peacetime the social prestige of military service was generally sufficient to prevent the outbreak of serious unrest. During the world wars, however, many African servicemen objected to their inferior terms of service in comparison to other imperial British troops. Their discontent invariably led to a rise in disciplinary problems in the East African forces. A certain degree of indiscipline is common to all armies, but acts of resistance in the KAR are significant because they also reflect the African soldiery's attempts to redefine their terms of service. Moreover, resistance in the colonial army was a particularly sensitive issue because it had the potential to undermine the illusion of superiority that enabled a small handful of British officers to control the African rank-and-file.

The final chapter of the book analyzes the demobilization of African ex-servicemen and explores their influence on colonial society. The East African governments found it difficult to return African servicemen to civilian life because askaris expected their privileged status to continue after discharge. While service in modern Western armies is considered a civic responsibility, colonial soldiers were denied the rights of full citizenship. Therefore, ex-askaris expected specific material rewards for their sacrifices. The colonial governments, however, were primarily concerned with reintegrating ex-servicemen into rural African society with a minimum of social disruption. Worrying that military service led to "detribalization," making African soldiers less inclined to subordinate their individual interests to their "tribal communities," civil officials sought to "retribalize" African veterans by stripping them of the perquisites that set them apart from African civilians.

This process worked fairly well in peacetime but broke down after the world wars, when tens of thousands of ex-servicemen were discharged in the span of only a few years. British officials worried combat veterans might use their training against the colonial regime and followed a policy of "reabsorption,"which attempted to keep ex-servicemen out of urban areas. The most educated and experienced former askaris, who had the potential to articulate veterans' grievances in political terms, received vocational training and jobs. As a result, educated veterans tended to become successful farmers, ranchers, civil servants, and businessmen, but the majority of rank-and-file askaris were frustrated in their attempts at social and economic advancement. Many historians have argued that disgruntled African veterans of the Second World War were in the vanguard of the anti-colonial movement. Yet with the exception of limited Kikuyu veteran participation in the Mau Mau Emergency, there is little direct evidence for this assertion in East Africa. There was considerable discontent among a large segment of African veterans, but lacking the means to transform their resentment into a viable political movement, they concerned themselves primarily with local economic issues.

NOTES

[1] The Swahili word "askari" is derived from the Arabic term for army, "askar."

[2] Under the British military system, a regiment is essentially an organizational distinction that rarely sees active service as a collective whole. The British Army's primary large-scale operational unit is a brigade group, made up of several battalions that can be affiliated with any number of regiments.

[3] Hubert Moyse-Bartlett, *The King's African Rifles*, (Aldershot: Gale & Polden, 1956), p. 701; Geoffrey Hodges, *The Carrier Corps: Military Labor in the East African Campaign, 1914–1918*, (Westport, CT: Greenwood Press, 1986), pp. 110–11; East African Report to the Colonial Secretary, July 1947, KNA, DEF 10/43/93.

[4] Mahmood Mamdani, *Citizen and Subject: Contemporary Africa and the Legacy of Late Colonialism*, (Princeton, NJ: Princeton University Press, 1996), p. 22.

[5] Defence Minister's ME Tour, June 1957, PRO, DEFE 7/2032; EALFO, Statement of Accounts, 1958/9, KNA, LF 1/259/45.

[6] Maury Feld, *The Structure of Violence: Armed Forces as Social Systems*, (Beverly Hills, CA: Sage Publications, 1977), p. 18.

[7] Myron Echenberg, *Colonial Conscripts: The* Tirailleurs Sénégalais *in French West Africa, 1857–1960*, (Portsmouth, NH: Heinemann, 1991); Nancy Ellen Lawler, *Soldiers*

of Misfortune: Ivoirien Tirailleurs of World War II, (Athens: Ohio University Press, 1992); Kenneth Grundy, *Soldiers Without Politics: Blacks in the South African Armed Forces*, (Berkeley: University of California Press, 1983), p. 13.

[8] Anthony Clayton and David Killingray, *Khaki and Blue: Military and Police in British Colonial Africa*, (Athens: Ohio University Press, 1989); Moyse-Bartlett, *The King's African Rifles*.

[9] Moyse-Bartlett, *The King's African Rifles*, p. xix; Amii Omara-Otunnu, *Politics and the Military in Uganda, 1890–1985*, (London: Macmillan Press, 1987), p. 10; O.J.E. Shiroya, *Kenya and World War Two: African Soldiers in the European War*, (Nairobi: Kenya Literature Bureau, 1985), pp. 9–10; S. Lwanga-Lunyiigo, "Uganda and World War One," *Makerere Historical Journal*, v. 3, (1977), p. 27.

[10] Frederick Cooper, *On the African Waterfront: Urban Disorder and the Transformation of Work in Colonial Mombasa*, (New Haven, CT: Yale University Press, 1987), p. xiii.

[11] Sharon Stichter, *Migrant Labour in Kenya: Capitalism and African Response, 1895–1975*, (London: Longman, 1982), p. 27; Jane Parpart, *Labor and Capital on the African Copperbelt*, (Philadelphia: Temple University Press, 1983), pp. 3, 7, 77.

[12] Melvin Page, "The War of Thangata: Nyasaland and the East African Campaign, 1914–1918," *Journal of African Studies*, v. 19, (1978), pp. 88–89.

[13] Bill Freund, *The African Worker*, (Cambridge: Cambridge University Press, 1988), p. 22; John Saul, "'The Labour Aristocracy' Thesis Reconsidered," in *The Development of an African Working Class: Studies in Class Formation and Action*, edited by Richard Sandbrook and Robin Cohen, (Toronto: University of Toronto Press, 1975), p. 303.

[14] Bruce Berman and John Lonsdale, "Crises of Accumulation, Coercion and the Colonial State: the Development of the Labour Control System," in *Unhappy Valley: Conflict in Kenya & Africa*, edited by John Lonsdale and Bruce Berman, (London: James Curry, 1992), p. 81.

[15] Terence Ranger, "The Invention of Tradition in Colonial Africa," in *The Invention of Tradition*, edited by Eric Hobsbawm and Terence Ranger, (Cambridge: Cambridge University Press, 1983), pp. 221–27; Leroy Vail, "Ethnicity in Southern African History," in *The Creation of Tribalism in Southern Africa*, edited by Leroy Vail, (Berkeley: University of California Press, 1989), p. 3; John Iliffe, *A Modern History of Tanganyika*, (New York: Cambridge University Press, 1979), p. 323.

[16] Cynthia Enloe, *Ethnic Soldiers: State Security in a Divided Society*, (Athens: University of Georgia Press, 1980), p. 26.

[17] Berman and Lonsdale, "Crises of Accumulation, Coercion and the Colonial State," pp. 79–81.

[18] Ann Laura Stoler and Frederick Cooper, "Between Metropole and Colony: Rethinking a Research Agenda," in *Tensions of Empire: Colonial Cultures in a Bourgeois World*, edited by Frederick Cooper and Ann Laura Stoler, (Berkeley: University of California Press, 1997), p. 24.

[19] Frederick Cooper, *Decolonization and African Society: The Labor Question in French and British Africa*, (Cambridge: Cambridge University Press, 1996), p. xi.

[20] The Kenya National Archives is in the process of reclassifying its holdings, and it will be necessary for future researchers to consult the appropriate finding aids to locate the files cited in this book.

[21] Report to GOC EAC, 21 July 1951, KNA, ED 2/17321/175a.

[22] Interviews, #1, #64, #117.

2

THE KING'S AFRICAN RIFLES

The willingness of Africans to serve in the King's African Rifles varied with the changing mission of the colonial army. In peacetime, askaris provided "internal security" by intimidating potential opponents of the colonial regime. Conversely, East Africans served the British Empire directly as front-line combat troops in both world wars. The changing nature of the colonial army framed the process of negotiation and accommodation that shaped African attitudes toward military service. Most askaris found peacetime soldiering relatively undemanding and were less inclined to question their level of compensation. The hazards of actual fighting, however, raised their expectations considerably, and problems often arose in combat units as African soldiers expected pay and benefits to match their greater personal risk. As "protected persons" rather than citizens, they did not serve out of loyalty to the British Empire. In both peace and war, askaris sought to redefine the terms of their service to enhance their status in colonial society.

The status of rank-and-file African soldiers was determined largely by the continuing debate between military and colonial authorities over the mission, control, and funding of the East African forces. On the military side, the War Office, the East Africa Command, and British KAR officers sought to turn the colonial army into a modern combat-ready formation. To this end, they argued for a unified command structure, with military efficiency the determining factor in setting policy. Yet colonial governments were financially responsible for their own defense in peacetime, and civil officials were concerned primarily with matters of economy. Unmoved by warnings that their penny-pinching encouraged civil unrest and external aggression, colonial administrators tried to tailor the KAR to their minimum internal security needs. East African governors usually favored economic development over defense spending and worried that the privileged status of African soldiers would disrupt the racial hierar-

chy of colonial society. Most considered the KAR an expensive luxury
and argued they would be better served by an armed constabulary or
gendarmerie under the control of the civil police.

These differences of opinion were never resolved conclusively. Instead,
external circumstances usually dictated whether civil or military authorities
would set colonial defense policy. During the world wars, the War Office
expanded and modernized the KAR after assuming full administrative and
financial control of the colonial forces. In peacetime, however, imperial funding dried up, and territorial governments insisted on a high degree of fiscal
austerity that left the Regiment poorly equipped and disorganized. The tensions generated by these conflicts created a level of mutual distrust at official levels that made it extremely difficult for the KAR to reward African
soldiers adequately or to keep pace with political change and military innovation. Throughout its history, the Regiment suffered a high degree of institutional paralysis, compounded by the British military establishment's long-
standing suspicion of change and innovation. KAR battalions were often run
on a shoestring, and African soldiers were least willing to endure military
discipline when disagreements between civil and military officials over the
proper role of the KAR led to poor working conditions and low pay for the
rank-and-file.

THE EARLY KAR, 1880–1914

The King's African Rifles was originally composed of informal territorial
forces recruited in the three British Protectorates in East Africa. Uganda, British Central Africa, and British East Africa were administered originally by
the Foreign Office, which usually allowed its consuls and representatives a
free hand in making local policy and recruiting soldiers.[1] The first colonial
armies were created in the 1880s and 1890s by British officers and administrators who needed an armed body of men to impose their will on the local
population. The informal units had no official standing, and when the British
Representative to the Kingdom of Buganda requested permission to enlist
his African soldiers as regular British troops, the Foreign Office informed
him that the pay and organization of colonial forces were a local responsibility.[2]

The colonial forces in what became Nyasaland consisted of African irregulars recruited by Captain Frederick Lugard to break the power of Muslim slave traders in 1888. After the British Central Africa Protectorate was
formally established three years later, the African militia became the Central
Africa Rifles (CAR). At that time, the CAR consisted of six companies of
120 men (primarily Tonga and Yao) and a 175-man "Sikh Contingent." In
1898, the CAR added a second battalion under direct War Office control. It
sent the second battalion to garrison the coaling station at Mauritius one year

later because the Anglo-Boer War created a shortage of metropolitan British troops. Over the next two years, the battalion also saw service in British Somaliland, the Asante Campaign, and the Gambia Expedition.[3]

The first colonial soldiers in Uganda were recruited by Lugard, who was employed by Sir William MacKinnon's Imperial British East Africa Company (IBEAC) in 1890 to strengthen British influence in the Kingdom of Buganda. Lugard's force consisted of 70 Sudanese recruited directly from the Egyptian Army in Cairo and 2,000 of the Khedive's soldiers who had been stranded in the southern Sudan after Khartoum fell to the Mahdi. Britain declared a Protectorate over the Kingdom of Buganda in 1894, and Lugard's Sudanese became the Uganda Rifles one year later. Many of these askaris rebelled in 1897 to protest infrequent pay and excessive campaigning, but the 700 "loyal" Sudanese who reenlisted after the mutiny became the backbone of Britain's colonial forces in East Africa.[4]

In the East Africa Protectorate, the IBEAC recruited an irregular paramilitary police force of Zanzibaris, Sudanese, Indians, and ex-slaves. When MacKinnon surrendered his Royal Charter in 1895, the Foreign Office reorganized the Company's armed forces into the East Africa Rifles (EAR). By 1900, the EAR was a thousand-man unit composed primarily of coastal Muslims and 350 Sudanese recruited from the remnants of the Egyptian Army in the Sudan.[5]

With the exception of Tonga soldiers in the CAR, the vast majority of the askaris in Britain's early colonial forces were foreign-born Muslims. Their primary mission was to force East Africans to surrender their sovereignty, and it was imprudent to recruit askaris from the same African communities targeted by British military operations. Yet the mutiny by the Uganda Rifles demonstrated that even these soldiers were not entirely reliable, and the British stiffened the early colonial forces with troops borrowed from the Indian Army. As the KAR's Inspector General put it in 1912: "The Indian contingents were introduced in order that we might have a body of troops with no religious or local sympathies, and therefore no incentive for throwing in their lot with the native inhabitants."[6] In Nyasaland, Sikhs served as drill instructors and section commanders, whereas the Uganda Protectorate retained the 400 Indian troops to balance its Sudanese soldiers.[7] The political reliability of these Indian forces, however, was offset by their unsuitability for African service. They required a special diet and were paid more than African soldiers. Moreover, the Indian government refused to lend Sepoys to the East African Protectorates on a long-term basis because of concerns about the Russian threat on its northwestern frontier. As a result, all of the KAR's Indian contingents were withdrawn by 1912, after military officials decided it was safe to rely exclusively on African soldiers.

While the early colonial battalions were relatively cheap and easy to run, they also had a number of serious weaknesses. Since each unit was raised to meet the minimum internal security requirements of its home territory, no reserve force existed to deal with emergencies. Uganda needed an Indian Army battalion to suppress the Uganda Mutiny because the other British Protectorates could not spare any troops, thus exposing the informal territorial organization of the colonial forces as a false economy. In 1902, the Foreign Office, which retained responsibility for the three East African Protectorates until 1905, amalgamated the Central Africa Rifles, the Uganda Rifles, and the East Africa Rifles to form the King's African Rifles. The various colonial battalions were then renumbered in order of seniority. The two Nyasaland battalions became 1 and 2 KAR, the East Africa Rifles, 3 KAR, and the Uganda Rifles and its Indian contingent, 4 and 5 KAR, respectively. For a time there was also a Somaliland unit known as 6 KAR, but it was disbanded in 1910 and eventually replaced by the Somaliland Camel Corps.

When the KAR became the responsibility of the Colonial Office in 1905, each territorial government continued to finance and administer its own KAR battalions with the help of a limited amount of imperial funding. The War Office offered advice on organization and training through the Inspector General of the KAR, who was attached to the Colonial Office as an adviser on East African military matters. In theory, the KAR battalions were interchangeable, but in practice, they differed in size and terms of service for African ranks. In reality, the only connection between them was their name, the British officer corps, and a set of common regulations and ordinances.

The early KAR continued the work of its predecessors in subjugating the East African population. The army occasionally collected taxes, rounded up laborers, and enforced land alienation, but it most commonly conducted punitive expeditions against communities that refused to acknowledge British authority. These expeditions were usually nothing more than large-scale cattle raids. Since livestock constituted the accumulated wealth of many pre-colonial African economies, these societies had little choice but to submit to British rule or face the grim reality of poverty and famine. Most early askaris were willing participants in such operations. As foreigners and Muslims, they had few ties to local populations and usually received a generous share of the captured livestock. Civil officials, however, found such organized looting distasteful. Sir Charles Eliot, the Governor of the East Africa Protectorate, sarcastically proposed awarding all officers two medals when they arrived in East Africa, with one to be forfeited for each punitive foray they instigated.[8] These civil-military tensions never came to a head because by 1910 colonial rule was secure in all but the most remote rural areas.

With the conquest of East Africa completed, colonial military authorities hoped to reorganize the KAR into a modern military formation, capable of undertaking full-scale, battalion-level operations in the greater service of the British Empire.[9] Civil administrators opposed this plan because it required them to assume a greater share of the KAR's operating expenses. Assuming that, aside from the East Africa Protectorate's troublesome northern frontier, there were no more threats to British rule in the region, the East African governors argued they would be better served by a cheaper, lightly armed civil gendarmerie. Their proposal was not as far-fetched as it might have seemed; most African police forces of the time were essentially paramilitary organizations that emphasized military-style drill and musketry training over conventional police work. Moreover, many colonial administrators resented the relative autonomy of the KAR and preferred the police because they were under civil control.[10]

While War Office pressure prevented civil officials from dismantling the KAR, most governments drastically shrank their battalions once the British government reduced its imperial military subsidy. In 1910, the Colonial Office disbanded 2 KAR and cut back the remaining three battalions. By the end of the year, the Regiment was at the weakest point in its history, with a total of only seventeen companies spread over three geographically remote territories. British officers hoped the discharged askaris would sign up for a three-year term with the KAR Reserves, but most found the reserve pay of 1 rupee (the equivalent of 1.5 shillings) per month too low. In fact, many men of 2 KAR crossed into German East Africa to continue soldiering with the *Schutztruppe* (Protection Force). Colonel G. H. Thesiger, the Inspector General of the KAR, warned that these changes left the KAR dangerously understrength, but with the subjugation of East Africa largely completed, the Colonial Office dismissed his concerns.[11]

THE FIRST WORLD WAR, 1914–1918

Thesiger was vindicated by the outbreak of the First World War. In August 1914, the KAR was entirely unprepared for battalion-level operations. This was due partially to force reductions brought on by fiscal austerity, but it also reflected official fears that "white prestige" would be dangerously diminished if Africans took part in a European war. As one contemporary historian put it: "The tradition of the inviolability of the white man must be maintained if a few hundred whites were to continue to impose their authority, in governing many thousands of blacks, in safety. It was thought that it would be most dangerous to employ black troops to fight against white men."[12]

As a result, the colonial governments did little to prepare the KAR for active operations. The War Office assumed unofficial responsibility for all East African forces in November 1914 but did not take over direct control and funding of the Regiment until 1916. The KAR therefore remained virtually unchanged for the first year and a half of the war, and the only new African combat units raised during this time were irregular "tribal" militias like the Nandi Scouts and the Baganda Rifles. The main focus of African recruiting in the early years of the war was for the Carrier Corps, an unarmed and unmechanized labor organization charged with transporting the stores and equipment of British and Indian combat units. This emphasis on labor over combat units was in keeping with Britain's overall policy goal of preserving European prestige. The Carrier Corps would eventually kill tens of thousands of African porters through wanton neglect and indifference, but settlers and colonial officials were reassured that it was not teaching them to fight.

During the opening months of the First World War, KAR battalions were deployed on the borders of Nyasaland and the East Africa Protectorate. The War Office assigned the immediate task of invading German East Africa to an Indian Expeditionary Force, known as Force B, which it diverted from the Middle East to seize the port city of Tanga. The invasion was an utter disaster because the Germans had sufficient warning to prepare for the assault, and Force B was evacuated after taking over 800 casualties. As a result, British commanders spent most of 1915 in defensive positions along the German border where they lost more men to disease than to combat.

The decision to shift the burden of the fighting to Africans came in 1916, after British forces had recovered sufficiently to renew the invasion of German East Africa. The collapse of German resistance in Southwest Africa one year earlier freed up South African troops, and Afrikaner General J. C. Smuts assumed overall command in East Africa. Although many South Africans loudly refused to serve alongside "Kaffirs," Smuts decided to expand the KAR. Heavy South African casualties were politically unacceptable in Pretoria, and British and Indian troops were too vulnerable to disease. Indian units suffered a sick rate of over twenty percent, whereas the British 2nd Loyal North Lancashires and the 25th Fusiliers lost almost eighty percent of their original strength.[13]

Once the War Office approved Smuts's plan, the various territorial KAR battalions came under a unified command structure for the first time in their history. A commandant based in Nairobi oversaw their overall administration and set uniform guidelines for African conditions of service. Smuts split all existing battalions to form daughter battalions (e.g., 4 KAR begot 2/4 KAR) and raised a new 5 KAR from the companies of 3 KAR garrisoning the East Africa Protectorate's northern frontier. In February 1917, all of the original battalions (except 5 KAR) divided again to create third and fourth battalions. The extent of the recruiting program required by these changes was enormous. The Regiment grew from 2,319 men in three battalions in 1914 to almost 31,000 men in twenty-two battalions in 1918.[14]

These new KAR battalions were larger and more sophisticated than the simple infantry units of the pre-war era. Moreover, the wartime KAR included an artillery arm, transport service, signal corps, medical department, intelligence wing, and military police detachment. While these changes were intended mainly to prepare the KAR to fight the Germans, they also transformed the military experience of Africans soldiers. In the pre-war KAR, the average askari was an illiterate rifleman, but after 1916 colonial military authorities needed to train African soldiers for the new specialized units. To be sure, the number of tradesmen and specialists produced by the KAR was very small in comparison to the total number of enlisted Africans; what is significant, however, is that for the first time some askaris left the KAR with more skills and education than they had when they enlisted.

While Britain's naval superiority prevented the Germans from reinforcing their African colonies, the conquest of German East Africa proved much more difficult than Smuts had imagined. Under the leadership of the *Schutztruppe*'s gifted commander, General Paul von Lettow-Vorbeck, less than 2,000 well-disciplined German and African troops waged a successful guerrilla campaign, tying down a British imperial force fifteen times their number for the remainder of the war.[15] Before finally surrendering after the Armistice in November 1918, he led Smuts on a frustrating chase that wound through German East Africa, Mozambique and Northern Rhodesia.

Transportation by road and railway was impossible in most of German East Africa, and the supplies and ammunition for British units pursuing von Lettow-Vorbeck were carried almost exclusively by African porters. Just as the KAR expanded in 1916, military officials conscripted almost 120,000 men for the Carrier Corps.[16] Only a few carriers died in actual combat, but huge numbers perished from disease and neglect brought on by overwork and inadequate food, clothing, and medical care. Many also deserted in large numbers. Estimates of total carrier losses by the end of the war range from 40,000 to half a million men, and colonial officials had no way of tracing or locating the thousands of carriers declared missing during the war.[17] While the askaris of the KAR were, by and large, better treated than the men of the Carrier Corps, they also suffered heavy casualties during the East African Campaign. By July 1918, combat and desertion shrank 3/3 KAR from an official complement of 1,018 African ranks to roughly 100 men (a ninety percent casualty rate). On the whole, the KAR lost over 3,000 men during the war to disease and malnutrition, compared to only 1,198 askaris killed in action.[18]

Nevertheless, most KAR battalions fought effectively throughout the campaign, and those askaris tested in combat earned high praise from the British troops who served with them. In 1917, an officer of the 25th Royal Fusiliers, who fought back-to-back with 1/2 KAR against an encircling German force, remarked: "It was here that one saw, and realised, the full fighting courage to which well-trained native African troops can rise . . . and we, who were an Imperial Unit, felt that we could not have wished for a stoughter, nor more faithful, regiment to fight alongside of."[19] The performance of the KAR during the war put to rest (at least for the time being) racist assertions that the Africans made inferior frontline troops. The war did little, however, to allay the fears of colonial officials and settlers about having to rely solely on the KAR for their security.

THE INTER-WAR YEARS, 1918–1939

The effectiveness of the KAR during the First World War convinced military officials that it was worthwhile to keep the colonial army under a unified command structure. Some even entertained hopes of retaining a few of the additional wartime battalions. These plans, however, were incompatible with the political and fiscal realities of the post-war years. The fighting in Europe strained British resources, and there was no money to keep the KAR under imperial control. Moreover, colonial governments still resented the independent status of the Regiment. The Colonial Office therefore returned the KAR battalions to local control and financing in 1920. It abolished the position of KAR Commandant and returned the Regiment to the nominal authority of the KAR Inspector General.[20]

Of the twenty-two wartime KAR battalions, ten were disbanded immediately after the Armistice. Upon the resumption of local control, the Regiment shrank again to six territorial battalions. Nyasaland was allowed to keep 1 and 2 KAR, and Kenya retained both 3 and 5 KAR. Uganda kept only its original 4 KAR, and the British mandated territory of Tanganyika (the former German East Africa) received a new 6 KAR formed from elements of 2/4 KAR and 7 KAR (a wartime battalion recruited in Zanzibar and the Swahili coast). Furthermore, the strength of each battalion dropped from a wartime high of over 1,000 men to roughly 400 askaris.[21]

The Colonial Office sanctioned these reductions because it assumed the future mission of the Regiment would be limited to internal security. KAR battalions trained to fight "a savage, or semi-civilized enemy in tropical Africa." The pre-war pacification campaigns were no longer necessary, but military intelligence officers cooperated with Criminal Investigation Departments to intimidate African opponents of the colonial regime. In Nyasaland, the KAR convinced delinquent villages to pay their taxes by conducting public training exercises, which included bayonet fighting and the destruction of demonstration huts using incendiary machine gun tracer rounds.[22]

In Kenya, the KAR spent the 1920s on the northern frontier to check cross-border raids from Somalia, Ethiopia, and the Sudan and to impose British authority in what was still a largely lawless region. The commander of 5 KAR assumed administrative control of the Northern Frontier Province with the full magisterial powers of a Provincial Commissioner. Junior KAR officers in command of individual detachments had the authority of District Officers. This was an unworkable arrangement, as few military officers had the training or inclination for civil administration. Civil officials resented the army's foray into their sphere of authority and regained control of the northern frontier in 1926 after 5 KAR was temporarily disbanded as an economy measure.[23]

Aside from the unpopularity of arduous duty in the northern frontier, most African soldiers found military service relatively easy during the inter-war years. The army allowed them to keep their families in the barracks, and as Chapter 3 will show, they were relatively well paid in comparison to the civilian population. Their primary mission was to provide a visible representation of overwhelming military force to discourage civil unrest. In practical terms, this entailed regular training missions in the countryside and parades in cities and towns. Except for operations against cross-border raiders in northern Kenya, inter-war askaris saw little actual fighting.

As a result, many colonial officials concluded that they could dispense with the KAR entirely. Europeans in Kenya were particularly hostile to the Regiment, and Sir Edward Grigg, the pro-settler Governor of the Colony in the late 1920s, favored replacing the African colonial army with a settler militia known as the Kenya Defence Force. As civil authorities were financially responsible for the colonial forces, a reduction in the KAR was inevitable. From 1920 to 1930, the total number of askaris in the KAR fell from 5,740 to 3,080, with 3 KAR losing over fifty percent of its strength in 1927 alone.[24] Most territories accomplished these reductions by eliminating individual companies, but Kenya disbanded the entire 5 KAR.

Although the KAR's Inspector General warned that these cuts left the Regiment dangerously unprepared for serious unrest, the colonial governments believed they could rely on inexpensive African reservists in an emergency. Under the terms of their enlistment, discharged askaris had a three-year reserve obligation requiring them to report for yearly training in return for one to two shillings per month. Yet the KAR Reserve never functioned properly. Askaris usually retired when they were too old for further service, reserve pay was too low to keep them interested in the army, and the yearly call-up was impractical and expensive, given that most reservists lived in remote rural areas.[25] Thus, the belief that the KAR Reserve was a viable, low-cost alternative to maintaining KAR battalions at full strength was basically wishful thinking on the part of colonial administrators. Given the widely held belief that British East Africa was in no danger from African unrest or external aggression, their faith in the KAR Reserve was just an excuse for further force reductions.

The civil impetus to abolish the KAR intensified during the worldwide depression in 1929. With the exception of Nyasaland, each territory faced severe budget deficits in the early 1930s. Kenya and Tanganyika experienced the worst shortfalls, with respective deficits of £250,000 and £307,000 in 1932. Although military spending constituted only a small percentage of colonial budgets (Tanganyika spent just five and a half percent of its income on defense in 1932), the ongoing controversy over the value of a colonial army made the Regiment particularly vulnerable.[26] Faced with severe cuts in administrative staffs and development projects to repay loans from the imperial treasury, settlers and administrators were adamantly opposed to diverting scarce funds to the colonial army.

The military establishment sought to justify its continued existence during these lean times by citing the need for military readiness and efficiency. One of the most worrisome concerns of senior officers was that the decentralized colonial army made it impossible for the forces of one territory to reinforce another in an emergency. By the end of the 1920s, the Regiment's various battalions had become dissimilar units ranging in size from two to six companies.[27] Brigadier H. A. Walker, the Inspector General of the KAR from 1927 to 1931, therefore offered the civil governments a compromise: The Regiment would be substantially reduced but reorganized under a unified command structure. He shrank all battalions to a standard two companies and grouped them into Northern and Southern Brigades. Each Brigade maintained two battalions on garrison duty, plus a third reserve battalion that could be sent to any East African territory in the event of trouble. The Brigades were integrated formations with a Headquarters Staff, Signals section, and a mechanized Supply and Transport Corps. Nyasaland and Tanganyika were responsible for the Southern Brigade, consisting of 1, 2, and 6 KAR. The Northern Brigade had the Kenyan and Ugandan 3 and 4 KAR, with 5 KAR reformed as its reserve battalion. (The Somaliland Camel Corps was not included in the restructuring.) Walker believed it was possible to reduce each battalion to only two companies because the new Supply and Transport units could deploy troops rapidly to even the most remote trouble spots. Trucks and armored machine gun carriers were more expensive than camels, wagons, and porters, but he argued their cost would be recovered through overall manpower reductions.[28]

The East African governments were happy to reduce their KAR battalions to two companies but had a number of misgivings about the other aspects of Walker's plan. The Ugandan government disliked being linked to Kenya through the Northern Brigade. With few permanent European residents in the territory, Ugandan officials objected to having to protect Kenyan settlers.[29] The real stumbling block, however, was the cost of the Supply and Transport Corps. Tanganyika and Nyasaland believed the relative stability of their territories made the rapid deployment of troops unnecessary, and the Colonial Office ultimately had to broker a compromise in which Tanganyika's civil transportation department served as the Southern Brigade's Supply and Transport Corps in emergencies.[30]

The bitterness generated by this debate gave new life to civil efforts to replace the KAR with an armed constabulary. With African nationalism still in its infancy, the early 1930s was the most stable period of British rule in East Africa. Colonial officials were confident this security could be preserved by giving Africans a share in local administration through indirect rule and saw little need to retain an expensive standing army. They found allies among the settler communities in Tanganyika and Kenya, who believed public funds should be spent on loans and subsidies to help them through the Great Depression. In Kenya, elected unofficial Legislative Council representatives introduced a resolution calling for the KAR to be amalgamated with the Kenya Police under civil authority. They cited Northern Rhodesia as their model, which until 1933 had relied solely a civil police force for its defense.[31]

The Colonial Office's military staff, however, was still opposed to relying on armed constabularies. Believing all colonies had an obligation to contribute to the defense of the empire, they argued that the sole function of the civil police was the preservation of law and order. Brigadier C. C. Norman, Walker's successor as Inspector General, believed a militarized police force was not a "positive deterrent" to rebellion. Deterrence was a role that could be filled only by the colonial military:

> There should be presented to the people at all times a detached and independent military force, so loyal, so powerfully armed and so highly trained that all idea of resistance to it, in spite of immense superiority of numbers and the vastness of the country, would be a hopeless and unthinkable undertaking.[32]

The Overseas Defence Committee (ODC) of the Imperial Defence Committee, which had ultimate authority over the strength and disposition of colonial troops, agreed with Norman. The ODC considered Britain's overseas defense commitments too overextended to allow East Africa to opt out of its imperial obligations. With no British or Indian troops available to reinforce East Africa in an emergency, the Committee ordered that the functions of the police and the KAR be kept separate. It also rejected an impossibly expensive and unrealistic plan to replace three KAR battalions with a Royal Air Force squadron.[33]

The East African governments became complacent about military readiness in the 1920s because there were no serious external threats to their security. This changed in October 1935, when Italian forces invaded Ethiopia. Where Kenya's northern threat had previously consisted of spontaneous raids by Ethiopian and Somali irregulars, British East Africa now faced a hostile modern Fascist army equipped with tanks, airplanes, and poison gas. The KAR was entirely unprepared to deal with such an enemy, and the Italian invasion exposed the deleterious effects of ten years of forced economy and neglect. Each KAR battalion consisted of only two rifle companies and a machine gun platoon.[34] Furthermore, the Southern Brigade's reserve battalion (1 KAR) was dangerously slow in deploying to Kenya's northern border because the KAR Reserve in Nyasaland was almost nonexistent. Many of the askaris in the battalion were elderly and due for immediate discharge, and the Southern Brigade's reservists were mostly World War I veterans.[35]

Britain was fortunate that Mussolini had no immediate plans to attack East Africa, and the situation on the northern frontier stabilized by the summer of 1936. Yet the presence of substantial Fascist forces in the Horn of Africa meant the weakened and disorganized state of the KAR could no longer be ignored. By 1937, an official in the Colonial Office was forced to admit: "The KAR at present is little more than a gallant sham. The battalions are so weak they could not take the field, even to jump on a riot."[36]

With internal security now a secondary concern, the Inspector General of the KAR, Major General G. J. Giffard, reorganized the Regiment to fight a modern war. He transformed the KAR's reserve battalions into "cadre battalions" for wartime expansion and built up the KAR Reserve through direct recruitment. Giffard equipped the remaining battalions with mortars, anti-tank rifles, and artillery and created new African support units, including a Field Ambulance Company and a Coast Defence Unit. He also assumed control of the Northern Rhodesia Regiment (NRR), which split off from the civil police in 1933, and reorganized it to conform to the standards of a frontline KAR battalion. To address the shortage of European leadership, the Kenya Defence Force became the Kenya Regiment, with the mission of training local Europeans to serve as officers and NCOs for the KAR.[37] For the first time since World War I, the overall strength of the Regiment increased, and the Kenyan KAR battalions grew by over twenty-six percent in 1937 alone.[38] The East African governors placed their forces under a unified command and laid the groundwork for an expanded mechanized transport service and a new military labor unit known as the East African Pioneers.[39]

In 1939, Sir Philip Mitchell, the Governor of Uganda, offered to raise an additional KAR battalion as an African territorial unit (roughly equivalent to the American National Guard) to allow young Ugandans to express their "loyalty." In a departure from established policy, he also proposed to give the battalion at least two African commissioned officers drawn from an Officer Training Corps at Makerere College.[40] Military officials accepted Mitchell's offer and designated the new territorial battalion 7 KAR. Three members of the Kabaka's family received commissions over the objections of senior KAR officers, who did not want Africans to have access to secret military documents. Most of the new battalion was composed of Ganda recruited within a seven-mile radius around Kampala and Jinja. With over 800 volunteers applying for fewer than 200 positions, 7 KAR had little difficulty raising two complete infantry companies. The unit included many Makerere graduates and was the best-educated battalion in the history of the Regiment.[41]

THE SECOND WORLD WAR, 1939–1945

When war with Germany came in 1939, the War Office took direct control of all East African units, and the Inspector General of the KAR, who happened to be in Nairobi at the time, became the General Officer Commanding (GOC) the East African forces. With Italy neutral until June 1940, East African units were under the overall authority of the Middle East Command to aid the defense of the Suez Canal. The direct security of East Africa was a secondary issue. Although the Royal West African Frontier Force and South Africa's Union Defence Force fought in the campaign to liberate the Horn of Africa, East Africa was largely on its own. There was never any doubt or debate about the wisdom of relying on African troops because the colonial governments simply had no choice in the matter.

On the infantry side, the KAR grew from seven battalions (plus the NRR) in 1939 to forty-three battalions (plus eight NRR battalions and the Rhodesian African Rifles) by the close of the war. As was the case in the First World War, the original senior battalions (except for 5 KAR) divided to form daughter units. Tanganyika's 6 KAR alone spun off five additional battalions, whereas the Ugandan 7 KAR shifted from a small territorial unit into a regular frontline infantry battalion, much to the distress of some of its members who had viewed it as a part-time job.[42] As the war progressed, military authorities raised additional battalions that had no connection to the pre-war KAR and were only nominally linked to specific territories. Nyasaland, however, insisted that its Chewa-speaking askaris serve in homogeneous units because it was concerned they would not mix well with Swahili speakers.[43]

While most Africans who saw direct combat during the war served in a KAR infantry battalion, the East African territories also raised a host of specialist and support units. The colonial forces fielded brigade and even division-level formations equipped and trained to the standards of their Axis opponents. KAR battalions were backed by the guns of the East Africa Artillery (EAA), supported by sappers of the East Africa Engineers (EAE) and the fighting vehicles of the East Africa Armoured Car Regiment, cared for by medics from the East Africa Army Medical Corps (EAAMC) and transported and supplied by the trucks of the East Africa Army Service Corps (EAASC). An East Africa Army Chaplains Department (EAAChD) ministered to the spiritual needs of Protestant African soldiers (Catholics had a separate organization). The East Africa Army Education Corps (EAAEC) trained Africans to serve in these new specialist units and also taught British personnel Swahili and African soldiers English.[44]

Even though the EAASC's trucks eliminated the need for another Carrier Corps, the military still required large amounts of unskilled manual labor. The East African Pioneer battalions were originally intended to fill this role but were promoted to full-fledged combat pioneers after striking in late 1939 to protest their inferior status.[45] To replace them, military officials raised the East Africa Military Labour Service (EAMLS), which was clearly and exclusively defined as a labor unit. Members of the EAMLS had the rights and status of fully attested soldiers, and the unit's name was carefully chosen to avoid association with the Carrier Corps. Yet despite repeated emphasis that the EAMLS was a military unit, it remained, without a doubt, the least prestigious and most disdained branch of the colonial forces.

Britain was fortunate the Italians did not enter the war in 1939, when the KAR was still entirely unprepared for full-scale military operations. When war finally broke out in East Africa in June 1940, Italy's colonial forces only occupied a few Kenyan border towns and overran British Somaliland after a short but fierce battle with its KAR garrison. In response, Britain waited until February 1941 to launch a counteroffensive.[46] Since a specific discussion of military tactics is not relevant here, suffice it to say that Britain's African forces enjoyed overwhelming success in the Ethiopian Campaign. East Africa's two colonial divisions advanced 1,687 miles (averaging 76.6 miles per day) to take Addis Ababa in just two months. They were supported by two Indian Divisions and elements of the Sudanese Defence Force, which attacked from the north. By July, British imperial forces had captured thirty Italian generals and over 170,000 Italian troops.

The Italians did not give up without a fight, however, and the KAR lost 108 askaris taking the fortified town of Gondar in November 1941. For the most part, however, disease and accidents were the greatest threats to the East Africans. Of the 1,935 fatalities over the course of the campaign, only eleven percent were due to combat.[47] Most African veterans of the Ethiopian Campaign fought to defend their homes and are proud of their victory over the Italians. Gaining confidence in their fighting abilities, they enjoyed singing "Mussolini has run away" to Italian prisoners of war (POWs). The settler press also hailed the victory and dismissed fears that fighting the Italians would undermine European prestige because African soldiers understood the Italians were "a sort of poor white man." British officers were proud the askaris were more than a match for the Fascist Blackshirts but worried that their men were not ready for the Germans or Japanese.[48]

With the total liberation of Ethiopia by the end of 1941, the KAR assumed responsibility for blockading pro-Vichy French forces in Djibouti and guarding vast numbers of Italian POWs. As a result, the East Africa Military Labour Service was no longer needed on the battlefield. The Kenyan settler community, which faced a severe wartime labor shortage, demanded the abolition of the EAMLS. Yet victory in Ethiopia did not reduce the military's demand for African labor. By early 1942, over 17,000 EAMLS askaris were serving in thirty-five companies employed on static tasks including stevedoring, camp hygiene, and construction work or were assigned to individual units as domestic servants.[49]

Moreover, British forces in North Africa were also desperately in need of military labor. With Australian troops withdrawn to counter the Japanese threat in Asia, and manpower at a premium in Britain, military planners turned to the colonies for laborers to release more Europeans for combat. The Director of Pioneers and Labour for the Middle East asked the East African territories to shift surplus labor from the EAMLS to the new African Auxiliary Pioneer Corps (AAPC), which also included companies from West Africa and the High Commission Territories of Swaziland, Basutoland and Bechuanaland. They were joined in the Middle East by other colonial Pioneers from India, Mauritius, Palestine, and Cyprus.

The AAPC was the first East African formation to serve under a military command that was not directly responsible to the colonial governments. Although the AAPC companies were recruited and raised in East Africa, they became imperial troops once they reached the Middle East. To allay fears that AAPC askaris might pick up unsuitable ideas while they were abroad, the Middle East Command promised never to send East Africans to Europe or to mix AAPC companies with other imperial units.

On an operational level, the AAPC was organized into companies of 300 men each, with six companies making up an AAPC Group. East Africa contributed a total of eight groups to the Middle East by the end of 1942.[50] To distinguish them from other imperial Pioneer units, each East African company was numbered with the prefix "18," thus producing 1801 Company, 1802 Company, and so forth. Although not formally part of the AAPC, elements of the East Africa Army Service Corps also served in the Middle East to augment the region's transportation network. During the North African Campaign, most East African AAPC companies provided labor for the British Eighth Army in its operations against the German Afrikacorps. When the Germans were finally defeated in 1943, these units switched to garrison duties and construction assignments that included railway lines, roads, and water pipelines. By 1944, the East African deployment in North Africa and the Levant consisted of fifty-six AAPC companies, six EAASC general transport companies, plus 5 NRR and 23 KAR, the only African combat units sent to the region during the war.[51]

Although civil and military officials in East Africa insisted the AAPC's primary mission was military labor, the East African AAPC companies in the Eighth Army saw more combat than most KAR battalions. The Pioneers helped keep the Libyan port of Tobruk open when it was besieged by the Germans in early 1942, and although they were never intended for the front lines, the East Africans earned high praise from their commanders for their coolness under fire. In other cases, however, the strain of combat proved too great, and a number of AAPC companies disintegrated during the British retreat from Libya. When Tobruk finally fell in May 1942, the men of 1823 Company were taken prisoner as British forces withdrew from the town. Italian guards murdered 202 of them, but 71 escaped to the British lines and 49 survived to become prisoners of war.[52] Two months later, 1808 Company was attacked by German planes at the Abu Hagag railway station. Forty-one pioneers burned to death when the bombing ignited gasoline stores and turned the station into an inferno. Surviving members of the Company made regular visits to Abu Hagag throughout the war to tend their comrades' graves.[53]

Service with a frontline unit was hard and dangerous work, and many Pioneers resented their inferior status in comparison to KAR askaris. African veterans of the AAPC blame their casualties on the failure of the British Army to give them enough combat training to defend themselves.[54] Many lost hope in the inhospitable desert. Their despair created disciplinary problems in the Pioneer Companies and was obvious in the letters they sent home to their families. A Ganda driver wrote: "Our position now is awful as we are facing the enemy who attacks us from time to time without warning. Were it not that I love you, I should be afraid, but I have taken my oath to the British."[55] Yet in spite of their substantial contribution to the much celebrated success of Montgomery's Eighth Army, military historians have taken little note of sacrifices by the African Pioneers.

Moreover, no mention has been made of the roughly 300 East African Pioneers taken prisoner during the campaign. Although the British tried to liberate them before the Germans evacuated North Africa, most were sent to Italy before they could be rescued. These men eventually wound up in POW camps in France and Germany after the Italian surrender.[56] Of 300 East Africans taken prisoner in North Africa, only 232 were eventually liberated at the end of the war. Four escaped to find their way back to the Allied lines, but the rest appear to have died in captivity from disease and neglect. Sensitive to potential charges that they had abandoned these men, the East African governments sent a special unit to Britain to ensure the ex-POWs arrived home in good health.[57]

Japan's entry into the war in December 1941 also had a number of important ramifications in East Africa. The fall of Malaya and Singapore left the entire Indian Ocean vulnerable to Japanese naval forces. With the Italian threat to Egypt now over, East African forces were divorced from the Middle East Command, and a new East Africa Command (EAC) covering all British territory between the Zambezi River and Eritrea was created under the command of Lieutenant General Sir William Platt.

More significantly, while East Africans served in support units in the Middle East, the KAR battalions were frontline combat units in Asia. In October 1939, the War Office drew up plans for a colonial African division for overseas service. Little was done while the KAR was tied down in Ethiopia, but after the fall of Gondar, the Commander in Chief of British forces in India specifically requested East African troops. His plea took on greater urgency in February 1942 after the Japanese began to overrun Burma, ultimately threatening the security of British rule in India. With 70,000 men taken prisoner at Singapore, the War Office sent an East African brigade to release Indian troops in Ceylon for the Burma front. In addition, KAR battalions also garrisoned Reunion, Mauritius, and the Seychelles.[58]

The KAR was also responsible for taking Madagascar from the Vichy French. As in Djibouti, French units in Madagascar remained hostile to the Allied cause, and their cooperation with Japanese submarines threatened vital supply routes to East Africa and the Middle East. In May 1942, British and South African forces carried out initial amphibious landings at the northern port of Diégo Suarez, but it fell to 22 (East Africa) Brigade to clear the island of pro-Vichy forces. Facing under-supplied and demoralized Vichy forces, 22 Brigade advanced 660 miles in eight weeks, capturing 3,500 French colonial troops at a cost of only five European and thirty-one African combat deaths.[59] The KAR's opponents were mostly local Malgaches and West Africans of the *Tirailleurs Sénégalais*. As in the First World War, Africans again found themselves pitted against each other solely because they wore the uniforms of rival colonial powers.

As Japanese forces prepared to invade eastern India, it became evident that the KAR would have to take a more direct role in the fighting. In late 1942, the War Office directed the East Africa Command to provide three infantry brigades (nine battalions) for service in Asia. Platt proposed to raise an entire East African division with a full complement of specialist and support units for service in Southeast Asia. Concerned that morale would suffer if Africans were used solely in a support role, he insisted that the division see active combat.[60] As was the case with most troops, askaris became harder to control on tedious garrison assignments. Platt was adamant that if the colonial governments went to the expense of raising a fully equipped African infantry division, the division had to be used against the Japanese.

The War Office agreed and ordered Platt to prepare an East African division plus two additional independent infantry brigades for the Southeast Asian Command (SEAC) in India and Burma. As was the case in all military decisions, no one consulted the African rank-and-file, many of whom had volunteered only to defend East Africa. While some refused to serve overseas, most askaris were willing to go to Burma if they were suitably compensated for their increased risk and long-term separation from their families. The military establishment's failure to address these concerns was at the root of most of the disciplinary problems that would arise in Asia.

East Africa's contribution to the SEAC amounted to eighteen full KAR and NRR battalions, which, including support and service units, came to a total of almost 50,000 men.[61] As was the case with the AAPC in the Middle East, KAR askaris in Southeast Asia served as imperial troops. The War Office originally intended 22 and 28 (EA) Brigades to be replacement units for the

East African division, but both eventually saw action as independent formations. Two of the battalions sent to the SEAC came from territories that did
not supply men to the peacetime KAR. In 28 Brigade, 71 KAR was drawn
from British Somaliland and Somali ex-POWs from the Italian Army. The
Matabele and Shona of Southern Rhodesia (and migrant laborers from
Nyasaland) comprised the Rhodesian African Rifles (RAR) of 22 Brigade.[62]
The 11th (EA) Division also included five regiments of artillery, five engineer field companies, three field ambulances, a stretcher bearer unit (a converted AAPC company), and three advanced engineering workshops. A complete AAPC Group consisting of four companies helped maintain the lines of
supply and communication for British forces operating in Burma. These units
were staffed by African personnel of the EAA, EAE, EAAMC, EAASC, and
EAEME and indicate the level of sophistication and training African soldiers
achieved during the war.[63]

The first East Africans arrived in Burma in the summer of 1944, just after
the tide of the war turned against the Japanese. The Japanese 15th Army was
in retreat after failing in a desperate and bloody attempt to capture the strategic towns of Imphal and Kohima in the eastern Indian province of Assam.
One of the main routes back into Burma was through the Kabaw Valley. In
August 1944, the SEAC ordered 11 Division to overrun the valley and seize
a bridgehead over the Chindwin River before the Japanese had time to so-
lidify their defenses. The high command expected the East Africans to have
the advantage of surprise because the Japanese would not expect an attack at
the height of the monsoon season.[64] The Kabaw Valley was, without a doubt,
one of the most difficult places the KAR was ever to fight. Hubert Moyse-
Bartlett, the official historian of the KAR, described it as

> [a] depression of thick teak forest and seething mud, continuously drenched
> with perpetual downpours of torrential rain. It was infested with malaria
> and scrub typhus, and was known locally as the Valley of Death. The floor
> of the valley was from ten to twenty miles wide, hemmed in by high moun-
> tain ranges. Beyond the eastern wall lay the Chindwin, running parallel to
> the valley from north to south. From the mountains on either side several
> rivers and numerous chaungs ran across the track, which they intersected
> every few hundred yards. All were full at this time of year. In the forest the
> teak stood close, often limiting visibility to a hundred yards.[65]

The SEAC chose 11 Division for this mission because it assumed African
soldiers were used to difficult jungle conditions and had a special resistance
to tropical diseases. Most askaris, however, were from the cooler highlands
of East Africa. They were as vulnerable to malaria and typhus as British and
Indian soldiers and found themselves fighting in an environment that, as one
British officer admitted, other troops would have rejected as impossible.[66]

These conditions were made all the more difficult by the tenacity of the Japanese resistance. Despite appalling casualties from disease and starvation, they were far from defeated. Individual companies and platoons dug in and fought what often amounted to a suicidal delaying action. KAR battalions usually had to take these fortified positions by direct assault, often without the aid of heavy artillery or air support. Heavy foliage made it easy for the Japanese to conceal their positions, which forced the East Africans to send out small patrols to feel out the enemy. This made for harrowing jungle fighting not unlike the American experience in Vietnam. Operations in the Kabaw Valley ultimately cost 11 Division 1,244 battle casualties (of which 1,099 were African). Nevertheless, the East Africans rushed the Japanese defenses and established a bridgehead over the Chindwin River at Kalewa in December 1944. This allowed other imperial formations to retake the Burmese capital of Rangoon several months later.[67]

Exhausted from the capture of Kalewa, the men of 11 Division were withdrawn to India for rest and retraining at the end of 1944. In their place, the SEAC used the two East African brigades, intended originally as replacements for 11 Division, in the push to liberate southern Burma. The 22nd (EA) Brigade helped recapture the Arakan region of coastal Burma, and 28 (EA) Brigade had the unenviable task of serving as a diversionary force while British and Indian formations outflanked Japanese units in Mandalay. The Japanese became well acquainted with the East Africans in the Kabaw Valley, and 28 Brigade pretended to be the entire 11 Division to draw their attention away from the main British advance. The Brigade was all too successful in this masquerade and provoked a full-scale Japanese counterattack when it reached the Irrawaddy River in February 1945.[68]

Although the East Africans constituted only a small percentage of the SEAC's forces and arrived relatively late in the campaign, they played an important role in the reconquest of Burma. While campaign tactics are not the focus of this study, it is worthwhile to analyze the performance of KAR askaris in Burma in some detail. Military organizations are by nature hierarchical and authoritarian, but in colonial armies these divisions were defined almost exclusively by race. The primary mission of KAR askaris in peacetime was to support an authoritarian colonial regime. Their reliability depended on formal discipline and the army's ability to make military service lucrative and worthwhile. Sociologists have observed that the pressure of war strips away the coercive underpinnings of military discipline, meaning that the effectiveness of a particular unit in combat depends on the willingness of individual soldiers to risk their lives for (in order of importance): their comrades, their unit, and the cause for which they are fighting.[69] The Burma Campaign was unquestionably the KAR's most trying and difficult mission. Thus, it offers key insights into what motivated Africans to serve in the wartime colonial army.

While the East Africans accomplished their assigned mission in Burma, their success did not come easily. Although Moyse-Bartlett's official history of the KAR makes only brief mention of these problems, a number of askaris broke under fire or used "collective insubordination" (strikes) to protest their conditions of service. Military organizations tend to attribute such incidents to moral weakness, cowardice, and a failure of leadership, and disciplinary problems are usually glossed over in official reports and censored in the civil press. To be sure, virtually every imperial unit suffered discipline and morale problems when first confronted with the hardships of fighting in the Burmese jungle. During the Allied counterattack in the Arakan in April 1943, a British staff officer concluded:

> Outstanding was the fact that our troops were either exhausted, browned off or both, and that both Indian and British troops did not have their hearts in the campaign. The former were obviously scared of the Jap and generally demoralised by the nature of the campaign, i.e., the thick jungle and the subsequent blindness of movement.[70]

Thus, the problems of the East Africans in Burma were not due to any particular racial or cultural failing, as some colonial officers seemed to infer.

In spite of its tactical success, 11 Division occasionally suffered lapses of discipline. Morale suffered when both the officers and men of the formation realized they were not as well supplied or paid as a comparable Indian Army division. As a result, some African soldiers were unwilling to face the hazards of combat. In February 1944, 11 Division's poorly trained scout battalion broke under heavy Japanese attacks while attached to 81 (West African) Division in the Arakan. Three British officers and 120 askaris were missing after the retreat, and most of the survivors refused to face the enemy in subsequent operations.[71] The SEAC withdrew the Scouts from Burma to prevent their low morale from infecting other African units but continued to put tremendous pressure on 11 Division to advance in the Kabaw Valley.

Few rank-and-file askaris were psychologically prepared for the intensity of these jungle operations. Transportation problems and poor visibility during the monsoon made artillery and air support very difficult, and on one occasion the Royal Air Force accidentally bombed 34 KAR, killing many askaris.[72] Moreover, the Japanese were experienced jungle fighters and a much more formidable foe than the Italians or Vichy French. They conducted nighttime raids, or "jitter parties," to harass the East Africans, and it was not unusual for nervous askaris to waste hundreds of rounds of ammunition firing into the undergrowth. A Somali company of 71 KAR was nearly wiped out because they held their fire after hearing cries of "Don't shoot" in their own language. In another incident, an askari ripped off his clothes and charged the enemy suicidally after breaking under a jitter attack.[73]

On a larger scale, askaris responded to this pressure by avoiding combat. During the Burma Campaign, a few KAR battalions were paralyzed when their men either refused to advance or broke under fire. In the best known incident, an entire battalion of 25 Brigade took part in a "mass refusal," rejecting orders to expand the Kalewa bridgehead. The askaris of 44 KAR informed their officers that they had been told Kalewa was their objective, and they refused to go any further.[74] British officers responded to these incidents in a number of ways. When a company of 22 KAR broke under fire, the battalion commander held a mass field court-martial and demoted the company's African NCOs. The company fought bravely after it was reorganized, probably because a Regimental Sergeant Major was posted in the rear with a bren gun to shoot any deserters. Another junior officer who experienced similar problems in 36 KAR immediately led his men on a counterattack to restore their courage.[75]

One of the main reasons for sinking African morale in Burma was that askaris had little hope of replacement or leave. Once 22 and 28 Brigade became frontline units, there was no longer a replacement pool for the East African forces. The SEAC expected askaris to remain in Asia for the duration of the war. While British and Indian soldiers received no leave either, they at least had clearer motives for fighting. It was much harder for an askari to accept the necessity of personal sacrifice when he was serving so far from home, particularly when many had only volunteered to defend East Africa.

To make matters worse, the Japanese recognized that any European in an African unit was a leader, and in a striking reversal of the peacetime racial hierarchy of the KAR, British personnel were ordered to paint their faces black and "copy the gait, bearing and mannerisms of their own troops."[76] A small handful of British officers were even removed for refusing to lead their askaris on patrols because they did not trust them to stand under fire. A company of 36 KAR lost so many junior leaders that promotion to Company Sergeant Major was regarded as a "death sentence." Yet jungle patrolling was equally dangerous for African NCOs, and the loss of experienced and respected African leaders was a major factor in many unit failures.[77]

These tensions, coupled with resupply problems in the Burma theater, led to the decision to take 11 Division out of action in late 1944. The Division accomplished its primary mission, but the high command of the SEAC had become increasingly concerned about its internal problems. In a secret letter to Lieutenant General Sir Oliver Leese, the overall commander of British ground forces, Sir William Slim, the commander of 11 Division's parent 14th Army Group, warned that the Division's mounting disciplinary problems made him "anxious" about using it again in combat. This prompted Leese, who was no great fan of African soldiers, to inform Admiral Lord Louis Mountbatten, Supreme Commander of Allied Forces in Southeast Asia, that "considerable unrest" in the Division was "prejudicing" his plans for using it in future operations.[78] As a result, Major General W. A. Dimoline, a successful brigade commander with considerable East African experience, was promoted to command the Division. He increased standards of discipline and training and purged frontline units of "undesirable" askaris. Dimoline was largely successful, and by the late spring of 1945, morale in the Division had improved considerably. The SEAC planned to use the East Africans in the reconquest of Malaya, but the unexpected Japanese surrender in August 1945 made this unnecessary.

In retrospect, the East African morale problems in Burma were hardly unique. Disciplinary records from the SEAC show British troops were equally disgruntled over lack of leave and poor treatment, and censorship reports warned they were suffering from a "general browned-offness" that made them "inclined to look for a catch in everything the Government does."[79] Most askaris fought out of loyalty to their friends and, to some extent, their units; few believed they were defending East Africa by inching their way down the Kabaw Valley. Although some officers estimated only twenty percent of their askaris were reliable in a direct assault, many Africans fought with extreme valor and bravery. African NCOs assumed key leadership positions when British officers were killed or wounded. To cite a few examples: Warrant Officer Platoon Commander Salika of 2 KAR won the Distinguished Conduct Medal for directing three consecutive assaults at Longstop Hill in spite of being badly wounded; Sergeant Jowana Odinga of 4 KAR earned a Military Medal for leading an attack on a Japanese bunker. Other askaris laid down their lives for their fellow soldiers: An askari of 71 KAR rescued a comrade by throwing his arms around an attacking Japanese soldier and dragging him over a cliff; Sergeant Mwanza Kimanzi of 5 KAR died while protecting his British Lieutenant from shell fire with his own body.[80]

The dangers of combat made the officers and men of the KAR mutually dependent, which, in turn, eroded racial barriers. The best British officers learned to rely on their askaris and developed strong emotional attachments to their men that survive to this day. Many Africans shared this bond and appreciated no longer being treated as inferiors. Waruhiu Itote, who later became "General China" during the Mau Mau Emergency, was profoundly influenced by his service in Burma:

> Among the shells and bullets there had been no pride, no air of superiority from our European comrades-in-arms. We drank the same tea, used the same water and lavatories, and shared the same jokes. There were no racial insults, no references to "niggers," "baboons" and so on. The white heat of battle had blistered all that away and left only our common humanity and our common fate, either death or survival.[81]

Surviving African veterans of the Burma fighting are still exceptionally proud of their exploits in Southeast Asia. They do not make much of their service to the British Empire but view their combat experience as an affirmation of their stamina, manhood, and personal courage.[82]

The record of East African forces in Ethiopia, Burma and the Middle East shows that askaris played a relatively small but significant role in the Second World War. Pre-war debates over the merits of the KAR were set aside in the face of the Axis threat to Britain and the Empire, and colonial military officials recruited some 323,483 East Africans over the course of the war. Roughly thirty percent of these men came from Kenya, twenty-seven percent from Tanganyika, twenty-four percent from Uganda, nine percent from Nyasaland and ten percent from Northern Rhodesia and other territories.[83] Approximately 80,000 men served in the AAPC and East African units in Southeast Asia, which meant roughly twenty-five percent of all askaris had some sort of overseas experience.

Official casualty reports for the East African forces list 7,301 dead out of 323,483 wartime askaris (two and three-tenths percent). Roughly 900 died when the transport *Khedive Ismail* was torpedoed in February 1944 by a Japanese submarine while transporting 11 Division's 301 Field Artillery Regiment from Mombasa to Ceylon.[84] Excepting this tragic loss, British officials took pride in these relatively low casualty rates. Yet the official statistic of only two and three-tenths percent casualties is inconsistent with campaign reports. For example, the official figure for losses from Nyasaland is 156 men, but in 1942, the East Africa Command informed the Colonial Secretary that some 230 Nyasalanders had perished in the Ethiopian Campaign alone.[85]

The most probable explanation for this discrepancy is that non-combat fatalities were underreported. While relatively few askaris were killed in combat, a great many East African servicemen died from accidents and disease. In the summer of 1943, only 11 of the 4,468 African patients in Nairobi's No. 1 (EA) General Hospital were being treated for war wounds, and of the 2,476 Kenyans listed as official fatalities during the war, only 490 were actually combat deaths.[86] British officials worked hard to avoid repeating the abominable suffering of the Carrier Corps. Yet although many Africans came from societies where debilitating diseases were endemic, askaris still suffered because, as Chapter 4 will show, they received inferior rations and medical care in comparison to European troops. It is difficult to determine whether the underreporting of disease-related fatalities was due to record keeping problems or to an attempt by colonial officials to avoid charges of exploiting African soldiers in a war that did not directly concern them.

THE POST-WAR KAR, 1945–1963

The end of the Second World War did not bring about an immediate resumption of the debate between civil and military officials over the proper role of the KAR. African soldiers had defended the East African territories, and internal security risks in the post-war era convinced administrators of the necessity of maintaining a standing colonial army. While direct African resistance to colonial rule had been minimal in the inter-war era, by the late 1940s, the colonial governments were increasingly concerned about the activities of African nationalists, trade unions, religious sects, and disgruntled veterans. The emergence of these groups signaled the end of tacit African acquiescence to British rule, and senior military officials warned it might be necessary to station one or two British battalions in the region if political and labor unrest continued to grow.[87]

In light of these problems, colonial officials dropped their opposition to funding the KAR, and debate shifted to how much of a role the Regiment should take in supporting the civil police. The British Army has always had a particular distaste for operations "in support of the civil power" requiring the use of lethal force against civilians.[88] Senior KAR officers believed their primary internal security role was to deter unrest through intimidation. To this end, they conducted public company and platoon-size training exercises, known as Company Safaris or Flag Marches, to demonstrate the effectiveness of their firepower. Convinced that the colonial army should be used only when all other options were exhausted, British officers opposed having their men sworn in as police constables because askaris were not trained in non-violent crowd control. In situations where the KAR confronted civilians directly, it followed the standard British military policy of firing on a mob's ringleaders if a crowd ignored sufficient warnings to disperse. Officially, the British Army believed warning shots were ineffectual.[89] Civil authorities, on the other hand, argued the KAR had to provide direct non-lethal support for the police in times of widespread disorder. Police forces in most East African territories could cope with minor incidents but were unequipped to deal with large-scale African resistance.

Although many African veterans insist that they sympathized with anti-colonial resistance movements, most KAR askaris continue to follow orders in the post-war era. In Kenya, 4 KAR reinforced the Kenya Police during the 1947 Mombasa dockworkers' strike, and three years later, the East Africa Armoured Car Squadron helped break up the Nairobi General Strike.[90] While these operations were largely non-violent, the Ugandan government called upon KAR askaris to use lethal force against African civilians twice in the late 1940s. In January 1945, a platoon from 28 KAR (a Kenyan unit) fired on approximately 2,000 civilians during a general strike in Kampala, killing four and wounding eleven.[91] Trouble flared up again in 1949, when widespread rioting against the Kabaka, who governed the Kingdom of Buganda as a British client, forced the Governor to call out the KAR. Kenya's 5 KAR garrisoned strategic points in Kampala because the EAC did not trust the Ugandan 4 KAR to fire on the local populace. When matters grew more serious, the KAR took direct control of the Kingdom of Buganda for four days to allow the police to rest and arrested rioters under the supervision of civil magistrates.[92] While these operations occasionally led to bloodshed, they did not tax the allegiances of Kenyan soldiers because the KAR did not ask them to shoot civilians from their home territories.

The KAR's increased internal security role did not preclude its use as an imperial force. In spite of 11 Division's problems in Burma, the War Office considered the experiment of using African soldiers overseas an unqualified success. Since Britain had promised the Indian nationalists independence during the war, imperial strategists now looked to Africa for military manpower. In as early as 1943, the EAC formulated plans for a modern post-war African force to replace the Indian Army. Metropolitan military officials expected to use African soldiers for "imperial policing" in "low-intensity" conflicts in the Middle East and Asia. The East African governments did not oppose the proposal because they assumed an imperial African army would be financed by metropolitan funds and therefore favored retaining the East Africa Command to keep the post-war KAR under centralized control.[93]

The KAR took on added importance for imperial planners when the regular British Army became overextended in the years immediately following the Second World War. Wartime British conscripts demanded immediate demobilization when the pending loss of India, the rising threat of Soviet Russia, and the vulnerability of the remaining overseas Empire increased Britain's foreign military commitments. Fiscal austerity, however, dictated a return to pre-war force levels, and most of the wartime KAR battalions (including the RAR) were disbanded. Increased internal security problems in Kenya convinced the government to retain three full battalions, and 11 KAR became a regular unit (under the new designation of 2/3 KAR) in recognition of its strong service in Burma. The wartime specialist and support arms shrank to small cadre units paid for by imperial funds, while the East African governments again became responsible for maintaining the KAR battalions. Under the new mobilization plans, these formations were the nucleus for a modern East African division that would be reconstituted rapidly in the event of a renewed global war.[94]

As the threat of war with the Soviet Union deepened in the late 1940s, East Africa's colonial forces became closely tied to the defense of the Middle East. Since Zionism and Arab nationalism made it difficult for Britain to retain extensive military bases in Palestine, Egypt, and Libya, in 1947 the War Office decided to shift extensive stock piles of weaponry and equipment from the Suez Canal Zone to the small railway town of MacKinnon Road, located just west of Mombasa. The "African Stores Holding Project" was intended to supply up to four divisions fighting in the Middle East and was to be ready by 1949, when treaty obligations required British troops to leave Egypt. The Royal Engineers began construction on the base in 1948 with the assistance of a special African military labor unit known as the East African Construction Force (EACF).[95]

These elaborate plans collapsed, however, after negotiations with the Egyptian government extended British tenure in Egypt. The project closed down entirely in 1950, as saner military minds realized MacKinnon Road was too far from the Middle East to be of much practical value in the event of a major war. Yet the demise of the African Stores Holding Project did not end East Africa's strategic connection to the Middle East. When the Egyptian government withdrew all civil labor from the Suez Canal Zone in 1951, the War Office raised a new East African military labor force to keep the Suez bases running. Ten thousand Africans from Kenya and Uganda served two-year overseas tours with the new East African Pioneer Corps until the Suez Crisis shut down the Canal Zone bases for good in 1955.[96]

The debate between military and civil officials over the KAR's fate was set aside in the immediate post-war years because the Regiment, funded sufficiently from imperial sources, easily served as both an internal security force and an imperial reserve. In 1948, the total cost of the East African colonial army was roughly £5.5 million per year. Of this, the Colonial Office contributed £3 million, the War Office, £1.5 million, and the East African governments, £1 million. In other words, eighty percent of the KAR's funding came from imperial sources. This was only a small fraction of Britain's total imperial defense budget of £750 million in 1949, but economic problems in Britain dictated a substantial reduction in overseas military spending. The War Office therefore proposed to make the East African governments responsible for a much greater percentage of the KAR's operating costs.[97]

This suggestion reignited the debate over the mission of the KAR. Although increasing African unrest was a problem, the East African governments hoped to rely upon the newly created paramilitary arms of the civil police. In 1948, the Kenyan Police established an Armoured Mobile Unit (later renamed the General Services Unit) under the command of an ex-army officer. The Kenyan government also revived the Kenya Regiment, and unofficial European representatives in the colonial legislatures were confident they could follow the Southern Rhodesians in eliminating their standing army. When representatives of the East African governments gathered in London for a conference on African defense in the fall of 1949, they unanimously rejected the War Office's suggestion that they assume a greater share of the colonial defense burden. The Ugandan and Tanganyikan delegates warned the conference that any decrease in social spending would lead to unrest and protested having to pay for the defense of the Middle East.[98]

With the imperial and colonial governments both refusing to fund the KAR at its current level, military officials had no alternative but to institute substantial cuts in the East African forces. Faced with a deficit of over £1 million, the War Office reduced the KAR battalions and eliminated most of the specialist cadre units for the wartime East African division.[99] In 1950, colonial military planners drew up a plan, code-named "Bludgeon," to return the colonial army to local control in five years. While it intended these reductions to preserve the core of the KAR as a viable military force, the cuts created an overall climate of apathy in the Regiment. The colonial governments rejected proposals to improve the pay and benefits of the African soldiery by updating and unifying their outmoded 1932 KAR Ordinances. The Regiment had difficulty retaining veteran soldiers with African pay fixed at 1946 levels, and British officers feared that the KAR's exclusive focus on internal security hurt their chances for promotion. Therefore the War Office had to draft officers to serve with the Regiment. With little experience leading African soldiers, these new men were bitter about being consigned to a "colonial backwater."[100]

In actual fact, however, the KAR was hardly inactive in the early 1950s. As Britain struggled to hold on to the peripheral regions of the Empire, the KAR became an ideal alternative to more expensive British units needed in Korea, Germany, and the Middle East. In 1951, military planners, still operating under the fallacious assumption that askaris were "natural" jungle fighters, sent 1 and 3 KAR to participate in counterinsurgency operations in Malaya as imperial troops. With the British government picking up the tab, the East African governments agreed to supply two battalions every two years on a rotating basis until the insurrection was over. To ensure internal security in East Africa was not compromised, Kenya and Tanganyika each raised a new KAR battalion. These were designated 23 and 26 KAR, respectively, and the old 2/3 KAR (which had been 11 KAR in Burma) was renamed 7 KAR. Thus, in spite of the "Bludgeon" plan, the infantry arm of the Regiment actually grew in the early 1950s.

The KAR's primary mission in Malaya was to provide small patrols for operations against Communist guerrillas. In this difficult counterinsurgency work, progress was measured in body counts rather than captured territory. Askaris were told they were going to Malaya to protect fellow subjects of the King from "armed bandits," and most of the younger men were eager to see combat and earn generous overseas pay.[101] The KAR battalions fought so well that British commanders wanted to replace them with new East African formations when their tour expired in 1953. Yet the outbreak of the Mau Mau rebellion in Kenya meant Kenyan, Ugandan, and Tanganyikan battalions could not be spared for overseas service. The War Office therefore relied exclusively on the two KAR battalions from Nyasaland, the Northern Rhodesia Regiment, and the newly reconstituted Rhodesian African Rifles.[102]

Civil and military authorities in Kenya were caught off guard entirely by the magnitude of the armed Kikuyu revolt. Mau Mau rebels fielded a military force that British intelligence officers estimated at 900 men organized in nine groups in the Aberdare Mountains, plus 4,500 men in nine "battalions" operating in the Mount Kenya region. While these figures may be high, the guerrillas were a coherent military force that threatened the security of British rule.[103] Using the cover of Kenya's mountainous Central Highlands, the Mau Mau fighters avoided being drawn into a full-scale set battle. In response, British commanders used their superiority in numbers and technology to divide Kenya's Central Province into zones of occupation, which were then swept of guerrillas by company and platoon-size patrols.

The KAR could not undertake such a mission on its own, and more to the point, the settler community did not trust African soldiers to put down an African rebellion. Thus, the regular British Army returned to East Africa for the first time since World War I. This did not mean, however, that the KAR was considered unreliable. In late 1952, a senior British officer confidently informed the War Office that the KAR was up to the job: "So far as I can see there should be no need to keep a British battalion in Kenya. The KAR are in excellent form and their loyalty so far is unshaken. They should prove fully sufficient backing for the police."[104] Nevertheless, Britain's Imperial General Staff sent a full British infantry brigade to Kenya to prevent the revolt from escalating as it had in Malaya. The East Africa Command also expanded the KAR during the Emergency. The four Kenyan battalions (3, 5, 7, and 23 KAR) were reinforced by the Ugandan and Tanganyikan battalions (4 and 6 KAR), and a fourth platoon was added to each Kenyan rifle company. As in Malaya, the counterinsurgency nature of the Mau Mau fighting required the KAR to conduct extensive forest patrols, and askaris also served in special operations teams under civilian intelligence officers. These measures were largely successful, and by the summer of 1955, the EAC declared victory over the Mau Mau's military wing.[105]

Although operations in Malaya and Kenya spared the KAR temporarily from "Bludgeon's" reductions, the plan was revived after the end of the Mau Mau insurrection. This time, however, the impetus for economy came from London rather than East Africa. In 1955, General Sir Gerald Templer reviewed Britain's armed forces and military commitments and concluded that thermonuclear weapons had diminished the likelihood of a protracted global war. Expecting nuclear hostilities to be short and confined to Europe, Templer believed there was no need to maintain the KAR as an imperial formation. The new mission of the Regiment in the event of war would be to defend East Africa and provide a single infantry brigade to reinforce the Middle East. With the full knowledge that colonial legislatures would insist on drastic reductions in the KAR, Templer recommended that the East African governments resume direct control of the Regiment for the first time since 1939. He assumed, however, that the development of long-range transport aircraft would prevent future "Mau Maus" by enabling a "fire brigade" of British infantry to be rapidly airlifted to Africa from Britain.[106]

The British government's decision to allow the Central African Federation (CAF) to take direct control of the Nyasaland KAR battalions and the NRR facilitated the devolution of military responsibility to the colonial governments. The federation of Nyasaland and Northern and Southern Rhodesia under the domination of Rhodesian settler interests enhanced Britain's strategic position in southern Africa and shifted more of the imperial defense burden to the colonies. In 1954, the Salisbury-based Central Africa Command (CAC) assumed responsibility for the defense forces of Nyasaland and Northern Rhodesia and replaced metropolitan British officers with men drawn from local settler communities.[107]

While the political future of African civilians in the CAF was decidedly uncertain, the general lot of African soldiers actually improved under the new regime. With African opinion in Nyasaland and Northern Rhodesia solidly opposed to federation with Southern Rhodesian settlers, the CAC needed to ensure the reliability of the armed forces. The Federation granted African soldiers substantial pay increases, improved living conditions, and service pensions at a time when their East African comrades suffered under the austerity of harsh budget cuts.[108]

Uganda and Tanganyika also welcomed the chance to resume direct control of their own KAR battalions. Unlike the Central African Federation, however, they were entirely unwilling to fund the Regiment beyond the bare minimum needed for internal security. While the War Office hoped to create a regional defense organization, Tanganyika and Uganda proposed to abolish all training and ordnance depots, engineering workshops, and even the EAC itself. Tanganyika, in particular, was confident that its Police Mobile Column could guarantee its internal security at a fraction of the cost of the KAR.[109] Sir Eveyln Baring, the Governor of Kenya, did not share this faith in the police after his territory's problems during Mau Mau and tried to persuade the British government to make up the difference between what was needed to maintain the KAR at full strength and what the colonial governments could afford. The War Office shared Baring's reservations but was willing to defer to Tanganyika and Uganda, provided they understood that they would not be able to call for external military assistance in an emergency.[110]

In response to this thinly veiled threat, the three East African governments grudgingly formed a regional defense organization to administer the KAR under a centralized command in February 1956. They originally proposed to place this body under the jurisdiction of the East African High Commission, but newly elected African representatives in the Kenyan and Ugandan legislatures blocked the plan because they suspected the High Commission would become a settler-dominated federation on the Central African model. In June 1957, the three governments therefore created an independent East African Land Forces Organization (EALFO) to administer the KAR.[111]

Under the EALFO's reorganization program the KAR absorbed all of the remaining specialist and support units created during the Second World War. The
EAASC shrank to two motor transport companies and an animal transport unit
for Kenya's northern frontier. The East African Corps of Signals became No. 1
Signal Squadron KAR, and the EAEME was replaced by a Workshop Detachment and three Light Aid Detachments. The EAAChD retained its autonomy
because church leaders would not allow religious personal to be attested as com-
batants. To ensure the KAR battalions could still function as a larger tactical
formation, a full brigade headquarters (designated 70 Infantry Brigade) was established in Kenya. One of the three remaining Kenyan battalions served as an
inter-territorial reserve battalion on a rotating basis. These changes were sanctioned in each territory by a new uniform KAR Ordinance that replaced the outmoded territorial 1932 ordinances.

As expected, the return to local control brought about drastic changes in
the scope and mission of the KAR. Under the EALFO, the Regiment shrank
from seven to five and a half battalions (not counting the two Nyasaland
battalions under the CAF). As the youngest battalion, 23 KAR was abolished
entirely, whereas two companies of 26 KAR became the garrison for
Mauritius, paid for by imperial funds. The fourth platoon added to each rifle
company during Mau Mau was also eliminated. Thus, the Regiment lost a
total of nine companies, or the equivalent of two entire battalions, forcing
the early discharge of over 700 African soldiers. Most askaris went will-
ingly, but a few saw the reduction as a "plot" by the EALFO to "take over"
the KAR. Those who remained found service in the new KAR much more
Spartan under the EALFO's new regime. Funding for new supplies or equipment dried up, and by the late 1950s, their appearance began to deteriorate,
with each man receiving only "one respectable shirt."[112]

The decision to establish the East African Land Forces Organization was
fundamentally flawed because it failed to account for the changing political
climate in East Africa. The Organization's fiscal austerity program was predi-
cated on the assumption that British rule in East Africa was relatively secure.
By the end of 1958, however, the East Africa Command had become increasingly concerned with the "deteriorating security situation" in the region.
In Kenya, intelligence officers worried about the reemergence of Kikuyu resistance, trade unionists, "fairly extreme" elected African legislative representatives, subversive independent African churches, and leftist elements at
Makerere University. Kenya's northern frontier also remained vulnerable to
cross-border raids by armed bandits from Somalia, Ethiopia, and the Sudan.[113]

In Tanganyika, the government's confidence that the civil police could
control large-scale unrest was unfounded. By 1959, Governor Sir Richard
Turnbull had to call in the KAR to maintain order. With all three companies
of 6 KAR tied down in Dar Es Salaam and Tabora, Tanganyika had to rely
on Kenya's 5 KAR to deal with rural unrest. The weakness of Tanganyika's

security forces was a key factor in Britain's decision to reach an accord with Julius Nyerere and the Tanganyika African National Union (TANU).[114] Similar problems existed in Uganda, where impatience with British rule, uncertainty over the future of the Kingdom of Buganda, and African hostility toward Indian merchants led to growing instability. Finally, the collapse of the colonial government in the Belgian Congo forced the EAC to add the western borders of Uganda and Tanganyika to its defense obligations.[115]

While no amount of military force could have driven the genie of African nationalism back into its bottle, the KAR's inability to deal with these new threats had an impact on Britain's sudden decision to relinquish its East African colonies. In 1958, the EAC concluded that it did not have sufficient forces to deal with an incident on the northern frontier if it coincided (by accident or intention) with a major internal uprising. Under the EALFO's reductions, only five KAR battalions existed in all of East Africa (not counting 26 KAR in Mauritius), whereas the EAC estimated that in a serious emergency it would need at least one brigade for internal security and two brigades (a total of nine battalions) on the northern frontier.[116] Thus, at a time when the East Africa Command faced a shortfall of at least four full battalions, civil officials often had to call upon the KAR to help suppress a variety of labor strikes and civil disobedience campaigns in all three territories.

Matters became equally serious in Nyasaland and Northern Rhodesia when African opposition to the Central African Federation turned violent in the late 1950s. Nyasaland had increased its police forces after 1 KAR and the NRR were called out to put down the first mass protests against federation in 1953. Yet the territory's security forces were still incapable of dealing with the massive unrest that rocked the Protectorate in 1959 after Kamuzu Hastings Banda returned from abroad to lead the Nyasaland African Congress. Although the CAF took better care of its African battalions than the East African governments, it did not consider 1 and 2 KAR sufficiently reliable to handle the situation. It supplemented the Nyasaland battalions with four companies from the RAR and NRR and sent three battalions of the all-European Royal Rhodesia Regiment to stiffen its African forces. Mass arrests of Congress supporters eventually smothered anti-federation resistance, but at a cost of at least thirty-seven civilian deaths and numerous complaints of beatings and rapes by the security forces. Three years later, the CAF had to use violence to control a similar rising in Northern Rhodesia's Northern Province.[117] While such operations were effective in the short term, the Federation's tactics only intensified African opposition to the point where it could no longer be contained by military means.

Yet colonial military authorities were caught off guard by Prime Minister Harold MacMillan's 1959 "Winds of Change Speech," which announced Britain's sudden intention to grant independence to her African colonies. They were therefore unprepared to transform their KAR battalions into the armed forces of independent African nations and were forced to scramble to keep up with the pace of political change. With only a single East African studying at the Royal Military Academy at Sandhurst in 1959, the East Africa Command had to undertake a crash program to recruit educated young men as officer candidates and prepare senior African NCOs for commissions. Unlike French colonial officers in Algeria, British strategists did not try to stand in the way of decolonization. Hoping to preserve their influence in the post-colonial era, they sought an orderly transfer of power to ensure that the new African armies would inherit the organization, traditions, and philosophy of the colonial army intact.

Colonial officials therefore tried to persuade African politicians in all three territories to accept some form of regional federation to keep the KAR battalions united under a centralized successor to the EALFO and the East Africa Command. With Tanganyika the first territory to gain independence in late 1961, the plan hinged on getting TANU's Julius Nyerere to agree to forgo the immediate creation of a national army. This proved impossible for a number of reasons. First, regional federation was incompatible with the nationalist aspirations of most Tanganyikan politicians, and second, Nyerere shared his colonial predecessors' belief that a sufficient police force would allow the country to dispense with an expensive standing army.[118]

Furthermore, the peaceful creation of new East African states depended on the ability of the colonial army and police to maintain order. With the KAR under local control, the Colonial Office's military advisers worried newly elected African members of the colonial legislatures would reduce their battalions to the point where they could not enforce British authority during the precarious period leading up to independence. Thus, in May 1959, W. L. Gorell Barnes asked the British Treasury to provide the £3 million per year that the War Office needed to resume full fiscal responsibility for the KAR. While publicly explaining the move as a gesture to allow the new African states to concentrate on economic development, in private he frankly admitted:

> You will see that our real reason for proposing these changes is political; that is, [it is] in the interests of Her Majesty's Government to ensure continued control of this service. . . . [This is] part of the price which we shall have to pay to maintain our influence and interests in the area for as long as we reasonably can. If the price cannot be afforded, we may well find ourselves considerably hampered in pursuing our main policy of the gradual approach in an area which is important to us for strategic as well as political reasons.[119]

Britain primarily feared the spread of Communist influence, but when a West German military mission visited Tanganyika in 1961, Governor Turnbull "seemed to detect quite an old-fashioned glint in the eyes of one or two of the Mission's members."[120]

The transfer of military power went even less smoothly in Central Africa, where the CAF tried to delay decolonization by force of arms. The Rhodesia-based officers of the Central Africa Command were frustrated by the Governor of Nyasaland's willingness to seek an accommodation with Banda and the Malawi Congress Party (the Nyasaland African Congress). The CAC's representative in Nyasaland counseled that military action should be used to hold the Federation together: "I feel if something of the sort is not done here very soon one can write this territory off as being a black state in the very near future agitating for independence continually. . . What I am concerned about is the fact that time is running out rapidly unless something to ease the political situation is put into effect by the Army now."[121] It is fortunate that this advice was never taken. African resistance to the CAF in Nyasaland had grown so strong that an attempted military solution to the problem would surely have resulted in considerable bloodshed.

Africans in Nyasaland were so hostile to the Federation's armed forces that recruiting for the KAR had become virtually impossible, and the War Office made secret plans to send British troops to Nyasaland and Northern Rhodesia if the CAC could not contain a major uprising.[122] Lacking the means and metropolitan support for further military action, the Rhodesian settlers had no choice but to allow the Federation to dissolve. Some Rhodesian officers favored retaining control of 1 and 2 KAR and continuing to recruit African soldiers in an independent Nyasaland just as the Gurkas were recruited in Nepal. In the end, however, the Federation transferred the African battalions of the CAC to the territories where they were stationed in 1964. Thus, 1 KAR became the Malawi Rifles in the former Nyasaland, and 2 KAR and the NRR became the national army of Zambia (Northern Rhodesia), even though the former battalion was composed almost entirely of Malawians.

In East Africa, the collapse of the proposed East African Federation doomed Britain's plans to continue the administration of the post-colonial armies under a unified military command. The various KAR battalions were therefore transformed into the Tanganyika, Uganda and Kenya Rifles as their countries achieved independence between 1961 and 1963. Britain maintained some military influence by seconding senior British officers to the new African armies, which preserved most of the KAR's traditions through national ordinances, regulations, and General Routine Orders that were virtually identical to their colonial predecessors.[123]

Thus, it appeared that Britain's direct involvement in the military affairs of East Africa was over. In January 1964, however, Tanganyikan askaris mutinied to protest low wages and slow promotions, which they attributed to the continued presence of expatriate British officers. In a matter of days, they were joined by members of the Uganda Rifles and one battalion of the

Kenya Rifles.[124] Eventually all three of the newly independent East African governments had to request military aid from Britain, and the revolts were ultimately crushed by Royal Marines and elements of the British Army still stationed in Kenya. Clearly, the institutions and culture of the colonial military could not be easily erased.

In retrospect, there were several main variables that determined the nature and character of African military service in colonial East Africa. As responsibility for running the colonial army swung back and forth between the War Office and the territorial governments, the African soldiery's compensation and terms of service shifted accordingly. Forced economy, official indifference, and civilian hostility allowed the King's African Rifles to deteriorate while under civilian control. Yet peacetime service was also relatively undemanding, and as we shall see in Chapters 3 and 4, askaris received considerably more privileges and benefits than the average African civilian. As imperial troops during the world wars, African soldiers received higher pay in return for enduring greater hardship and significant personal risk, but they were also more likely to resort to "collective insubordination" to contest their terms of service. Ultimately, African attitudes toward colonial military service were shaped by the nature of their mission, how much they were paid, and where and when they were asked to serve. Their reactions to this shifting set of variables ranged from reliable service to outright mutiny.

NOTES

[1] In 1904 the Central Africa Protectorate was renamed the Nyasaland Protectorate, and in 1920 the East Africa Protectorate became the Kenya Colony and Protectorate.

[2] Hubert Moyse-Bartlett, *The King's African Rifles*, (Aldershot: Gale & Polden, 1956), p. 63.

[3] Ibid., pp. 19–41.

[4] H. R. Wallis, *The Handbook of Uganda*, (London: Crown Agents for the Colonies, 1913); Moyse-Bartlett, *The King's African Rifles*, pp. 51–55.

[5] Historical Record of 3 KAR, PRO, WO 106/270; Moyse-Bartlett, *The King's African Rifles*, p. 96.

[6] Memorandum by Colonel G. Thesiger, 17 April 1912, PRO, WO 106/254.

[7] Moyse-Bartlett, *The King's African Rifles*, pp. 27, 135.

[8] Charles Eliot, *The East African Protectorate*, (London: Edward Arnold, 1905), pp. 200–201.

[9] Great Britain Colonial Office, *Regulations for the King's African Rifles*, (London: Waterlow and Sons, 1908), p. 111.

[10] Tour of Inspector General G. H. Thesiger, April 1912, NAM, 8201-42 1; Robert Foran, *The Kenya Police, 1887–1960*, (London: Robert Hale Limited, 1962), pp. 36, 40.

[11] Moyse-Bartlett, *The King's African Rifles*, p. 153; Tour of Inspector General G. H. Thesiger, March 1913, NAM, 8201–42.

[12] C. P. Fendall, *The East African Force, 1915–19*, (London: HF&G Witherby, 1921), pp. 22–23.

[13] Lewis Greenstein, "Africans in a European War: The First World War in East Africa with Special Reference to the Nandi of Kenya," (Ph.D. dissertation, Indiana University, 1975), p. 53.

[14] 3 KAR During the EA Campaign 1914–18, PRO, WO 106/273; Reorganization of the KAR, 1916, PRO, WO 106/277; History of the 5th Battalion, KAR, PRO, WO 106/279; Moyse-Bartlett, *The King's African Rifles*, p. 701.

[15] Paul von Lettow-Vorbeck, *East African Campaigns*, (New York: Speller & Sons, 1957), p. 293.

[16] Geoffrey Hodges, *The Carrier Corps: Military Labor in the East African Campaign, 1914–1918*, (Westport CT: Greenwood Press, 1986), p. 209.

[17] Report by Director of Military Labour to the BEA Expeditionary Force, 1919, (Nairobi: No publisher, no date); Hodges, *The Carrier Corps*, pp. 110–11.

[18] 3 KAR During the EA Campaign 1914–18, PRO, WO 106/273; Moyse-Bartlett, *The King's African Rifles*, p. 701.

[19] Angus Buchanon, *Three Years of War in East Africa*, (New York: Negro Universities Press, 1969), p. 193.

[20] Accounting for KAR, 30 August 1919, MNA, S2/45/19/2; Notes for the Inspector General, 5 December 1919, MNA, S1/1996/19.

[21] Memorandum on Defence Organization in East & West Africa, July 1936, PRO, WO 32/4141.

[22] IGR, 1 KAR 1927, PRO, CO 820/3/4; O/C Troops NY to CSNY, 1 December 1923, MNA, S2/8/20/4; Francis De Guingand, *African Assignment*, (London: Hodder and Stoughton, 1953), p. 62.

[23] NFP HoR, 1925, KNA, PC NFP 2/1/1; IGR, 3 KAR, 1927, PRO, CO 820/2/12; Re-Organization of the NFP, by PC NFP, 23 October 1928, KNA, PC NFP 4/1/4.

[24] See Table A.1.

[25] Lieutenant Colonel Davies to PC NZA, 24 November 1925, KNA, PC NZA 3/19/3; AR, 4 KAR Reserve, 1926, PRO, CO 820/1/16; B. F. Montgomery to DCs, 31 March 1933, KNA, DC KSM 1/22/29.

[26] Report by Bishop, 1932, PRO, WO 32/4128.

[27] Defence in East Africa, IGR, 15 September 1927, PRO, CO 820/2/23.

[28] Brigadier H. A. Walker to Colonial Secretary, 28 January 1929, KNA, AG 4/627/1c; Organization of the KAR, 14 January 1930, PRO, CO 820/8/6.

[29] Uganda Governor to Colonial Secretary, 13 April 1931, PRO, CO 820/11/10.

[30] Tanganyikan Governor to Colonial Secretary, 20 December 1929, PRO, CO 820/8/6; Nyasaland Governor to Colonial Secretary, 8 February 1930, PRO, CO 820/8/6.

[31] Defence and Public Security Forces in Tanganyika, by Tanganyikan Governor, 28 February 1932, PRO, CO 820/13/6.

[32] Minute by Inspector General C. C. Norman, 25 April 1932, PRO, CO 533/421/10; Minute by Norman, 9 May 1932, PRO, CO 820/13/6.

[33] Overseas Defence Committee, "KAR," 13 October 1932, PRO, CO 820/13/6; Defence Problems BEA & NR, 1934, by Brigadier C. C. Norman & Vice Air Marshall C.N.L. Newall; Minute by Colonel R. Cidan, 23 May 1935, PRO, WO 32/4127.

[34] Brigadier G. H. Cree, RHL, Mss.Afr.s.1715/57.

[35] O/C S Bde to CST, 15 November 1935, MNA, GOB G97; IGR, S Bde, 1935, PRO, CO 820/21/13.

[36] Minute by J.E.W. Flood, 13 September 1937, PRO, CO 820/26/15.

[37] Reorganization of the Forces in Our EA Colonies, by Inspector General Giffard, August 1937, PRO, CO 820/26/15; Memorandum on Defence of Mombasa, 17 January 1938, KNA, CNC 10/90/17b; W. V. Brelsford, ed., *Story of the Northern Rhodesia Regiment*, (Lusaka: The Government Printer, 1954), p. 78.

[38] Annual Unit Returns, 1927–1938, PRO, CO 820.

[39] Conference of Governors of British EA Territories, June 1939, PRO, WO 201/2676.

[40] British territorial units were roughly the equivalent of the U.S. National Guard. Uganda Governor to Colonial Secretary, 10 March 1939, PRO, CO 820/38/3.

[41] 7 KAR Officer List, 1939, PRO, CO 820/38/2; O/C N Bde to Bishop, 14 July 1939, PRO, CO 820/38/3; Uganda Governor to Colonial Secretary, 22 July 1939, PRO, CO 820/38/2.

[42] CSNY to Colonial Secretary, HoW, 4 February 1941, MNA, S33/2/1/1/97; 7 KAR Intelligence Summary, PRO, WO 169/778; Sir Anthony Swann, RHL, Mss.Afr.s.1715/268.

[43] Rear HQ ALFSEA to Adv HQ, 22 November 1944, PRO, WO 203/1995; CSNY to CSEAG, 16 October 1942, MNA, S41/1/17/12/12; LCN to CSNY, 29 December 1944, MNA, S41/1/23/4.

[44] Military Units Ordinance (No. 25) of 1939, KNA, MP 66/3.

[45] Memorandum by Fazan, "The Pioneer Corps," 27 September 1939, KNA, PC NZA 2/3/21/57; Michael Blundell, *A Love Affair with the Sun*, (Nairobi: General Printers, 1994), pp. 55–71.

[46] M. W. Biggs, "The Liberation of Addis Ababa–Fifty Years On," *Royal Engineers Journal*, v. 105, (August 1991), p. 162.

[47] Moyse-Bartlett, *The King's African Rifles*, pp. 521–67; CSEAG to Sir Arthur Dawe, 4 June 1942, PRO, CO 980/93.

[48] GOC to Colonial Secretary, 16 July 1941, PRO, CO 820/48/23; Anthony Clayton, *Communication for New Loyalties: African Soldier's Songs*, (Athens: Ohio University Press, 1978), p. 38; Kenneth Gandar Dower, *Askaris at War in Abyssinia*, (Nairobi: East African Standard, n.d.), p. 6; Interviews, #38, #59, #98, #114.

[49] DA & QMG EAC to CSEAG, 8 November 1941, KNA, DEF 15/57/4b; Investigation of the Military Labour Position, 10 June 1942, KNA, DEF 15/73/1.

[50] Kenya Secretariat Meeting with the EAC, 29 April 1941, KNA, MD 4/5/137/22; Notes for the WO Liaison Officer, 5 May 1942, PRO, WO 106/5099; African Manpower Conference, 7 May 1943, KNA, DEF 15/27/70a.

[51] EAPLO's Visit to EA Troops in the Middle East, 19 July–20 August 1944, KNA DEF 15/12/45a; EAC Conference Minutes, 25 July 1944, PRO, WO 169 18211.

[52] Report by Lieutenant J.E.V. Ross, Welfare Officer, 27 July 1942, KNA, MD 4/5/66/26a.

[53] Ross to Director of Pioneers and Labour, July 1942, KNA, PC NZA 2/3/97/1; PC NZA to Director of Pioneers and Labour, 11 November 1944, KNA, PC NZA 2/3/97.

[54] Interviews, #61, #78.

[55] Censorship Summary, Mail by EA Personnel in the MEF, June–July 1943, KNA, MD 4/5/116/5.

[56] PTE Kabichi Saidi to Akulu Kawanga, 24 July 1943; James Nkhoma, M-Stammlager VIII B Germany, to Thekerani (mother), 19 October 1943, MNA, S45/3/2/2.

[57] WO to CnC MELF, June 1944, PRO, CO 820/56/3; Bildad Kaggia, *The Roots of Freedom, 1921–1963*, (Nairobi: EA Publishing House, 1975), pp. 43–44.

[58] CnC India to WO, 1 December 1941, PRO, CO/968/11/5.

[59] Operations of 22 (EA) Brigade, September–November 1942, LHC, DP/VIII/5; Report by Consultant Surgeon EAC, July–December 1942; PRO, WO 222/1806; Moyse-Bartlett, *The King's African Rifles*, pp. 608–9.

[60] GOC EAC to WO, 7 December 1942, PRO, WO 106/4499.

[61] The battalions of 11 (EA) Division were organized as follows: (a) 21 Brigade: 2 (Nyasaland) KAR, 4 (Uganda) KAR, 1 NRR; (b) 25 Brigade: 26 (Tanganyika) KAR, 34 (Uganda) KAR, 11 (Kenya) KAR; (c) 26 Brigade: 22 (Nyasaland) KAR, 36 (Tanganyika) KAR, 44 (Uganda) KAR; (d) Division Protection Battalion: 13 (Nyasaland) KAR; (e) Division Scout Battalion: 5 (Kenya) KAR. The two independent brigades were: (a) 22 (EA) Brigade: 1 (Nyasaland) KAR, 3 NRR, 1 RAR; (b) 28 (EA) Brigade: 7 (Uganda) KAR, 46 (Tanganyika) KAR, 71 (Somali) KAR.

[62] Christopher Owen, *The Rhodesian African Rifles*, (London: Leo Cooper, 1970), pp. 4–16; Interview #152.

[63] 11 Division Support Units, 15 August 1944, PRO, WO 172/6484; Labour Situation in SEAC, 29 May 1945, PRO, WO 253/12.

[64] Lecture by Major General C. C. Fowkes, Operations on Assam-Burma Border, August–October 1944, LHC, DP/IX/5; Louis Allen, *Burma: The Longest War*, (London: J. M. Dent and Sons, 1986), p. 389.

[65] Moyse-Bartlett, *The King's African Rifles*, p. 614.

[66] Medical Aspects of the 4th (U) Bn KAR's Advance Upon Mawlaik and Kalewa, December 1944, PRO, WO 172/6531; Richard Stone, Staff Captain, 21 Brigade, RHL, Mss.Afr.s. 2114.

[67] Biggs to Major General E. Mansergh, O/C 11 Division, 3 January 1945, Biggs Collection; Lieutenant-General Sir Oliver Leese to Major-General W. A. Dimoline, O/C 11 Division, 27 May 1945, PRO, WO 172/9439.

[68] History of the 28th (EA) Independent Infantry Brigade, Burma 1945, LHC, DP/IX/9; Moyse-Bartlett, *The King's African Rifles*, pp. 667–71.

[69] Jacques van Doorn, "Ideology and the Military," in *On Military Ideology*, edited by. Morris Janowitz and Jacques van Doorn, (Rotterdam: Rotterdam University Press, 1971).

[70] Quoted in Allen, *Burma: The Longest War*, p. 114.

[71] The SEAC replaced the Scouts with 5 KAR, a veteran pre-war unit that had seen fighting in Ethiopia and Madagascar. 11 Army Group SEA to HQ 14th Army, 29 April 1944, PRO, WO 203/161; GOC 14 Army Group to 11 Army Group HQ, 13 May 1944, PRO WO/203/161; 11 Division Circular, "11 (EA) Division Scouts," 21 June 1944, PRO, WO 172/6484.

[72] Morale of British, Indian and Colonial Troops of ALF SEA, August–October 1944, PRO, WO 203/2268; Biggs to Mansergh, 3 January 1945, Biggs Collection; John Woodcock, RHL, Mss.Afr.s.1715/306; Interviews, #135, #142.

[73] Infantry Battalion Commanders Notes on 11 (EA) Division's Ops on the Burma Front, July to December 1944, by Lieutenant Colonel T. H. Birkbeck, IWM, 83/21/1, Birkbeck Papers; History of the 28th (EA) Independent Infantry Brigade, Burma 1945, LHC, DP/IX/9; D.F.T. Bowie, RHL, Mss.Afr.s.1715/24.

[74] Biggs to Mansergh, 3 January 1945, Biggs Collection; Cree, RHL, Mss.Afr.s.1715/57.

[75] Bowie, RHL, Mss.Afr.s.1715/24; Interview, #143.

[76] This order amused some askaris, whereas others took it as a sign of cowardice. After the war an African veteran wrote a letter to *Sauti ya MwaAfrica,* declaring: "We saw how brave the Africans were in Burma. While European bravery was by painting

their bodies with boot polish in order to disguise themselves from their enemies." 28 (EA) Infantry Brigade Training Instruction, No. 11, 26 November 1944, LHC, DP/IX/1; Kibutu P. Njogu to Editor of *Sauti ya MwaAfrica*, 30 April 1948, KNA, MAA 8/102/52; Interview, #81.

[77] 5 (EA) FSS, War Diary, 26 October 1944, PRO, WO 172/6585; Morale of British, Indian and Colonial Troops of ALF SEA, November 1944–January 1945, PRO, WO 203/2268.; Major K.W. Davies, RHL, Mss.Afr.s.1715/64; Bowie, RHL, Mss.Afr.s.1715/24; Interview, #143.

[78] Slim to HQ ALF SEA, 1 February 1945, PRO, WO 203/1794; Leese to Admiral Lord Louis Mountbatten, 9 February 1945, PRO, WO 203/2021.

[79] Court Martial Cases, SEAC, August 1944–October 1945, PRO, WO 203/2045; 2268; Morale of British Indian and Colonial Troops of ALF SEA, February–April 1945, PRO, WO 172/9544.

[80] Visit to EA Troops in SE Asia, by EAPLO, June 1945, KNA, DEF 15/12/80a; History of the 28th (EA) Independent Infantry Brigade, LHC, DP/IX/9; Anonymous (Major P. F. Vowles), *The Eleventh (Kenya) Battalion, The King's African Rifles, 1941–1945,* (Ranchi, India: Catholic Press, 1946).

[81] Waruhiu Itote, *"Mau Mau" General,* (Nairobi: EA Publishing House, 1967), p. 27.

[82] Interviews, #58, #80, #81, #82, #91, #112.

[83] East African Report to the Colonial Secretary, July 1947, KNA, DEF 10/43/93.

[84] GOC EAC to WO, February 1944, PRO, WO 106/4501; EAC to 11 Army Group SEAC, 15 February 1944, PRO, WO 203/161.

[85] Report to the Colonial Secretary, July 1947, KNA, DEF 10/43/93; CSEAG to Colonial Secretary, 4 June 1942, PRO, CO 980/93.

[86] Registrar's Report, 1 GH, July - September 1943, PRO, WO 222/1827; Kenyan Casualties, September 1940–September 1946, KNA, DEF 10/24/76.

[87] EAC Circular, "Internal Security," 11 July 1946, PRO WO/269/1; EAC, "Peace Time Order of Battle," 14 June 1948, PRO, WO 269/8; Appendix A, HQ Nairobi Sub-Area Operational Instructions Nos. 3, 7, February 1949, PRO, WO 276/102.

[88] Great Britain, *Imperial Policing and Duties in of the Civil Power,* (London: HM Stationery Office, 1949); Interview, #151.

[89] Nairobi Sub-Area Operational Instruction No. 1, 29 January 1946, PRO, WO 276/102.

[90] PC Coast Province to CSK, 26 February 1947, KNA, SEC 1/12/6/3; Diary of Events on Active Internal Security Service, EA Armoured Car Squadron, 13–24 May 1950, PRO, WO 269/238.

[91] Background to Buganda, PRO, WO 276/73; EAC Circular, "Aid to the Civil Power," 19 January 1945, PRO, WO 276/81; Buganda Riots, 18 January 1945, RHL, Mss.Afr.s. 1512.

[92] Report by Brigadier A.C.F. Jackson, O/C Northern Area, to GOC EAC, 26 May 1949, PRO, WO 269/67.

[93] Platt to Under Secretary of State, WO, 26 April 1943, PRO, CO 820/55/7; EA Governors' Conference, 4 November 1944, PRO, WO 106/5217; Post-War Organisation of Military Forces in African Dependencies, 25 January 1944, PRO, CO 820/55/7; Conference of EA Governors: Post-War Defence, 20 April 1946, LHC, DP/X/5.

[94] Post-War Garrisons of Colonial and Mandated Territories, 2 July 1945, PRO, WO 106/5217; Chief of the Imperial General Staff's African Tour, 18 December 1947, PRO, WO 276/251.

[95] Kenyan Secretariat Circular, "Directorate of East Africa Construction Forces (Civil)," 18 September 1947, KNA, DC ELD 1/17/5/48; MacKinnon Road IR, February 1948, KNA, PC CST CA/1/16/93/2.

[96] Sandfly Instruction No. 1, 23 November 1951, KNA, PC NZA 3/19/11/6a.

[97] EAHC Defence Committee Proceedings, 21 September 1948, PRO, WO 276/75; WO Minute, Colonial Forces: Financial Problems, 20 September 1949, PRO, WO 32/13267.

[98] African Forces Conference, 10 October 1949, PRO, WO 32/13267.

[99] WO to GHQ MELF, 18 November 1949, PRO, WO 32/13267; EAC "G" Branch, QHR, 1949, PRO, WO 269/11.

[100] Lieutenant General Sir A. M. Cameron, GOC EAC, to CSEAG, August 1951, KNA, DEF/6/4/1; Cameron to Kenya Governor, 29 July 1952, KNA, DEF 30/1/15.

[101] Report by Brigadier D. M. Shean, 1 Malay Infantry Bde, 25 August 1952, KNA, GH 4/705/1/3; 3 KAR Newsletter No. 6, 1 February–20 May 1953, KNA, GH 4/705/7; African Troops for the Malaya Project, July 1951, KNA, PC NKU 2/21/5/12a; WO Minute, 4 September 1951, PRO, WO 216/432; Interviews, #19, #33.

[102] Lieutenant General Harold Redman to W. L. Gorrell Barnes, CO, 12 June 1953, PRO, WO 216/853; W. V. Brelsford, ed., *Handbook to the Federation of Rhodesia and Nyasaland*, (Salisbury: Government Printer, 1960), p. 670.

[103] In 1953, the EAC offered the following assessment of their fighting abilities: "Good initiative is displayed by the leaders and the gangs are well disciplined. Their training is not to be despised, except in musketry." Brief for C-in-C by Major General W.R.N. Hinde, 5 June 1953, RHL, Mss.Afr.s. 1580/12; Future Military Policy in Kenya, 1954, PRO, WO 276/516.

[104] GHQ MELF to WO, 5 November 1952, PRO, WO 216/811.

[105] Operational Situation in Kenya in July 1955, 4 August 1955, KNA, WC CM 1/5/704; Anthony Clayton, *Counterinsurgency in Kenya: A Study of Military Operations Against the Mau Mau, 1952–1960*, (Manhattan, KS: Sunflower University Press, 1984).

[106] Report on Colonial Security, by General Sir Gerald Templer, 23 April 1955, IWM, Erskine Papers, 75/134/4; Colonial Secretary Lennox Boyd to Baring, 30 September 1955, PRO, WO 276/57.

[107] Lieutenant Colonel W. H. Hyde, CO 1 KAR, to HQ CAC, 2 September 1955, MNA, F/248/2072.

[108] Secretary BESL to KAR Colonel-Commandant, 17 June 1956, LHC, DP/XIV/B/3; Nyasaland Battalions–Changes Since Federation, June 1962, MNA, F/248/2073.

[109] EAC Circular, "Longshot III," 19 November 1955, PRO, WO 276/57.

[110] Chief of Staff Brief for GOC EAC, 11 November 1955, PRO, WO 276/57; GOC EAC to Under Secretary of State, WO, 12 December 1955, PRO, WO 276/57; EA High Commissioner to Colonial Secretary, 1 May 1956, PRO, WO 276/15.

[111] Proceedings of Ugandan Legislative Council, 11 March 1957, PRO, CO 986/593; EA Defence Working Committee, 3 April 1957, KNA, LF 1/48.

[112] Future of the KAR in Kenya After the Emergency, 1956, Birkbeck Papers, IWM, 83/21/1; 9th EADWC, April 1957, KNA, LF 1/49; Interview, #108; Lieutenant Colonel J.C.T. Peddie, RHL, Mss.Afr.s.1715/213.

[113] GOC's Talk to the U.S. National War College Group, 20 May 1958, KNA, LF 1/38/14; Report on the East African Land Forces in 1959, by GOC EAC, KNA, LF 1/212/3a.

[114] Sir Richard Turnbull to F. D. Webber, CO, 14 February 1959, PRO, CO 822/1322; John Iliffe, *A Modern History of Tanganyika*, (New York: Cambridge University Press, 1979), p. 564.

[115] EAC Circular, "Standing Instructions for Operational Moves," 29 July 1960, KNA, LF 1/152/9.

[116] Report on the East African Land Forces in 1959, by GOC EAC, KNA, LF 1/212/ 3a; Chief of Staff EAC to Kenya Defence Minister, 10 February 1959, KNA, LF 1/55/1.

[117] Organization of Nyasaland Operations, February–March 1959; Casualty Figures, MNA, F/248/2072; O/C 1 KAR to O/C NR District, 20 October 1961; "The Voice of UNIP: A Grim Peep in the North," MNA, F/248/2072.

[118] Future of the KAR in Tanganyika, by GOC EAC, 6 June 1961; R. J. Vile to A. N. Galsworthy, CO, 27 June 1961, PRO, CO 968/724.

[119] W. L. Gorell Barnes to A. D. Peck, Treasury, 11 May 1959, PRO, DEFE 7/1014.

[120] Turnbull to W.B.L. Monson, CO, 27 April 1961, PRO, CO 968/724.

[121] O/C Nyasaland Area to Chief of Staff CAF Army, 19 August 1960, MNA, F/248/ 2072.

[122] 1 KAR Recruiting Tour, October–November 1961, MNA/F/248/2072; O/C 1 KAR to CAC HQ, 17 February 1962, MNA, F/248/2076; WO Minute to CIGS, 25 February 1960, PRO, WO 216/923.

[123] J. T. Lisle to Colonial Secretary, 2 September 1961, PRO, CO 968/725; Dimoline to Goodwin, 16 November 1961, LHC, DP/XIV/14/A/6; "The Kenya Military Forces Bill 1962," 15 November 1963, KNA, WC CM 1/13/195.

[124] Major General R.W.N. Mans, RHL, Mss.Afr.s.1715/178; Interviews, #4, #25, #148.

3

RECRUITING AND THE DOCTRINE OF "MARTIAL RACE"

This chapter focuses on the shifting political economy of recruiting and its connections with stereotypes of "martial race," enlistment patterns, and the creation of ethnicity. Most Africans joined the colonial army out of necessity, attracted by lucrative military wages and the security and privilege of government service. Colonial military authorities only resorted to outright conscription to recruit military laborers during the world wars. They were extremely selective in recruiting combat soldiers, believing certain "tribes" had inherently militaristic characteristics. The King's African Rifles, therefore, divided East African ethnic groups into two categories: martial and nonmartial. Most accounts of the colonial army tend to accept these recruiting categories as a constant unit of analysis, but in reality, individuals, not "tribes," enlisted in the KAR.

Nevertheless, martial stereotypes are a useful index of the changing political economy of recruitment. Although portrayed by British officers as an innate cultural attribute, in reality martial race signified an acceptance of military discipline. The willingness of an ethnic group to serve in the colonial army was based on the extent of its integration into the East African economy and therefore changed over time. Askaris from martial races were usually illiterates from remote, economically disadvantaged regions who were attracted by the KAR's relatively high rates of pay for unskilled labor. Nonmartial races came from wealthier areas where there was greater opportunity for education and lucrative employment. Therefore, African societies were most martial when they were in a transitional stage of economic development, operating under the constraints of colonial rule.

Military authorities used martial categories to recruit specific ethnic groups for the three main branches of the colonial army: combat battalions, technical arms, and military labor units. Labor historians have been careful to document distinctions in the nature of skilled and unskilled civilian African labor, but works on colonial armies tend to use the term *African soldier* as a generic category. British officers believed specific ethnic groups were naturally suited to particular types of service. Only martial races had the necessary qualities for combat, but non-martial peoples could be laborers and military specialists. Colonial recruiting therefore involved matching a specific ethnic group with the appropriate branch of military service. Thus, military specialization and ethnicity also shaped African perceptions of military service.

MARTIAL RACES

The use of ethnic stereotypes to recruit soldiers did not originate in colonial East Africa. Scotch and Irish soldiers were the martial races of the British Army, and seconded officers and NCOs from the Indian Army spread the recruiting biases of the British Raj to the early KAR battalions. While virtually every colonial officer had his own personal views about which "tribe" made the best soldiers, it is possible to sketch a composite picture of the prototypical East African martial race. KAR recruiters preferred Africans from remote impoverished regions. According to the 1908 KAR Regulations, "[S]uch men are, as a rule, capable of undergoing prolonged exertion without regular food, and have a natural aptitude for observing and tracking."[1] The commander of 11 KAR in Burma observed that "our African askari definitely has a sixth sense in the jungle, which enables him to 'point' the enemy in the same manner as a good pointer gun dog."[2] Many officers believed education and affluence spoiled potential soldiers and were unequivocal in their preference for "illiterate savages." Some ethnic groups like the Kamba acquired a reputation for being "mechanically minded," but recruiters considered most educated Africans potential cowards and "bush lawyers."

KAR officers respected ethnic groups like the Nandi of Kenya, who had actively resisted colonial rule. As with the Highland Scots and Nepalese Gurkas, they believed a former enemy could be transformed into a reliable soldier if properly led. There was also room for the right kind of rogue. With regard to the potential enlistment of a convicted cattle thief, the commander of 3 KAR enthused: "The man sounds just the sort to make a soldier of some initiative! Call him by all means."[3] Civil administrators looked to the KAR to provide a disciplined outlet for the martial aspirations of youths who would have been warriors in pre-colonial times but had gravitated to brawling and stock theft under British rule. While these young men often disdained wage labor, they were attracted by the prestige of *kazi ya bunduki* (military service, or literally, "work of the gun").

Martial recruiting also had an important strategic function. Given that internal security was the KAR's primary peacetime mission, the army encouraged askaris to see themselves as different from, and superior to, the mainstream African population. Military authorities recruited ethnically balanced companies to avoid having to ask askaris to fight their own "kith and kin." Yet successful military organizations are built on homogeneity and conformity, and British officers also encouraged Africans to think of the KAR as their "tribe." They forbade askaris to wear earrings, bangles, or other examples of ethnic dress, and Swahili and Chinyanja (Chewa) were the Regiment's only official African languages.[4] During the Second World War, many askaris abandoned "tribal traditions" by sewing up split earlobes and buying dentures to replace filed teeth. In Ethiopia, army medical units were deluged by requests for circumcisions by men who came from societies that did not normally engage in the practice because many prostitutes would not have sex with uncircumcised men.[5] Civil authorities, on the other hand, viewed these developments with alarm, worrying that military service would "detribalize" askaris and thereby disrupt the institutions of indirect rule.

The KAR's recruiting policies also encouraged the creation of ethnic identities linked with military service. Leroy Vail has attributed the origins of tribalism in southern Africa to European missionaries who acted as "cultural brokers" by codifying languages, writing tribal histories, and disseminating ethnic symbols.[6] KAR officers played a similar role by celebrating, and sometimes even inventing, "martial traditions" for African soldiers. As was the case in the Scots Highland Regiments, the KAR turned African cultural institutions to military use. KAR battalions in Burma used African drums and horns to pass messages and unnerve the Japanese, who believed the East Africans were cannibals. After the war, the Regiment sponsored dancing exhibitions featuring askaris in "traditional tribal regalia" and established a KAR Museum in Kenya to display "tribal dress and finery as well as items which are or used to be important factors in tribal life."[7] While there was an important public relations element in these activities, they also educated individual askaris as to how their particular ethnic groups were "martial."

Conversely, Africans also manipulated martial identity for their own purposes. The label "Kalenjin," a term for the linguistically related Elgeyo, Kipsigis, Marakwet, Nandi, Pokot, Tugen, and Terik peoples of the central Rift Valley, was invented, in part, by African soldiers during the Second World War who disliked being referred to as "Nandi-speaking tribes" by the army. "Kalenjin" (meaning "I tell you") came into widespread use as an opening salutation during wartime radio broadcasts to African servicemen.[8] Kalenjin cultural brokers adopted the term to counter the influence of the more populous Luo and Kikuyu peoples in post-war Kenya. Military officials sympathized with this goal. The new label encouraged martial pride and sharpened divisions between askaris and more politically active Kenyan ethnic groups.

"Kalenjin" became an official recruiting category, and KAR battalions reinforced this supra-ethnic identity by distributing copies of vernacular newsletters for "Kalenjin" askaris.[9]

THE POLITICAL ECONOMY OF RECRUITING

Most Africans joined the KAR for economic reasons. In Kenya, European
settlers appropriated the best agricultural land in the Central Highlands. Africans could not own land outside their "native reserves" and had to carry a
special registration certificate, or *kipande*, if they left to seek work. By the
1930s, eighty-six percent of Kenya's African population lived in reserves
comprising only twenty-two percent of the arable land in the colony, which
left no room for population growth.[10] The Kenyan government claimed the
reserves protected African "tribal systems" from Western influence, but in
reality, their primary purpose was to generate labor for European farms. Driven
by regressive taxation policies that required payment in currency, Africans
from reserves with high population densities or limited productive capacities
had little choice but to sell their labor.

Yet ethnic groups from the most densely populated reserves did not necessarily produce the most soldiers. While taxation and land pressure encouraged wage laborer, many Africans had far more lucrative employment opportunities than military service. Taxation stimulated commodity production
in fertile reserves blessed with a suitable climate and access to the main transportation routes. Africans in these regions also tended to be better educated
because of their proximity to European missions and could therefore command higher wages. These factors explain why the Kikuyu, Meru, and Embu
peoples of the Central Highlands and the Luo and Luhya of western Kenya
were usually classified as non-martial; they simply had better prospects than
the KAR. Moreover, Kikuyu were politically unreliable from the British perspective because they lost the most land to European settlement.

Most of Kenya's martial races came from pastoral or semi-pastoral communities in less prosperous regions of the colony. The Kenyan government
lacked the means and inclination to enforce taxation and restrictive land
policies in these areas. Colonial officials considered pastoral societies unduly conservative because of their resistance to change, but in reality, livestock allowed African pastoralists to ignore the pull of wage labor by selling
cattle to pay their taxes. Pastoral and semi-pastoral peoples became martial
races when population growth, unfavorable climatic conditions, and colonial
economic policies began to limit their ability to maintain large herds.

The Kenyan government seized 10,000 head of cattle in the Nandi Pacification Campaign of 1905 and tried to "depasturize" the Nandi and Kipsigis
by alienating large tracts of grazing land to encourage a shift to agriculture.
District officers considered cultivation "progressive" and an effective means

of discouraging young men from cattle raiding. While colonial officials claimed the Nandi had more than enough land, none of the Kalenjin Reserves were large enough to support an exclusively pastoral economy.[11] Some Nandi and Kipsigis acquired grazing land by becoming "squatters" on European farms, but others enlisted in the KAR. Young Kalenjin saw *kazi ya bunduki* as a prestigious alternative to stock raiding and used army wages to purchase cattle.

A similar process took place in the Kamba reserves. In colonial times, the Kamba practiced a semi-pastoral economy in the arid regions of eastern central Kenya. Although higher and wetter areas in the northern corner of the Machakos Reserve supported extensive cultivation, most Kamba depended on their cattle during the region's periodic droughts, locust infestations, and famines. The reserve system severely restricted their ability to function as pastoralists. By the 1930s, large numbers of Kamba turned to wage labor as wealthy agricultural entrepreneurs began to appropriate most of the communal land that their poorer kinsmen had used for grazing. The Kenyan government accelerated the process by trying to force the Kamba to cull their herds and build hillside terraces to prevent soil erosion.[12] Together, these changes produced an economically disadvantaged class of men who needed paid employment. Some Kamba became squatters, but most chose the KAR, which offered the highest wages for unskilled work. Lacking the education and financial opportunities of their more fortunate Kikuyu neighbors, Kamba soldiers found *kazi ya bunduki* appealing because it was lucrative and "the most suitable job for a man."[13]

The influence of colonial economic policies on the formation of martial identity is most striking in the case of the Maasai and the Samburu. Both are Maa-speaking peoples who share a common cultural heritage stemming from what was an almost exclusively pastoral economy in the late nineteenth century. The colonial government separated the two groups in the early twentieth century when it alienated the central Rift Valley for European settlement and moved the Maasai to a 14,000-square-mile-reserve in southern Kenya. The Samburu sprang from a smaller group of Maa-speakers that remained on the northern Leroki Plateau.

In pre-colonial times, Maa-speakers were the dominant power in the grasslands of the Rift Valley, and British officials hoped to harness their martial expertise for the KAR. Yet the Maasai showed absolutely no interest in the army, as their pastoral economy remained largely intact. As the only Kenyan ethnic group to sign formal treaties with the British government, they received sole legal title to their sizable southern reserve in return for surrendering the central Rift Valley. In 1933, colonial officials estimated 48,381 Maasai owned over 720,000 head of cattle, an average of roughly seventy-four cows and bulls per household. The Kenyan Land Commission described them as "the most wealthy tribe in Africa, both in the matter of land and the

Table 3.1
Ethnic Composition of Kenyan KAR Battalions, Military Labor Units, and Support Arms (by percentage)

Ethnic Group	1927	1938	1942	1945	1959
Kamba	7.4	23.2	26.7	19.4	36.3
Kikuyu, Embu, and Meru	0.9	0.1	14.8	21.7	3.3
Kalenjin	9.3	25.1	6.7	7.2	25.8
Luo	18.1	14.2	27.3	16.0	9.7
Luhya	2.5	1.7	13.5	9.4	5.3
Samburu	0	1.0	0.5	0.5	3.6
Somali and Other Northern Pastoralists	19.9	9.8	1.2	0.8	11.6
Foreign-Born Askaris	22.3	13.4	0	0	0
Other	19.6	11.6	9.3	25	4.4
Total Number of Enlisted Kenyan Askaris	963	1,087	41,351	76,797	2,383

Sources: PRO, CO 820; KNA, DC TAMB 19/6/273; KNA, DEF 1/130/1; KNA, LF 1/210.

stock which they are able to keep on it."[14] Therefore, the Maasai had little interest in wage labor, and no amount of persuasion, short of conscription, could convince them to enlist in the KAR.

The Samburu, on the other hand, were in a far more precarious position than their Maasai cousins. With no recognized legal claim to their grazing lands, the Samburu depended heavily on the well-watered Leroki Plateau to pasture their livestock. The rest of the region was so dry that a District Officer in the 1920s estimated Samburu herdsmen would lose fifty percent of their cattle in the first protracted drought if they lost the plateau.[15] Unfortunately a handful of politically influential European ranchers also coveted the Leroki, and the Kenyan government imposed strict grazing controls on the plateau in the 1930s in response to settler complaints that it was becoming overused. Therefore, the Samburu had to rely on wage labor to supplement their pastoral economy. With virtually no civilian businesses in northern Kenya, the KAR was the most logical employer.

Kazi ya bunduki had a particular attraction for young Samburu who had formerly proven their manhood and courage by stock raiding. Most used their

Table 3.2

Ethnic Composition of the Kenyan African Population, Based on Census Estimates
(by percentage)

Ethnic Group	1927	1948	1962
Kamba	11.4	11.6	11.2
Kikuyu, Embu, and Meru	31.3	29.6	26.9
Kalenjin	6.0	6.5	10.7
Luo	16.3	13.2	13.7
Luhya	15.3	12.5	13.0
Samburu	0.3	0.5	0.6
Somali and Other Northern Pastoralists	5.3	1.5	6.6
Other	14.1	24.6	17.3
Estimated Total Population	2,771,264	5,251,120	8,365,942

Sources: 3 KAR Intelligence Report, 31 December 1927, KNA, PC NFD 3/1/1; 1948 Census
   Report; 1962 Census Report.

army pay to purchase cattle. Tables 3.1 and 3.2 show that by 1962 the Samburu
enlisted at a rate roughly six times their percentage of the overall Kenyan
population, and their willingness to serve brought about a drastic reordering
of the KAR's martial hierarchy. Where the Samburu had previously been
considered weak relatives of the more militaristic Maasai, British officers
now concluded the Samburu were in fact more martial because they were
"purer Maasai" than the Maasai themselves. They reasoned that the Maasai
living in the colony's southern reserve lost their "natural" warlike qualities
by inter-marrying with non-martial Kikuyu.[16]

Thus, a Kenyan ethnic group's martial identity depended on the extent of
its integration into the colonial economy. When pre-colonial economic systems remained largely intact, most African societies had little interest in
military service. Enlistment figures for 1927 (outlined in Table 3.1) show the
Kamba, Kalenjin, and Samburu constituted only 16.7 percent of the Kenyan
battalions. During this period, the KAR was composed mostly of foreign-
born askaris and locally recruited Luo. As the century progressed, taxation,
destocking, and soil conservation changed recruiting patterns significantly
by drawing more Kenyans into the colonial economy. By the late 1950s, over
65 percent of all Kenyan askaris were either Kamba, Kalenjin, or Samburu.

Conversely, when social and economic differentiation in African societies reached an advanced stage, ethnic groups usually lost their martial status. This happened to the Luo, who were the backbone of the KAR in the 1920s and 1930s but were deemed politically unreliable by the close of the colonial era. Kenyan societies were therefore most martial when they were in a transitional stage of economic development and suffering under the political constraints of colonial rule.

Martial recruiting in Kenya and Nyasaland differed in a number of important ways. In Nyasaland, few African societies could be termed exclusively pastoral, and the colonial administration found it relatively easy to get Africans to accept paid employment. Although the Protectorate did not have a "native reserve" system, European planters in the Shire Highlands convinced the government to encourage wage labor through taxation and direct coercion. Nyasaland usually had a labor surplus (particularly in the north) because most farmers could not sell enough produce to pay their taxes. Thus, many Africans left the Protectorate to work on mines and farms in southern Africa. In 1937, the colonial government estimated 90,087 Nyasalanders were working abroad, which amounted to more than eighteen percent of all able-bodied males in the Protectorate.[17] Similarly, in 1921, roughly eighty-three hundreths percent of all Nyasaland men were in the military, as compared to twenty-nine hundreths percent in Kenya and eleven hundreths percent in Uganda.[18] Nyasaland's mission graduates also were in great demand in South Africa and the Rhodesias, and employers in these territories easily outbid the Shire planters for unskilled African labor.

Patterns of labor migration in Nyasaland were far from uniform. In 1939, an estimated forty-three percent of all able-bodied males in the Northern Province were labor migrants, as compared to only seventeen percent of the work force in the Southern Province.[19] Northern farmers had few markets for their produce, and it was more lucrative for them to travel to southern Africa than to work on plantations in southern Nyasaland. The colonial government allowed South Africa's Witwatersrand Native Labour Association (WNLA) and Southern Rhodesian farmers to hire Nyasaland laborers directly in the north. The Shire planters, however, used their political influence to bar foreign labor recruiters from the southern half of the Protectorate.[20] Moreover, many Southerners were ineligible for a mission education because they were Muslims, and most Northerners were therefore wealthier and better educated than their southern countrymen.

From a military standpoint, it is not surprising that most Nyasaland askaris were recruited in the south. While the early KAR considered the northern Tonga and Ngoni to be the Protectorate's premier martial races, by the 1930s, the draw of migrant labor made them far less interested in military service. In 1938, the commander of the Southern Brigade worried that the martial races of Nyasaland were "past their prime as soldiers."[21] These fears were premature. While Northerners became less interested in military service, the restrictions on labor migration in the south made the KAR an extremely popular alternative to unskilled wage labor on settler estates. In 1943, sixty-nine percent of the 22,018 Nyasalanders in the military came from the Southern Province, and twenty-four percent of these askaris were from Zomba District alone.[22] While military authorities tried to recruit as many Northerners as possible to maintain an ethnic balance, by the end of the Second World War, the Nyasaland KAR battalions were almost entirely composed of Southerners. Thus, the evolution of martial identity in Nyasaland was intrinsically tied to labor migration; the KAR was the most popular form of paid employment for those who could not make the journey south.

EARLY RECRUITING, 1902–1918

During the first two decades of the twentieth century, most rural East African societies were largely isolated from the colonial economy. With little need for paid employment, they were uninterested in *kazi ya bunduki*. For example, 3 KAR disbanded its experimental "Masai Company" in 1907 after officers concluded Maasai warriors were a class of "idle rich," totally unadaptable to conventional military discipline.[23] With most of the ethnic groups that would eventually become martial races still in armed opposition to the colonial regime, the early KAR battalions were composed largely of Muslims or foreign-born Africans. The only exceptions to this rule were 1 and 2 KAR's Tonga and Ngoni askaris from northern Nyasaland.

As a universalistic faith, Islam conveyed a sense of cultural superiority that made Muslim askaris less likely to view their African opponents as kith and kin. Moreover, Britain's emphasis on Christian education circumscribed their opportunities under the colonial system, giving military wages more appeal. Most of the original askaris were recruited from Muslim communities involved in the East African caravan trade. These included coastal Swahili peoples, Somalis, and the Yao, who comprised more than half of the early Nyasaland battalions. Yet the commercial bent of many East African Muslim communities ultimately diminished their military value. Trade was still profitable under British rule and was much more lucrative than military service.

As a result, British military recruiters had to look outside East Africa for the bulk of their rank-and-file askaris. These foreigners were usually nominal Muslims recruited in Egypt, the Sudan, the Belgian Congo, Ethiopia, or Somalia but were known collectively as Sudanese or Nubians. Many were former slave soldiers of the Egyptian Khedive, and as foreigners and military professionals, they had no emotional ties to the East African population. They comprised as much as three-quarters of the early KAR battalions because many recruiters considered them a natural martial race. As one officer put it: "When recruits are wanted, it is only necessary to walk through their village and select the most likely looking youngsters. You find them ready-made soldiers, for the children drill each other as soon as they can walk."[24] In reality, the military orientation of these southern Sudanese communities was a vestige of military slavery and not some innate cultural characteristic. Most askaris were hired by Afro-Arab military recruiters in famine-ridden rural villages or the slums of Cairo and Khartoum, a process that some informants describe as enslavement. As a former Sudanesese corporal recruited in 1904 put it: "We had no choice.... [T]here was no food and if we resisted we would be punished."[25]

Colonial military authorities would have preferred to rely exclusively on Sudanese askaris, but by the 1910s, it had become extremely difficult to obtain replacements for men lost to injury or old age. While partially a result of the Sudan's ban on further recruiting, the shortage of Sudanese soldiers was due primarily to the demise of military slavery in northeastern Africa. The niceties of colonial rule made it impossible to simply impress large numbers of young men. In 1908, KAR officers recruited several hundred Ethiopians in Addis Ababa as a stopgap measure, but they were equally difficult to replace because of their foreign status. Moreover, it was difficult to integrate these "Abyssinians" into the KAR because they tended to look down on the Sudanese as "slaves."

By 1912, 3 KAR's recruiting difficulties led the Regiment's Inspector General to raise an "experimental" company of Nandi, Kamba, Meru, and Kavirondo askaris in a search for new martial races.[26] The trial produced mixed results. The KAR found the Nandi sufficiently martial and recruited them in large numbers. The Luo and Luhya received mixed reviews, and British officers labeled the Meru "unusually backward and stupid" and deemed the Kamba a complete "waste of money."[27] The verdict on the Kamba is particularly interesting, given that they ultimately became the premier martial race of colonial Kenya.

Military officials claimed these locally enlisted East Africans were volunteers. Most recruiting for the early KAR, however, was carried out by African chiefs, who supplied "recruiting safaris" with set quotas of men. This process often involved a degree of coercion, but the KAR's generous pay rates also provided a powerful incentive for those in need of paid employment. In the 1910s, the KAR paid a private the equivalent of thirty-eight shillings per month, as compared to the five to eleven shillings earned by an unskilled African civilian. In Nyasaland, KAR privates received a monthly wage of eight to ten shillings, whereas their civilian counterparts earned about three.[28] The colonial army needed these generous pay levels to secure the cooperation of askaris. While pressure from civilian employers would eventually act as a brake on military wages, the foreign status of most askaris meant the early KAR was not in direct competition with European settlers for unskilled labor. Military officials were free to pay their soldiers as much as their budgets would allow, which in turn helped to build the overall prestige of *kazi ya bunduki*.

With the outbreak of the First World War in 1914, the colonial governments and settlers believed Africans should only contribute to the war effort by providing military labor. The poorly developed rail system and lack of motor transport in East Africa meant supplies and ammunition had to be hand carried. Each armed combatant needed at least one carrier at the front, plus two additional carriers on the lines of communication. The army originally recruited these porters by offering wages that were much higher than civilian rates. In early 1915, an experienced Swahili carrier earned twenty shillings per month in the army, almost twice the going wage for unskilled labor on the coast.

Yet as the war progressed, harsh working conditions and high mortality rates in the Carrier Corps made it increasingly difficult for the army to meet its military labor needs. By March of 1915, the offer of twenty-seven shillings per month in Malindi attracted just three volunteers.[29] Moreover, private employers and government departments protested the inflationary influence of carrier wages on civilian pay scales. The Kenyan government therefore resorted to limited conscription under the "Native Followers' Recruitment Ordinance of 1915." It required chiefs and headmen to produce a set quota of carriers, which enabled the army to reduce carrier pay to seven shillings per month for new recruits.[30]

Military authorities relied on informal conscription until 1917, when the invasion of German East Africa created a huge demand for more carriers. Under the Mass Levy of 1917, civil administrators directly conscripted tens of thousands of Africans for the Carrier Corps. As a general rule, most carriers came from non-martial ethnic groups. In Kenya's Machakos District, civil officials conscripted three out of every four unmarried Kamba males. They captured conscripts at sporting events and in night raids on villages in South Kavirondo District.[31] In all, the East Africa Protectorate impressed approximately 120,000 men by the first half of 1917. Uganda also supplied large numbers of carriers, and advancing imperial forces in German East Africa impressed the "liberated" African population. While Nyasaland was not formally under the jurisdiction of the Nairobi-based Carrier Corps, the Protectorate also conscripted over 100,000 Nyasalanders as carriers, or *tenga-tengas*. Senior officials in the East Africa Protectorate only abandoned the Mass Levy in August 1917, after district officers warned that the African population was on the verge of open revolt.[32]

Service in the Carrier Corps was so oppressive and lethal that Africans went to extreme lengths to avoid conscription. Some went to work for Europeans to secure an exemption, but most simply fled to the bush at the first sign of a recruiting party. Many conscripts deserted two or three times, and others purposely starved themselves to get a medical discharge.[33] To overcome this resistance, district officers ordered chiefs to seize the wives and cattle of resisters, and their African policemen indulged in rape and theft in the course of rounding up conscripts. In Nyasaland, bitterness generated by widespread labor conscription was a primary cause of John Chilembwe's uprising in January 1915, and angry civilians often assaulted chiefs who cooperated with the recruiters.[34] Military labor conscription therefore threatened the foundations of indirect rule, and the negative legacy of this grim episode affected colonial recruiting policies for the next forty years.

Recruiting for the KAR was far less problematical. During the first two years of the war, when political opposition prevented the full deployment of KAR battalions against the Germans, recruiters focused solely on replacing casualties. It was not until 1916, when General J. C. Smuts used the KAR to spearhead the invasion of German East Africa, that colonial authorities initiated a full-scale recruitment campaign. Even then, the KAR's manpower needs were relatively small compared to the vast numbers of men conscripted by the Carrier Corps, and the Regiment totaled slightly more than 30,000 African soldiers in 1918.

British military authorities formally renounced conscription as a recruiting method for the infantry. Unofficially, however, KAR recruiters often resorted to coercive methods that qualified as conscription. The KAR's Chief Recruiting Officer informed the East African governments of his manpower needs, and civil officials in turn divided their quota among the various districts in their territories. They left it to African chiefs and headmen to actually bring in recruits using whatever methods they saw fit. In a study of Nandi veterans of the First World War, Lewis Greenstein found that all of his fifty-two informants were volunteers. Most believed, however, that the government would have confiscated their land and cattle if they refused to enlist. In Nyasaland, chiefs received a bonus payment of "head money" for each recruit they produced.[35]

It is difficult to determine exactly how often traditional authorities resorted to outright compulsion to fulfill their quotas. There are a number of reasons to believe many of the askaris who served during the war did actually volunteer. While pressure from civil employers continued to drive down military pay rates, the KAR still offered the highest wages for unskilled labor. In 1917, an African private earned the equivalent of twenty-one shillings per month, compared to the seven to ten shillings received by an agricultural laborer. In 1916, the army standardized KAR pay rates at 3 KAR levels as the various territorial battalions came under a unified command structure, which led to a considerable raise for Nyasaland askaris.[36]

Furthermore, if these relatively generous pay rates alone were insufficient inducement to join the KAR, there was always the incentive of volunteering to avoid the Carrier Corps. To most Africans, *kazi ya bunduki* was considerably more prestigious than military labor, as KAR askaris had better uniforms, rations, and pay than army porters. Military authorities also used the threat of carrier conscription to drive men into the KAR. Officials at carrier depots offered conscripts a chance to volunteer for the infantry, and in 1916, three of Smuts's new battalions were recruited directly from the Carrier Corps.[37] In a practice reminiscent of Sudanese military slavery, the KAR also conscripted its opponents. The new wartime 6 KAR was composed almost entirely of ex-German askaris, some of whom were actually former members of the pre-war 2 KAR. Many askaris saw little difference between the British and the Germans, and the ease at which they moved back and forth between the two European armies indicates few had any real allegiance to either side. They simply sought the most advantageous terms of service.[38]

An important consequence of the KAR's expansion during the First World War was the designation of new martial races. The pre-war shortage of Sudanese continued, and British efforts to recruit foreign askaris in Ethiopia, Portuguese East Africa, and the Belgian Congo were blocked by their respective governments. Nyasaland still drew on the Yao, Tonga, and Ngoni, but by 1916, the East Africa Protectorate had to find new sources of manpower for the KAR. The Nandi and Kipsigis had proved themselves in 1912, but most of the new transfers to the KAR were Kamba and Kavirondo carriers who had shown bravery on the front lines. With the elevation of these groups to martial status, civil officials filled out the ranks of the Carrier Corps with conscripts from the Kikuyu, Mijikenda and other non-martial peoples of the East Africa Protectorate. Some ethnic groups, however, refused to become martial races. In 1918, the Purko Maasai fought a pitched battle with army recruiters who were attempting to conscript 175 young men for the KAR. The Maasai never produced the required recruits, and the incident only deepened their distrust of the colonial military.[39]

THE INTER-WAR ERA, 1919–1939

Two main factors influenced KAR recruiting patterns in the period between World War I and II. The shift from foreign to locally recruited martial races continued, and the Regiment entered into more direct competition with European civilian employers for African labor. Table 3.3 shows that from 1927 to 1938 the Kenyan KAR battalions had an average strength of 943 askaris. They recruited an average of 182 men per year and returned another 191 to civilian life. These are hardly significant figures, given the estimated 213,743 Kenyan Africans in civil employ in 1936, but European farmers and the KAR were often in direct competition for the same ethnic groups.[40] This was the case with Nandi and Kipsigis in the Rift Valley and, to a lesser extent, with the Luo of western Kenya. Civilian employers pressured the Kenyan government to block the military from driving up wages or "signing off" laborers who wished to escape their labor contracts.[41]

Table 3.3
Manpower Turnover in the Kenyan KAR Battalions, 1927–1938

	1927	1928	1929	1930	1931	1933	1934	1935	1937	1938	Averages
Number of New Enlistments	134	175	215	150	154	138	183	193	266	215	182.3
New Enlistments as a Percentage of Total Unit Strength	13.9	17.1	22.4	18.1	19.9	15.5	19.7	19.5	26.9	19.8	19.3
Number of Men Discharged	499	160	173	220	152	131	150	143	202	76	190.6
Discharges as a Percentage of Total Unit Strength	51.8	15.6	18	26.6	19.7	14.7	16.1	14.5	20.4	7	20.4
Total Unit Strength	963	1,023	959	827	772	890	931	988	989	1,087	942.9

Sources: Annual Unit Reports, 1927–1938, PRO, CO 820.

The KAR was one of the most popular employers in inter-war Kenya. The continued burden of taxation, coupled with the onset of the depression, ensured the Regiment had no difficulty recruiting combat askaris. It had little need for coercive recruiting tactics, and annual unit reports for the inter-war years show KAR battalions lost only a handful of men to desertion. It was not as easy, however, to recruit porters and educated soldiers. British officers tried to raise the status of carriers by placing them in uniform and offering the chance to earn promotion to infantrymen, but inferior pay and the negative legacy of the Carrier Corps made military labor recruiting extremely difficult.[42] To some extent, the problem was solved by the introduction of mechanized transportation in the early 1930s, but this further exacerbated tensions with civilian employers by creating a need for skilled African drivers and mechanics. Even though the KAR's Supply and Transport Corps trained its own personnel, the army had to pay them an extremely generous wage to retain them after their initial term of service expired. In 1935, a trained driver in the S & T Corps made as much as 110 shillings per month, compared to a rifleman who earned only twenty-eight shillings.[43]

Political pressure from European employers forced the KAR to halve these inflationary wages by the end of the decade. Military authorities therefore had considerable difficulty attracting specialist African soldiers needed to modernize the Regiment in the years leading up to the Second World War. The KAR especially needed signallers with a command of basic arithmetic and simple written Swahili and English. These were skills acquired only through formal education, and the army competed directly with civilian employers for African mission school graduates. Military service had little appeal for men with the educational credentials for more lucrative and comfortable clerical work, a primary reason why better-educated ethnic groups were considered non-martial. Therefore, in 1935, the Northern Brigade began a program at the Government African School in Machakos to train fifteen Kamba boys per year as army signallers, which assured the Regiment of a steady supply of trained men from a sufficiently martial race.[44]

The elevation of the Kamba to full martial status reflected the final shift of the KAR's recruiting base from foreign to local sources. While the War Office's report on British colonial forces for 1925 confidently declared that "with the exception of the Kavirondo and Nandi, there are few tribes in Kenya Colony that make efficient soldiers," the report for 1934 described an entirely different picture:

> The present system of recruiting is to recruit from Kenya tribes only with the exception of a proportion of Nubians and Acholis, chiefly the latter, from Uganda. The supply of Sudanese recruits from Kenya has ceased. The recruiting of Tanganyikan tribes and Somalis from British Somaliland has been discontinued.[45]

Table 3.4

Ethnic Composition of Kenyan KAR Battalions, 1927–1938 (by percentage)

Ethnic Group	1927	1928	1929	1930	1933	1934	1935	1937	1938
Kamba	7.3	7.4	13.9	12.0	13.6	16.0	17.8	19.1	23.2
Kikuyu, Embu, and Meru	0.9	1.1	1.1	1.5	0	0	0	0.3	0.1
Kalenjin	9.3	10.3	8.2	12.0	16.6	23.2	21.1	18.5	25.1
Luo	18.1	14.9	16.0	14.3	8.8	8.3	12.3	14.9	14.2
Luhya	2.5	4.3	4.5	3.0	7.3	8.3	2.6	1.2	1.7
Samburu	0	0	0	0	0	0	0	0.2	1.0
Maasai	0	0	0	0	0	0	0	1.6	0
Somali and Other Pastoralists	19.9	15.7	14.2	16.7	12.1	12.6	13.4	11.3	9.8
Mijikenda	0	0.2	0.5	0.7	0	0	0	0	0
Sudanese	8.5	7.8	6.6	5.2	6.2	3.5	4.3	3.9	2.8
Foreign-Born Askaris	22.3	23.9	16.2	19.8	24.6	17.1	15.3	13.7	13.4
Other	11.1	14.5	18.9	14.9	10.8	11.1	13.2	15.3	8.8
Total Enlisted Kenyan Askaris	963	1,023	959	827	890	931	988	989	1,087

Sources: Annual Unit Reports, 1927–1938, PRO, CO 820.

This shift in official military thinking was born out in annual battalion reports. Table 3.4 shows that from 1927 to 1938 the percentage of foreign-born askaris serving in Kenyan KAR battalions declined from 22.3 to 13.4 percent, whereas Somalis and other northern frontier groups (whose nationality was always uncertain) dropped from 19.9 to 9.8 percent. At the same time, there was a 7.3 to 23.2 increase in the percentage of Kamba in the army, and Kalenjin groups rose from 9.3 to 25.1 percent.[46]

It is useful to compare these enlistment figures to the general civil population estimates listed in 3 KAR's intelligence report for 1927, an admittedly imprecise source. Table 3.3 shows that by the late 1930s, ethnic groups considered the primary martial races of Kenya enlisted at rates two to four times their comparable percentage in the overall African population of the Colony.[47] It could be argued that these figures simply reflect the racial biases of the colonial military establishment. Yet in examining KAR recruiting patterns over time, it is clear that martial stereotypes were principally derived from officers' awareness of the enlistment rates and military performances of various African ethnic groups. The intransigence of the Maasai demonstrates that KAR recruiters did not have the power to force an ethnic group to become martial.

The KAR expanded its Kenyan recruiting base in the 1920s and 1930s as many of the ethnic groups it had previously recruited became less dependent on unskilled wage labor. This was particularly true for the second generation of Sudanese who, for the most part, were the children of discharged KAR askaris and local women. Few Sudanese soldiers retained any connection to their original homes, and most took their discharge in the territories in which they served. Founding small communities of ex-soldiers near KAR garrisons, they used their accumulated pay and benefits to become traders and butchers. The KAR originally tolerated these settlements because it expected Sudanese boys to follow their fathers into the army. In reality, however, the second generation of Sudanese had far more lucrative employment opportunities, including overseeing Kikuyu sharecroppers on their farms, renting rooms to African migrant laborers, stock trading, and clerical work in Nairobi.[48] The Sudanese joined with Somali veterans in lobbying the Kenyan government to grant them "non-native" status on par with the Colony's Arab and Asian communities, which reflected a level of political and economic sophistication entirely incompatible with colonial military service.

Civil officials were thoroughly contemptuous of the well-to-do non-martial Sudanese. In 1931, Nairobi's District Commissioner wrote: "The old Nubi is a man to whom the Colony owes much, but the second generation and the hybrids arising from mixed unions are degenerate and generally a disgrace to their fathers."[49] During the inter-war period, the few Sudanese who enlisted became musicians in the KAR Band. In Uganda, where a veterans' community flourished near 4 KAR's cantonment at Bombo, there was also a

shortage of Sudanese recruits. The declining martial reputation of the sec-
ond-generation Sudanese embarrassed older veterans, who depended on military patronage to protect them from unsympathetic and often hostile civilian
officials. In 1931, the Kenyan Sudanese invited the colonial government to
conscript their sons. While this may have been a political ploy, 4 KAR's
Sudanese Regimental Sergeant Major actually impressed young Ugandan
Sudanese at a specially organized soccer game.[50]

In Nyasaland, a similar shift in the KAR's recruiting base took place during the inter-war years. The increasing demand for Nyasalanders in southern
Africa made the Tonga and Ngoni less interested in military service. During
the depression years, the colonial government actually encouraged labor
migration from the Northern Province to reduce African unemployment. As
a result, the KAR found it increasingly difficult to fulfill its Tonga and Ngoni
quotas in the north by the mid-1930s. Conversely, the Yao and other southern ethnic groups continued to join the inter-war KAR because the Nyasaland
government restricted labor migration from Southern Province to appease
the European planters in the Shire Highlands.

The KAR, however, could not compete with the mines and farms of southern Africa. In 1926, a private in 2 KAR earned ten shillings per month, more
than the six shillings paid to agricultural laborers in Nyasaland but far less
than the £3 offered by South African mines during this period. The
Witwatersrand Native Labour Association also offered better transportation,
food, and clothing than the KAR. Furthermore, most European farmers in
Southern Rhodesia also paid wages that were at least comparable to army
rates.[51] Thus, the Nyasaland battalions had a particularly difficult time recruiting educated men. Many Nyasaland missions had strong anti-military
biases, and most mission school graduates aspired to become clerks in the
Rhodesias and South Africa.[52]

The weakness of Nyasaland's KAR Reserve in the 1930s was also due to
the army's inability to counter the appeal of migrant labor. Reserve obligations required ex-servicemen to remain in their home territories, and most
Nyasaland reservists preferred to travel south to look for work. In an effort
to make the Reserve more attractive, the Nyasaland government grudgingly
granted reservists special privileges. They received preference in hiring for
government jobs, and the Governor pardoned reservists who were jailed for
not paying their taxes. These measures were largely ineffectual, and by 1938,
the KAR had to allow its reservists to work in southern Africa.[53]

THE SECOND WORLD WAR, 1939–1945

The unprecedented expansion and modernization of the East African forces
during the Second World War necessitated a total departure from pre-war
recruiting patterns. The size and complexity of the wartime KAR and its

Table 3.5
Percentage of Kenyan Ethnic Groups in Military Service, by Unit, 30 April 1942

Unit	Luo	Luhya	Kalenjin	KEM*	Kamba	Mijikenda	Other
KAR	23.8	11.7	23.1	4.3	30.4	0.9	5.9
EAASC	23	13.6	5.8	17.4	33	1.9	5.3
EAAMC	18.5	18.3	1.4	46.0	11.8	1.5	2.5
Signals	13.9	5.7	2.8	19.3	46.3	10.9	1.1
EAE	47.7	12.5	2.1	14.4	20.1	1.0	2.3
EAAC	24.4	15.7	7.1	29.1	15.7	1.6	6.3
Pioneers	81.7	15.7	0.4	0.7	0	0	1.5
EACMP	23.9	10.6	5.5	12.7	42.9	1.6	2.9
EAAOC	28.6	25.3	0	33.6	9.6	0.7	2.2
EAA	23.6	7.8	10.8	7.6	45.6	1.4	3.1
AAPC	40.1	18.1	0.4	18.9	17.3	1.2	4.0
EAMLS	27.9	21.2	0.5	26.6	12.6	6.0	5.2
Miscellaneous	24.3	10.5	18.6	20.0	18.8	2.0	5.8

*KEM = Kikuyu, Embu, and Meru.

Source: KNA, PC NZA 2/3/84.

Table 3.6
Number of Kenyans in Military Service, by Unit and Ethnic Group, 30 April 1942

Unit	Luo	Luhya	Kalenjin	KEM*	Kamba	Mijikenda	Other	Total
KAR	1,340	657	1,300	242	1,713	50	334	5,636
EAASC	2,985	1,765	750	2,256	4,279	243	691	12,969
EAAMC	436	430	33	1,082	278	36	58	2,353
Signals	172	70	35	238	572	135	13	1,235
EAE	777	203	35	234	327	16	37	1,629
EAAC	31	20	9	37	20	2	8	127
Pioneers	906	174	4	8	0	0	17	1,109
EACMP	92	41	21	49	165	6	11	385
EAAOC	155	137	0	182	52	4	12	542
EAA	281	93	129	90	542	17	37	1,189
AAPC	2,152	975	20	1,014	932	66	213	5,372
EAMLS	1,354	1,028	23	1,289	609	292	251	4,846
Miscellaneous	519	223	397	426	401	43	123	2,132
Total Enlisted	11,200	5,816	2,756	7,147	9,890	910	1,805	39,524
Total % Enlisted	28.3	14.7	7.0	18.1	25.0	2.3	4.6	

* KEM = Kikuyu, Embu, and Meru.

Source: KNA, PC NZA 2/3/84.

supporting units made it impossible to rely entirely on martial races, and military authorities were forced to recruit ethnic groups they had previously scorned. Relying on a mixture of generous wages and outright conscription to induce men from non-martial races to join the military, the army's full-scale entry into the wage labor market diminished civilian labor supplies. As a result, colonial governments took direct control of the recruiting process to minimize the economic impact of military recruiting.

When the war began in September 1939, the East African governments recalled their reservists but made no plans to expand the KAR's peacetime recruiting base. By the summer of 1940, however, it became clear that Allied reverses in Europe ruled out the possibility of metropolitan British reinforcements for East Africa. Colonial authorities therefore raised eight new wartime battalions and the first African technical and support units. Each battalion required approximately 1,200 askaris, and by March 1941, 38,084 Kenyan Africans were serving in the military. Only 4,488 of these were in the KAR; the majority of new recruits went into the East Africa Military Labour Service. Enlistment reports shown in Tables 3.5. and 3.6. indicate recruiters originally followed pre-war martial stereotypes.[54] The EAMLS was drawn largely from non-martial races, and the East African Pioneer Battalions were entirely Luo.

Most of the military laborers of the EAMLS were Kenyan because the Ethiopian Campaign began on the Colony's northern frontier. Yet even though they had the most to lose in an Italian invasion, the settlers strenuously protested this drain on their African labor supply. In September 1941, Kenya faced a civilian labor shortfall of 17,000 men, which led the government to order a temporary three-month ban on all military recruiting.[55] The prohibition did not unduly tax the army because the Italians were largely defeated by the summer of 1941. At that time, most recruiting was geared primarily toward raising the roughly sixty men per month that each KAR battalion lost to disease and desertion.

These low recruiting levels lasted until the War Office decided to send East African units to the Middle East and Southeast Asia. In 1942, the East Africa Command raised three new brigades (twelve battalions) for overseas service, in addition to recruiting 40,000 men for the African Auxiliary Pioneer Corps. Combined with demands for the various East African support and technical units, the total military manpower burden for all East African territories (including Northern Rhodesia and Nyasaland) in 1942 was approximately 93,000 men.[56]

While this quota would not have been burdensome if spread evenly over East Africa, practical and political considerations dictated that it fell most heavily on Kenya. In September 1942, nine and three-tenths percent of the African labor force in Kenya was in the army, as compared to five and two-tenths percent in Uganda, four percent in Nyasaland, and only three and a half percent in Tanganyika.[57] Kenyan officials used these figures to protest the new recruiting program and lobbied to have most of their quota shifted to Tanganyika and Uganda. The inter-territorial recruiting committee ruled, however, that the needs of Kenyan industry did not outweigh those of the military. In October 1942, the Colonial Secretary issued a directive that ranked the various of uses of East African labor in order of importance: (1) the defense of East Africa, (2) essential foodstuffs for local consumption, (3) strategic materials vital to the war effort (rubber, sisal, pyrethrum, and zinc), (4) foodstuffs for export, (5) the defense of the Middle East, and (6) local civilian industry. Under these guidelines, the Kenyan government did not have much of a case.[58]

The situation changed in 1943, however, when Kenya convinced the Colonial Office that military recruiting was endangering the Colony. Kenyan officials blamed the army for disrupting food production in the African reserves by siphoning off labor. Estimating African food supplies depended on forty-five percent of all African males remaining in the reserves, they warned the figure had fallen to only thirty-five percent. While it was true that the 74,684 Kenyan Africans in the military was 16,319 more than Kenya's official quota for 1943, military recruiting was not the sole cause of the civil labor shortage.[59] The wartime economic boom in Kenya created new markets for African agriculture, and the expansion of key industries drove up labor costs. Nevertheless, civilian employers blamed Kenya's labor problems on the East Africa Command, and the Kenyan government ultimately convinced the Colonial Secretary to ban recruiting for all combat and labor units. The army was only allowed to recruit educated Kenyans for specialist units.[60]

By late 1943, Tanganyika and Uganda replaced Kenya as the primary source of manpower for the East Africa Command. Military recruiting was much more difficult in these territories, and by the end of the year, the EAC experienced its first serious manpower shortfall. In Tanganyika, where the First World War left a general distrust of military service, a severe famine in the first quarter of 1943 forced the government to suspend recruiting. Neither territory had a "native reserve" system, and their African populations were less dependent on wage labor than many Kenyan societies. Moreover, transportation problems and the outbreak of spinal meningitis in overcrowded recruiting depots slowed the enlistment process. Large numbers of Tanganyikan and Ugandan Africans also failed to meet the military's minimum physical qualifications. Thus, both countries' statistical labor surpluses were largely fictitious. These problems limited the EAC's ability to raise new units, and the East African governments abandoned all recruiting for the AAPC in August 1943.[61]

By 1944, the East Africa Command was concerned primarily with recruiting enough replacements to keep its forces in Southeast Asia at full strength, but this proved impossible, as East African manpower reserves were largely expended by the end of the year. In Tanganyika and Nyasaland, roughly thirteen percent of all able-bodied males were in the army, whereas enlistment rates in Kenya and Uganda were over twenty percent.[62] Recruiting more men would have required either a drastic reordering of civil labor priorities or wholesale conscription. The War Office had hoped to expand the East African forces for the planned invasion of Malaya, but as it was, the EAC had barely enough trained men to maintain its existing formations. With insufficient trained replacements to allow askaris home leave, many KAR battalions experienced morale and discipline problems in Burma.[63]

In terms of actual recruiting, there was no shortage of Kenyan volunteers in the first years of the war. The EAC never allowed its pay scales to drop below comparable civilian levels, and for the most part, army pay far outpaced the going rate for unskilled Kenyan labor. In 1941, civil wages averaged between 8 and 12 shillings per month, whereas a newly trained private in the KAR earned 28 shillings. Moreover, the army offered extremely generous wages for skilled labor to meet its desperate need for educated recruits. A private in the East Africa Army Medical Corps earned 46 shillings per month, whereas a Driver I in the East Africa Army Service Corps received 60 shillings. Army clerks earned up to 150 shillings per month, as compared to their civilian counterparts, whose wages usually topped out at 90 shillings. The military also offered uniforms, housing, full rations, medical care, and rapid promotion. A trained African artisan in the Kenyan Public Works Department would have had to work seven to ten years to earn the same pay as an army tradesman with the rank of corporal. It would have taken twenty to thirty years to qualify for a sergeant's pay.[64]

Military service, therefore, was understandably popular in many parts of Kenya. The Nyanza Provincial Commissioner observed: "Every recruit who joins the forces from Nyanza at present is a volunteer. Our trouble is to select from the large numbers that present themselves in answer to every call."[65] It is easy to see how Kenya's military quota became oversubscribed when the military conducted its own recruiting. The colonial government therefore assumed direct control of the recruiting process in 1940 to prevent the army from driving up labor costs. Military authorities agreed to the change because it conserved their manpower and resources.[66] The system worked relatively well in the early years of the war, and the other East African governments eventually copied it.

Kenya's Chief Native Commissioner (CNC) had primary responsibility for balancing civil and military recruiting needs. After receiving manpower requests from the various branches of the colonial military, he met with the Colony's Provincial Commissioners to set ethnic recruiting quotas. While the CNC was supposed to be objective, a close examination of the way esti-

Table 3.7
African Manpower Reserves, 2 February 1945, Compiled by East African Governments

Line	Category	Kenya	Tanganyika	Uganda	N Rhodesia	Nyasaland
A	Adult Males	642,000	842,000	841,000	300,000	300,000
B	Adult Males Available for Wage Labor	343,100	462,000	261,000	189,000	205,000
C	Adult Males in Civil Employ	310,358	320,442	155,204	167,000	175,000
D	Percentage of Adult Males Needed for African Food Production	45%	45%	68%	37%	32%
E	Percentage of Adult Males Actually Engaged in African Food Production	35%	55%	66%	Unknown	58%
F	Official Estimate of Adult Males Available for Military Enlistment (Line B – Line C)	32,742	141,558	105,796	22,000	30,000
G	Adult Males Actually Serving, March 1945	76,045	63,569	56,313	13,000	27,595
H	Percentage of Adult Males Serving, March 1945	22.2%	13.7%	21.6%	6.9%	13.5%
I	Estimated Adult Males Available for Military Service, March 1945	0	78,789	49,483	9,000	2,405
J	Number of Adult Males Actually Available for Military Service, March 1945	0	8,000	9,000	900	2,405

Sources: KNA, DEF 15/29/88a; KNA, MD 4/5/140/170.

mates of available military manpower were calculated clearly shows that, in spite of the Colonial Secretary's directive on recruiting priorities, settlers had priority over the army. As shown in Table 3.7, the Kenyan government determined the number of Africans to be recruited by taking the estimated number of working African males not needed for food production in the "native reserves" and subtracting the number needed by civilian employers. Thus, according to the government, the maximum number of Kenyan Africans available for service without disrupting the Colony's economy was only 32,742 men, as compared to the 76,045 askaris serving at the end of the war.[67] This discrepancy explains the Kenyan government's increasing opposition to military recruiting as the war progressed. All requests for African recruits were routed through the CNC, and depot commanders who transgressed received a tart bureaucratic rebuke from the Kenyan Secretariat.[68] Under these strict guidelines, the government barred unit commanders from accepting casual applicants, and recruiters were forbidden to exceed assigned quotas. Thus, when 120 Kamba volunteers presented themselves at the EAASC's Motor Transport Depot in 1944, Kenya's Labor Commissioner ordered them to go home. All would-be recruits also had to present their *kipandes* to show they were not under contract to a European employer. While these restrictions ensured that the army kept closer track of askaris than it did in the First World War, Kenyan officials were most concerned with protecting the civilian labor supply (see Tables 3.8–3.10).[69]

This inability to reign in military enlistment was the motive behind the Kenyan government's push for a total prohibition on recruiting in 1943. Members of the civil administration were genuinely concerned about food shortages in the African reserves, but the ban was due largely to the political influence of settler representatives in the Legislative Council. The war created unprecedented economic opportunities for European agriculture and industry in Kenya that could be exploited only with inexpensive African labor. The Colony's farmers and businessmen blamed military recruiting and the payment of remittances to soldiers' families for pushing up wages and drying up labor supplies.[70] The EAMLS was the primary target of the settlers' wrath because it competed for the same non-martial ethnic groups that made up the bulk of the civil labor force. Kenya's Labor Commissioner held it responsible for the decline in the Colony's overall agricultural output during the war:

> I personally think it is useless at the present time to try and get natives to do more work so long as the EAMLS remains as an example to the civilian native labourer. The agricultural employee is well aware that his brothers are well paid, receive better food, work under better conditions and do less work than he is expected to do and no amount of propaganda will do any good until the position is changed.[71]

Table 3.8
Kenyans in Military Service, by Ethnic Group, 1942–1946

Ethnic Group	1942	1943	1944	1945	1946
Luo	11,803	16,845	20,691	19,330	6,647
Luhya	6,451	10,706	13,627	12,736	4,989
Kikuyu, Embu, and Meru	7,633	*12,073	17,009	15,607	5,857
Kamba	9,993	12,707	15,003	14,389	4,256
Kalenjin	3,077	3,961	4,341	4,340	2,092
Maasai	89	*123	247	219	116
Kisii	1,001	2,064	2,459	2,142	703
Northern Frontier Pastoralists	769	786	1,002	618	479
Other	743	1,116	1,469	1,765	446
Total Enlisted	41,559	60,381	75,848	71,146	25,585

*Estimates.

Note: The Kenyan Labour Department defined an "able-bodied male" as being between the ages of fifteen and forty in 1942 and 1943 and between the ages of sixteen and forty-five from 1944 on.

Sources: Kenya Labour Department, Manpower Bulletins, 1942–1946, KNA, PC NZA 2/3/84.

Table 3.9
Percentage of Adult Males of Selected Kenyan Ethnic Groups in the Military, 1942–1946

Ethnic Group	1942	1943	1944	1945	1946
Luo	10.5	15.0	18.0	16.6	5.7
Luhya	8.6	14.2	15.3	13.5	5.3
Kikuyu, Embu, and Meru	4.6	*7.3	9.7	9.0	2.9
Kamba	13.8	17.6	19.8	19.4	5.8
Kalenjin	8.4	10.8	8.8	8.7	4.2
Maasai	1.3	1.8	2.6	2.1	1.2

*Estimates.

Note: The Kenyan Labour Department defined an "able-bodied male" as being between the ages of fifteen and forty in 1942 and 1943 and between the ages of sixteen and forty-five from 1944 on.

Sources: Kenya Labour Department, Manpower Bulletins, 1942–1946, KNA, PC NZA 2/3/84.

Table 3.10
Percentage of Adult Males of Selected Kenyan Ethnic Groups in Civil Employ, 1942–1946

Ethnic Group	1942	1943	1944	1945	1946
Luo	35.1	36.9	38.6	35.1	40.6
Luhya	57.1	64.3	55.1	49.0	52.6
Kikuyu, Embu, and Meru	47.0	47.2	44.8	44.3	37.0
Kamba	30.7	28.4	30.1	35.8	34.1
Kalenjin	61.1	60.2	43.9	35	38.9
Maasai	25.0	25.0	18.6	16.5	18.7
Total Percentage of Employed Adult Males	61.1	60.2	43.9	35.0	38.9

Note: The Kenyan Labour Department defined an "able-bodied male" as being between the ages of fifteen and forty in 1942 and 1943 and between the ages of sixteen and forty-five from 1944 on.

Sources: Kenya Labour Department, Manpower Bulletins, 1942–1946, KNA, PC NZA 2/3/84.

The Kenyan government tried to alleviate the wartime labor shortage by conscripting more than 20,000 Africans for civil labor by 1945. The "Defence (African Labour for Essential Undertakings) of 1942" compelled them to work for any enterprise designated an "essential undertaking." The settlers' political influence ensured that virtually every European business fell under this heading, including such "vital" activities as coffee picking. Most African labor conscripts despised the low pay and unpleasant working conditions in the civil labor camps.[72] Many realized that if they were going to be forced to serve the government, it would be better to join the army, where pay and working conditions were far superior. When Kenya banned most forms of military recruiting, Kenyans sneaked into Uganda and Tanganyika to enlist. In 1943, roughly one percent of the 18,897 men who passed through Uganda's Tororo civil recruiting depot listed a home address in Kenya. While this number does not appear significant, colonial officials complained that cross-border traffic undercut civil conscription and abetted the illegal flow of Kenyan manpower into the military.[73]

Military service was less popular in Nyasaland than in Kenya. The lessons of the 1930s showed that the army could not compete with migrant labor, and it was difficult to meet the military's manpower needs during the war. The KAR had made extensive plans to recall reservists working in the

South African mines, but only forty-seven men returned to the army when war broke out. In Southern Rhodesia, newspaper advertisements appealing to Nyasaland veterans to reenlist produced only a single response. While recruiting went well in Nyasaland's Southern Province, it was a dismal failure in the north. By October 1940, Nyasaland had filled only sixty percent of its quota for the KAR.[74] Moreover, many of the Northerners who did volunteer were either too old, sick, or small to be infantrymen.

Sir Donald Mackenzie-Kennedy, the Governor of Nyasaland, therefore imposed a temporary ban on labor migration until the military's manpower needs were met. The first interruption lasted only from September to October 1939 and allowed the army to fill out the pre-war KAR battalions. Nyasaland officials, however, needed a more lasting ban to meet their quota of 7,000 men during the first big recruiting push in 1940. With the approval of the Colonial Office, Kennedy placed a temporary moratorium on the issuance of identity certificates, which Nyasalanders needed for legal employment in Southern Rhodesia. The new rules allowed applicants rejected by the army for medical reasons to emigrate but denied healthy men exit permits "so that they may appreciate, after further thought, the desirability of enlisting for military service in the King's African Rifles."[75] The WNLA voluntarily suspended its operations and, in the spirit of wartime cooperation, lent its labor recruiters to the military. Many Africans signed up expecting to be sent to the mines, only to find themselves in uniform. The migration ban succeeded in bringing in higher-quality recruits and was lifted in May 1941, after Nyasaland met its recruiting quota.[76]

With a comparatively small settler population, Governor Kennedy was free to make military recruiting his first priority. When full-scale recruiting resumed in 1942 to raise East African units for overseas service, Kennedy promised to produce 14,000 men if he was allowed to reinstate the temporary ban on labor migration.[77] Once again the WNLA shut down its Nyasaland operations, and the Protectorate stopped issuing exit permits. While many Nyasalanders still illegally made their way south, military recruiters attracted more volunteers than they needed.

Unlike 1940, however, South African and Southern Rhodesian employers were less willing to accept even a temporary halt in the supply of migrant labor. When Nyasalanders working in Southern Rhodesia dropped from 18,819 in January 1942 to just 7,747 one year later, the Southern Rhodesian government protested the migration ban to the Dominions Office and threatened to hire Nyasalanders without identity certificates. This was an effective tactic because Nyasaland officials relied on the permit system to ensure their African subjects received fair wages and treatment in the south. The WNLA was also less cooperative in 1942 and warned it would hire any Nyasalander who made his way to South Africa on his own. In making this threat, the WNLA played to the worst fears of civil officials, who worried Nyasalanders would fall victim to abusive South African "touts and sharks."[78] Thus, even though the Colonial Office and the Nyasaland government agreed military recruiting was the Protectorate's first priority, the prospect of unregulated labor migration was a sufficient threat to cause them to lift the ban on foreign labor recruiting in the summer of 1943. The East Africa Governors Conference reduced Nyasaland's enlistment quota from 14,000 to 11,000 men, and for the rest of the war Nyasaland relied primarily on casual recruiting to keep its KAR battalions at full strength.[79]

The extent to which Africans found military service lucrative and appealing largely determined the level of coercion needed to secure recruits. The East Africa Command preferred volunteers because they made better soldiers. In Kenya, where there was a surplus of recruits, the government rarely had to conscript Africans for combat and specialist units. In most cases, if the army received men from the civil recruiting depots who claimed they had been conscripted, military authorities refused to accept them. In 1943 the EAC sent the following letter to Kenya's Chief Native Commissioner: "[F]our of the recent 125 recruits received from Machakos refused to sign their attestation papers stating that they were forced to join up by their chiefs. As the [Motor Transport Depot commander] considered that they would only make a nuisance of themselves . . . he returned them to the District Commissioner."[80]

Many East African veterans admit to volunteering for the colonial military. A man's family often urged him to join, for, as Robert Kakembo observed, the prosperity of askaris home on leave was a powerful recruiting incentive:

> The soldiers go home on leave smartly dressed in His Majesty's uniform and with plenty of money. A man leaves his village and goes into the Army; he disappears for some eighteen months, and on his return home on leave he is 100 percent changed. He is fat and strong, clean and clever, with plenty to talk about and lots of money to spend. The young girls of the village worship him; the young men follow him about. He stands them drinks, while a box of matches to an old man produces blessings and love. The soldier becomes the center of worship to everybody except those whose girls have fallen for him. In other words, he makes very good propaganda for the Army.[81]

Most informants cite poverty and the perquisites of military service as their main reasons for enlisting. While the wartime food exports were an economic bonanza for European farmers, they produced famine conditions in many rural African communities. In Tanganyika's Central Province, the situation was so bad in 1943 that askaris even gave up their home leave to stay in the army.[82] Some informants joined the army to protect their lands and families:

"I didn't want my country taken by the Italians. . . . [O]ur teachers told us what would happen to us if Mussolini's soldiers came." Educated askaris were well aware of Hitler's racist pronouncements about Africans and fought to help Haile Selassie, the only independent African ruler during the colonial era.[83]

In spite of these sentiments, however, British authorities still resorted to forced recruiting in certain circumstances. When the East Africa Governors Conference asked for permission to rely on full-scale conscription in 1942, the Colonial Secretary left the decision as to when and how much compulsion would be used to the individual territorial governments.[84] Kenya conscripted Africans primarily for the EAMLS and the AAPC. Yet there was never a shortage of volunteers for these units. Kenyan's Chief Native Commissioner saw conscription primarily as a way of selectively rationing labor: "I am strongly adverse to calling for volunteers as it inevitably upsets normal labour working in the Colony. It is far preferable to select natives for conscription than to allow general volunteering."[85] Conscription allowed Kenyan officials to block military recruiting in areas that supplied labor to settler farms and industry. Conversely, the Tanganyikan and Ugandan governments used conscription to protect food production by spreading recruiting evenly throughout the African population.

While Kenya and Uganda only conscripted military laborers, Tanganyika actually used conscription to recruit infantrymen. Tanganyikan officials relied upon volunteers at the outbreak of the war, but by 1940, the rising rate of medical rejections made it difficult to fill their manpower quotas. By 1945, thirty-four percent of all potential Tanganyikan recruits failed their physical exams, and some districts had rejection rates that reached ninety-nine percent.[86] Tanganyikan officials were initially concerned that the League of Nations mandate prevented the conscription of "protected" peoples, but once the Colonial Office ruled that overseas service was needed to defend the territory, Tanganyika shifted to near universal conscription. District officers working in conjunction with African chiefs took volunteers first, then the "merely indifferent," and "falling back as a last resort on the reluctant and definitely unwilling."[87] The government made no distinction between civil and military conscription, and officials in the recruiting depots used health as the sole determinant of whether an African would become an askari or a civil labor conscript. Thus, many men from non-martial races became infantrymen, and some British officers in Burma attributed morale problems in the Tanganyikan KAR battalions to the fact that some askaris were unwilling draftees.[88]

In spite of its recruiting problems, Nyasaland was the only East African territory to eschew conscription entirely. The South African and Southern Rhodesian governments used their influence to oppose compulsion because it threatened their labor supplies, and Nyasaland officials agreed that the practice was futile. With no corner of the Protectorate more than fifty miles from a foreign border, Africans could easily flee to escape impressment. Many men living in the Southern Province had families in Portuguese East Africa and even paid taxes in both territories. Finally, the Protectorate government expected opposition from "pacifist" European missions, and intelligence reports from Portuguese East Africa warned "Axis agents" would use discontent generated by conscription to foment unrest.[89]

Yet in practice, some Africans were pressed into military service even in territories that officially disavowed coerced recruiting. The enlistment pipeline began with district officers and chiefs, who had wide latitude in filling their manpower quotas. Traditional authorities often got rid of men who displeased them, and several informants recall being conscripted as a result of disputes over land or women. "The chief wanted my [fiancee]. . . . Because I couldn't read, he sent me to Embu with a letter telling [the recruiters] I wanted to be an askari."[90] During Nyasaland's 1942 recruiting drive, civil officials unofficially assigned quotas (usually about three men per village) to each headman, a tactic that a dissenting recruiting officer charged amounted to "unofficial compulsion." He warned: "It would be unfair—in fact dangerous—to allow the East Africa Command to believe that all our 1942 recruits are true volunteers."[91]

Some civil recruiting officers stayed within the letter of the rules barring outright conscription but ridiculed the bravery and manhood of Africans who refused to volunteer. In Kenya's Nyanza Province, a district officer ordered one such resister to be dressed in women's clothes and paraded before a large crowd. Nyasaland's Director of Recruiting issued similar guidelines for recruits who refused to take the oath of attestation:

> They should not be forced to sign or [be] detained, but if, after discussion with them before other recruits in the same area who are willing to attest, the individual still refuses to do so, he should be ridiculed and his military clothing taken from him. He should then be sent to his village and both the village Headman and Native Authority informed and asked for an explanation.[92]

In other cases, criminal activity stripped a man of his protection from conscription. One of the first drafts of recruits for the EAMLS was composed largely of Nairobi "scalawags" rounded up by the Kenya Police. In the Rift Valley Province, district officers conscripted stock thieves, and in Uganda, Sudanese prisoners were released from jail so they could be impressed. Nyasaland officials gave would-be labor migrants convicted of trying to leave the Protectorate illegally a choice of joining the KAR or paying a twenty-shilling fine.[93]

Oral testimonies of African veterans corroborate these reports. Contrary to Kenyan rules prohibiting conscription for combat units, many Kamba in-

formants were impressed in Machakos Town.[94] Jackson Mulinge, one of
Kenya's most famous soldiers, a man who eventually rose to command the
National Kenyan Army, was conscripted as a schoolboy.

> I was fifteen years old. I went with my older sister to Machakos market to
> sell chickens to buy a school uniform. There was a recruiting party in the
> market. . . . I had never seen an *Mzungu* [European] before . . . and pushed
> to the center of the crowd to get a better look. . . . [They] ordered me to the
> center of the circle . . . and then threw me into a truck and took me to a
> training center in Uganda.[95]

Civil officials also conscripted educated men for the Signal Corps, and promising schoolboys were a ready target. Most wartime Kamba signallers were
conscripted in virtually the same way: "I had almost finished school . . . [when]
the teachers told me I was being taken to a better school. . . . Instead they
sent me to the army to learn signaling." This "better school" was the Army
Signals School at Ngong where signals recruits took a dictation test in English that included a statement that they had their parents' permission to enlist and were volunteering of their own free will. They were then ordered to
sign the statement.[96]

There were, however, many avenues of escape for those determined to
stay out of the army. Wealthier Africans simply bribed or intimidated other
men into taking their places, whereas others fled to neighboring territories. A
common tactic in western Kenya was to insert a foreign substance into the
penis to simulate gonorrhea, and medical officers received detailed instructions on how to recognize false symptoms.[97] For legally astute Kenyans, the
most effective tactic was simply to refuse the oath of attestation. The Kenyan
government had no legal power to force a man to join a combat unit, and
KAR battalion commanders usually rejected unwilling recruits who claimed
to have been so conscripted.[98]

Kenyan conscripts also had the right to appeal to an exemption tribunal
composed of District Officers, traditional authorities, missionaries, and settlers. The tribunals had the power to excuse men who were supporting aged
relatives, men regularly employed by a European, men who were "genuine
working farmers," men attending school, or men who were too old or sick
for military service. They also excused conscripts with family members in
the army. Exemptions were hard to come by, however, and the burden of
proof was on the applicant. The tribunals rejected appeals from men with
male relatives who could look after their farms, cattle, and wives and refused
to release men from villages that had not produced enough recruits.[99]

Once a recruit was accepted, either by conscription or voluntary enlistment, a medical officer determined his suitability for military service. The
only physical qualifications for prospective askaris in the pre-war army was

Figure 3.1 Recruiting askaris in Kenya, c. 1941. Illiterate recruits provided a thumb-print in place of a signature. Courtesy of the Trustees of the Imperial War Museum, London (K1528). Reprinted with permission.

general good health, a "supple trigger finger" and sufficient height of five feet seven inches tall.[100] By 1942, the rising rate of medical rejections forced the East Africa Command to lower its height limit to five feet three inches in Kenya and five feet one inch in Nyasaland (see Table 3.11). Medical officers reserved the most healthy men for frontline KAR battalions and sent recruits considered too small, underweight, or old for combat to labor units.[101] Re-cruits then spent two to three weeks in a civil recruiting depot to acclimatize them to military life, then were passed on to their parent units for more spe-cialized training.

Martial stereotypes decided an African soldier's branch of service and determined the skills and social standing he would retain in civilian life. The EAMLS and AAPC were the least prestigious branches of the East African forces and were generally composed of men who did not meet the physical and intellectual qualifications for frontline or technical units. Combat askaris in particular often taunted military laborers about their inferior status. While the AAPC eventually received combat pay in 1942, EAMLS privates earned fourteen shillings less than their KAR counterparts.[102] Civil officials opposed the army's efforts to make military labor more prestigious because they wor-ried that it would denigrate manual labor. In rejecting proposals to assign

Table 3.11
African Recruiting Standards, by Branch of Service, 1942

Unit	Age	Height	Weight (lbs.)	Sight	Intelligence
KAR, EAA, and EAASC	18-30	5'3"*	120*	Normal	Normal
EAAMC	18-30	5'3"	120	Glasses allowed	Standard V–VI
Signals	15-18	Variable	Variable	Variable	Standard IV
EAMLS	18-40	5'2"†	120	One normal eye	Normal
AAPC	18-40	5'3"†	120	Normal	Normal
Clerks and Tradesmen	18-40	5'	110	Glasses allowed	Variable

*Nyasaland askaris could be five feet one and weigh 112 pounds.

†Tanganyikan laborers could be five feet one and weigh 112 pounds.

Source: Physical Standards and Medical Examination of African Recruits, 8 July 1942, KNA, DEF 15/12/1b.

AAPC askaris to more "interesting" jobs, the Director of Pioneers and Labour candidly declared: "If we allow ourselves to think for a moment that manual work is in any sense derogatory, what is to happen to these thousands of Pioneers after the war? They cannot all be tradesmen, their living must for many years be on the land, either their own or a European farm."[103]

Yet Nyasaland never raised African labor units. When war broke out in 1939, Governor Kennedy reassured the civilian population there were no plans for a new Carrier Corps. In 1942, the Nyasaland government cited Kennedy's promise to justify its refusal to recruit for the EAMLS and AAPC. It claimed that Nyasalanders' martial traditions made them unsuitable for military labor, but in reality, civil officials knew labor conscription would have produced mass resistance and desertion. Only the most high-paying forms of military service could compete with the appeal of labor migration. Nyasalanders did not object to well-paying military labor and volunteered in large numbers for the higher-paying South African Native Labour Corps and High Commission Territory AAPC companies.[104]

Conversely, the demands of modern warfare forced the East Africa Command to compete actively for skilled African labor. During the early days of the conflict, many colonial officers were seconded from the civil administra-

Figure 3.2 Bayonet training, World War II. Courtesy of the Trustees of the Imperial War Museum, London (K5150). Reprinted with permission.

tions of East Africa, but by 1942, these governments were pressing for their return. Manpower shortages in Britain ruled out the possibility of importing extensive imperial reinforcements, and in 1943, the War Office mandated that Europeans could comprise no more than one-quarter of the total East African forces. As a result, the EAC's Assistant Adjutant General called for "intelligent and educated African boys" to serve as medical orderlies, clerks, ordnance men, signallers, teachers, censors, gunners, engineers, and tradesmen, thereby allowing local Europeans to receive commissions.[105]

Finding men with proper educational qualifications for these jobs was no easy matter because private employers usually offered higher pay and more comfortable working conditions. As a general rule, the army needed recruits with at least a Standard IV level of elementary education. Yet most African boys who fit this criteria were between the ages of twelve and fifteen and

Figure 3.3   Training drivers for the East Africa Army Service Corps, Nairobi, World War II. Courtesy of the Trustees of the Imperial War Museum, London (K4943). Reprinted with permission.

were therefore too young to serve. Conversely, older teenagers who passed their Primary School Certificate Examination rarely found military service attractive. Recruiters therefore had to entice fifteen-year-old boys, who were in Standard IV or Standard V, to forgo their schooling. To make military service more appealing, the Nyasaland government declared every wartime civil service appointment temporary and promised any African who left school to join the army could resume his education after he was discharged.[106]

These promises were not very convincing, and the EAC soon realized it would have to produce its own educated soldiers. It formed the East African Army Education Corps and established a special school at the Maseno Depot to train recruits marked for specialist units. The East Africa Command also offered more money to attract educated Africans (Table 3.12). After 1942, an army driver earned forty-six shillings per month, as compared to a KAR private's monthly pay of twenty-eight shillings.[107] Thus, the Second World War marked the only time during the colonial era when the military outbid civil employers for skilled African labor.

This pressing need for educated Africans also forced the EAC to abandon its ethnic prejudices. While many officers believed the Kikuyu were too physically small or politically unreliable to make good soldiers, they were undeni-

Table 3.12
East Africa Military Pay Rates, by Branch of Service, 1940–1941 (in shillings per month)

Unit	Recruit	Private or Driver I	Corporal	Sergeant	Sergeant Major
EAMLS	12	17	32	42	-
KAR	20	28	48	64	90
EAE or Signals	-	28	55	75	100
EAAMC	28	46	73	94	115
EAASC	15	60	90	100	120

Sources: GROs on Pay 1941, KNA, DEF 1/39/53 & 64.

ably the best-educated ethnic group in Kenya. Moreover, the Kikuyu were actually interested in the army's high wartime wages, and their vernacular press protested the army's discriminatory recruiting policies.[108] Colonial military authorities refused to allow the non-martial Kikuyu in the KAR, but their insatiable demand for African manpower eventually forced the army to recruit them for every other labor and technical unit. In 1942, the Kikuyu comprised forty-six percent of the EAAMC, thirty-three and six-tenths percent of the East Africa Army Ordnance Corps, nineteen and three-tenths percent of all signallers, and seventeen and three-tenths percent of the EAASC. By the war's end, the Kikuyu, Embu and Meru constituted twenty-one and eight-tenths percent of the Kenyan military, more than any other Kenyan ethnic group.[109]

World War II therefore put the colonial military's martial stereotypes to the test and reordered the martial hierarchy of East Africa. Military officials tried to reserve martial races for frontline KAR battalions but ultimately had to broaden their recruiting base. Results were mixed. Some martial races failed to live up to expectations, whereas other peoples previously disdained as non-martial showed themselves to be willing askaris.

The war solidified the reputation of the Kamba as the premier martial race of Kenya. In 1940, they made up a significant portion of the East Africa Military Labour Service, but by 1942, their reputation as the most reliable and technically skilled Kenyan askaris led the Chief Native Commissioner to limit their recruiting to infantry and support units.[110] In comparison, the Luo lost their martial status during the war. While they were well respected in the early KAR, Luo askaris acquired a reputation for being childish, "boneheaded," and "bush lawyers" in the 1940s. These new stereotypes reflected the declining value of military service in Nyanza Province. As the Luo acquired extensive experience as labor migrants, they often struck to protest unfair treatment in the army. By 1942, the EAC would recruit them only for the EAMLS and AAPC. Many Luo askaris resented this demotion and were unwilling to accept the low pay and prestige of military labor.[111]

Not surprisingly, Nyasaland's ethnic recruiting policies during the Second World War were dictated almost entirely by patterns of labor migration. British officers pressured the Nyasaland government to produce Tonga and Ngoni recruits, but both groups preferred civilian work in the south. In 1940, Governor Kennedy informed the army that it could not expect more Tonga askaris because "they are so accustomed to bowler hats and mouth organs in Johannesburg that their fibre has been sapped and the older men quite openly accuse the younger generation of cowardice."[112]

Therefore British recruiters had no choice but to turn to the previously non-martial Lomwe. Also known as Nguru, Lomwe is a modern term for an ethnically diverse collection of peoples that migrated to southern Nyasaland from Portuguese East Africa around the turn of the twentieth century. Most Nyasalanders were uninterested in the low pay offered on Shire Highland estates, but the Lomwe found these wages relatively attractive in comparison to the dearth of employment opportunities in Mozambique. Portuguese authorities even encouraged Africans who could not pay their taxes to cross the border to join the KAR. Since most of the new immigrants had no legal claim to land in Nyasaland, they became clients of Yao and Nyanja chiefs. This subservient relationship earned the Lomwe the label of *akapolo* (slave). Many were uneducated and undernourished when they arrived in Nyasaland, and they acquired an undeserved reputation in the colonial army for being stupid, cowardly, and subservient.[113]

The ban on foreign labor recruiting in Southern Province made it difficult for the Lomwe to become labor migrants, and their lack of land tenure required them to stay close to home to prevent their families from being evicted. Thus, the army was appealing because military service paid more than estate labor, and the colonial administration was obligated to look after Lomwe soldiers' interests while they were away. When military authorities complained that civil officials were recruiting too many Lomwe, the Governor told them to abandon their pre-war prejudices because the Lomwe were the only local group willing to volunteer in large numbers. By all accounts, the Lomwe served bravely during war. Table 3.13 shows they comprised over twenty-six percent of the Nyasaland KAR battalions in 1943. In March 1944, 750 of the 2,720 Nyasalanders in Ceylon training for Burma were Lomwe, making them the largest Nyasaland ethnic group in 11 Division.[114]

Yet the strong combat record of the Lomwe does not mean they suddenly became martial during the war. Ethnic identity was quite fluid in southern Nyasaland, and in the pre-war KAR, many Lomwe had simply called them-

Table 3.13
Military Enlistment in Nyasaland, by Ethnic Group, 1943

Ethnic Group	Percentage of the Overall Civil Population	Percentage of the Nyasaland Colonial Forces	Number of Adult Males Enlisted in the Military
Chewa	23.2	11.8	3,520
Nyanja	17.2	17.8	5,306
Yao	15.4	20.0	5,646
Lomwe (Nguru)	14.7	26.7	7,945
Ngoni	13.6	15.7	4,667
Tumbuka	6.9	2.9	874
Tonga	3.5	2.0	582
Chikunda	3.0	1.2	348
Nkonde	1.9	0.3	85
Wemba	0.4	0.2	58
Others	0.2	2.3	678
Total Number Enlisted			29,709

Source: Nyasaland Ethnic Distribution by District, 1943, MNA, S41/1/23/2.

selves Yao in order to enlist. When the East Africa Command polled KAR officers on the martial qualities of Nyasaland askaris, they ranked the "Nguru" at the top and the "Ampotola" at the bottom. Most officers had no idea that both groups were technically part of the same "tribe." Nyasaland's ethnic identities were at least partly determined by a man's receptivity to military service. If a Southerner refused to enlist or was a bad soldier, he was a Mpotola; if he did enlist and served with distinction, he was a Nguru or even a Yao.[115]

THE POST-WAR ERA, 1945–1963

The War Office's decision to maintain the KAR as a post-war imperial reserve placed a considerable recruiting burden on the East Africa Command. The EAC hoped to retain as many trained African soldiers as possible, but most wartime askaris, wanting to return home as quickly as possible, refused to sign on for a peacetime term of service. In Kenya, only Kamba veterans rejoined the army in large numbers, and the EAC had to find new askaris to fill out the post-war KAR battalions.[116]

Peacetime recruiting in the late 1940s was much more difficult than it had been during the war because the EAC was not free to compete with civilian employers. Although the army comprised only two and a half percent of all African wage laborers in 1950, private employers pressured the Kenyan government not to let the army drive up African wages. European farmers in particular wanted to have their squatters declared off limits to military recruiters. The Kenyan government therefore required all potential recruits to prove they were not still under contract to a civilian employer and forbade KAR battalions from accepting casual applicants at the barracks door.

When Kenya agreed to host the East African Stores Holding Project, the government assumed responsibility for recruiting the East African Construction Force to prevent the military from offering too much pay for African labor. Civil officials promised to reject Africans discharged from private employment within the previous three months and held wages for unskilled EACF askaris to twenty-five shillings per month, which was only slightly above prevailing civilian rates. Yet although these parsimonious wages pleased private employers, they provided little incentive for hard work. Military engineers blamed the project's severe construction delays on the indifferent attitude of the African work force. EACF askaris were barely considered soldiers. Many informants who served with the "Fanya Corps" (from the Swahili for "to make or do") are unwilling to discuss their service because they are teased by peers who served in combat units.[117]

Yet the East Africa Command was also unable to raise base wages for the KAR in the late 1940s. Colonial officials put off army pay increases because of the uncertainty over whether the Regiment would remain an imperial responsibility or would return to local control. In 1946, the EAC dropped its proposal to raise the pay of African privates to 100 shillings per month because the Kenyan and Tanganyikan governments objected that the increase was too large. Kenya's Labour Commissioner argued that while military wages in Britain were double the average civilian rate, the EAC was proposing to raise military pay to five times the prevailing civilian wage for unskilled African labor.[118]

As a result, askari wages in the late 1940s failed to keep pace with inflation. In Kenya, the price index of consumer goods rose 217 percent between August 1939 and December 1949, whereas KAR wages increased only 160 percent during the same period (from twenty-eight to forty-five shillings per month for a private). Many Nyasaland askaris sold their equipment to support their families, and it became difficult even to recruit in Southern Province. Senior officers naturally became concerned that these developments would undermine the overall reliability of the KAR:

Unless the African is given pay compatible to his position and value recruiting will undoubtedly suffer, and dissatisfaction and lowering of morale will result. A dissatisfied Askari is seldom of any use to anyone, and as regards pay he is steadily becoming more and more discontented.[119]

Yet uncertainty over the basic mission and status of the KAR continued to derail proposals to increase African wages throughout most of the 1950s. The War Office had to approve monthly bonuses of 82 to 315 shillings (depending on rank) for KAR askaris in Malaya to ensure they were paid as much as Gurkha and Fijian imperial soldiers. The East African governments approved the increases because they only applied to overseas duty and were paid from imperial, rather than local, funds.[120]

Nyasaland askaris received substantial raises in 1954 when 1 and 2 KAR became part of the Central Africa Command. The wages of Kenyan, Ugandan, and Tanganyikan askaris, however, remained fixed until the East African Land Forces Organization took over the remaining KAR battalions in 1957. The EALFO increased the base pay of African privates to 80 shillings per month, and the highest-ranking African Warrant Officers received up to 300 shillings. While this constituted a thirty-three percent pay increase, its actual value was wiped out by inflation. By the early 1960s, British officers renewed their warnings that low military wages threatened morale and discipline. KAR askaris received another small pay increase in 1961, but lingering discontent over inadequate pay was a primary cause of the dissatisfaction that produced the wave of army mutinies in 1964.[121]

This is not to say, however, that the KAR was no longer a popular form of unskilled labor in post-war East Africa. By definition, martial races came from relatively impoverished ethnic groups, and although KAR wages failed to keep pace with inflation, they were still higher than the going rate for unskilled labor. In 1946, the Kenyan Labour Department calculated that agricultural workers earned only ten to twelve shillings per month, whereas casual laborers could command from two to three shillings per day. By Rosberg and Nottingham's estimates, the average unskilled monthly wage in Kenya rose to roughly twenty-five shillings in 1950. In Nyasaland, rates for unskilled African labor averaged between eight and ten shillings per month during the same period. Although Frederick Cooper has calculated that Kenyan dockworkers earned as much as eighty-two shillings per month in 1947, the forty-five shillings per month earned by KAR privates in 1949 was still a relatively lucrative wage for most East Africans.[122]

Interviews with African veterans who served during this period bear this out. While many grumbled about racial inequity in army wages, most agreed they could not have earned more in civilian life. As one man put it: "We made more money in the army, but it was like slavery because we couldn't negotiate our wages." For the bulk of these informants, poverty was still the common inspiration for enlistment. Some also cite a lack of school fees or a need to earn money for bride price cattle as their reason for enlisting. "My brothers needed school fees and. ... there was no other well-paying job like the KAR." One man joined to get treatment for kala-azar, which reached epidemic proportions in northern Kenya in the early 1950s.[123] Other recruits were attracted by the perquisites of military service. As one veteran explained: "The army paid compensation if you were hurt or injured. ... None of the [private European employers] would pay this." KAR recruiting posters also offered the chance to learn to shoot, drive a truck, and operate telephones and radios and promised free education, housing, clothing, medical care, and a generous family support allowance.[124]

Thus, the KAR continued to attract more applicants than it required during the post-war period and rarely resorted to informal conscription. Most askaris were enlisted by recruiting safaris, which visited the home regions of martial races. Chiefs publicized these visits and helped district officers and African NCOs weed out men with "unsavory reputations . . . or who belong to sections or families of the tribe who are likely to prove troublesome to the units."[125] Potential recruits ran and threw spears to demonstrate their physical qualifications and were asked to pitch a tent and engage in casual conversation to gauge their general intelligence. The army's overall physical requirements were generally less rigorous than in pre-war times as the necessity of recruiting Africans from less affluent regions lowered height requirements. As a general rule, a man had to be under twenty-five years of age and stand over five feet three inches tall. In 1950, however, with military pay at its lowest point compared to civilian wages, recruits could be up to thirty years of age and only five feet tall.[126]

While the KAR still found it relatively easy to attract unskilled Africans, recruiting educated men also remained a problem. The increasing sophistication of military weaponry required better educated rank-and-file askaris, and the EALFO hoped to replace most British NCOs with lower-paid Africans. Yet the KAR even had difficulty retaining its own trained skilled soldiers. Specialist pay lagged far behind civilian wages, and most askaris left the army after earning their nine-year service gratuity. A tradesman who received an average of only 135 shillings per month in the KAR could earn as much as 550 shillings in civilian life.[127] In 1957, only six of the fifty-three time-expired vehicle mechanics and electricians of the EAEME agreed to reenlist. Since it would take three years to train their replacements, the East Africa Command begged for more money to pay army tradesmen. Civil officials, however, would sanction only an average raise of less than 10 shillings per month. With the forced economy brought on by the return of the KAR to local control, the army lacked the authority and financial resources to compete for skilled labor.[128]

Table 3.14
The Ethnic Composition of the Late Kenyan KAR, 1959 (by percentage)

Ethnic Group	Official Recruiting Quota, 1959	Actual Enlistment Figures, 1959	Overall Population, 1962 Kenyan Census Estimates
Kamba	34.0	36.3	11.2
Kalenjin	34.0	25.8	10.7
Samburu	7.5	3.6	0.6
Northern Frontier Pastoralists	12.5	11.6	6.1
Maasai	2.0	0.6	1.8
"Unspecified"	5.0	9.0	29.0
Luo	Under "Unspecified"	9.7	13.7
Kikuyu, Embu, and Meru	Under "Unspecified"	3.4	26.9

Sources: EAC Circular, "Tribal Structure 1959/60," 22 December 1959, KNA, LF 1/255/28; Report on the EALF & the Kenya Regiment in 1959, by GOC EAC, KNA, LF 1/210; Kenya Ministry of Finance and Economic Planning, *Kenya Population Census, 1962*, (Nairobi: Government Printer, 1964).

The changing political economy of military service also transformed the KAR's martial stereotypes. The ideal askari came from a society in which reliance on pastoralism or subsistence agriculture made them only partially dependent on paid employment. The army could then keep wages low, and askaris were less inclined to strike over labor issues. In Kenya, rapid population growth and a shortage of productive land made this arrangement increasingly unworkable in the 1950s. The East Africa Command became particularly distrustful of the large numbers of partially urbanized young men unwilling or unable to participate in the agricultural economy of the "native reserves" and warned recruiters to avoid the large numbers of "spivs and drones" who congregated in urban areas.[129] Nyasaland experienced similar problems in its Northern Province, where African hostility toward the Central African Federation made military recruiting impossible. In 1961, a recruiting safari in Nkata Bay District produced only a single recruit and was told by a young supporter of the Malawi Congress Party: "You are not the KAR, you are Welensky's invaders."[130] Therefore, recruiting safaris in both territories had to venture deeper into the countryside to find recruits willing to accept the discipline and relatively low wages of the KAR.

As a result, the EAC's "Tribal Composition Committee" drafted new recruiting quotas which substantially altered the ethnic composition of the KAR.
Table 3.14 shows that the Kamba and Kalenjin retained their status as preferred martial races, but recruiters worried about the large numbers of Mau
Mau sympathizers and unemployed spivs among the Kamba. The army therefore shifted its Kamba recruiting base from Machakos District to the more
pastoral Kitui District.[131] The Tribal Composition Committee also reclassi-
fied the Luo as a non-martial race, and the East Africa Command quietly
issued a directive restricting them to specialist and support units. Yet the Luo
still constituted almost ten percent of the Kenyan KAR battalions in 1957,
which indicates the limits of these ethnic recruiting quotas.[132]

As more and more of Kenya's agricultural peoples became politically suspect, KAR recruiters concentrated on pastoral societies. The East Africa
Command took as many Samburu as it could get and targeted the nomadic
Rendille and Turkana, who had previously been uninterested in military service. Yet the most striking shift in post-war recruiting came with the sudden
interest of the Maasai in the KAR. They had successfully resisted the Kenyan
government's attempts to lure them into the army during the Second World
War, but political and economic changes in post-war Kenya forced them to
rethink their opposition to military service.[133] By the 1950s, large tracts of
underused Maasai land in the Trans Mara region attracted migrants from the
more densely populated Kikuyu, Luo, and Kalenjin Reserves. While the
Kenyan government restricted immigration into the "Masai Extra-Provincial
District" to those Africans formally adopted into a Maasai clan, the Maasai
realized the end of British colonial rule would make it impossible for them
to retain sole title to their substantial grazing lands. They therefore lobbied
the British government to guarantee their land rights after independence and
pushed for an increase in Maasai enlistment in the police and KAR to ensure
adequate representation in the new nation's security forces.[134] Although few
young Maasai were really interested in a military career, the political and
economic uncertainty generated by the prospect of independence stimulated
recruiting, and for the first time, the Maasai joined the army in statistically
significant numbers.

In retrospect, it is clear that most Africans joined the colonial army in
response to specific social and economic stimuli. While the colonial governments conscripted military laborers during the world wars, most Africans
joined the army out of necessity, attracted by generous wages and the privileges of government service. Martial stereotypes were simply an index of the
changing political economy of recruitment. Although portrayed by British
officers as an innate cultural attribute, "martial race" was actually a descriptive label that signified an acceptance of military discipline. The willingness
of an ethnic group to serve in the army was based on the extent of its integra-

tion into the colonial economy and therefore changed over time. When pre-colonial economic systems were still largely intact, most East Africans were considered poor soldiers because they had viable alternatives to military service. Restrictive government policies and social differentiation brought on by subordination to the colonial economy pushed martial races to join the army. Yet once this process reached an advanced stage, these ethnic groups lost their martial status because they once again had viable economic alternatives to the army. Therefore, African societies were most martial when they were in a transitional stage of development, operating under the constraints of colonial rule.

NOTES

[1] Employment of KAR Overseas, 14 April 1920, MNA, GOA 2/4/7; Great Britain, *Regulations for the King's African Rifles*, (London: Waterlow and Sons, 1908).

[2] Infantry Battalion Commanders Notes, by Lieutenant Colonel T. H. Birkbeck, IWM, 83/21/1, Birkbeck Papers.

[3] O/C 3 KAR to DC Tambach, 7 September 1935, KNA, DC TAMB 1/9/1.

[4] Great Britain, *Standing Orders of the 6th Battalion, the King's African Rifles*, (n.p., 1930); Lieutenant Colonel the Lord St. Helens, KNA, MSS 78/3.

[5] Gerald Hanley, "Resettling the East African," *Army Quarterly* v. 52, (1946), p. 128; Visit to the Mid East, by Brooke-Anderson, 26 July 1943, KNA, MD 4/5/65/216a; Bowie, RHL, Mss.Afr.s.1715/24.

[6] Leroy Vail, "Ethnicity in Southern African History," in *The Creation of Tribalism in Southern Africa*, edited by Leroy Vail, (Berkeley: University of California Press, 1989), pp. 11–12.

[7] O/C 2/3 KAR, to PC RVP, 19 July 1952, KNA, PC NKU, 2/21/5/51/1a; O/C 7 KAR to HQ Northern Area, 26 September 1952, KNA, DC KAPT 1/12/51/16/1; Interview, #146.

[8] B. E. Kipkorir, *The Marakwet of Kenya: A Preliminary Study*, (Nairobi: EA Literature Bureau, 1973), p. 73; A. T. Matson, "Reflections on the Growth of Political Consciousness in Nandi," in *Hadith 4: Politics and Nationalism in Kenya*, edited by B. A. Ogot, (Nairobi: EA Publishing House, 1972), p. 20.

[9] Kericho District AR, 1946, KNA, MAA 2/3/10/IV/1aii; KIO to DC Nandi, 21 June 1952, KNA, DC KAPT 1/13/10/75; KAR Recruiting Guide, July 1960, KNA, DC KAPT 1/12/12/1.

[10] Kenya Land Commission, *Evidence, Volume II*, (Nairobi: Government Printer, 1933).

[11] Kenya Colony and Protectorate, *Report of the Kenya Land Commission*, (Nairobi: Government Printer, 1933).

[12] Machakos HoR, by AH Bailward, 1938, KNA, DC MKS 2/26/1/10; J. Forbes Munro, *Colonial Rule and the Kamba: Social Change in the Kenya Highlands 1889–1939*, (Oxford: Clarendon Press, 1975), p. 219.

[13] Interviews, #26, #49.

[14] Kenya Colony and Protectorate, *Report of the Kenya Land Commission*.

[15] Memorandum on Samburu Grazing Question, by DC Embu, 2 June 1924, KNA, PC NFP 4/2/1; Samburu HoR, 1928, KNA, PC NFP 1/9/1.

[16] Interview, #146.

[17] Adult Male Population and Labor Statistics, Nyasaland Protectorate, October 1937, MNA, S1/96/37.

[18] Nyasaland Governor to Colonial Secretary, 14 July 1921, MNA, GOA/2/4/7.

[19] Secretariat Meeting on Effects of Emigration, 13 April 1939, MNA, S1/174AV/35/106.

[20] Labour Commissioner to SP Native Labour Advisory Committee, 15 December 1938, MNA, S1/96/37/130; Cholo District AR, 1938, MNA, S1/96/37/135; Governor's Permit for WNLA, 2 January 1951, MNA, LB/10/4/7/1.

[21] O/C S Bde, Fowkes, to IG KAR, Giffard, 17 October 1938, PRO, CO 820/32/11.

[22] Nyasaland Recruiting, as of 31 December 1943, MNA, DMP 1/6/1/1.

[23] G. R. Sandford, *A History of the Masai Reserve*, (London, 1919), p. 73.

[24] C. A. Sykes, *Service and Sport on the Tropical Nile*, (London: John Murray, 1903), p. 26.

[25] Interviews, #40, #41, #42, #43.

[26] Until the 1920s, British officials referred to the Luo and Luhya peoples of western Kenya as "Kavirondo" (sometimes Nilotic and Bantu Kavirondo). It is usually impossible to determine whether early reports were referring to either the Luo or the Luhya. William Lloyd-Jones, *Havash!*, (London: Arrowsmith, 1925), p. 27; Nyanza Province IR, August 1948, MAA 2/3/17/III/185.

[27] Tours of Inspector General Thesiger, 1911–1913, NAM, 8201-42.

[28] Some of these figures are converted from rupees using Clayton and Savage's formula of one rupee being equal to sh. 1/4d. Anthony Clayton and Donald Savage, *Government and Labour in Kenya, 1895–1963*, (London: Frank Cass, 1974), pp. xxiv, 49; Uganda Protectorate, *Standing Orders of the 4th Battalion, the King's African Rifles*, (Entebbe: Government Printer, 1934); IGR, 1 KAR, 1919–1920, MNA, S1/484/20; Robert Bension Boeder, "Malawians Abroad: The History of Labor Migration from Malawi to Its Neighbors, 1890 to the Present," (Ph.D. Dissertation, Michigan State University, 1974), p. 292.

[29] Donald Savage and J. Forbes Munro, "Carrier Corps Recruitment in the British East Africa Protectorate, 1914–1918," *Journal of African History*, v. 7, (1966), pp. 316–17; DA & QMG to PC Mombasa, 10 April 1915, KNA, PC CST 1/13/136/54; DC Malindi to PC Mombasa, 4 March 1915, KNA, PC CST 1/13/136/38.

[30] PC Mombasa to DC Malindi, 2 November 1915, KNA, PC CST 1/13/134/228; Kenyan Secretariat Circular no. 91, 8 December 1915, KNA, PC CST 1/13/6/1.

[31] Kenyan Secretariat Circular, no. 12, "Recruitment for Carrier Corps," 22 February 1917, KNA, PC CST 1/13/8/350; Ukamba Province AR 1917–18, KNA, DC MKS 1/5/11; South Kavirondo AR, 1946, Appendix on the History of South Kavirondo, KNA, MAA 2/3/10/IV/1ai.

[32] Boeder, "Malawians Abroad," p. 99; Kenyan Secretariat Circular, no. 55, 8 August 1917, KNA, PC CST 1/17/114/637.

[33] MKS AR, 1917–18, KNA, DC MKS 1/1/10; Captain H. A. Bodeker, EAMS Kisumu Depot, 16 May 1917, KNA, PC CST 1/13/8/525.

[34] DC Gazi to PC Mombasa, 9 January 1917, KNA, PC CST 1/1/234/12 & 14; George Shepperson and Thomas Price, *Independent African*, (Edinburgh: The University Press, 1958); Melvin Page, "The War of Thangata: Nyasaland and the East African Campaign, 1914–1918," *Journal of African Studies*, v. 19, (1978), pp. 87–100.

[35] Lewis Greenstein, "Africans in a European War: The First World War in East Africa with Special Reference to the Nandi of Kenya," (Ph.D. dissertation, Indiana Univer-

sity, 1975), p. 85; D.W.J. Cuddleford, *And All for What? Some Wartime Experiences,* (London: Heath Cranton Ltd, 1933).

[36] Provisional Schedule for the KAR, PRO, WO 106/276; Clayton and Savage, *Government and Labour in Kenya,* p. 99.

[37] 3 KAR Recruits from Carrier Corps, 10 April 1917, KNA, PC CST 1/13/8/406; Geoffrey Hodges, *The Carrier Corps: Military Labor in the East African Campaign, 1914–1918,* (Westport, CT: Greenwood Press, 1986), p. 98.

[38] 3 KAR During the EA Campaign 1914–18, by T. O. Fitzgerald, PRO, WO 106/273; Interview, #87.

[39] Historical Record 3 KAR, PRO, WO 106/270; Sandford, *A History of the Masai Reserve,* p. 77.

[40] Bruce Berman, *Control and Crisis in Colonial Kenya: The Dialectic of Domination,* (Nairobi: EA Publishers, 1990), p. 302.

[41] DC Nandi to F. J. Weynman, 27 March 1934, KNA, DC KAPT 1/12/44/6; Kenyan Secretariat Circular, Recruitment for KAR, 1 June 1935, KNA, DC KSM 1/22/12/4.

[42] Uganda Protectorate, *Standing Orders of the 4th Battalion*; IGR, N Bde, 1935, PRO, CO 820 34/10; DC Central Kavirondo to O/C 5 KAR, 3 October 1938, KNA, DC KSM 1/22/12.

[43] O/C Northern Bde to Colonial Secretary, 3 April 1935, PRO, CO 820 20/11.

[44] Staff Sergeant C. W. Catt, RHL, Mss.Afr.s.1715/55; Stoney, RHL, Mss.Afr.s.1715/263; Government African School Machakos, AR 1938, KNA, ED 1/932/269.

[45] Great Britain, War Office, *Notes on Land and Air Forces of the British Overseas Dominions, Colonies, Protectorates and Mandated Territories,* (London: HM Stationery Office, 1925); Great Britain, War Office, *Notes on Land and Air Forces of the British Overseas Dominions, Colonies, Protectorates and Mandated Territories,* (London: HM Stationery Office, 1934).

[46] KAR Annual Unit Reports, 1927–1938, PRO, CO 820.

[47] 3 KAR Intelligence Report, 31 December 1927, KNA, PC NFD 3/1/1; Annual Unit Reports, 1927–1938, PRO, CO 820.

[48] Timothy Parsons, "'Kibra Is Our Blood': The Sudanese Military Legacy in Nairobi's Kibera Location, 1902–1968," *International Journal of African Historical Studies,* v. 30, (1997), pp. 87–122.

[49] DC Nairobi to Commissioner of Lands, 13 May 1931, KNA, BN 46/4/49.

[50] Testimony of Mohamed bin Abusaker, Kenya Land Commission, *Evidence, Volume I,* (Nairobi: Government Printer, 1933); Lieutenant Colonel J.R.V. Thompson, IWM, 79/11/1.

[51] Great Britain, *Standing Orders of the 2nd (Nyasaland) Battalion, the King's African Rifles,* (Nairobi: Uganda Railway Press, c. 1926), appendix IV; Boeder, "Malawians Abroad," p. 292.

[52] O/C 2 KAR to PC Northern Province, 24 September 1938, MNA, NN 1/18/1/29.

[53] PC Southern Province to CSNY, 22 January 1937, MNA, S1/240/34/54; CSNY to PCs; DCs, 23 January 1937, MNA, NCN 1/13/1.

[54] EAF HQ to EA Governments, 9 July 1940, KNA, MD 4/5/132/53a; EAF Circular, "New Battalions KAR and NRR," 30 September 1940, KNA, CNC 10/129/10; Kenya Recruiting, August 1940 to March 1941, KNA, MD 4/5/139.

[55] CNC to PC NZA, 27 September 1941, KNA, MD 4/5/140/6.

[56] EAC Circular, "Formation of New and Reinforcement of Existing Units, 1942–1943," 10 May 1942, KNA, MD 4/5/140/157a; Colonial Secretary to Nyasaland Gover-

nor, 9 June 1942, MNA, S41/1/16/4; Nyasaland Governor to Colonial Secretary, Nyasaland HoW 1942, MNA, S33/2/2/1/1.

[57] Civil Labor Estimates, September 1942, KNA, MD 4/5/140/170.

[58] Colonial Secretary to CSEAG, 26 October 1942, KNA, DEF 15/27/2a.

[59] NZA AR 1942, KNA, MAA 2/3/10/III/1a; Kenyan Executive Council Circular, African Manpower, 21 October 1943, KNA DEF/15/28/74.

[60] Meeting, Kenyan Governor; GOC EAC, 21 July 1943, KNA, DEF 15/27/115; Kenyan Secretariat Meeting on African Manpower, 3 February 1944, KNA, DEF 15/28/127.

[61] African Manpower Conference, 7 May 1943, KNA, DEF 15/28/142a; CSEAG to CST, 31 July 1943, KNA, DEF 15/28/6a; African Manpower Conference, 15 November 1943, KNA, DEF 15/28/84a.

[62] Civil Labor Estimates, 2 February 1945, KNA, DEF /15/29/88a; KNA, MD 4/5/140/170.

[63] Appreciation—Leave for African Ranks in EA Forces in Eastern Theatre, February 1945, PRO, WO 203/4668; EAC to CSEAG, 28 March 1945, KNA, DEF 10/151/1.

[64] Clayton and Savage, *Government and Labour in Kenya*, p. 244; GRO 281, "Pay—African Personnel," 2 January 1940, KNA, MD 4/5/117/II/1; Pay and Grading of Enlisted African Tradesmen, 17 February 1942, KNA, DEF 15/61/1b; Divisional Engineer Mombasa to DPW, 6 May 1942.

[65] PC NZA to CSK, 24 July 1943, KNA, DEF 15/27/120.

[66] Dickinson to Kenyan Governor, 8 July 1940, KNA, MD 4/5/132/68; Hosking to CSK, 20 July 1940, KNA MD/4/5/132/74; Kenyan Secretariat, Recruiting for EAMLS and AAPC, 16 December 1941, KNA, DEF 15/57/5a.

[67] Civil Labor Estimates, 2 February 1945, KNA, DEF /15/29/88a; KNA, MD 4/5/140/170.

[68] CSK to CSEAG, 12 August 1941, KNA, DEF 15/45/9.

[69] LCK to DC MKS, 4 January 1944, KNA, DEF 15/28/112.

[70] Kenya Sisal Grower's Association to CSK, 22 September 1943, KNA, DEF 15/74/103; Ian Spencer, "Settler Dominance, Agricultural Production and the Second World War in Kenya," *Journal of African History*, v. 21, (1984), pp. 497–514.

[71] The Commissioner and his staff spent an entire morning peering out their office windows to document a detachment of EAMLS askaris sleeping on the job. One has to wonder which group was using their time more productively. LCK to CSK, 17 November 1943, KNA, DEF 15/75/21a.

[72] "Defence (African Labour for Essential Undertakings) 1942," KNA, DEF 9/4/167; Meetings on Labour Policy, November 1943, KNA, DEF 15/74/151; Wyn-Harris to CSK, 16 April 1945, KNA, DEF 15/86/34.

[73] PC NZA to CSK, 28 January 1944, KNA, DEF 15/28/123; O/C Tororo Depot to PC NZA, 14 February 1944, KNA, PC NZA 2/3/98/7.

[74] Recruiting in Nyasaland, by Director of Recruiting, n.d., MNA, S41/1/17/4/1; Boeder, "Malawians Abroad," p. 180; Nyasaland Governor to Colonial Secretary, HoW, 23 July 1940, MNA, S33/2/1/1/40; Civil Recruiting Officer to CSNY, 24 October 1940, MNA, S41/1/17/8/47/1.

[75] CSNY to PC Southern Province, 6 November 1940, MNA, GOB G141a.

[76] Nyasaland Governor to Colonial Secretary, HoW, 26 October 1940, MNA, S33/2/1/1/69; CSNY to Colonial Secretary, HoW, 4 February 1941, MNA/S33/2/1/1/97.

[77] Nyasaland Governor to Colonial Secretary, 12 May 1942, MNA/S41/1/16/4; Nyasaland Governor to Colonial Secretary, HoW, 1942, MNA/S33/2/2/1/1.

[78] Salisbury Conference on Manpower, 3 March 1943, MNA/S41/1/16/6; Nyasaland Governor to CSNY, 6 January 1942, MNA/S41/1/5/2; Nyasaland Governor to Colonial Secretary, 14 October 1942, MNA, S41/1/17/12/18.

[79] African Manpower Conference, 7 May 1943, KNA, DEF/15/27/70a; Nyasaland Governor to Colonial Secretary, HoW, 31 January 1945, MNA, S33/2/2/1/5.

[80]EAC to CNC, 2 July 1943, KNA, DEF/15/27/99.

[81] Robert Kakembo, *An African Soldier Speaks*, (London: Livingstone Press, 1947), p. 9.

[82] Tanganyika Territory, *Annual Reports of the Provincial Commissioners, 1939–1945*, (Dar Es Salaam: Government Printer, 1940–1946).

[83] Bildad Kaggia, *The Roots of Freedom, 1921–1963*, (Nairobi: EA Publishing House, 1975), p. 21; Okete J. E. Shiroya, "The Impact of World War II on Kenya: The Role of Ex-Servicemen in Kenyan Nationalism," (Ph.D. dissertation, Michigan State University, 1968), p. 25; Interviews, #59, #61, #62, #63, #67a, #79, #92, #98, #112, #114.

[84] CSEAG to Under Colonial Secretary, 19 February 1942, PRO, CO 820/48/12; CSEAG to CSU; CST, 14 February 1942, KNA, MD 4/5/140/65a.

[85] CNC to CSK, 17 December 1940, KNA, MD 4/5/135/78; Minute by E. M. Hyde-Clark, 10 December 1941, KNA, MD 4/5/140/35.

[86] CST to PCs Lake Province & West Province, 9 September 1940, KNA, MD 4/5/136/82; CSEAG to EAC, 2 February 1945, KNA, DEF 15/29/88.

[87] GRO 747, "Military Units Ordinance—Attestation of Tanganyikan Natives," 20 July 1940, KNA, MD 4/5/117/II/50; Inquiry into Compulsory Recruitment of Civilian Labour in Kenya and Tanganyika, by Sir Julian Foley, 14 December 1944, KNA, DEF 15/76/1.

[88] Lieutenant Colonel G. G. Robson, RHL, Mss.Afr.s.1715/231.

[89] Nyasaland Governor to Northern Rhodesian Governor, 3 August 1942, MNA, S41/1/16/5; Conference on Nyasaland Recruitment, 19 August 1942, MNA, S41/1/16/4; Political Intelligence Bulletin, No. 6, 1942, MNA, S34/1/4/1.

[90] Interviews, #72, #103.

[91] Report by Major Kenyon-Slaney, December 1942, MNA, S41/1/17/2/128b; Minute to CSNY, 23 December 1942, MNA, S41/1/17/2.

[92] Memoirs of an Administrative Officer, by K. L. Hunter, RHL, Mss.Afr.s. 1942; Director of Recruiting to Civil Camp Commandant Mpata, 27 November 1942, MNA, S41/1/17/2/110.

[93] DC Nairobi to PC Central Province, 20 January 1941, KNA, MD 4/5/135/100a; 7 KAR War Diary, September 1940, PRO, WO 169/778; DC Dowa to PC Northern Province, 8 October 1940, MNA, LB 10/4/1/81.

[94] Interviews, #10, #97.

[95] Interview, #25.

[96] P. G. Goodeve-Docker, RHL, Mss.Afr.s.1715/110; Interviews, #13, #36, #37, #80, #84.

[97] Examination of Military Recruits and Conscript Labor, by MO Central Kavirondo, 7 September 1942, KNA, DC KSM 1/29/7/71.

[98] O/C Maseno Depot to DC Machakos, 14 March 1944, KNA, DC KSM 1/22/31/78.

[99] Memorandum by Fazan, PC NZA, 11 August 1941, KNA, PC NZA 2/3/65/3; District Exemption Tribunal, North Kavirondo, 10 September 1941, KNA, PC NZA/2/3/65/15.

[100] Standard of Physique—KAR Recruits, 17 August 1935, KNA, DC TAMB/1/9/1; O/C 3 KAR to DC Nakuru, 17 October 1938, KNA, DC NKU 2/29/12.

[101] Physical Standards and Medical Examination of African Recruits, 8 July 1942, KNA, DEF 15/12/1b; R. R. Scott, *Medical Examination of Recruits for Service with the Forces*, (Dar Es Salaam: Medical Department Tanganyika Territory, 1942), para. 5.

[102] African Manpower Conference, 7 May 1943, KNA, DEF/15/28/142a.

[103] Brooke-Anderson to CSEAG, 16 October 1942, KNA, MD 4/5/137/125a.

[104] Chief Political Liaison Officer to Nyasaland Governor, 18 October 1939, MNA, S41/1/17/4/21; Nyasaland Governor to CSEAG, 26 July 1942, MNA, S41/1/16/4; EAC Conference Report, 28 August 1942, PRO, WO 169/6893; CSNY to Nyasaland Governor, 9 October 1942, MNA, S41/1/10/1.

[105] Platt to General Sir Alan Brooke, CIGS, 22 January 1942, PRO, WO 216/72; African Manpower Conference, 30 September 1942, KNA, MD 4/5/140/170; African Manpower Conference, 7 May 1943, KNA, DEF 15/27/70a.

[106] Kenya Director of Education to CSK, 4 December 1941, KNA, DEF 15/42/5; EAC Circular Letter to EA Headmasters, 5 January 1943, KNA, DEF 15/31/48a; Nyasaland Governor to the "Educated Young Men of Nyasaland," May 1942, MNA, S41/1/17/11/17.

[107] African Manpower Conference, 15 March 1944, KNA, DEF 15/37/57.

[108] Central Province AR, 1939, KNA, PC CP 4/3/2; Chief Political Officer to CNC, 26 March 1940, KNA, CNC 10/129/4; Survey of Tribal Composition of KAR, 22 April 1940, KNA, CNC 10/129/8a.

[109] Kenya Natives in Military Service, Analysis by Unit, 30 April 1942, KNA, PC NZA 2/3/84; Kenyan Tradesmen by District, 1945, KNA, DEF 10/9.

[110] Colonial authorities preferred to believe the Kamba enlisted in such large numbers out of loyalty to the British Empire. Yet the substantial rise in their wartime enlistment rates was due largely to increased economic differentiation and wartime famine. Many Kamba referred to these food shortages as the *Yua ya Makovo* (Famine of the Boots) in recognition of the crucial role of army remittances in feeding the general population. CNC to Humphrey Slade, 8 October 1942, KNA, DEF 15/118/42; Kenya Colony and Protectorate, Native Affairs Department, *Report on Native Affairs, 1939–1945*, (London: HM Stationery Office, 1948), p. 59; Interviews, #37, #114, #133a.

[111] Survey of Tribal Composition of KAR, 22 April 1940, KNA, CNC 10/129/8a; AAG EAC to CNC, 15 September 1942, KNA, PC NZA 2/3/67/235; Interview, #147.

[112] Nyasaland Governor to Major General D. P. Dickinson, April 1940, MNA, S41/1/17/4/112.

[113] Nyasaland Governor to Colonial Secretary, HoW, 26 October 1940, MNA, S33/2/1/1/69; Great Britain, General Staff, *Military Report and General Information Concerning Nyasaland*, (London: HM Stationery Office, 1909), p. 67; R. B. Boeder, *Silent Majority: A History of the Lomwe in Malawi*, (Pretoria: Africa Institute of South Africa, 1984), pp. 13–33.

[114] Nyasaland Governor to EA Governor's Conference, 9 August 1940, MNA, S41/1/8/1/92.

[115] Minute to CSNY, 8 April 1943, MNA, S41/1/20/4; Minute to CSNY, 27 March 1944, MNA, S41/1/23/5.

[116] 11 Division Commander's Conference, 10 November 1945, PRO, WO 172/9439; CSNY to PCs, 13 December 1946, MNA, PCS 1/18/8/2; AAG EAC to CSEAG, 22 November 1946, KNA, MD 4/5/134/95a.

[117] EACF (c) Circular No. 3, Recruiting in Settled Areas, 14 November 1947, KNA, CA 6/46; East Africa News Review, 19 February 1948, KNA, MAA 8/102/26; MacKinnon Road IR, March 1948, KNA, PC CA 1/16/93/3; Interview, #100.

[118] Conference on Pay of African Ranks, 10 January 1946, KNA, DEF 15/29/233a; LCK to CNC, 12 January 1946, KNA, DEF 15/61/43; Inter-Territorial Conference on Post-War Rates of Pay for African Soldiers, 1946, PRO, CO 537/2103.

[119] GOC EAC to GHQ MELF, 1949, KNA, DEF, 1/39/230/a/14; also see Chief of Staff Conference Minutes, 4 August 1950, KNA, MD 4/5/84/I; Colonel Humphery Williams, RHL, Mss.Afr.s.1715/300.

[120] Information Concerning African Troops for the Malaya Project, July 1951, KNA, PC NKU 2/21/5/12a.

[121] EALF, Standing Orders, Section I/VIII, "Pay of Officers and Other Ranks," 1957, KNA, DEF 13/470; GOC EAC to Kenya Governor, 7 November 1961, PRO, CO 968/723; EA Defence Committee, Report on the Army in EA, 1961, PRO, WO 305/531.

[122] Kenya Colony and Protectorate, *Labour Department Annual Report 1946*, (Nairobi: Government Printer, 1948); Carl Rosberg and John Nottingham, *The Myth of "Mau Mau": Nationalism and Colonialism in Kenya*, (New York: Praeger, 1966; reprint, Nairobi: TransAfrica Press, 1985), p. 204; Frederick Cooper, *On the African Waterfront: Urban Disorder and the Transformation of Work in Colonial Mombasa*, (New Haven, CT: Yale University Press, 1987), p. 159; Boeder, "Malawians Abroad," p. 292; GOC EAC to all EA Governments, 2 May 1949, KNA, DEF 1/39/230/a/9.

[123] Kala-azar is a severe infectious disease caused by a parasite spread by the bite of the sand fly. It is potentially fatal and causes fever, anemia, and enlargement of the liver and spleen. Interviews, #8, #22, #23, #56, #57, #101, #110.

[124] KAR Recruiting Poster, "In The Service of the Queen: Join the K.A.R. and Lead a Man's Life," c. 1952, MNA, 1DCZA/1/20/26; Interviews, #4, #21, #52, #116.

[125] Standing Orders, EALF, Section I/VI, "Recruiting," 1957, KNA, DEF 13/470 7; see also Interviews, #18, #32.

[126] EAC Circular, "African Recruiting," 27 August 1947, KNA, MD 4/5/134/188; Kenyan Secretariat Circular, "Recruitment of African Other Ranks," 28 May 1951, KNA, DC TAMB 1/9/18/80; Standing Orders, EALF, Section I/VI, "Recruiting," 1957, KNA, DEF 13/470; KAR Recruiting Guide, July 1960, KNA, DC KAPT 1/12/19/1.

[127] Chief Signals Officer to G(SD) EAC, 18 February 1959, KNA, LF 1/254/50.

[128] EAC Circular, "KAR (EAEME) Tradesmen," 13 November 1957, KNA, LF 1/254/1; EAC Circular, "Tradesmen—KAR," 5 December 1958, KNA, LF 1/254/30.

[129] *Partridge's Concise Dictionary of Slang and Unconventional English* defines a "spiv" as (1) one who lives by his wits, or (2) one who earns a living by not working. 11 KAR Recruiting Safari in Machakos and Kitui, September 1959, PRO, WO 305/997; KAR Recruiting Guide, July 1960, KNA, DC KAPT 1/12/12/1.

[130] 1 KAR Recruiting Tour, October–November 1961, MNA, F/248/2072.

[131] EAC Circular, "Tribal Composition of Units," October 1949, KNA, GH 4/451/282; Report on the EALF in 1959, by GOC EAC, KNA, LF 1/210.

[132] PC RVP to Brigadier A.C.F. Jackson, 14 January 1950, KNA, PC NKU 2/21/100; Visit of Nyanza Party to KAR Units, 25 May 1961, KNA, DC HB 2/18/2/1.

[133] AAG EAC to CNC, 15 September 1942, KNA, PC NZA 2/3/67/235; DC Narok to KIO, 24 March 1945, KNA, PC NGO 1/15/7.

[134] Southern Province AR, 1959, KNA, PC SP 1/1/4; Meeting, Kenya Governor and Masai Leaders of Narok and Kajiado, 15 August 1960, KNA, OPE 1/130/141/1

4

MILITARY LIFE

African perceptions of military service were determined largely by the degree to which the army transformed and reordered their daily lives. While Chapter 3 explored links between recruitment and ethnicity, this chapter deals with the nature of military service and its implications for askaris' identity as a class. Colonial military authorities understood the importance of encouraging loyalty and obedience. The security of British rule in East Africa depended on the effectiveness of the KAR, and British officers could not afford to take chances with the reliability of rank-and-file askaris. While military service was not as prestigious as clerical or railway work, both of which required more education and training, it was the most lucrative unskilled employment in colonial Africa. To a degree, the African soldiery was a "stabilized" work force that enjoyed benefits and perquisites that set them apart from other African wage laborers.

African soldiers who acceded to military discipline did so because the KAR fostered a distinct military culture that fostered a sense of superiority to the civilian population. Generally speaking, these military traditions were informal and improvised before the Second World War but became increasingly institutionalized in the final decades of colonial rule. When a man joined the colonial army, his instructors tried to separate him from the society into which he was born. As an askari, he learned a new language, experienced new styles of food and clothing, learned new forms of entertainment, and was often converted to a new religion. African soldiers cannot be studied in isolation from their social origins, but the army's goal was to detach askaris from their "kith and kin" by creating a distinctly privileged military culture. This was a relatively uncomplicated process in peacetime, when the demands of colonial soldiering were relatively light, but became much more problematical when askaris expected greater rewards for serving overseas and risking their lives in combat.

While these policies offered attractive incentives to serve in the KAR, they also disrupted colonial society. The military establishment's main concern was to ensure the cooperation of the African soldiery by making military service attractive. The East African governments, however, worried that the privileged status of African soldiers would undermine the racial hierarchy of colonial society. This was particularly true after the Second World War, when their greatest fear was that military service would create a class of "detribalized" ex-servicemen who would reject the authority of their chiefs, thereby disrupting the framework of indirect rule. Most askaris were instinctively aware of this dilemma and sought additional benefits and concessions by playing civil and military authorities against each other. This made the colonial army a valuable source of patronage. Although military discipline was restrictive and oppressive, the KAR offered a unique opportunity for social advancement, and askaris invariably endeavored to renegotiate the obligations of their service in the most advantageous terms. By bringing their own values and beliefs to the colonial army, the African rank-and-file tried to redefine the military culture of the KAR.

MILITARY HIERARCHY

Officially, the military culture of the KAR was based on the traditions of the metropolitan British Army. As in Britain, colonial officers were taught to consider their regiment an extended family, in which "brother officers" led obedient soldiers whose loyalty was based on bonds of affection, friendship, and tradition. Frederick Lugard, the founder of both the Central Africa and Uganda Rifles, warned: "Men who have sympathy with and are proud of their soldiers will be followed with blind devotion, while the martinet who despises his men, loses his temper, and strikes or abuses them . . . should be got rid of as a public danger."[1] Consequently, the KAR admonished new British officers to learn as much as they could about their African soldiers. Many tended to view African soldiers as children, and the military correspondent for the *East African Standard* in Burma, who was himself an ex-officer of the Somaliland Gendarmerie, observed:

> When you meet an African unit that has had its officers for a long time, you meet a family. That applies to most army units, but in an African unit it is a little different. An officer or sergeant is like a father, and he has about the same responsibilities. The troops rely on his decision about cattle sales and rain, just as much as about the setting up of a three-inch mortar. . . . "My Africans," says an officer, and he means just that. They know they are his Africans, and when he knows them well and they know him, he speaks of them possessively, for it is likely that besides knowing their regimental numbers, he knows how many children they have as well, or what songs they sing when the rain comes.[2]

The most effective officers acquired a sophisticated understanding of African languages and customs through extended contact with askaris and recruiting visits to their home areas and developed strong, albeit paternalistic, emotional attachments to their men.

This is not to say, however, that all colonial officers shared these views. British officers were usually seconded to the KAR from their home regiments for a two to three-year tour that could, on average, be extended only once. A representative of the Colonial Office or the KAR Inspector General interviewed prospective candidates in London to find the "right kind of man" for East Africa. While some applicants sought adventure, hunting, and combat experience, the Regiment also attracted inferior men unwanted by their parent units. This was especially true before the First World War when Richard Meinertzhagen described fellow officers in 3 KAR as a cast of "regimental rejects," including alcoholics, gamblers, and pedophiles.[3]

As a general rule, the KAR experienced the greatest problems with its officer corps when imperial manpower shortages forced colonial officials to be less selective. The growing demand for experienced platoon commanders in the British and Indian Armies before World War II produced the notorious "court-martial draft" in which twenty-five of the thirty officers sent to East Africa in a single year were brought up on charges for a variety of offenses. These difficulties continued during the war, when the War Office had no choice but to randomly draft men for the colonial forces. As a result, senior KAR officials complained that their battalions had become a "dumping ground" for rejects from metropolitan units. Some of the new men became effective officers, but others openly abused their African soldiers. Settlers from Kenya and Southern Rhodesia also received commissions and tended to treat askaris like farm-workers.[4]

There were further problems with officers required to "volunteer" for the KAR in the early 1950s, but, for the most part, the quality of KAR officers improved after the war. Many of the men who saw combat with the East African forces as young Lieutenants and Captains returned to the KAR as company and battalion commanders. They tried to foster a sense of pride and community in the Regiment and took their obligations to the African soldiery quite seriously.[5]

African soldiers expected fairness and consistency from their officers and responded well to good treatment. While the majority of ex-servicemen described their treatment as "relatively fair," some had particularly strong opinions about their superiors. On one extreme were veterans who detested the racial inequality of the KAR and believed that no *mpereru* (a derogatory term for Europeans) could ever be fair. As one man put it: "A European [officer] is no good. He rolls you like a ball at his will. And you have to live by his commands." Not surprisingly, most of the informants with serious complaints about British officers served in labor units rather than the KAR itself.

On the other extreme, a few ex-servicemen recall their former officers warmly: "I overstayed my leave for six months to get married; Major Carter saved me from punishment. . . . He was a true friend and comarade." It was also not unusual for veterans to name children after former commanders.[6]

As in all modern military organizations, non-commissioned officers played a vital role in the KAR. With primary responsibility for enforcing discipline and executing orders, in the British Army, they were the link between the gentlemen of the officer corps and rank-and-file soldiers drawn almost entirely from the lower classes. While colonial military authorities may not have sensed the depth of it, African NCOs were the "glue" that held the KAR together. They made European and African cultural values mutually intelligible and interpreted the British military system for rank-and-file Africans.[7] The discipline of a KAR battalion depended on its African NCOs; they were expected to report the grievances of askaris instead of leading them in strikes or protests. Since most British officers served short tours, senior African NCOs established and preserved a battalion's collective memory and traditions by tutoring new arrivals in Swahili or Chewa. African Company Sergeant Majors quietly corrected inexperienced platoon commanders on the parade ground and often steadied young officers during their first taste of combat.[8]

Military officials would have preferred to have done without European NCOs because of their high salaries and benefits, but prevailing biases in the colonial army held that Africans lacked the initiative and education to serve as drill instructors, clerks, and specialists. The KAR therefore considered British NCOs a necessary evil. Yet these men were in a difficult position because racial barriers in the colonial army made it hard for them to relate to African soldiers, and class distinctions kept them apart from British officers.[9] During the early years of the Second World War, the East Africa Command unwisely assigned a British Sergeant to every KAR platoon. This undermined the authority of senior African NCOs and brought in metropolitan junior leaders who had no sympathy for African troops. Many were unable or unwilling to learn Swahili, and the EAC considered most of the new British NCOs lazy, tactless and foul-mouthed.[10]

Many officers believed Africans lacked the intelligence to command platoons, but African NCOs often rose to command positions in Burma. In one instance, an African Sergeant Major in 11 KAR assumed temporary command of an entire company after its commander was killed in action.[11] As a general rule, however, promotion to the KAR's junior noncommissioned ranks was based on a candidate's intelligence, initiative, and a simple command of written and spoken Swahili, but advancement to more senior positions was determined by ethnicity.[12] During the Second World War, even the most junior European Private had "precedence" over the most senior African NCO. While the EAC went to great pains to avoid assigning rank-and-file Britons to African units, this rule meant a

European could always command an African in an "emergency."[13] The hierarchy of the KAR reflected the color bar in East African civil society, and in both peacetime and at war, ultimately race, rather than ability, was the true measure of authority in the colonial army.

Many African NCOs resented the extension of the color bar to the KAR. Robert Kakembo, a Ganda graduate of Makerere College and Regimental Sergeant Major, was demoted from 7 KAR after arguing with junior British NCOs about the welfare of African soldiers. The Chief Secretary of the East Africa Governors Conference acknowledged that Kakembo was treated unjustly and arranged for his transfer to the East Africa Army Education Corps, where his schooling and intelligence were deemed an asset. Kakembo's case was far from unique.[14] Bildad Kaggia was reprimanded for disciplining an insubordinate European Corporal while serving as a Sergeant with the African Auxiliary Pioneer Corps in the Middle East. Kaggia's superiors told him: "A European is not to be judged by his rank but by his civilisation."[15] These incidents were the primary reason that only senior British NCOs were posted to the KAR during peacetime.

Although a handful of Sudanese "Native Officers" in the early KAR held the equivalent status of Viceroy's Commissioned Officers in the Indian Army, the first significant increase in the authority of African NCOs came during the Second World War. In 1942, General William Platt, the head of the East Africa Command, feared discontent over racial discrimination in discipline and promotions was undermining discipline and morale. He therefore created a new rank, known as Warrant Officer Platoon Commander (WOPC), to accommodate Africans with leadership potential. WOPCs were first introduced in the British Army in 1939 to compensate for a shortage of commissioned officers. With the growing dearth of British manpower in East Africa, Platt intended the new rank to enhance the prestige of senior African NCOs while allowing more local Europeans to become officers. The settler community accepted the proposal because it stopped short of granting Africans full commissions.[16]

While Platt intended that one platoon of each KAR rifle company would be commanded by a WOPC (four WOPCs per battalion), in reality a shortage of qualified men, as well as the resistance of some British commanders, meant that many units never received African platoon commanders. Nevertheless, the most effective KAR battalions in Burma had a full complement of able WOPCs. In the two Kenyan battalions in 11 Division, WOPCs were popular and showed courage and initiative in leading jungle patrols. In describing WOPC Nelson's leadership in capturing an entrenched Japanese position, the unofficial historian of 28 (EA) Brigade noted: "It was the first time within the Brigade that a purely native platoon had operated without European leadership, and the success of the operation proved [without] a doubt that the African is fully competent as a Platoon Commander."[17] In the

1950s, African WOPCs replaced British National Service men whose two-year commitment expired halfway through the KAR's tour of duty in Malaya. Many qualified Africans became platoon commanders because it took too long for new metropolitan officers to learn Swahili and jungle operations.[18]

Many British officers who served in combat with senior African NCOs and WOPCs firmly believed they were qualified for commissions, but intense political pressure from the settler community maintained the racial segregation of the colonial officer corps. Nevertheless, a handful of East Africans did receive full commissions during the Second World War. When 7 KAR was raised as a territorial battalion, Sir Philip Mitchell, then the Governor of Uganda, ensured that several members of the Kabaka's family became Lieutenants. In addition, a few Ugandans with Diplomas in Medicine from Makerere held commissions in the East Africa Army Medical Corps. While these men generally received the full military courtesies due an officer, the color bar prevented them from commanding European troops. The East Africa Command therefore considered the experiment a failure.[19] In spite of the unqualified success of WOPCs in the field, most senior African NCOs lacked the education to assume the full administrative and clerical duties of a platoon commander. Colonial military authorities therefore argued that East Africans were unfit for commissions.[20] Yet most Ugandan officers were college graduates, and there was no reason why a man like Robert Kakembo would not have made a good field officer.

The prohibition on African commissions became increasingly unsustainable in the post-war era as the rising tide of anti-colonialism made the metropolitan British government more sensitive to charges of racial injustice.[21] In 1945, Eliud Mathu, an appointed representative for African interests in Kenya's Legislative Council, voiced the grievances of rank-and-file askaris by formally asking the Kenyan government to explain the absence of African officers in the colonial forces.[22] As a result, the East Africa Command convened a joint civil and military committee one year later to discuss promoting Africans to officer rank. Predictably, the delegates concluded there were no African candidates with proper educational qualifications.[23] They were responding in part to pressure from the Southern Rhodesian government, which threatened not to provide European officers for another wartime East African Division if Africans received commissions. Yet the political embarrassment caused by racial exclusivity in the KAR would not go away—particularly after 1947, when the British Cabinet cleared the way for all "protected persons" to receive commissions in the regular British Army. This made it impossible to retain a blatant color bar in the colonial forces.[24]

While the Royal West African Frontier Force granted regular "King's Commissions" to qualified Africans, colonial officials in East Africa reintroduced the rank of Native Officer (known as an Effendi) for select African

NCOs and WOPCs. While British KAR officers received their commissions from the Monarch, Effendis were commissioned by the territorial Governor and, as such, could only command African troops. Europeans did not salute them, and they had no authority to order disciplinary action. Thus, they were politically acceptable to the European settler community. Even so, the first Effendis were not commissioned until 1957 because of the distraction of Mau Mau and the uncertain status of the colonial forces. By 1959, there were only thirty-nine Effendis in the entire KAR.[25]

The new rank did not satisfy the critics of the colonial army. Africans recognized that Governor's Commissions were inferior to Queen's Commissions. The KAR was therefore still open to charges of racial discrimination, this time from the new guard of nationalist politicians elected when the African franchise was expanded in the late 1950s. Caught off guard by the rate of political change in East Africa, military authorities scrambled to find African candidates with the educational qualifications for Queen's Commissions. Serving African NCOs and WOPCs were generally considered too uneducated, and a special selection board in each territory chose civilians to attend the Royal Military Academy at Sandhurst.[26]

Yet qualified candidates were hard to find. Military authorities had hoped to attract students who failed intermediate examinations at Makerere, but even these men had employment opportunities in civilian life that were far more lucrative than the army. Of the eight African candidates who met the army's minimum qualifications in 1956, three chose to attend Makerere, one failed to show up, and four were rejected for being Kikuyu. There were no eligible candidates in 1957, and it was not until 1958 that the first East African was chosen to attend Sandhurst.[27] The sudden prospect of independence in the early 1960s forced the army to accelerate the Africanization of the KAR, and senior African NCOs and Effendis finally received commissions once the East Africa Command created a special training school to raise their educational qualifications.

CULTURE

The East African colonial army was first and foremost an African institution. British officers and NCOs rarely constituted more than six percent of a peacetime KAR battalion. Colonial soldiers were usually illiterate rural Africans who became trained askaris through a process of acculturation that touched virtually every aspect of their personal lives. While all armies have their own intrinsic values and rhythms that set soldiers apart from the civilian population, in East Africa military service had an especially potent influence. In most cases, it represented an askari's first introduction to the ideals and material culture of the West. Yet as an overwhelmingly African organization, the King's African Rifles' institutions were also heavily influenced by African social norms. Regimental traditions had to be understandable and accessible to the average askari. Ultimately, the military culture of the KAR evolved from the daily interaction of Western and African values. This distinct culture served a useful military function by encouraging askaris to see themselves as different from, and superior to, mainstream African society. Civil authorities, however, tried to ensure military training did not lead to "detribalization" by divorcing African soldiers entirely from their home societies.

The process of turning Africans into askaris usually began with a four-month training course. During wartime, recruits trained at special depots, but in peacetime, they joined training companies attached to individual KAR battalions.[28] There was nothing particularly complex about the training of infantrymen. The KAR relied on drill and repetition to teach simple military tasks, an approach that differed little from the methods used to train poorly educated lower class recruits in the regular British Army. All British officers understood the link between drill with discipline:

> Close order drill . . . secures the whole attention of the man to his commander by requiring: 1) absolute silence, 2) the body rigid and motionless, 3) eager expectation of the word of command and the instant readiness to obey it. . . . Thus close order drill compels the habit of obedience, and stimulates by the combined and orderly movement of the platoon, the man's pride in himself and his unit.[29]

The KAR carried this philosophy to an extreme by using drill to teach everything from anti-gas precautions to the use of flush toilets. Although the average African infantryman learned to use his weapons and equipment by rote, he easily mastered basic military tasks, and most askaris were skilled in marksmanship and close order drill.[30]

Yet colonial military training went far beyond teaching men to follow orders. Most African recruits came from societies where conceptions of time were dictated by seasonal agricultural rhythms; in the KAR, they met the tyranny of the clock. In the 1930s, 6 KAR's day began at 5:30 A.M., when the electric lights in the barracks were turned on, and ended at 9:15 P.M., when they were shut off. Those unable or unwilling to adapt to the army's sense of time were punished severely. Askaris who fell asleep on guard duty before the Second World War were often flogged or received ninety days' imprisonment at hard labor.[31]

Military training also altered a man's appearance by imposing new standards of hygiene. In the 1930s, platoon commanders in the NRR conducted "tooth inspections" and kept a "bath book," which confirmed that each man bathed at least twice per week. Askaris found to be sloppy or dirty were punished, and one ex-serviceman recalls having to run in place with a gun over his head for being "untidy."[32] KAR battalions also required askaris to keep their heads shaved, a rule that led to disciplinary problems when East Africans served alongside longer-haired imperial troops during the Second World War. Most askaris considered the KAR's hair regulations a form of racial discrimination, and British officers had to allow longer hair after dissatisfaction with the rule led to strikes. Robert Kakembo wrote: "It is long hair that counts in Africa. . . . Pay is given according to whether you are white or wear long hair."[33] On the positive side, Africans were usually much healthier in the army than in civilian life. Medical care and an improved diet helped recruits to gain up to twenty pounds during basic training.[34]

New recruits also learned to speak the KAR's distinct military dialect of Swahili. Although the colonial military avoided recruiting native Swahili speakers on the grounds that coastal peoples were non-martial, Swahili still served as the lingua franca of the Kenyan, Ugandan, and Tanganyikan KAR battalions. The early KAR used Sudanese soldiers' "KiNubi" (a language with an Arabic vocabulary and African grammar) as the language of command, but as the KAR's recruiting base shifted to East Africa, the army switched to a more accessible language. Since African soldiers came from diverse ethnic backgrounds, they needed a common medium of communication. The colonial military establishment believed it was too difficult for illiterate Africans to learn English, and recruits were therefore taught an extremely simple version of Swahili that came to be known as "KiKAR." As one education officer put it: "It is easier to debase Swahili to suit the Uganda askari than to improve it to suit the Coast askari."[35] Ugandan askaris used KiNubi until the Inspector General ordered 4 KAR to adopt Swahili in 1927. In a departure from standard recruiting policies, the KAR enlisted several clerk/interpreters from the coast to improve the language skills of the battalion. In practice, however, these native-Swahili speakers had to learn KiKAR to communicate with the Ugandan soldiery.[36]

KiKAR was more complex than the "kitchen Swahili" spoken by settlers but not as advanced as the *safi* (pure) Swahili spoken by coastal peoples and colonial administrative officers. As with other forms of training in the KAR, recruits were drilled in military Swahili through repetition and simple songs. KiKAR ignored most of the grammatical rules of proper Swahili and invented words and phrases that were unique to the colonial military. The Tanganyikan 6 KAR, however, prided itself in its *safi* Swahili. Chinyanja (or Chewa as it is known today) was the language of command in 1 and 2 KAR, and Nyasaland askaris resisted the East Africa Command's attempts to force them to learn Swahili.[37] Both KiKAR and its Chinyanja counterpart developed into unique languages spoken only by members of the KAR and their immediate families and thus were key factors in isolating them from the greater civilian population.

Figure 4.1 Conversational Swahili instruction for officers, Jeanes School (Command School of Education), Kenya, World War II. Courtesy of the Trustees of the Imperial War Museum, London (K4953). Reprinted with permission.

During peacetime, British officers were not eligible for leave or promotion until they passed a simple oral Swahili test. Those who learned to read and write Swahili received a bonus. During the Second World War, the EAC developed a simple Swahili primer for new officers, which taught such useful phrases as, "The Germans are worse than the Italians" and "The soldier annoyed me: I woke him up and he refused to follow my orders."[38] Yet many wartime officers were unwilling or unable to master Swahili, and the army had to designate English-speaking askaris as interpreters. African soldiers who passed a simple English conversation test wore circular cloth badges consisting of a black "E" on a red background on the left sleeves of their uniforms. They received no special pay or status, and the whole program was generally distrusted by both British and African personnel. Intelligence officers worried the "E" badges identified educated Africans to Axis agents, and some askaris believed the badges warned officers not to discuss their "secrets" in the presence of educated Africans.[39] No military organization can function effectively when officers and men do not understand each other, and colonial military authorities concluded that it might be easier to teach African soldiers English than to teach Britons Swahili.

JEANES SCHOOL
LANGUAGE
COURSE

"CHAMP" 45

" WELL — what d'you want to know THIS time? "

Figure 4.2 A British perspective on conversational Swahili instruction for officers, Kenya, World War II. Note the diminutive depiction of African soldiers. From *Jambo*, c. 1945, p. 67. Courtesy of Rhodes House Library, Oxford (Mss.Afr.s.1715/Box 18/295). Reprinted with permission.

The early KAR had a strong bias against teaching English to African soldiers. British officers considered educated Africans too undisciplined to be good soldiers, and before the Second World War, they considered it "presumptuous" for an askari to address an officer in English, even if the soldier was fluent in the language. The first significant change in these policies came in the late 1930s when Inspector General G. J. Giffard realized the wartime KAR would have to depend on metropolitan officers who had no familiarity with Swahili or Chinyanja. He directed the KAR battalions to begin English classes for rank-and-file soldiers, which were especially popular with Nyasalanders, who appreciated that fluency in English would bring higher wages in the south.[40] During the Second World War, General Platt placed an equally heavy emphasis on English instruction to improve military efficiency, but there were not enough African Education Instructors to bring the language into widespread use.[41]

These ongoing communication problems inspired the EAC to try to make English the primary language of command in the post-war KAR. Without absolving British officers of the responsibility to learn Swahili, military authorities envisioned that all basic commands would be given in English by 1951. They linked African promotions to a command of basic English and barred askaris from turning English words into KiKAR by adding an "i" suffix to them (e.g., "blanketi").[42] In reality, it proved difficult to teach English to men who were illiterate in their own vernacular tongues. Most askaris disliked the invasiveness of the new language rules and avoided speaking English unless it was absolutely necessary. The EAC failed to meet its 1951 deadline and settled for requiring recruits to learn English words for basic military terms and commands. By the end of the 1950s, a British education officer estimated that all senior African NCOs spoke fluent English, but less than fifteen percent could read or write it. While most rank-and-file askaris attended daily English classes, few understood more than a handful of simple commands, and as independence loomed, the EAC shifted its training emphasis to making African soldiers fully literate in Swahili.[43]

One of the most overlooked aspects of colonial military service has been that the army was the third largest educational institution in East Africa (after the mission and government primary schools). Since they distrusted mission school graduates and could not offer sufficient wages to attract skilled African labor, military authorities produced their own educated soldiers. This was in keeping with a tradition in the regular British Army, which held that educated soldiers were more efficient and easier to discipline. By the 1920s, most KAR battalions ran their own unit schools for signallers, senior African NCOs, and any interested rank-and-file askaris.[44] During the Second World War, the East Africa Army Education Corps was based at Kenya's Jeanes School, which became the "Command School of Education" under the direction of the former principal of Alliance High School. The EAAEC was born in late 1941 when General Platt developed a comprehensive education program to convince African veterans of the Ethiopian campaign to contine fighting in a war that was largely finished in East Africa. He created the Education Corps in the face of strong opposition from the Kenyan settler community, which worried about the destabilizing impact of unregulated African education.[45]

The EAAEC's official mission was to teach specific military skills, provide language instruction in Swahili, Chinyanja, and English, train African junior leaders, and explain British war aims. Yet British army education officers also believed their mission was to improve the welfare of East African society as a whole and eventually broadened the EAAEC's brief to include courses on land preservation, crop cultivation, cattle management, hygiene, and "citizenship." As an African Education Instructor, Robert Kakembo was an ardent supporter of the EAAEC:

> General Platt . . . has done something that will take its due place in the history of this war and that of African progress by introducing the East Africa Army Education Corps. This Corps is doing wonders, both to increase the efficiency of the Army's capacity to win the war and to educate the African soldier generally. He has started African adult education. Many things that will be done for the welfare and education of African adults after the war will be based on the foundations laid by the East Africa Army Education Corps.[46]

While Kakembo may have slightly exaggerated the legacy of the EAAEC, there can be no doubt that military education programs had a significant impact on the African soldiery. In Burma, Gerald Hanley encountered an African artillery battery in which Swahili literacy rates had increased seventy percent during its time overseas.[47] The average African veteran of the Second World War left the army substantially better educated than his civilian counterparts.

The EAC's emphasis on military education continued into the post-war era. The EAAEC was reorganized after the war to become the "Command Pool of African Education Instructors," which mustered approximately 100 trained African teachers assigned to individual units and the East African Training Centre at Nakuru. Its primary mission was to help African soldiers work through the EAC's standard educational curriculum. The regular British Army had made these tests of basic knowledge a prerequisite for promotion to non-commissioned ranks since the nineteenth century. In East Africa, they evolved into a comprehensive curriculum consisting of three levels of Army Education Certificates. To earn these certificates, and win promotion to the non-commissioned ranks, askaris had to demonstrate increasing levels of competency in written and spoken Swahili (or Chewa) and English, mathematics, hygiene, "citizenship," imperial geography, and the regimental history of the KAR. By 1951, almost half of the 12,405 African soldiers in the KAR had earned a Third Class Education Certificate. Thirteen percent held a first- or second-class certificate, which meant that slightly more than one in ten askaris could speak some form of English.[48]

Military education standards continued to improve throughout the 1950s, and by the end of the decade, most civil authorities recognized the First Class Education Certificate as being equal to the "Kenya African Preliminary Examination." British military authorities never intended to create an alternative to the missions, but by the 1950s, the colonial army became a viable means of advancement for Africans who could not pay for a civilian education. More significantly, since British education officers were concerned solely with producing military specialists, the army's curriculum did not have the non-literary industrial emphasis that many Africans distrusted as intentionally inferior and backward. Yet just as mission schools imbued their students with a distinct set of ethics and values, an education in the KAR was entirely geared to transforming Africans into disciplined askaris.

Thus, African soldiers were part of a closed world in which virtually every aspect of their daily lives marked them as different and separate from the general African population. In terms of appearance, all armies rely on uniforms to establish a group identity, suppress individualism, and integrate their wearers into a hierarchical military system. In the KAR, however, the influence of army uniforms was especially potent because they were based on Western styles of clothing that were too expensive for the average unskilled African laborer. More significantly, askaris coveted their uniforms because they symbolized the authority and privilege of the colonial government. Conversely, unique military clothing in East Africa was also a disciplinary tool. When Kenyan Africans were impressed into the East Africa Military Labour Service, authorities at the Maseno Depot burned their old clothes and replaced them with a new set of clothing that marked the recruits clearly as military conscripts.

> The uniform is easily identifiable in respect of the vest—white with red on black trimming on the neck and down the front—and the shirt—khaki, without buttons, open neck shaped something like a sailor collar but without the big flap on the back, no belt or belt slots; and the cap—khaki similar to the old Pioneer Corps cap, round shape without stiffening and having a sun-flap at the back and a little peak in front. Any native seen wearing any article of this uniform is a deserter or a receiver of stolen property.[49]

Until the 1950s, rank-and-file askaris were always required to wear their uniforms unless at home on extended leave. Even when they finally received official civilian "walking out dress" later in the decade, they still wore a special web belt in their battalion colors that readily identified them as soldiers.[50]

The style of dress in the colonial army was influenced largely by the uniform of the Egyptian Army, brought to East Africa by the KAR's original Sudanese askaris. The fez was standard headgear until the eve of the Second World War, when it was replaced by an Australian-style bush hat, but remained the Regiment's ceremonial headdress until the early 1960s. Basic operational dress for most KAR battalions consisted of a simple collarless khaki shirt, flyless khaki shorts, and a blue pullover for warmth. In addition, all askaris wore an identity disc and the unit flashes and insignia of their parent battalions.[51]

This uniform reflected the racial hierarchy of the KAR. On the one hand, in a society where Western styles of clothing were expensive or unavailable, the uniform's various components were valuable in and of themselves. Thus, the promise of a military uniform was an effective recruiting inducement.[52] On the other hand, African soldiers were acutely aware that their uniforms were inferior to those worn by British personnel. Until the late 1950s, the standard African uniform had no collar, pockets, belt loops or fly. In 71 KAR, Somali soldiers rejected the Regiment's basic battle dress as "too African" and thus a mark of slavery. Askaris in Malaya grumbled about their "inferior" khaki uniforms in comparison to the jungle-green Far East battle dress worn by other Commonwealth soldiers. As one man recalled: "They were insulting . . . and brought us no respect." Colonial officers maintained that distinctive uniforms fostered unit pride, but askaris knew that officers wore a version of the KAR uniform with collars and pockets. The African Sergeant who led the protest put the entire issue in perspective: It was demeaning to have to drop his pants to urinate because the standard-issue African shorts lacked a fly. In the late 1950s, Justus Kandet ole Tipis, a veteran of the Second World War, attacked the "degrading" uniforms of African soldiers in the Kenyan Legislative Council, and as independence approached, KAR askaris received uniforms that more closely matched their officers.[53]

Boots were probably the most controversial article of clothing in the early KAR. Before the Second World War, colonial authorities believed African soldiers did not need footwear because they had naturally tough feet. The 1908 KAR Regulations explicitly ordered:

> Care is to be taken to preserve the natural mobility and marching power of the native African soldier. . . . [Their] excellent marching power . . . is undoubtedly due to a large extent to their being independent of footgear, and all tendency to introduce the latter into general use is to be discouraged.[54]

Askaris had sandals for long marches, but only senior African NCOs and British officers wore boots. Most Africans saw this policy as discriminatory and were pleased when the threat of Italian poison gas in the late 1930s forced the army to issue boots. Yet the new boots had exceptionally wide toe caps because many Africans had splayed feet from not wearing shoes. This made them unpopular with askaris who wanted "boots like the Bwanas'," even though the narrow European-style caused painful blisters. As the war progressed, boots became a standard part of the KAR uniform, although the EAMLS still wore sandals.[55]

Since the KAR uniform marked its wearer as a government servant, military authorities tried to control its unauthorized use to prevent Africans from masquerading as soldiers. In most territories, impersonating an askari was a crime punishable by a fine of 1,500 shillings and two years' imprisonment at hard labor. Soldiers were forbidden to wear uniforms while on extended home leave, and worn-out or obsolete military clothing was burned. Yet since askaris often sold parts of their equipment to supplement their pay, it was relatively easy for civilians to acquire a uniform. During the Second World War, Kenyan prostitutes used illicit uniforms to sneak into army camps, and civilians were occasionally arrested for using military clothing to extort money from shopkeepers. KAR impostors were a particular problem during the Mau Mau Emergency, and the Kenyan War Council required all owners of secondhand military clothing to register their goods with the government.[56] When surplus military clothes were sold to civilian merchants, they were usually dyed a different color or stamped with a special identifying mark to signal they no longer represented the authority of the colonial government.

Military decorations and medals also conveyed special status. In general, armies use medals to recognize that a soldier has performed in a particularly meritorious fashion, but there are rarely specific material benefits associated with military decorations. KAR medals, however, came with a generous gratuity and lifetime tax exemption. Furthermore, askaris who gave eighteen years of good service were awarded the Long Service and Good Conduct Medal, which conferred similar privileges.[57] Veterans of the First and Second World Wars also received service stars commemorating their various campaigns, which did not grant a specific cash reward but, rather, symbolized the debt that the colonial government owed their holders for loyal service. These decorations represented the status of military service, and the government of Nyasaland bought back the medals of deceased ex-askaris to ensure they did not fall into the hands of impostors. While most African veterans and their families valued their decorations, some World War II veterans rejected their medals, believing they were a trick to entice them into a new war.[58]

The KAR also housed and fed its African soldiers. As was the case with military uniforms, these amenities were generally better than what African soldiers received in civilian life but inferior to what was given to British personnel. In terms of housing, most askaris lived in wattle and daub huts until disease problems forced a switch to wooden barracks with corrugated iron roofs before the Second World War. Soldiers and their families slept on "bed boards" instead of sheets to reduce the threat of bed bugs. During the war, most servicemen lived in temporary housing, which became permanent when the KAR returned to peacetime status. By the 1950s, these barracks had deteriorated to the point where the head of the East Africa Command described Nairobi's Buller Camp as a "military slum of the first order."[59] These conditions caused discontent, and as an African veteran recalled: "We slept on boards like animals while the Europeans had sheets and mattresses." Conditions did not improve until the late 1950s, when the transfer of the KAR to local control embarrassed the East African governments into spending more on military buildings.[60]

Similarly, most African veterans recall that military rations were substantially superior to their diet in civilian life. The first Sudanese askaris in the Uganda Rifles grew their own food, and from 1902 to 1914, soldiers purchased their own rations. Officers often shot wild game for meat, which was the most prestigious part of an askari's diet. African soldiers received free rations during the First World War, which in theory consisted of a daily issue of a half pound of meat or beans and a full pound of rice or posho (maize meal). In practice, however, inadequate supply lines meant askaris usually received a few cups of posho—and in some instances, not even that. This diet was totally inadequate for men engaged in strenuous physical activity and was a direct cause of the high mortality rates suffered by African soldiers and carriers during the war.[61] During the inter-war period, boiled maize meal continued to constitute the bulk of African rations. In Nyasaland, the medical officer in charge of the African hospital at Zomba blamed the deteriorating physical state of 2 KAR askaris on a diet entirely deficient in fresh fruit and vegetables. While these inadequate rations could be blamed in part on budget problems, they were also due to the opposition of private employers, who used their political influence to prevent the army from offering substantially better food than European settlers gave their civilian laborers.[62]

Military rations improved markedly during the Second World War, when the East Africa Command paid much greater attention to the health and welfare of African soldiers. Medical authorities carefully calculated the caloric needs of an askari on active service to avoid the morality rates of the First World War. The EAC's guidelines called for 3,500 to 4,000 calories per day, depending on the climate. Whenever possible, frontline African soldiers received regular servings of meat, plus a full ration of fresh fruits and vegetables. When operations made this impossible, they were issued vitamin supplements in the form of tablets, specially brewed millet beer, or ground bone meal in their posho.[63] Despite problems with spoiled or "weevily" posho in the Middle East, censored soldiers' letters revealed they were satisfied with their food. In Burma, askaris received the same rations as other imperial troops, which included fresh or canned meat and vegetables, maize meal, rice or potatoes, and tea and sugar.[64] Many of these foods were virtually unknown to unskilled African laborers, and a European farmer in Kenya complained the army was setting impossibly high standards:

> Much as I want to give employment to as many ex-askaris as I can after they are discharged, I am not at all happy that they will like their 2 lbs of posho after being used to rations supplied in [the Southeast Asia Command] . . . not that I approve of the present farm rations (2 lbs posho) but I do think that it will be an awful "come-down" to the askari to have to face farm rations, quite apart from their wages in SEAC—45/—per month. Fifty cigarettes and a jam issue in lieu of butter! Just what hopes have I got of giving rations on this basis: at present prices it would amount to sh1/25. . . [I]t is difficult enough to make farms pay in peace-time on the present rations.[65]

Such protests did little to convince the EAC to reduce African rations after the Second World War, and for the most part, KAR askaris continued to enjoy a healthy and varied diet. In 1952, the monetary value of an askari's rations in Nyasaland was over fifty-six shillings per month, which was almost as much as a Private's total wages.[66]

This is not to say, however, that askaris were always satisfied with their food. As was the case with the other aspects of the KAR's material culture, the overall quality of the Regiment's rations was determined by race. British personnel enjoyed a diet costing roughly three times that of African soldiers. The few Asians and Arabs who served in the KAR as tradesmen and medics also received special rations, which included more meat and rice than the official African diet. African soldiers rightfully considered these distinctions discriminatory. In the 1950s, they refused to eat ground nuts because they were referred to as "monkey nuts," and during the Mau Mau fighting, they rejected certain types of canned meat that were also used to feed "war dogs."[67] It was possible, however, for an askari to qualify for improved rations if he could convince the military authorities that African rations were not "similar to what he was accustomed to before enlistment." The few Maasai who served in the KAR exploited this loophole to get more meat.[68] Somali askaris also demanded Asian rations. They detested maize meal and refused to eat the army's canned bully beef, even though it was certified "hallal" by Muslim clerics. The most logical solution to these problems would have been to grant all askaris Asian or European rations, but the EAC considered this too expensive. In reality, the supposed ethnic basis of KAR rations was actually determined by economic considerations.[69]

After meat, beer was probably the most controversial and status-laden item in an askari's diet. Military authorities would have preferred that

African soldiers remain sober, but denying askaris access to alcohol created too many disciplinary problems. As is the case in many armies, colonial African soldiers tended to believe drinking was a perquisite of military service and thought nothing of fighting the civil policemen who tried to prevent them from finding strong alcohol. Furthermore, since much of the illegal distilling in colonial East Africa was carried out by prostitutes, the army blamed the spread of venereal disease among African soldiers on illegal drinking.[70] The army therefore tried to control where and when askaris consumed alcohol. Most battalions brewed their own African-style beer (*pombe*) and ran wet canteens monitored by senior African NCOs. In some units British officers wisely kept out of the way while their men got "roaring drunk" during special *pombe* nights.[71] These policies had serious social repercussions. In many East African cultures, only respected elders were allowed to drink beer, and colonial administrators restricted African drinking to create a more reliable work force. In an effort to reduce disciplinary problems, the KAR undercut prevailing institutions of civil authority by providing askaris with alcohol.[72]

The army's alcohol-related disciplinary problems illustrate the contested nature of leisure in the colonial military. As is the case with soldiers the world over, askaris expected to spend their free time as they saw fit, but unregulated drinking and fraternization with civilians undermined the authoritarian underpinnings of the KAR. Thus, recreation was an important aspect of military discipline. Music, games, and athletics improved morale, but British officers introduced Western diversions into the KAR primarily to better control how askaris spent their leisure time. Yet African soldiers did not blindly assimilate Western popular culture and frequently adapted European pastimes to suit their own tastes.

In terms of music, military brass bands were an extremely effective recruiting device, and many Africans joined the army to learn to play an instrument. The vast majority were disappointed, but askaris often formed their own informal bands equipped with makeshift instruments to play popular African tunes.[73] On the Swahili coast, Africans used European martial music and parades as the basis of a new satirical style of dance known as Beni. Organized into competing, hierarchically organized societies, Beni dancers wore costumes based on military uniforms and Western dress. Each group had an African King, Kaiser, or General who was saluted by underlings holding appropriate subordinate ranks. KAR veterans and former German askaris spread Beni throughout East Africa after the First World War. In northern Nyasaland, a local version of Beni known as *malipenga* (trumpet) sprang up as Africans copied the performances of KAR bands. Military officials worried the popularity of Beni would undermine military discipline. An officer in Nyasaland noted: "I discovered that my acting Company Sergeant Major was saluting the local butcher, as the former was a General of the Beni, and the latter was the King."[74] Time proved these fears groundless, but in a classic illustration of how the colonial army co-opted elements of African culture, KAR bands adopted many of the Beni marches.

KAR battalions also sponsored their own *ngomas* (dances). During these celebrations, the racial hierarchy of the KAR partially relaxed as British officers joined in the festivities. A company *ngoma* for 250 men in 36 KAR during the Second World War consumed several forty-four gallon drums of *pombe* and enormous quantities of roasted mutton and beef. The celebration was paid for by unit funds and organized by an African NCO, who served as the "General Officer Commanding *ngoma*." As was the case in the Beni societies, the dancers wore officers' uniforms and exchanged salutes and reports with their subordinates. British officers attending the *ngoma* did not wear their badges of rank in deference to the "GOC *ngoma*."[75] The colonial military establishment believed these performances reinforced the ethnic pride of the Regiment's martial races, and in the 1950s, staged formal *ngomas* for visiting dignitaries. A certain amount of risk, however, came with putting aside the protection of race and rank. A few *ngomas* in Burma turned into general "European beat-ups," as askaris took advantage of the festivities to settle accounts with unpopular officers.[76]

Clearly, recreation could also be used to challenge prevailing institutions of authority in the colonial army. British officers used songs to raise morale and build battalion traditions. The Regiment's official songs were usually based on simple European tunes like "Men of Harlech" or "My Darling Clementine" but were sung in Swahili with new lyrics. Some songs spoke of the pain and homesickness that came from being separated from loved ones, whereas others such as "God Protect the Colonel" fostered unit pride.[77] Yet not all KAR songs were official, and askaris often made up their own satirical and ribald songs either praising favorite officers or mocking and ridiculing tyrants and buffoons.

As in the regular British Army, athletic competitions were also an approved form of recreation in the KAR. Not only did physical exercise improve stamina and fighting ability; sports built unit pride by teaching men to work together. Officers also hoped athletics would reduce disciplinary problems by providing an alternative to the attractions of women and drink.[78] Sports became a sanctioned activity in the KAR in the 1930s, but it took a while to interest askaris in the new games. During the Second World War, however, athletics became an integral part of army welfare programs and an increasingly popular form of recreation for most askaris. In the 1950s, the East Africa Command established a formal series of inter-battalion sporting competitions, and KAR recruiters sought out Africans who demonstrated athletic ability. KAR soccer teams also played against civilian teams, but these matches were discontinued in the late 1950s when British officers became concerned that losing to civilians undermined the KAR's prestige.[79]

Team sports had special significance in the KAR because they were the one activity (aside from informal *ngomas*) where racial distinctions were relaxed. The army encouraged officers to play alongside their askaris to build unit morale and reduce tensions. The KAR even had its own official game known as "Karamoja Football," which was a type of anarchic rugby that one young British subaltern described as "terrifying."[80] There were no rules governing tackling, and an unlimited number of men could participate. As one officer explained it: "You played with a football and ran, kicked and passed in all directions until you scored a goal [soccer type]. On the way you were kicked, tackled and generally submitted to many forms of grievous bodily harm, all to the accompaniment of great peals of laughter."[81] Another officer viewed the game as an important safety valve where "rank did not matter," and an African "could take it out on a European with no repercussions." Karamoja Football worked well in units that had good race relations, but in Burma, where tensions between officers and men ran high, 11 Division instituted new rules that prohibited free-form tackling.[82]

Boxing was another popular sport with strong racial overtones. Although the East Africa Command approved its introduction in the early 1950s, the Kenyan government barred African soldiers from boxing non-commissioned Europeans (officers never participated) because of racial tensions in the Colony. This was not a problem in the Ugandan 4 KAR, which often sponsored inter-racial matches. Adi Amin was one of the best boxers in 4 KAR, but in 1952, he lost his match with a European NCO. However, his teammate Lance Corporal Sebi was victorious.[83] Clearly, sports were some of the riskiest forms of recreation in the KAR. While they could improve unit morale, they had the potential to undermine the racial hierarchy of the Regiment by puncturing the illusion of European superiority, an essential part of discipline in the colonial military. Moreover, the sports field and the boxing ring were the only venues where African soldiers could take out their aggressions on their officers with impunity.

Finally, religion was the last major cornerstone of military discipline in the colonial army. For many African soldiers, enlistment in the KAR led to conversion to a new faith. Before the First World War, the majority of Sudanese, Swahili, and Somali askaris were Muslim, and were instrumental in converting new recruits to Islam. This did not bother early KAR officers with experience leading Muslim troops in India and Egypt. In terms of discipline, Islam helped set rank-and-file askaris apart from the general populace. Many British officers during the period considered African converts to Christianity impertinent and unreliable and believed missionaries stirred up unrest among Muslim troops. East Africa church authorities, however, worried that Islam would spread through the KAR to the general population. During the First World War, many of the askaris who converted to Islam in the army became *Shaykhs* and religious teachers when they returned home.[84]

Most Muslim askaris served reliably during the war, and British officers remained confident that Islam was compatible with military service. The few wartime army chaplain positions were abolished in the early 1920s, and there were no official Christian religious leaders attached to the colonial army until the Second World War. Most battalions, however, had a "Haji" or "Qadi" to lead religious services for Muslim askaris. Uganda's 4 KAR, which was the most Muslim battalion in the inter-war era, observed all major Islamic festivals and counted both Friday and Sunday as holy days. Nevertheless, Muslim veterans found it hard to adhere strictly to their faith while in the army, and many condemned the KAR's tolerance of drink and prostitution, common vices among their fellow soldiers. As one veteran recalled: "The army was bad for our religion, we were surrounded by immorality and there was never enough time for us to [observe] the proper [religious] festivals."[85] These grievances became more pronounced when Islam lost its predominant position in the 1930s as the KAR's recruiting base shifted to locally enlisted Africans who were often Christians.

During the Second World War, the East Africa Command tried to co-opt Islamic religious leaders to serve as unit "Maalims" in the same manner as Christian chaplains. The plan proved unworkable, however, because there were not enough politically acceptable East African Muslim leaders sufficiently interested in joining the army.[86] Most Muslim askaris found military service more difficult in the post-war era when the army's official attitude toward Islam shifted considerably. KAR battalions lost their unofficial Muslim clerics, and Islamic holidays were no longer officially recognized. Somali irredentism on Kenya's northern frontier and Egyptian anti-British radio broadcasts made colonial authorities wary of Muslim askaris, and the Kenyan government refused to recruit *Shaykhs* for Somali askaris on active duty during the Mau Mau operations. Muslim askaris tried to reestablish Friday as a holiday in 1959, but the East Africa Command would only excuse them from duty on Fridays during Ramadan.[87]

The declining status of Muslim soldiers was linked directly to the change in askaris' primary religious affiliations. The army shifted to local recruiting in the 1930s because there were not enough politically reliable Muslims to fill out the KAR battalions. While British officers distrusted graduates of mission schools, the success of evangelism in East Africa gave the army little choice but to recruit Africans who were professed Christians. In 1934, over forty-eight percent of all askaris listed themselves as Christian, as compared to thirty-five percent Muslim and sixteen percent classified as "Pagan."[88]

During World War II, the increasingly Christian character of the colonial forces led the East Africa Command to appoint a Senior Chaplain to the Forces (RC) to oversee the army's Roman Catholic priests. The East Africa Army Chaplains Department, under the command of a Deputy Assistant Chaplain General, was responsible for Protestants. Yet in spite of the large numbers of

Christians serving in the colonial forces, the EAAChD faced a chronic short-age of qualified chaplains. Most East African missions, particularly those with an anti-military bent, were unwilling to release their members for mili-tary service. In August 1942, there were only twenty-three European and twelve African chaplains for the 35,000 Protestant troops in East Africa. To compensate for this shortfall, the EAC created the position of African Staff Sergeant Catechist to provide simple religious services for Christian askaris.[89]

Christianity was an important disciplinary tool during war. While KAR officers from the old school still believed its emphasis on racial equality undermined their authority, senior military authorities saw religion as a means of encouraging obedience and temperance. Army chaplains urged askaris to shun drink and "unwholesome" women and emphasized the moral correct-ness of the Allied cause. In the Middle East, military authorities tried to con-trol unrest in East African AAPC companies by assigning each unit an Afri-can Staff Sergeant Catechist.[90] Serving in the Christian Holy Land had a profound influence on many AAPC askaris, who took the existence of Jerusa-lem and Bethlehem as literal proof of the Bible's veracity. Military authori-ties made good use of these sentiments. Bildad Kaggia attended a "Church leader's course" in Jerusalem to be trained as a lay minister for his unit.

> On my return . . . my friends were very eager to hear about what I had seen in the Holy Land. I too was very proud to relate all the Bible stories, not just from the usual reading of the Bible but from seeing the sites with my own eyes. With these new stories my classes became very popular, and the Chaplain was very pleased.[91]

Yet religion could be a doubled-edged sword. Kaggia came to distrust the military's "official" brand of Christianity after he encountered racial discrimi-nation in the army. He gave up his post as a company church leader and helped to found an independent African church when he returned to Kenya after the war.

Although the colonial military establishment ordered religious leaders to refrain from overt proselytizing, the semi-official status of Christianity in the East African forces made the colonial army a potent evangelical force during the Second World War. Many askaris saw a link between Christianity and the benefits of Western material culture, and army chaplains received numerous petitions for baptism in the AAPC companies in the Middle East.[92] Candi-dates for baptism had to know the Lord's Prayer and the "vows of Repen-tance, Faith and Obedience" and needed at least one Christian sponsor. If married, they had to sign a statement promising to register their marriage as a "Christian monogamous marriage according to the Regulations of my Church and Country." Crucifixes, rosaries, baptismal cards, and souvenir postcards from Jerusalem were all common items in the personal effects of deceased AAPC askaris. By 1945, Christians constituted roughly sixty percent of the East African forces, and General Platt estimated over 20,000 African soldiers were baptized during the war.[93]

The EAAChD was generally pleased to perform baptisms, but civil officials and senior army chaplains worried African soldiers might develop their own interpretations of Christianity, thereby undermining the authority of the missions in colonial society. They urged baptismal candidates to work toward Confirmation by accepting regular religious instruction from the nearest local mission after they returned home. It is difficult to determine the strength of these wartime conversions. Christian veterans tell a mixed story of their religious experiences during the war. Some found that the hardships of military service and close contact with army chaplains strengthened Christian convictions; others, however, found chaplains hypocritical or lost their faith when they succumbed to smoking, drinking, gambling, and womanizing. As one man recalled: "I became addicted to free beer [in the army] . . . and as an alcoholic, I almost forgot that I was a Catholic." Moreover, Chapter 7 will demonstrate that many Christian veterans like Kaggia played an important role in founding independent African churches.[94]

Nevertheless, the Christianization of the KAR continued into the postwar era. Budget cuts shrank the EAAChD, and most of the duties of the Staff Sergeant Catechists were subsequently assumed by "unit elders." In the 1950s, the EAC relaxed the formal ban on proselytization, and many KAR veterans recall being converted to Christianity by army chaplains. Under the EAC's regulations, askaris could choose a Christian denomination simply by applying to their commanding officer for appropriate religious instruction. Yet even during this period the exact religious composition of the KAR is uncertain. In 1958, the East Africa Command estimated fifty-seven percent of all askaris were Christian, whereas the EAAChD put the figure at eighty-five percent. The most likely explanation for this discrepancy is that the EAAChD listed all self-professed Christians, but the EAC counted only baptized, practicing Christians.[95]

While official sources paint an impressive picture of the increasingly Christian character of the colonial military, indigenous African concepts of faith and the supernatural continued to play an important role in the daily life of the KAR. The East Africa Command considered "Pagan" an officially recognized religious classification, and recruits were either sworn in on a Bible or were permitted "to make a solid affirmation in such a manner as he may declare most binding on his conscience."[96] Furthermore, many African soldiers, regardless of their official religious affiliation, believed in witchcraft. Respect for supernatural forces was not unusual in many East African societies. Few of the askaris in the early KAR fully understood the medical causes of illness and often blamed the outbreak of disease in a battalion on witchcraft. In 1912, 3 KAR's "C" Company in Jubaland was nearly wiped out by an outbreak of beriberi. Believing they had been bewitched by local Somalis, the incident left such a strong impression on the askaris that 3 KAR did not raise another C Company until after the First World War.[97]

Accusations of sorcery disrupted morale and discipline, and in the inter-war years askaris caught practicing witchcraft were brought up on formal charges for "disgraceful conduct." During the Second World War, however, combat soldiers still used "African medicines" to protect themselves from bullets and charms to help their unit athletic teams. If the NRR was winning at soccer because its fullback had a talisman strapped to his leg, then 2 KAR deployed its own "battalion witch doctor" to cast an even stronger spell. Thus, there was little British officers could do to stamp out the practice. Askaris who became physically ill after being bewitched often received home leave to consult traditional healers and exorcists.[98]

Clearly, the popular culture of the KAR demonstrates that African attitudes toward everyday life in the army followed a distinct pattern. When a man first joined the Regiment, he was generally appreciative of the overall improvement in his standard of living but eventually became aware of racial discrimination in the colonial military's terms of service. Poor-quality uniforms, inferior barracks and bad food were less problematical in the early KAR, when African soldiers came from relatively simple backgrounds. In the more politically charged atmosphere after the Second World War, the KAR had to pay much greater attention to African welfare. Yet when racial distinctions were based on cost or settler political pressure, the colonial army had little room to maneuver. In such cases African discontent often led to the strikes and other forms of collective protests discussed in Chapter 6. While recreation and religion played a role in reducing this unrest, they also provided askaris with an effective means of subverting the authoritarian underpinnings of the colonial army.

AFRICAN SOLDIERS IN COLONIAL SOCIETY

Military authorities believed it was necessary to win the cooperation of askaris by granting them privileges and benefits that set them apart from the general population. KAR askaris were the only African group with access to the instruments of lethal force. Although Africans in the colonial police were drilled in musketry training, they were not a cohesive military unit. KAR askaris were trained combat soldiers, and veterans of the world wars had firsthand experience in fighting Europeans. As a result, colonial authorities paid much more attention to their aspirations and grievances than they did to those of African civilians. The KAR did not directly encourage African soldiers to consider themselves superior, but most British officers believed a trained askari was a better man than his civil counterpart. KAR regulations minimized the African soldiery's contact with the greater population, and as compensation, military life generally provided askaris with a higher standard of living than that of unskilled laborers.[99]

Colonial governments accepted these arrangements not only because they understood the need for a contented soldiery but, more significantly, because they had little control over day-to-day military life. As a general rule, civil administrators granted African policemen a package of benefits that was roughly comparable to KAR askaris'. Civil and military officials sharply disagreed, however, over whether African soldiers should receive special legal status because of their unique service to the colonial state. The East African governments feared military service would lead to "detribalization" by creating a privileged class of soldiers with no further ties to their home societies. One of the most powerful inducements for askaris to submit to military discipline was the promise of a lifetime exemption from the hut or poll tax and a generous cash gratuity or service pension. While British officers believed these perquisites were absolutely necessary to ensure the reliability of their soldiers, civil officials attacked them as unreasonable privileges that encouraged African servicemen to think of themselves as a class apart. Ultimately, colonial governments had the upper hand in this argument because the army needed civil legislation and funding to enact all regulations governing tax exemptions, gratuities and service pensions.

In the early KAR, military authorities expected most discharged African soldiers to be "reabsorbed" into "tribal society" and therefore considered a large service gratuity or pension unnecessary. Nevertheless, the army still had to offer a suitable incentive for reliable service, and excusing ex-servicemen from paying taxes had the added benefit of being inexpensive. The colonial governments used taxation to promote wage labor by forcing young men, who might have been warriors in pre-colonial times, to seek paid employment. This need to earn money to pay the poll tax was one of the driving forces that brought Africans into the army, and the promise of a tax exemption restored some of the prestige of the old warrior classes. Concerned freedom from taxes would "detribalize" African veterans by removing their incentive to work, most colonial officials considered the army's pay and status sufficient inducements to attract recruits. The Governor of Uganda, W. F. Gowers, led the push to abolish tax exemptions by maintaining that KAR askaris should not receive better treatment than civilian government employees. By the 1930s, Uganda had won over every East African government except Nyasaland, which still believed the KAR needed a lifetime tax exemption to compete with the pull of migrant labor.[100]

The colonial military establishment strongly opposed the Ugandan proposal. KAR officers preferred to preserve the status quo but felt that if change was necessary, the military tax exemption should be replaced with a service pension. Civil officials, however, considered pensions a greater evil than tax exemptions. Not only would they release African veterans from the burden of working, but pensions were expensive and difficult to administer. Lord Passfield, the British Colonial Secretary, ultimately ruled in favor of the Ugandan proposal: "It must, I think, be conceded that the continuation of a special class in a privileged position as regards taxation, however justifiable in the early stages of British rule in East Africa, is open to objection in principle, and must become more so as the Dependencies progress."[101] In 1932, each East African territory enacted new KAR Ordinances that abolished lifetime tax exemptions, replacing them with a lump service gratuity. In Kenya, a KAR Private was eligible to receive £7 after nine years, £9 after twelve years and £13 after eighteen years. Men who enlisted before 1932 retained their lifetime exemptions but had the option of converting them into a cash payment. Most significantly, askaris still did not have to pay taxes for as long as they were in the army.[102]

In 1949, the Kenyan government revived the debate by proposing to abolish all tax exemptions for serving soldiers. Kenyan officials argued askaris used tax-supported services provided by the civil governments and considered it "contrary to modern ideas to regard the armed forces as a separate community."[103] The pending return of the KAR to local control made it difficult for the colonial military establishment to oppose such recommendations. The move was not particularly burdensome, however, because taxation was imposed in conjunction with the long-awaited post-war pay increase. In theory, KAR officers collected taxes from askaris and forwarded them to their men's home African District Councils. In 1960, these taxes were light, ranging from twenty-three to thirty-five shillings per year when KAR Privates earned a minimum of eighty shillings per month. Most askaris, however, avoided paying them on the grounds their service entitled them to special consideration from the colonial state.[104]

While civil officials were quick to condemn the military tax exemption as outdated and unprogressive, they were far less willing to grant askaris long service pensions, despite the fact that soldiers in most modern armies enjoyed this benefit. Even after the Second World War, the colonial governments continued to assume askaris did not need pensions because they would return to "tribal life." Moreover, as colonial administrators pushed to end tax exemptions for serving soldiers, the KAR's service gratuities remained fixed at 1932 levels. African veterans of the Second World War knew that soldiers in other Allied armies received pensions and criticized the army for denying them similar rights. They did not understand that the colonial governments were primarily to blame. British officers who served with African troops during the war genuinely believed their soldiers were entitled to service pensions, and in the summer of 1945, the East Africa Command recommended that askaris with eighteen years of reliable service be allowed to convert their gratuities into life pensions. General Sir William Slim, the former Commander of the British 14th Army in Burma, personally lobbied the colonial governors to approve the recommendation.

> I hope you will forgive me if, as a Commander who had many thousands of African troops under him in a most arduous campaign, I suggest that the granting of a pension to Regular African troops for long and faithful service should be considered. Apart from the fact that the excellent service rendered to the Empire by these men, especially those who serve outside Africa, deserves recognition, there are, I think, many reasons why a small population of pensioned native soldiers would be as good and stabilizing an influence in Africa as it has been in India.[105]

The various East African governments, however, deferred the question to an inter-territorial conference of territorial Financial Secretaries in late 1946, which ultimately reaffirmed that African soldiers could not be treated better than African civil servants.[106]

While the EAC and the British Legion in Africa pushed for service pensions throughout the remainder of the decade, civil officials refused to assume financial responsibility for the measure. The various territorial governments could not agree on a unified pension policy, and the army's proposals perished from bureaucratic neglect. When the Northern Rhodesia Regiment and 1 and 2 KAR joined the Central Africa Command in 1954, Federation officials finally granted service pensions in a bid to win over African soldiers. Each askari with more than twenty years of service was eligible for an average annual pension of £54 pounds; those with at least ten years of experience received a gratuity of one month's pay for each year served. In East Africa, pensions for askaris were a dead issue until the remaining KAR battalions came under the authority of the East African Land Forces Organization. With the issue of local control finally resolved, KAR askaris finally became eligible for service pensions in 1957.[107]

Relations between African servicemen and civil officials were often tense because KAR askaris considered themselves a privileged class. Soldiers frequently appealed to their officers for help in overturning or circumventing unfavorable government policies. During the First World War, Nandi servicemen tried to regain grazing land lost to European settlement by offering to form a special colony of ex-soldiers that would provide reservists and future recruits. KAR officers supported their proposal, but civil officials rejected it outright on the grounds that privileges for Nandi veterans would set a precedent for other ethnic groups.[108] Yet as they enlisted in larger numbers during the inter-war era, the Nandi used their military status to extract concessions from the Kenyan government. When Nandi and other Kalenjin elders raised the issue of land alienation and the loss of grazing rights during the Second World War, the government relented and gave them permission to pasture their stock in forest reserves and areas closed to civilians from non-martial races.[109]

In addition to pushing for collective privileges for their own people, African servicemen also believed their status as armed government servants exempted them as individuals from civil laws and regulations. During the Second World War, soldiers on leave in Nyasaland refused to pay for train tickets and commandeered trucks to take them home. Askaris also expected special consideration from the colonial administration in applications for grazing permits and trade licenses, and tried to use their military connections to overturn decisions by civil magistrates and "native tribunals."[110] The East Africa Command unintentionally encouraged this behavior by requiring officers to take an interest in their soldiers' domestic problems. Usually, an askari would explain his *shauri* (a matter requiring advice) to his unit commander, who would either pass on the problem to the EAC's "African Enquiry Bureau" or write directly to the man's District Commissioner. While some *shauri* dealt with serious welfare issues, soldiers also asked their officers to reopen twenty-year-old land or bride price cases.[111]

Most civil administrators resented these challenges to their authority and grumbled that KAR officers were duped too easily. District officers also complained that African soldiers on leave did not show proper respect and deference to Europeans. After visiting Kenya's Central Province in 1943, an army Public Relations Officer issued the following report:

> Askaris have often refused to accept summonses to attend tribunals, to salute their District Officers and to listen to reason or obey instructions given them. What is going to be the reaction of askaris to civil discipline in the post-war epoch if this state of affairs is not remedied in the near future? District Commissioners should, I feel, be given strong powers to punish askaris of this kind on the spot. At present they have little power at all to do anything to an insulting, disagreeable, saucy askari but to let him go on his way unchecked.[112]

Incidents such as these complicated relations between the army and the civil administration. Colonial officials resented military interference in their sphere of influence and accused KAR officers of interceding in the domestic affairs of their soldiers to buy "cheap popularity." As a result, one former military officer candidly recalled a "them and us" attitude toward civil officials.[113] Relations between the army and the civil governments improved somewhat after the war, when a number of former KAR officers joined the district administration.

Friction between civil and military officials often translated into open hostility between KAR askaris and African policemen. The latter group had the unenviable task of forcing African soldiers to obey civil laws and regulations, and servicemen looking for women or drink often fought policemen. In Nairobi, African prostitutes gravitated toward askaris because they knew the police feared them. A particularly serious incident took place in Kenya in 1949 when askaris at the EAC's Command Ammunition Depot at Gilgil attacked a European Police Inspector investigating theft, prostitution, and bootlegging in the nearby African Location. While the Kenya Police charged an army driver named Dalmasius with leading the attack, a military Court of Inquiry found him innocent on the grounds army records showed he was not in camp at the time. Police officials accused KAR officers of covering for Dalmasius to protect the army's reputation and brought civil charges against him. They were again frustrated, however, when the EAC hired an English lawyer to represent him, and three officers testified to his good character.[114]

While strained relations between soldiers and civil policemen are not unusual, in colonial East Africa these clashes represented a struggle for dominance between the armed African servants of the civil government and the military. A. E. Swann, who served as both a KAR officer and a District Commissioner, noted: "One had to beware terribly of friction between the Police and the ex-soldiers, because generally speaking the Army and the Police had always loathed each other, although they were [from] the same tribes."[115] In another case, a KAR Private on leave told an African Police Sergeant: "Who are you? You are only a civilian, I am KAR!"[116]

The privileged status of African soldiers reflected in these sentiments seriously complicated the colonial administration's policy of indirect rule. The East African governments lacked the financial and manpower resources to administer directly their large and scattered African populations and relied upon African chiefs and tribunals to enforce their authority. Chiefs and headmen mediated social disputes and were the primary representatives of the colonial government in the countryside. Colonial policy held that every African belonged to a "tribe" and was therefore the subject of a "native authority." In theory, indirect rule simply integrated indigenous African systems of authority into the colonial administration. In reality, however, most East African "traditional authorities" were handpicked men who derived their power from collaboration with the colonial regime.

These chiefs and headmen played an important role in disciplining African soldiers. They rounded up "volunteers" for recruiting safaris and acted as soldiers' representatives while they were away from home. During the Second World War, African chiefs visited every theater where East African forces were on active duty. In the Middle East, Chief Kasina wa Ndoo, a former Kamba Sergeant Major, dressed down rebellious AAPC companies and provided British officers with a list of untrustworthy African NCOs. In Southeast Asia, chiefs raised morale by bringing news to homesick soldiers, but their primary task was to identify the troublemakers responsible for unrest in the KAR battalions.[117] Traditional authorities also helped "reabsorb" discharged soldiers into rural society. Most askaris spent their savings on land and cattle and therefore depended on chiefs to protect their rights and investments until they retired. A soldier who failed to show proper deference might return home to find a chief or tribunal had awarded his farm, livestock, or in the case of bride price disputes, even his wife to another man.[118]

Many askaris understandably resented these autocratic powers and used their status as colonial soldiers to challenge the legitimacy of traditional authorities. This was a particular problem during the Second World War, when the relative wealth and experience of young African soldiers made them less inclined to defer to their elders. Askaris often persuaded their officers to appeal the rulings of African tribunals, openly flaunted the authority of chiefs when home on leave, and beat traditional authorities who tried to break up drinking parties or arrest deserters. Askaris sent threatening letters to chiefs who enforced unpopular colonial policies too vigorously or who ordered them not to protest unfair working conditions in the army. A Luo askari stationed in Ceylon complained:

> Every chief is against us and so when they are asked what ought to be done with we soldiers, no chief says that we may have a rest, but every one says that we must keep on working and must not ask for leave. . . . We soldiers do not feel well, though our Chiefs tell the White man that we feel well and that the White men rule us nicely; that is just mere praise which we oppose very greatly.[119]

It was also not unusual for visiting chiefs to extort money from askaris, and in Burma, many soldiers refused even to meet with them. Kenyan askaris accused their chiefs of having been bribed by the army to say positive things about the war; Nyasalanders told them that they should be home looking after military families, and since they were in Burma, they should fight.[120]

Colonial administrators worried African soldiers would retain this disdain for traditional authority after discharge. Under pressure from the territorial governments, the EAC ordered unit commanders to impress upon askaris that military service did not change their status in civil life or their obligation to obey their chiefs.[121] This admonishment was particularly relevant to educated servicemen with overseas experience, who were openly critical of unsophisticated and reactionary chiefs. A Nyasaland askari in Southeast Asia called for traditional authorities to be replaced by an "Advisory Council" chosen from the "most enlightened members of the community."

> The majority of the present chiefs can hardly be the medium of development. Most of them still entertain the "Ancient" African Culture. How can such leaders who are so closely concerned with the African development

put up with ideals of the many plans and programmes that are intended to improve the country?"[122]

With good reason, the East African Political Liaison Officer warned that autocratic chiefs were in for a rude surprise when veterans with overseas experience returned home. Civil officials interpreted the declining status of traditional authorities as evidence of the "detribalization" of African soldiers and worried about unrest among a large class of ex-soldiers who considered themselves exempt from the system of indirect rule.

The KAR was an effective instrument of colonial authority because the social isolation of African servicemen ensured they had little sympathy for the greater African population. While the privileges granted to askaris made for a stable soldiery, these same factors created tensions when askaris interacted with non-soldiers. Few veterans admit to abusing civilians, but most consider themselves braver and better disciplined than those who did not serve. Most also believe that military service made them more sophisticated: "[The army] gave me the opportunity of traveling far and wide in Africa—Kenya included—and other parts of the world. I was able to meet different races and people of the world." Even those ex-servicemen who disliked the colonial army labeled civilians "foolish," "cowardly," and "useless." As one man put it: "They were unfortunate and now lack awareness." Prosperous veterans still tend to look down on their civilian agemates because they were not members of the military fraternity. Malawian veterans, claiming to have been respected by their peers for their knowledge and courage, also admit they were feared by many of these same civilians.[123]

While the consequences of these superior attitudes should not be overstated, it was almost inevitable that the colonial soldiery's lack of respect for civilians would lead to trouble. The African soldiery's sense of self-confidence and superiority often turned into open contempt. In peacetime, British officers were usually able to control off-duty soldiers, but during the Second World War, it was much harder to keep them from mistreating civilians. In Kenya, askaris openly extorted money and goods from African traders. In 1944, a band of armed Somali deserters terrorized Central Province, and the government of Nyasaland charged six askaris with assault and extortion.[124] These incidents are graphic evidence of the social isolation of African servicemen.

African civilians often had to take their defense into their own hands when the civil police could not protect them. While they were occasionally able to intimidate African soldiers through collective action, such tactics often provoked more serious problems. During the Second World War, African troops stationed in Kenya spent their free time in nearby African Locations, where drinking and arguments over women erupted into violence. This was a particular problem in the Nairobi military camps that bordered the Kikuyu Reserves. The military, however, claimed civilians provoked most incidents and refused to pay compensation for damage caused by its soldiers. Despite the EAC's insistence that African soldiers were adequately disciplined, a serious riot between askaris and Kikuyu civilians broke out in December 1943. Men from the No. 1 Sub-Depot and the 101 (EA) Tyresole Repair Unit rioted after being charged a one-shilling admission fee for a soccer match at a local school. The soldiers claimed they had been charged more than civilians and were attacked while peering through the fence surrounding the field. The school's African headmaster, on the other hand, blamed the riot on askaris trying to force their way into the game. The fighting spilled over into a nearby market, where shops were looted and two civilians had their skulls crushed. Askaris also vandalized a car owned by a local chief, and many were arrested by the Kenya Police during the fighting. After the EAC refused to accept liability for the damage and loss of life caused by the ensuing riot, the District Commissioner of Kiambu warned anti-military feeling was so high that "any native soldier, other than Kikuyu of this district, who enters the reserve is likely to be set upon."[125]

The end of the war did not put an end to these problems. In February 1953, a handful of 2 KAR askaris in Zomba fought with African employees of the Government Forestry Department over a married woman. When false rumors spread to Cobbe Barracks that two soldiers had been murdered in town, an entire company turned out to assault the foresters with bayonets and *pangas* (machetes). They burned twenty-three houses and, in the words of the Nyasaland Governor, "attacked every civilian they could find." Fortunately, there were no fatalities. In this case, responsibility for the incident was clear, and the army paid compensation to civilians who lost property in the fighting.[126]

Incidents such as these made askaris understandably unpopular with the greater African population. Soldiers were usually respected in their home communities, but civilians from non-martial ethnic groups tended to view African servicemen as tyrannical and oppressive. Although only a small minority of African soldiers were involved in these incidents, their conduct affected the reputation of the entire colonial army. When Kenya's Committee on African Post-War Employment asked an African employee of the Veterinary Department, "What part can discharged trained soldiers play in development in the Native Reserve after the war apart from their general influence?" he replied: "Commonly speaking nothing but to exploit the country."[127]

While the East Africa Command was embarrassed by this anti-military sentiment, tensions between African soldiers and civilians also served a useful strategic function. Askaris were more reliable when they were alienated from the general population. British officers became concerned, however, when it appeared that hostility toward the military might undermine discipline. A soldier was of no value in a civil jail. The behavior of askaris on leave during the Second World War was so poor that the East Africa Command worried that such behavior would hinder recruiting. The army therefore launched a propaganda campaign to remind askaris to be on their best behavior while they were home. Soldiers in the Rift Valley Province were told: "The people around Nakuru did not get along too well for some-time with some of you askaris coming on leave or stationed in the vicinity, because they felt that many of you had become too conceited and treated the civilian like dirt."[128] These problems became less of a factor in the post-war era, when askaris kept their families in the barracks. Thus, the social isolation of rank-and-file askaris served an additional purpose: Not only did it ensure African soldiers were ready and willing to use lethal force when called upon, it also protected African civilians from the consequences of the KAR's aggressive and potentially destructive esprit de corps.

As the only group with access to the instruments of lethal force in East Africa, African soldiers were in a unique position in colonial society. Ever concerned that askaris might side with the African majority, colonial authorities sought to insulate them from the civilian population. The evolution of a distinct military culture granted African soldiers a package of benefits that encouraged them to see themselves as different from, and superior to, African civilians. Yet although the privileged status of African servicemen made military discipline more palatable, it also created severe social tensions. Military officers were concerned primarily with addressing grievances that affected the overall effectiveness of the KAR; rarely were they troubled by the social consequences of military policy. Colonial administrators, on the other hand, worried the army's efforts to create a stabilized African soldiery would lead to "detribalization" and the collapse of indirect rule. African soldiers tried to exploit these tensions by using their access to military patronage to improve conditions of service and challenge their subordinate position in colonial society. As a result, the boundaries of military life in colonial East Africa were never fixed. Each party endeavored to redefine the nature of military service to conform to its own vested interests.

NOTES

[1] Frederick Lugard, *The Dual Mandate in British Tropical Africa*, (London: Frank Cass, 1965), p. 577.

[2] Gerald Hanley, *Monsoon Victory*, (London: Collins, 1946), p. 209.

[3] Richard Meinertzhagen, *Kenya Diary 1902–1906*, (Edinburgh: Oliver & Lloyd, 1957; reprint, New York: Hippocrene Books, 1984), p. 10.

[4] Minute by Lieutenant Colonel S. J. Cole, 2 January 1942, PRO, CO 820/48/23; E.G.W. Haigh, RHL, Mss.Afr.s.1715/122; Tour of Central Province, Kenya, by Assistant Public Relations Officer, December 1943, KNA, MD 4/5/71/II/89; Interviews, #135, #137.

[5] Interviews, #140, #143, #146, #149, #150.

[6] Interviews, #5, #7, #36, #69, #81, #110, #111.

[7] Great Britain, *Standing Orders of the 6th Battalion, the King's African Rifles*, (n.p., 1930), para. 131.

[8] Major J. W. Howard, RHL, Mss.Afr.s.1715/143; Interviews, #134, #141, #147, #150.

[9] Shields, RHL, Mss.Afr.s.1715/247; Staff Sergeant C. W. Catt, RHL, Mss.Afr.s.1715/55.

[10] Swann, RHL, Mss.Afr.s.1715/268; CO 2/3 KAR to HQ 25 Bde, 17 February 1942, PRO, WO 169/6965; GOC EAC to Secretary of State for War, 11 June 1943, PRO, WO 106/5102.

[11] Anonymous (Major P. F. Vowles), *The Eleventh (Kenya) Battalion, the King's African Rifles, 1941–1945*, (Ranchi, India: Catholic Press, 1946); W. V. Brelsford, ed., *Story of the Northern Rhodesia Regiment*, (Lusaka: Government Printer, 1954), p. 97.

[12] Uganda Protectorate, *Standing Orders of the 4th Battalion, the King's African Rifles*, (Entebbe: Government Printer, 1934), Section 42; 3/4 KAR Progress Report, 24 September 1942, PRO, WO 169/7028.

[13] GRO 133, "Precedence and Command," 25 February 1941, KNA, MD 4/5/117/II/84; Kenyan Secretariat Minute, 27 March 1941, KNA, MD 4/5/132/132.

[14] CSEAG to AAG EAC, 25 April 1942, KNA, DEF 15/64/1b.

[15] Bildad Kaggia, *The Roots of Freedom, 1921–1963*, (Nairobi: EA Publishing House, 1975), p. 32.

[16] GOC EAC, to CSEAG, 20 April 1942, KNA, DEF 15/64/1a; Platt to WO, 5 June 1942, KNA, DEF 15/64/5a; African Manpower Conference, 7 May 1943, KNA, DEF 15/27/70a.

[17] History of the 28th (EA) Independent Infantry Brigade, Burma 1945, 2 February 1945, LHC, DP/IX/9; Malcom Montieth, *Ceylon to the Chindwin, Burma 1944*, (Lusaka: Government Printer, 1945); Major Patrick Barnes, RHL, Mss.Afr.s.1715; Shields, RHL, Mss.Afr.s.1715/247; Interview, #147.

[18] GRO 114, "African Infantry Warrant Officer Platoon Commanders," 23 June 1952, KNA, MD 4/5/83/II/39/1; 3 KAR Newsletter No. 3, August 1952, KNA, MD 4/3/10/1/1; Interview, #152.

[19] Uganda Governor to Colonial Secretary, 9 June 1939, PRO, CO 820/38/2; 7 KAR Officer List, 1939, PRO, CO 820/38/2; J. E. Goldthorpe, *An African Elite: Makerere College Students, 1922–1960*, (Nairobi: OUP, 1965), p. 10; Major A. S. Watts, RHL, Mss.Afr.s.1715/290; Sir George Gator to African Governors, 24 May 1944, PRO, CO 820/55/7.

[20] Platt to Sir Henry Moore, Kenya Governor, 17 June 1944, PRO, CO/820/55/7.

[21] CO Minute, "Future of Colonial Forces," 1944; Minute by E. E. Sabben-Clare, 9 March 1944, PRO, CO 820/55/7.

[22] Kenya Legislative Council Question by Eliud Mathu, 4 July 1945, KNA, DEF 15/25/43; Meeting of 15 Chiefs, 8 September 1945, MNA, S41/1/23/5/72a.

[23] The committee entertained a series of proposals to establish military training programs to remedy the situation but eventually dropped them because of a lack of money and interest. Joint Civil and Military Committee of the EAC, 12–13 September 1946, PRO, CO 820/55/6; East Africa Governors Conference, 9 October 1946, KNA, CS 2/2/17/130a.

[24] Colonial Secretary to E. Shinwell, MP, 25 January 1948; Colonial Secretary to Defence Secretary, 24 May 1948, PRO, DEFE 7/418.

[25] Brief on Governor's Commissioned Officers, 9 April 1954, PRO, WO 276/162; Report on the East African Land Forces in 1959, by GOC EAC, KNA, LF 1/212/3a.

[26] Chief of Staff EAC to Major General K. Bayley, WO, 12 February 1954, PRO, WO 276/162; Territorial Selection Board, 12 October 1956, KNA, OPE 1/803/21; 9th Meeting of EADWC, April 1957, KNA, LF 1/49.

[27] A. R. MacDonald to Selection Board Members, 25 March 1956, KNA, OPE 1/803/25; E. Ross Magenty, Ministry of Defence, to Kenyan Director of Information, 27 February 1958, KNA, OPE 1/803/37.

[28] After the Second World War, recruits were sent to the East African Training Centre at Nakuru, Kenya, until it was shut down in the mid-1950s as an economy measure.

[29] Great Britain, War Office, *Infantry Training: Volume I, Training*, (London: HM Stationery Office, 1926), p. 42.

[30] D.T.F. Bowie, RHL, Mss.Afr.s.1715/24a; Interview, #137.

[31] Great Britain, *Standing Orders of the 6th Battalion*, para 122; GRO 1458, "Discipline—Convictions by Court Martial," 20 April 1941, KNA, MD 4/5/117/II/101.

[32] Northern Rhodesia, *Standing Orders of 2nd Battalion, the Northern Rhodesia Regiment*, (Lusaka: Government Printer, n.d.), Section 7; Interview, #64.

[33] Robert Kakembo, *An African Soldier Speaks*, (London: Livingstone Press, 1947), p. 8; Uganda Protectorate, *Standing Orders of the 4th Battalion*, Section 94; Lieutenant Colonel R. C. Glanville, KNA, MSS 78/4; C. F. Broomfield, RHL, Mss.Afr.s.1715/31; Interviews, #143, #147.

[34] Operation "Dik Dik," May 1951, PRO, WO 276/255; O/C 92 MT Company to DCs, 13 March 1959, KNA, DC KAPT 1/12/4/165.

[35] Deputy Uganda Governor to Colonial Secretary, 12 March 1928, PRO, CO 820/3/17.

[36] E.V.H. Hudson, "The East African Education Corps," *Army Education*, v. 25, (June 1951), p. 78; IGR, 4 KAR, 1927, PRO, CO 820/3/17; Major General H. A. Borradaile, KNA, MSS 78/1.

[37] H. W. Newell, *Notes on Ki-Swahili as Spoken by the K.A.R*, (n.p., 1930); Anthony Clayton, *Communication for New Loyalties: African Soldier's Songs*, (Athens: Ohio University Press, 1978), p. 45; *Lazima kila askari kujua maneno haya* (Every askari must know these words), KNA, PC CST 2/26/56; Final Report of the EAPLO, 12 February 1946, KNA, DEF 15/12/111a; Interview, #148.

[38] Great Britain, *Standing Orders of the 6th Battalion*, para 73; GRO 2307, "Language Tests," 20 April 1942, KNA, MD 4/5/117/III/35a; East African Army Education Corps, *Kiswahili: A Kiswahili Instruction Book for the East African Command*, (Entebbe: Government Printer, c. 1942), pp. 35 & 41.

[39] GRO 2718, "Interpreters—African," 21 September 1942, KNA, MD 4/5/117/III/58; 11 Division Intelligence Summary, No. 8, August 1943, PRO, WO 172/3985; O.J.E. Shiroya, *Kenya and World War Two: African Soldiers in the European War*, (Nairobi: Kenya Literature Bureau, 1985), p. 41.

[40] Reorganization of Forces in EA, by Major General Giffard, August 1937, PRO, CO 820/26/15; IGR, Northern Bde, 6 March 1938, PRO, CO 820/30/3; O/C Nyasaland Troops to CSNY, 5 February 1938, MNA, S1/26/38/3.

[41] Harold Palmer & H. A. Harman, *The Teaching of English to Soldiers*, (London: Longmans, 1940); Extracts from African Mail, May 1945, KNA, DEF 10/64/36.

[42] Division Commander's Conference, 10 November 1945, PRO, WO 172/9439; EAC Circular "African Education," 11 November 1947, KNA, ED 2/17321/7; Northern Bde

Circular, "Teaching of English to African Personnel," 15 September 1948, PRO, WO 269/66.

[43] 4 KAR, QHR, 9 February 1950, PRO, WO 269/233; GRO 173, "African Education," 3 July 1951, KNA, MD 4/5/83/I/30; Report on the East African Land Forces in 1958, by GOC EAC, KNA, LF 1/210; Interviews, #22, #57, #139.

[44] AR, 4 KAR, 1926, PRO, CO 820/2/2; Great Britain, *Standing Orders of the 1st (Nyasaland) Battalion, the King's African Rifles,* (Zomba: Government Printer, 1927), Section 21.

[45] William Platt, "The East African Soldier," *National Review,* v. 126, (January 1946), p. 46; Educating the EA Soldier, by T.D.T. Thompson, RHL, Mss.Afr.s. 1158/2; Hudson, "The East African Education Corps"; T. H. Hawkins and L.J.F. Brimble, *Adult Education: The Record of the British Army,* (London: Macmillan, 1947), p. 252; G. K. Young, RHL, Mss.Afr.s.1715/309.

[46] Kakembo, *An African Soldier Speaks,* p. 6.

[47] Hanley, *Monsoon Victory,* p. 150.

[48] EAC Circular,"African Education," 11 November 1947, KNA, ED 2/17321/7; GRO 300, "Education Certificates—Africans," 20 November 1951, KNA, MD 4/5/83/II/6; EALF Standing Orders, Section I/XIV, "Education," 1957, KNA, DEF 13/470; Interview, #139.

[49] O/C Maseno Depot to Superintendent of Police, 23 September 1940, KNA, DC KSM 1/22/81; Robson, RHL, Mss.Afr.s.1715/231.

[50] Nathan Joseph, *Uniforms and Nonuniforms: Communication Through Clothing,* (Westport CT: Greenwood Press, 1986), pp. 65–68.; Uganda Protectorate, *Standing Orders of the 4th Battalion,* Section 58ii; Northern Rhodesia, *Standing Orders of 2nd Battalion,* Section 39; EALF Standing Orders, Section I/XXXIV, "Miscellaneous," 1957, KNA, DEF 13/470; Interview, #146.

[51] Provisional Schedule for KAR, 1916, PRO, WO 106/276; O/C Northern Bde to DMS, 9 December 1938, KNA, MOH 2/249/1.

[52] Nyasaland Governor to CSNY, 24 February 1942, MNA, S41 1/17/10/37; CSEAG to CSK, 13 September 1943, KNA, DEF 15/53/26a; EAC Circular, "Recruiting Parties," 19 November 1946, KNA, MD 4/5/134/92.

[53] Captain R. R. Darlington, RHL, Mss.Afr.s.1715/62; Kenyan Legislative Council Debates, 15 October 1958, KNA, DEF 6/4/125; 8th Meeting of the Regimental Working Committee, 3 April 1959, LHC, DP/XIV/C/II; Interviews, #35, #111, #139.

[54] Great Britain, Colonial Office, *Regulations for the King's African Rifles,* (London: Waterlow and Sons, 1908), paras. 114, 117.

[55] Cockcraft, KNA, MSS 78/2; Broomfield, RHL, Mss.Afr.s.1715/31; GRO 900, "Clothing and Equipment EAMLS," 25 September 1940, KNA, MD 4/5/117/II/62.

[56] Kenya KAR Ordinance, 1932, Section 95; Great Britain, *Standing Orders of the 6th Battalion,* paras. 169, 243; DO Embu to DC Nyeri, 21 September 1942, KNA, DC NYI 2/10/6/8; Kenya Colony and Protectorate, *Emergency Regulations Made Under the Emergency Powers Order in Council 1939,* (Nairobi: Government Printer, 1953).

[57] Minute by S. J. Cole, 26 March 1941, PRO, CO 820/49/4; "Medals for Distinguished Conduct in the Field and for Long Service and Good Conduct," 1925, KNA, DEF 1/158/64.

[58] Nyasaland Governor to Colonial Secretary, 13 February 1929, PRO, CO 820/7/2; RVP AR, 1950, KNA, MAA 2/3/38/VIII/1/1; Interview, #79.

[59] Housing and General Sanitary Conditions of 2 KAR Lines, 22 November 1938, MNA, M2/24/39/75b; GOC EAC to Kenya Governor, 26 March 1954, KNA, DEF 1/83/1.

[60] 8th Meeting of the Regimental Working Committee, 3 April 1959, LHC, DP/XIV/C/II; Interview, #108.

[61] Director of Military Labour to PC Mombasa, 30 June 1915, KNA, PC CST 1/13/135/113; Geoffrey Hodges, *The Carrier Corps: Military Labor in the East African Campaign, 1914–1918*, (Westport, CT: Greenwood Press, 1986), p. 121.

[62] O/C African Hospital Zomba to DMS, 7 March 1939, MNA, M2/24/39/85; Williams, RHL, Mss.Afr.s.1715/300.

[63] Medical Research Laboratory to DMS, 5 April 1939, KNA, BY 49/25/2; Ethiopian Campaign, Hygiene and Principal Diseases, 21 February 1942, PRO, WO 222/1806; Lieutenant Colonel T. F. Anderson to ADMS, 7 November 1942, PRO, WO 222/1809.

[64] Censorship Summary, EA Personnel in the Middle East, May 1943, KNA, MD 4/5/116/1; 11 Division Circular, "Field Service Scale (African)," 9 February 1944, PRO, WO 172/6484.

[65] A. Kincaid-Lennox to Principal Civil Reabsorption Officer, 7 July 1945, KNA, DEF 11/1/3.

[66] Estimated Caloric Needs for Soldiers, 19 August 1949, KNA, DEF 1/139/241; GRO 23, "Operational Scale Africans," 16 January 1950, KNA, MD 4/5/83/I/6; Notes on the KAR, c. 1952, MNA 1DCZA/1/20/26.

[67] GRO 2294, 27 March 1942, KNA, DEF 30/2/3/96; GRO 29, January 1957, KNA, DEF 6/6/1/2; E.D.H. Williams, RHL, Mss.Afr.s.1715/299.

[68] EAEME Circular, "Application for African/Arab/Somali Diet," 19 February 1953, KNA, DC FH 3/12/13/366; O/C Masai EPD to EAC, 16 February 1943, KNA, DEF 15/45/137; Interview, #35.

[69] 72 KAR War Diary, April 1944, PRO, WO 169/18362; EAC to CSK, 12 March 1955, KNA, DEF 6/61/125; Report on Tropical Ulcers, 1943, PRO, WO 222/1808; Darlington, RHL, Mss.Afr.s.1715/62.

[70] "M" Branch, 12 (A) Division, July–September 1941, PRO, WO 222/1808; PC NZA to CNC, 19 June 1944, KNA, PC NZA 2/14/39; Lieutenant Colonel H.K.P. Chavasse, RHL, Mss.Afr.s.1715/42.

[71] Great Britain, *Standing Orders of the 2nd Battalion*, Section 36; Great Britain, *Standing Orders of the 6th Battalion*, paras. 122, 310; EAC Standing Committee for Combating VD, 3 March 1944, KNA, BY 13/91/19a; Lieutenant Colonel P. E. Langford, RHL, Mss.Afr.s.1715/161.

[72] John H. Duncan to Secretary CCK, 10 July 1944, CPK Archives; D. J. Penwill, *Kamba Customary Law*, (Nairobi: Kenya Literature Bureau, 1986), pp. 97, 100.

[73] Melvin Page, "Malawians and the Great War: Oral History in Reconstructing Africa's Recent Past," *Oral History Review*, v. 8, (1980), pp. 54–55; General Secretary of the Red Cross to PC NZA, 4 July 1945, KNA, DC KSM 1/22/196/242.

[74] Nyasaland Police Commissioner on Beni, 24 February 1921, MNA, S2/1/21/2; James C. Njoloma, "The King's African Rifles and Colonial Development in Nyasaland (Malawi), 1890–1914," (M.A. thesis, Chancellor College, University of Malawi, 1988), p. 182; Terence Ranger, *Dance and Society in Eastern Africa, 1890–1970*, (London: Heinemann, 1975), pp. 42–49.

[75] John Nunneley, a Captain in 36 KAR, noticed a possible connection between KAR *ngomas* and the fanciful ranks and titles adopted by Mau Mau leaders. Waruhiu Itote, who was a Mess Corporal with 36 KAR in Burma, adopted the nom de guerre "General

China" when he commanded a Mau Mau unit in the 1950s. It is possible that Mau Mau ranks were at least partially derived from the boastful and mocking nature of Beni dances and military *ngomas*. John H. Nunneley, *Tales from the King's African Rifles*, (London: Askari Books, 1998), pp. 21–23.

[76] 11 Division Circular, 4 December 1945, LHC, DP/IX/2; D.N.W. Irven, "KAR Subaltern," *The Gunner*, v. 65–66, (April–May 1976), p. 21; Iain Grahame, *Jambo Effendi, Seven Years with the KAR*, (London: J. A. Allen, 1966), p. 223.

[77] Clayton, *Communication for New Loyalties*, pp. 3–38.

[78] Notes for British Officers, October 1939, KNA, PC NZA 2/3/21/68; SMO Native Hospital Kisumu to PC NZA, 20 August 1940, KNA, PC NZA 2/3/49; Great Britain, *Infantry Training: Volume I*, p. 42.

[79] 11 KAR Football Report, 1960–1961, PRO, WO 305/998; Flag March by A Coy, 11 KAR, February 1958, PRO, WO 305/262.

[80] Anthony Clayton, "Sport and African Soldiers: The Military Diffusion of Western Sport Throughout Sub-Saharan Africa," in *Sport in Africa*, edited by Baker and Mangan, (New York: Africana Publishing, 1987), pp. 115–19; Interview, #136.

[81] Mans, RHL, Mss.Afr.s.1715/178.

[82] Sports Conference at 11 Division HQ, 14 September 1945, PRO, WO 172/9439; Interview, #150.

[83] Operation "Dik Dik," May 1951, PRO, WO 276/255; Private Secretary to Governor Baring, to Colonel G. A. Rimbault, 13 January 1954, KNA, GH 4/457/20; AHR, 4 KAR, 1952–1953, PRO, WO 305/257.

[84] H. A. Wilson, *A British Borderland: Service and Sport in Equatoria*, (London: John Murray, 1913), p.169; Chaplain to the Force to Senior Chaplain of the Church of England, 21 August 1918, CPK Archives.

[85] Uganda Protectorate, *Standing Orders of the 4th Battalion*, Section 111; Kenya Governor to Colonial Secretary, 11 May 1935, PRO, CO 820/19/17; Borradaile, KNA, MSS 78/1; Interviews, #41, #42, #79.

[86] Meeting, AAG EAC; Liwali of the Coast, 3 June 1944, KNA, DEF 15/37/67; EAC Circular, "Spiritual Welfare—Moslems," 3 May 1945, KNA, DEF 15/37/105b.

[87] PC Northern Province, 1955, KNA, DEF 1/89/9; Tour by DCs, DOs & Chiefs to the KAR, by DC Isiolo, 19 May 1959, KNA, DC LDW 2/18/1/349.

[88] East African Unit Returns, 1934, PRO, CO/820.

[89] DACG, to CSEAG, 21 August 1942, KNA, DEF 15/37/5a; EAC Circular "African Chaplains," 7 December 1943, PRO, WO 169/13956.

[90] Major C. D. Trimmer to CO 2/3 KAR, 17 February 1942, PRO, WO 169/6965; Confirmation Tour of the Middle East, July–August 1943, CPK Archives.

[91] Kaggia, *The Roots of Freedom*, p. 30–39.

[92] P. A. Unwin to DACG, 25 February 1943, CPK Archives.

[93] Baptism on Active Service, by W. P. Low, 22 October 1940, CPK Archives; EAAChD Certificate of Baptism Form, October 1942, MNA, UCMA 1/3/2; EA Military Records to DC Central Kavirondo, 27 February 1945, KNA, DC KSM 1/22/77/3; William Platt, "East African Forces in the War and Their Future," *Journal of the Royal United Services Institute*, (August 1948), p. 410.

[94] Interviews, #20, #61, #64, #91, #111.

[95] EALF Standing Orders, Section I/XXXIII, "Chaplains," 1957, KNA, DEF 13/470; Report on the East African Land Forces in 1958, by GOC EAC, KNA, LF 1/210; Inter-Territorial Committee on Chaplaining Service in East Africa, 17 April 1958, CPK Archives; Interviews, #1, #19, #24.

[96] KAR Ordinance 1958, Schedule 1, KNA, DEF 1/153/4/1; Shirreff, RHL, Mss.Afr.s.1715/248.

[97] Tour of KAR IG, April 1912, NAM 8201-42; 3 KAR During the EA Campaign 1914–18, PRO, WO 106/273.

[98] IGR, SCC, 11 March 1928, MNA, S1/2161/23/11a; QMR, Station Hospital Gilgil, September 1945, PRO, WO 222/1842; Major T. D. O'Connell, RHL, Mss.Afr.s.1715/205; John S. Harrison, Unpublished Memoirs; *Jambo Effendi;* Interview, #13.

[99] The relative prosperity of KAR askaris can be seen in the inventories of personal effects of dead soldiers, which included a vast array of books, clothing, and household goods. None of these artifacts were army issue, and their diversity and value reflected the wealth and Western tastes of many askaris. EA Military Records, 8 November 1945, KNA, DC KSM 1/22/77; O/C Field Records, 21 August 1953, KNA, DC KAPT 2/16/5/32; O/C Field Records, 6 July 1959, KNA, DC KAPT 2/16/5/73.

[100] Uganda Governor to Colonial Secretary, 28 November 1927, MNA, S1/1709/23/12a; O/C Troops Nyasaland to CSNY, 30 April 1930, MNA, S1/1709/23 .

[101] Colonial Secretary to Nyasaland Governor, 20 November 1930, MNA, S1/1709/23/17; G.A.S. Northcote to Kenya Governor, 24 November 1926, KNA, PC CST 1/11/68; Uganda Governor to Colonial Secretary, 7 August 1931, MNA, S1/1709/23/32a.

[102] Kenya KAR Ordinance 1932, Section 84/8-9.

[103] CSK to Kenyan PCs, 12 July 1949, KNA, MD 4/5/80/206.

[104] GRO 85, "African District Council Rates," 26 April 1955, KNA, MD 4/5/83/IV/41/1; "KAR Recruiting Guide," July 1960, KNA, DC KAPT 1/12/12/1.

[105] General Sir William Slim to Nyasaland Governor, 27 February 1946, MNA, S41/1/8/5/70.

[106] Item 3, Pensions for African Soldiers, Financial Secretaries Conference, 1946, MNA, S41/1/8/5/74.

[107] Chair British Legion Tanganyika to CST, 2 November 1949, PRO, CO 820/73/6; "Service with the King's African Rifles," 1955, MNA, 1DCZA/1/20/26; Breakup of Federation from the Defence View Point, June 1962, MNA, F/248/2073.

[108] O/C 2/3 KAR to KAR Headquarters Nairobi, 25 September 1916, KNA, PC NZA 3/19/1.

[109] CS EAP to KAR Commandant, 8 November 1916, KNA, PC NZA 3/19/1; Assistant Conservator of Forests to DC Tambach, 16 September 1942, KNA, DC TAMB 2/13/1/239.

[110] A. B. Dickson, "Studies in Wartime Organization: Mobile Propaganda Unit, East Africa Command," *African Affairs*, v. 44, (1945), p. 14.

[111] African Enquiry Bureau, February 1945, KNA, PC NGO 1/15/7.

[112] Tour of Central Province, by Assistant Public Relations Officer, December 1943, KNA, MD 4/5/71/II/89; DC Nandi to O/C 5 KAR, 1 June 1955, KNA, DC KAPT 1/12/37/128.

[113] DC Samburu to PC RVP, 1 November 1955, KNA, PC NKU 2/21/6/117; Interview, #138.

[114] O/C 303 Regiment EAA to Superintendent of Police, 30 June 1949, KNA, DEF 13/114/180b; K. P. Hadingham, Provincial Superintendent of Police to Kenyan Commissioner of Police, 17 June 1949, KNA, DEF 13/114/175; Crown Council to Kenyan Attorney General, 10 September 1949, KNA, DEF 13/114/194.

[115] Swann, RHL, Mss.Afr.s.1715/268.

[116] Assistant Warden of Mines Nyanza to DC Central NZA, 10 May 1949, KNA, MD 4/5/80/200/2.

[117] Visit of Wakamba Chiefs to Gilgil, 3 September 1942, KNA, DEF 15/60/8a; "The Story of My Life by Chief Kasina Ndoo," told to J. B. Carson, 1957, KNA, OPE 1/381/ 5/2; Report by O/C Chief's Party, 20 October 1945, MNA, S41/1/23/5/81e.

[118] Interview, #61.

[119] Censored letter by Romanus Onyango s/o Wasiyo, 1943, KNA, DEF 15/27/63; also see Visit to EA Troops in SE Asia, by EAPLO, 30 June 1945, KNA, DEF 15/12/80a; Kenyan Director of Internal Security to EAC, 19 November 1945, DC, MKS 1/10b/17/ 1.

[120] 5 FSS, Security Report Week Ending 17 July 1945, PRO, WO 172/9544; Report by Rev. J. M. Rose on 22 Brigade, Summer 1945, MNA, S41 1/23/5/92.

[121] EAC Circular, "Tribal Discipline—African Ranks," 7 June 1943, KNA, MD 4/5/ 151/43.

[122] Corporal J. MacHamilton Mawle, 1883 Company, Unpublished letter to Editor of *Nyasaland Times*, c. 1945, MNA, S41/1/23/5/60b.

[123] Interviews, #2, #8, #19, #21, #32, #65, #80, #94, #110; Njoloma, "The King's African Rifles and Colonial Development," pp. 153–54.

[124] Central Province AR, 1944, KNA, MAA 2/3/8/V/7a; Kenyan Secretariat Meeting on Crime, January 1945, KNA, MD 4/2/29/I/137; Political Intelligence Bulletin, No. 6, 1943, MNA, S34/1/4/1.

[125] Military Court of Enquiry into the Riot at Udhera School, Kabete, 7 January 1944, KNA, DEF 13/114; DC Kiambu to PC Central Province, 19 June 1944, KNA, DEF 13/ 114/144a.

[126] O/C 2 KAR to EAC, 10 February 1953, PRO, WO 276/111; Nyasaland Governor to Colonial Secretary, 13 August 1953, PRO, CO 968/315.

[127] Testimony of J.M. Omino, 2 September 1942, KNA, DC KSM 1/1/174/13.

[128] "Native Newsletter to HM Forces," 19 February 1945, KNA, DC NKU 2/29/7/5.

5

ARMY WOMEN
AND MILITARY FAMILIES

Just as Chapter 4 dealt with the contested place of askaris in colonial society, this chapter explores competing attempts to define the nature of "family" within the context of the army. The conjugal relations of African soldiers were also shaped by their perceptions of military service. Colonial officers sought to foster the social isolation of African servicemen by regulating their relations with women. In keeping with biases in the metropolitan British Army, officers in the King's African Rifles tended to regard females as a threat to the morale and efficiency of the rank-and-file. They worried women might spread both venereal disease and politically unacceptable ideas. On the other hand, KAR officers encouraged African servicemen to develop formal relations with women to reward reliable service and reproduce future generations of soldiers. Just as mine owners in the Northern Rhodesian Copperbelt worked to stabilize their labor force by granting skilled African miners married quarters and family benefits, the KAR also tried to discipline askaris by giving them the means to begin families within the framework of the colonial army.[1]

Most African servicemen considered access to women a perquisite of military service that ameliorated the hardships of army life. Women provided companionship, sexual gratification, and domestic labor, but more significantly, askaris also used their military connections to circumvent established social norms governing marriage and procreation. While many African societies regulated conjugal relations by requiring young men to produce a substantial bride wealth payment before they could marry, the KAR provided askaris with alternative access to women. This was an important benefit that went beyond the personal satisfaction that came with marriage and starting a family. Women and children had considerable value in many East African societies as a source of agricultural labor and were an important form of old-age insurance.

While the benefits of military families to askaris are relatively straightfor-
ward, it is harder to determine what motivated African women to enter into
conjugal relationships with soldiers. Official military records tend to treat
women as either property or predators. It is also much harder to locate female informants with specific firsthand knowledge of the KAR. Most African veterans identify themselves readily as ex-askaris, but for most former
military women, the army was simply a passing stage in their lives. Although
many retain strong impressions of their time in the barracks, they had little
knowledge of the greater scope of military life. Interviews reveal soldiers'
wives often lived in a very different world from their men, and a separate
study would be needed to do full justice to their experiences. Nevertheless,
there were some basic factors that drew African women to the colonial military. Some wed soldiers from their home areas under established social norms.
Others saw the army as a source of wealth and patronage and associated
themselves with askaris out of necessity or economic hardship.

The army classified military women as "official" or "unofficial," depending on whether they had permission to live in the barracks, but in reality,
these were largely artificial labels. Askaris, African women, and the military
establishment all concurred on the desirability of incorporating women into
the military culture of the KAR, but fundamental contradictions existed within
each group's definition of what constituted a military family. The army could
accommodate soldiers' wives only during peacetime, and the necessity of
denying askaris access to women in the field led to low morale, poor health,
and disciplinary problems. African soldiers resisted the KAR's attempts to
divide women arbitrarily into official and unofficial categories and used their
military connections to undermine the bride wealth system, which allowed
their elders to monopolize access to young women. Colonial administrators
therefore worried that the army's willingness to let askaris flout established
social norms would lead to "detribalization." Finally, although African women
derived material benefits from their association with servicemen, they also
resisted the army's attempts to regiment their lives. They disliked mandatory
medical inspections and chafed under the paternalistic hierarchy of the KAR
that subordinated them to askaris.

FAMILY POLICIES

The KAR based its regulation of African soldiers' conjugal relations on
racial and gender stereotypes inherited from the metropolitan British Army
and on colonial fears about the "predatory" sexuality of African males. Many
officers believed lower-class men, particularly Africans, were governed by
unquenchable sexual appetites. During the Second World War, the East African Political Liaison Officer warned: "It would not be practical to keep the
African troops entirely from women. It is true that, if they are kept strenu-

ously at work they think less of sex matters, but . . . it is necessary for Africans' health and peace of mind that they should have access to women occasionally."[2] This official depiction of the African soldier was strictly heterosexual. While metropolitan authorities worried British soldiers might turn to homosexuality if denied access to women, no similar concern existed in the KAR. Sexual relations between men were a criminal offense in the colonial army, but officers tended to attribute "homosexual incidents" to "mental instability."[3] Military officials based their family policies on the assumption that askaris would create serious disciplinary problems if denied female companionship.

During peacetime, every KAR battalion had a substantial complement of African women and children, but few formal guidelines governed their status. The colonial army's regulations and ordinances made little mention of the conjugal relations of African soldiers. In most early KAR battalions, individual commanders drafted the Regiment's family policies. In 1930, 6 KAR's Standing Orders directed: "Every endeavour will . . . be made to encourage NCOs and men to be lawfully married." In practice, however, the early KAR cared little about the precise marital status of soldiers' women, and an askari could designate virtually any woman as his military "wife." The army accepted little responsibility for these women, and with only occasional supervision by the most junior British officers, individual soldiers looked after the needs of their families by themselves.[4]

When the colonial army expanded during the world wars, it could no longer accommodate the families of rank-and-file soldiers. In 1939, most African families in military housing were sent home, and in a sharp break with the KAR's peacetime policies, military authorities actively discouraged African soldiers from marrying.[5] Most askaris on active duty worried about the wives and children they left behind, and in the interests of morale, the colonial military establishment pushed the colonial governments to look after the welfare of African military families.

The army finally accepted full responsibility for supporting soldiers' families after the Second World War, when the East Africa Command assumed direct control of peacetime KAR battalions. Senior officers believed family welfare policies improved morale and military efficiency. In the post-war KAR, askaris received a family support allowance, modern married quarters, free medical care, and low-cost education for their children. In 1949, military officials estimated seventy-five percent of the Regiment's 5,428 rank-and-file soldiers lived with their wives and children, which meant approximately 4,000 women were residing in military camps throughout East Africa.[6] British officers in this period were allowed to marry, and their wives assumed most of the responsibility for seeing that wives and children of African soldiers were cared for.

The peacetime KAR subscribed to a paternalistic ideal that the families of British officers and African enlisted men were part of a larger "regimental family," which, in addition to military discipline, was bound together by ties of loyalty and affection. Most Africans, however, had a different sense of the colonial military. Career African soldiers subscribed to some of the KAR's familial sentiments, but most rank-and-file askaris viewed the army more as a job and a source of patronage than as an emotive family.

FAMILY LIFE IN PEACETIME

During peacetime, it was usually possible to accommodate askaris' families in the barracks. From the British standpoint, the incorporation of women and children into the regimental family had considerable advantages. General W. A. Dimoline, the commander of the EAC in the late 1940s, strongly believed married askaris were easier to discipline: "When their families are present with them, [askaris] are contented and of good nature. The reverse applies when separated, and they tend to get into mischief. The morale of the unit is directly dependent (in normal peace conditions) upon whether families are present."[7] A Quarterly Historical Report for 2 KAR in 1946 observed: "It is hoped that by the end of the year there will be 100% married families in barracks. This will mean that petty crimes such as AWOL and breaking out will cease entirely."[8] British officers considered a married soldier less likely to become drunk and that a wife improved his overall health.

Soldiers' wives also helped KAR battalions run more smoothly by providing domestic labor. Units without military women often experienced disciplinary problems because askaris considered it unmanly to cook or clean. During the Second World War, the army told new recruits: "If you are chosen at one time or another to be a cook do not feel that this is women's work for we cannot take women into battle, and it is usual to choose an askari to cook for his platoon."[9] Kalenjin askaris often claimed "tribal law and tradition" barred them from domestic labor, and only intervention by their chiefs overcame their resistance. Nevertheless, some soldiers purposely burned their platoon's rations to be excused from what they considered demeaning duty. In peacetime, however, African wives conveniently assumed responsibility for cooking rations and cleaning uniforms, equipment, barracks, and latrines. The KAR was so dependent on female domestic labor that African NCOs often hired women to care for young unmarried askaris.[10]

This last case offers an important example of how the colonial military secured the cooperation of African soldiers. Pre-modern armies that relied on military slavery often supplied obedient rank-and-file soldiers with women. During the early nineteenth century, British West Indian Regiments purchased female slaves to serve as wives for reliable soldiers, who were themselves ex-slaves. At the end of the century, French officers rewarded their West

Figure 5.1   Malawian askaris and their families, c. 1941. Courtesy of the Trustees of the Imperial War Museum, London (K43). Reprinted with permission.

African soldiers in Chad by allowing them to capture over 600 women.[11] These practices were also common in the first East African units. The Uganda Rifles often treated captured women as booty. As one officer explained: "In the evening the question of the looted ladies had to be decided, and finding no better solution, I served them out to the most deserving of my men. In those climes marriages are quickly arranged, and the preliminary love-making is perhaps too hurried to suit our tastes."[12] While these arrangements could scarcely be termed "marriages" by Western standards, they offer a realistic picture of the role of women in the early colonial militaries.

Once the KAR was established, it was harder to treat females as blatant property. The army, however, still used women to attract recruits and reward reliable service. British rule in East Africa put an end to communal warfare, and many askaris, who would have been warriors in pre-colonial times, saw enlistment as an opportunity to prove their manhood. This view reflected a conception of manliness linked with military service. Borrowing a phrase from the British Army, a recruiting poster in Nyasaland challenged young men to "Join the KAR and Lead a Man's Life." The colonial military portrayed the KAR as an appropriate occupation for the men of East Africa's martial races. African veterans themselves speak with pride of having en-

dured harsh discipline and the challenges of combat: "The army was a suitable job for a warrior. . . . It showed that we were men."[13]

Many askaris believed *kazi ya bunduki* (military service) made them attractive to women and refused to serve in unarmed labor units. As one veteran recalled: "I wanted to join the army because women preferred to go
with an askari in uniform." British recruiters exploited these sentiments by
encouraging young men to believe women would mock them if they refused
to become infantrymen.[14] Once a man enlisted, the KAR reinforced this
militaristic definition of heterosexual masculinity by ensuring that he had
access to women. After the Second World War, the Northern Rhodesia Regiment induced askaris to reenlist by offering them married quarters, and the
KAR promised new recruits the right to have a woman in the barracks after
completing nine months of training.[15]

In many East African societies, a young man could not marry without first
paying his in-laws a gift of cattle or, in some cases, cash or labor. This system of bride wealth enabled older men to control their sons and nephews
because few young men could afford a wife without their assistance.[16] Colonial military service was a form of migrant labor in which demobilized soldiers, like African miners, returned home flush with accumulated wages. As
with civil labor migration, generous military pay disrupted "martial" societies by empowering young men to challenge the authority of their elders. As
a result, older men increased bride wealth prices to retain control over the
younger generation. This was especially the case after the Second World War.
Among the Kipsigis of Kenya, for example, bride prices quadrupled over the
course of the war, whereas in Uganda, Acholi veterans complained elders
conspired to appropriate their savings by making it more costly to marry.
Military censors also noted a large increase in the number of askaris complaining about inflationary bride prices, and educated Kikuyu veterans formed
an "Anti-Dowry Association" to eliminate the practice altogether.[17] Their
efforts were largely ineffective, however, because most askaris invested their
savings in land and cattle and thus remained dependent upon chiefs and elders to protect their interests.

Brasher African soldiers used military patronage to circumvent the bride
wealth process entirely. Some "eloped" with prospective brides and relied upon the army to protect them from prosecution for "abduction" in
African tribunals. In many cases, civil officials forced soldiers to return
such women, but in others, KAR officers loaned their men enough money
to keep their "wives."[18] When it was impossible for African soldiers on
active duty to get leave to marry, British officials interceded with traditional authorities to secure special dispensation. During the Second World
War, Kipsigis elders allowed an askari to place a "downpayment" with
his fiancée's father to ensure she would not marry another man before he
returned to complete the marriage ceremony. In other cases, chiefs and

district officers acted as "marriage brokers" by conducting courtship negotiations for absent soldiers.[19]

Officers in the early KAR encouraged askaris to establish semi-permanent relationships with women out of necessity, but the military establishment did not concern itself with the origins and marital status of these women until the very end of the colonial era. Thus, the labels of "wife" and "family" had ambiguous meanings within the context of the colonial army. While the KAR was aware its soldiers came from cultures in which polygyny was common, it maintained the fiction that each askari was monogamous. Paragraph 158 of the Standing Orders for 6 KAR explicitly stated: "No native is allowed to have more than one wife in the barracks and no native rank is officially recognized as having more than one wife."[20] British officers, however, were relatively unconcerned with the actual marital status of military women, and it was not uncommon for askaris to change "wives" after returning from leave. The army happily endorsed an askari's ethnic marital traditions but was equally willing to sanction any relatively stable relationship, no matter how brief. In many cases, soldiers' "marriages" were quite temporary and amounted to little more than an extended form of contractual prostitution. Before the 1950s, an askari could name any woman as his "wife" as long as she did not cause trouble.[21]

The one rule strictly enforced in all KAR battalions was that unapproved women were not allowed in the barracks. Every female living in the lines had to be endorsed by a District Officer, medical officer, and trusted African NCO to ensure she was healthy and of good character. The army severely punished askaris who secreted unsanctioned women and sent away wives who arrived in the lines without proper authorization. Yet in spite of these regulations, many soldiers concealed extra or unapproved women in nearby villages.[22]

In some battalions, African NCOs simply hired women to tend to the sexual and domestic needs of their askaris. Military authorities generally turned a blind eye to the practice if the "temporary wives" accepted military discipline. During the 1930s, KAR garrisons in Kenya's Turkana District regularly passed on their women to the men who relieved them. Temporary wives were particularly common in inhospitable places where women who had the status of a recognized marriage refused to go. The exact origins of these "professional wives" are unclear, but most came from the communities of "detribalized" Africans that sprang up around army camps.[23]

Askaris often abandoned these temporary wives in considerable hardship when they moved to new postings. In 1939, the wife of a 6 KAR Signalman became blind and destitute in Kenya's Northern Frontier Province after she tried to follow her husband when his battalion was mobilized. By the end of the Second World War, the problem of discarded "wives" became so pronounced that the EAC froze the pay of discharged askaris until they made arrangements to support their women.[24] In the post-war era, the desperate plight of temporary wives, coupled with the introduction of family benefits, forced the army to pay closer attention to marital status. Military authorities refused to spend limited resources on temporary wives and required askaris to prove they were formally married to the women with whom they were living. The army asked chiefs and District Commissioners to certify soldiers' marriages were either sanctioned by a Christian church or had taken place "according to tribal law and custom." By the early 1960s, askaris had to produce a marriage certificate to apply for married quarters.[25]

Most African veterans acceded to the post-war army's shift to formal marriages and enjoyed having their families in the barracks. They viewed the army's family benefits as a valuable perquisite of military service. In the words of one veteran: "There was no drawback to having your wife with you. It built solidarity and made it easier to handle family matters." Another single veteran envied married soldiers because they got "better food, better houses and [sexual] satisfaction."[26] Some ex-servicemen, however, disliked subjecting their families to military discipline. Many hated having their wives inspected by military doctors: "If your wife lived in the army she had to parade for the *daktari* [doctor] just like an askari." Another private in 11 KAR recalled that the army's free beer and cigarettes "taught children to drink and smoke while they were still too young."[27]

Moreover, as African soldiers were denied service pensions until the 1950s, they had to maintain a strong agricultural stake in their rural homes to ensure a comfortable retirement. A man's farm was often neglected when his wife joined him, and only wealthy soldiers with multiple wives could readily afford to have a spouse in the barracks. In many cases, askaris waited until they were promoted to non-commissioned rank before they sent for a wife.[28]

Once a woman received formal permission to live with an askari in the KAR lines, she became an unofficial junior member of the Regiment and was subject directly to military discipline. Many of these women joined the KAR while still in their early teens. In 1938, the District Commissioner for Elgeyo-Marakwet refused to send a very young wife to 5 KAR without an escort: "She is not capable of coming to Meru by herself. She is a complete *Mchenzi* [rustic], wears skins, cannot speak a word of Swahili, and has never left the Reserve before."[29] Life in the barracks therefore introduced military women to a distinct military culture with its own values and social norms. As soldiers' wives, young African women often adopted clothing, hairstyles, perfume, and cosmetics linked to a Western conception of "femininity." When the first Africans were commissioned in the early 1960s, British officers' wives developed a YWCA course for the new African wives promoting the use of bras, deodorants, and contraception. Most askaris approved of these changes and sent money for their wives to buy Western clothing before joining them in the barracks. Askaris in London for the 1946 Victory Parade even spent their pay on perfume, cosmetics, and dresses.[30] Just as African men were trained to be efficient askaris, the military culture of the KAR indoctrinated young African women in the role of obedient soldiers' wives.

The KAR did not pay much attention to African wives until the close of the Second World War, when military authorities took steps to improve their quality of life. British post-war military doctrine held that family welfare had a positive influence on morale and military efficiency. Furthermore, the KAR also needed to compete with civilian employers, who had begun to offer better pay and benefits for unskilled labor. In 1949, the commander of the KAR's Northern Brigade appealed to the Kenyan government to help fund social welfare courses to train military women in cooking, homecrafts, hygiene, and child care: "It is, of course, very important for the morale of the Askaris that their wives should be trained in homecrafts, etc., and know how to look after their babies and be hygienic in their methods and in the running of their houses and children."[31] By the 1950s, most KAR battalions supported a chapter of the *Maendeleo ya Wanawake*, an African women's club that served a similar function. While these programs were certainly beneficial to military families in general, their main function was to teach wives to care for African soldiers.[32]

Women and children living in the barracks also received free medical care because colonial military authorities learned through experience that askaris held the army responsible when their immediate families became ill. Moreover, British officers worried childhood diseases like colds and chicken pox might spread to African soldiers, thereby undermining military efficiency.[33] In the early KAR, civil medical officers or visiting nursing sisters treated soldiers' families; wives usually went home to have their babies. After 1945, military families were cared for in special wards of civilian hospitals or in military hospitals when such facilities were unavailable. Most battalions also established family clinics staffed by a trained African midwife, and 4 KAR recorded 140 births in a single year. As a result, the army's pre-natal care programs ensured these children were generally healthier than their civilian age mates.[34]

As junior members of the regimental family, soldiers' wives were subordinate to their husbands in the military hierarchy of the KAR. The army required them to wear an identity disc bearing their husbands' regimental number and disciplined them through a system of authority that paralleled the command structure of the KAR. The wife of the senior African NCO was usually responsible for controlling the women of a battalion; she wore a military sash or chevrons as a badge of rank and carried a *kiboko* (a rhino hide whip). In the 1920s, the spouse of a Company Sergeant Major in 6 KAR was the battalion's "ex-officio beater-in-chief of troublesome wives."[35] Before the Second World War, askaris needed only an officer's permission to discipline their women, but striking a wife without official permission was a punishable offense. After the war, beating was unnecessary because trouble-some wives were simply sent home. The considerable benefits and amenities military women enjoyed in the barracks of the post-war KAR made expulsion an effective deterrent to misbehavior.

Nevertheless, many servicemen's wives were strong-willed individuals who exerted a significant influence on the colonial soldiery. An officer in the early KAR described the spouses of Sudanese askaris as having "a powerful physique and villainous temper" that intimidated their men. They had a reputation for looting, and on at least one occasion, 4 KAR had to put down a "wives riot." Sudanese women also had a reputation for using witchcraft to keep their men in line.[36] While overt acts of female resistance disappeared over time, African wives often chafed under their subordinate status and found ways to challenge the army's patriarchal system of authority. In addition to mundane domestic quarrels, soldiers' wives occasionally beat, cuckolded, and even robbed their husbands.[37]

Many military women did not consider themselves formally "married" and insisted on the right to choose their own partners. Occasionally a woman found a particular soldier too stingy or abusive, or perhaps she simply preferred another man. Military authorities usually gave women a free hand in choosing a "husband" but were unwilling to let them readily switch mates within a particular unit because competition over women often led to serious violence. Adultery, or "seduction of the wife of a comrade," was a grave offense. In one case, a soldier's spouse was at the center of one of the most notorious disciplinary incidents in the inter-war KAR. After discovering his wife having intercourse with another askari, an African Sergeant in 6 KAR "ran amok," killing several soldiers and threatening the local District Commissioner before he was eventually captured. Adulterous askaris were flogged during the inter-war era, and the Commander of the Southern Brigade used this incident to mount a general defense of corporal punishment:

> The importance of a sufficient punishment for adultery cannot be over-stressed, since experiences of this offence clearly prove that unless full justice is given in the form of a heavy punishment, and the native considers a whipping a just punishment, the dire trouble that may ensue is a very pertinent danger: in other words the injured party will take the matter into his own hands, usually with murderous intent.[38]

British officers believed askaris were the masters of their wives, but these incidents demonstrate that neither the KAR nor African soldiers could fully control military women.

The difficulty of locating large numbers of surviving ex-military women precludes drawing definitive conclusions about female perspectives on army life. Few archival records deal even indirectly with their opinions and aspirations, but it is safe to assume soldiers' wives in the early KAR would not have had much praise for their indifferent treatment by the colonial military. In comparison, female informants who lived with askaris in the late 1940s and 1950s generally appreciated the army's family welfare policies. The wife of a Kenyan Private who chose to join her husband found the Langata barracks to be "a fair place to live," recalling that "I enjoyed remaining close to my husband." Many of these women seemed almost reluctant to criticize military life. While maintaining that the army was a good place to raise children, one veteran's wife worried that boys and girls "lost their tradition" because they could not be circumcised in the barracks.[39]

Children did have considerable value in the peacetime KAR. Since they were old-age insurance for professional soldiers who lacked pensions, the KAR rewarded reliable service by providing askaris with an opportunity to father children. During peacetime, African soldiers were also military assets. The KAR's policy toward children was based on a long-standing tradition in the metropolitan British Army that viewed military children as future soldiers or soldiers' wives.[40] The early KAR also enlisted African boys (including many sons of askaris) as drummers and simple laborers. These "band boys" and "line boys" were subject to military discipline and usually trained as full-fledged soldiers when they came of age.[41]

Colonial military authorities worked to make soldiering a family tradition and organized boys' platoons and Scout troops to introduce them to discipline at an early age. As a result, boys who grew up in the barracks often chose the army as a career. Many officers preferred to enlist the sons and nephews of serving soldiers or veterans because they already understood the military culture of the KAR.[42] Askaris often served alongside their sons, and most KAR battalions gave special preference to recruits whose relatives had belonged to the same unit. In the 1950s and early 1960s, a large number of boys in 4 KAR were named "Jack Torry" after a popular British Company Sergeant Major who was an eleven-year veteran of the battalion.[43] While some officers worried barracks life made the sons of askaris too worldly to be good soldiers, most believed a family tradition of military service fostered discipline and loyalty.[44]

It is difficult to determine the exact number of African children who lived in the KAR lines before the Second World War. Although KAR battalions were ostensibly required to keep careful track of military children, unit-level censuses were informal, and none have survived to the present day. Fortunately, after the Second World War, the East Africa Command kept more detailed records of soldiers' families. Generally speaking, when not on active duty, a 600-man KAR battalion usually supported about 100 children, mostly under the age of ten.[45] The number of children in a particular battalion varied with the unit's operational status, the availability of married quarters, and the age and wealth of individual askaris.

Most askaris sent their children home when they were old enough to tend cattle or engage in agricultural labor, but a few soldiers chose to keep their older children in the barracks. For most Africans, education during the colonial era was exclusive and expensive. As a result, the army's primary schools were a valuable perquisite of military service because they assured African soldiers they would have relatively prosperous children to support them in their old age. Before the Second World War, most officers preferred to recruit illiterates and believed it unnecessary to educate military children. In the post-war era, however, the KAR offered a rudimentary primary curriculum for army children to create a cadre of future tradesmen and specialists.[46] Soldiers' children usually attended local civilian primary schools, but when distance or overcrowding made this impossible, the army established its own battalion-level schools. Some were staffed by African teachers seconded from civilian Education Departments; others were run by the East Africa Army Education Corps. The army subsidized school fees, and the KAR's involvement often meant these schools were better equipped than their civilian counterparts.[47]

Colonial military authorities also saw the sons of African soldiers as potential commissioned officers. After the Second World War, political pressure to commission Africans inspired a number of proposals to create "cadet battalions," "boys companies," and "young soldiers platoons" to train future African officers.[48] Settler opposition and the EAC's financial problems prevented their implementation until 1957, when the KAR established a Junior Leader Company (JLC). Each year, fifty fourteen-year-old African boys were admitted to a four-year program that combined military training with a conventional secondary school education. The Junior Leader Company was exclusive and prestigious, and the prospect of a commission was a strong recruiting inducement during the period of soaring unemployment in the last years of the colonial era. Most recruits passed their secondary school examinations, and in 1958, the Company ranked thirteenth in "order of merit" among the fifty-three African secondary schools in Nairobi.[49]

Candidates for the Junior Leader Company were chosen on the basis of their ethnic background, educational qualifications, physical fitness, character, and political reliability. Recruiting generally followed the ethnic guidelines of the KAR; JLC selection boards rejected otherwise qualified Kikuyu youths because of political concerns brought on by the Mau Mau Emergency. Yet despite the army's bias that mission school graduates were "politically indoctrinated," over ninety-three percent of the JLC's first class in 1958 were Christians.[50] Military authorities preferred boys who passed their primary school examinations but had failed to earn one of the limited places in a civilian secondary school. Nevertheless, political connections also played a role in admissions. The aide-de-camp to the Kenyan Governor personally

Figure 5.2 Outfitting recruits for the KAR Junior Leader Company, Kenya, c. 1958. Courtesy of the Kenyan National Archives, Nairobi. Reprinted with permission.

lobbied for the selection of the son of the African Chief Commissionaire at Government House, and chiefs' sons also received glowing recommendations. The army did give limited preference to the sons and younger brothers of serving soldiers, but many were rejected because they did not meet the JLC's minimum educational requirements. This angered askaris and ex-servicemen who believed the Junior Leader Company should be restricted to the African military community.[51]

The colonial military establishment worried about the implications of enlisting educated Africans and monitored the Junior Leader Company carefully for signs of instability or unrest. The East Africa Command assigned the JLC an "extremely loyal" African Company Sergeant Major and reassured the Colonial Office that "by the time these boys are old enough to think politically, we feel that they will be sufficiently advanced mentally to be able to weigh carefully all anti-British facts with the pro-British facts that they know to be true."[52] Yet despite these precautions, the teenagers who joined the JLC were more politically aware than the average KAR recruit.

They were referred to as "Junior Privates" because of their dissatisfaction with the term *boy soldier* used in metropolitan Junior Leader units.

Since the JLC had the status of an exclusive secondary school, most disciplinary problems were solved by simply expelling the offender. A "bright lad" who suggested the Company's favorable review by a visiting dignitary merited a pay raise suffered this fate.[53] For the most part, the JLC had relatively few serious disciplinary problems until the eve of Kenyan independence when the Company struck for higher pay. Although an African Education Instructor instigated the unrest, worried military officials placed the entire unit under the authority of the Commander of 3 KAR for increased discipline. They jailed or dismissed a number of Junior Privates, and the new Kenyan government disbanded the entire Company in March of 1963.[54]

UNSANCTIONED RELATIONSHIPS

While the KAR's family policies were comprehensive and far-reaching, African soldiers often entered into informal and unauthorized relations with women. Occasionally askaris objected to the army's attempts to regulate their personal lives, but in most cases, they sought out unapproved women when engaged in active operations. Families were a liability to military formations in the field. The early colonial forces made no distinction between peacetime and active service and were often weighed down by the wives and children of African servicemen. In Mauritius in 1899, an inspection parade of the Central Africa Rifles turned up a soldier carrying a small baby under his uniform because his wife was ill.[55] There was no "day care" in the early KAR. Military authorities sent soldiers' families home during wartime, but 2 KAR experienced similar problems on internal security operations in Somalia in 1948. The unit's Quarterly Historical Report complained: "The Battalion contains more African wives and children than it does Askari, and this long tail is slowly strangling us. . . . Companies cannot move anywhere without leaving an appreciable proportion of [their] strength to guard women and children."[56] When called on to fight, the KAR had to temporarily abandon its commitment to military families.

Many wartime askaris refused to accept the army's insistence that they should remain celibate until they received home leave. While few men were willing to expose their families to the dangers of combat, many still sought the company of women while off duty. Some soldiers in support units found ways to continue to meet their wives clandestinely, whereas other askaris formed short-term informal ties with local women. Many of these arrangements could technically be termed prostitution, but in other cases, servicemen forged strong and lasting emotional attachments to the women they met while on active service. A veteran of the Second World War credits an Ethiopian woman with curing his throat disease and saving him from a prison sentence for absenteeism by appealing directly to Emperor Haile Selassie: "We were in love . . . but I lost her after [the war]."[57]

"Unofficial" military women formed relationships with African soldiers for a variety of reasons. Prostitutes traded sexual gratification for money; other women sought the protection of servicemen during troubled times or simply fell in love. Colonial military authorities, however, considered the sexuality of African soldiers a dangerous and volatile force. They tended to assume "unofficial" military women were either "victims" of this sexuality or harlots who exploited it for personal gain.

While aggression toward women has been an unfortunate reality in armies of all nationalities, colonial military officials believed African soldiers had uncontrollable sex drives that made them particularly dangerous to women. They cited a few notorious incidents of rape by askaris during the Second World War to justify this unfair racial stereotype. Sexual assaults by Africans in the Southeast Asia Command produced a political backlash in the Ceylon State Council and led to fighting between askaris and civilians in India.[58] In a few cases, African soldiers were convicted of assaulting female European missionaries and nursing sisters, which fueled colonial phobias about the "black peril" posed by the unrestrained sexuality of African males. Paranoid medical officers in Southeast Asia assigned guards to European nurses and kept flares burning around their quarters at night. In wartime Nairobi, an African EAASC Sergeant was tried and executed for the rape and murder of a female European Staff Sergeant largely on the basis of circumstantial evidence.[59] As a result, the East African governments became more reluctant to allow army bases near population centers.

There is, however, no evidence that askaris were more inclined to sexual assault than other imperial troops. Reports from the Southeast Asia Command during the war reveal the incidence of disciplinary action taken against askaris (including rape) was no higher than that of Indian or British troops.[60] Yet African soldiers serving overseas were often victimized by derogatory racial stereotypes. In Southeast Asia, askaris complained British officers warned local women that Africans had penises "down to their knees," which would kill anyone who had sexual intercourse with them.[61] These stories undoubtedly helped poison relations between African soldiers and Indian civilians and may explain the rash of rape charges. British officers attributed disciplinary problems in non-African units to a variety of causes, including boredom and homesickness, but tended to blame African unrest on problems over women.

Many of the problems relating to women in the colonial forces actually stemmed from a widely held perception among askaris that the army unfairly denied them access to women. During the inter-war era, a pair of Yao askaris in the Somaliland Camel Corps were charged with plotting to murder their British company commander and his wife. Both men had lost spouses in childbirth but were denied permission either to send for new women from Nyasaland or marry local Somalis. During their court-martial, the askaris implied they intended to murder their commander's wife in retaliation.[62] To put it another way, if they could not have a woman, neither could their Captain. Many askaris considered the army's efforts to control their conjugal relations discriminatory because they believed British officers could have women whenever they liked. African soldiers therefore reacted violently when military policemen tried to bar them from areas where women congregated. As one Samburu Corporal recalled: "We often left the barracks to look for women. . . . If they tried to stop us we would fight them."[63]

The privileged status of African servicemen increased during wartime, when askaris were particularly well paid and fed in comparison to African civilians. During World War II, a combination of drought, increased food exports, and a drain on the civilian labor supply led to famine in rural Kenya and Tanganyika. While the colonial military portrayed women who had relations with soldiers as harlots, it is more likely that economic hardship drove them to seek the company of relatively affluent soldiers. Servicemen returning to Kenya on leave often carried hundreds of shillings, and desperate or ambitious women frequented trains and ferries and plied askaris with drink to rob them of their clothes and money.[64] More significantly, the army blamed such women for subverting soldiers' loyalty by encouraging them to overstay their leaves.

British officials blamed the alarming wartime increase of venereal disease (VD) in the colonial army on these unsanctioned women. During the Ethiopian campaign, medical officers believed every local woman was a "potential prostitute and source of VD." Approximately 350 of the 900 men in 1/6 KAR were infected, and the battalion formed a special "VD Company" to allow them to continue training while undergoing treatment. Many officers attributed this problem to "immoral" Ethiopian women, but six years of Italian occupation and a year of fighting had led to severe economic hardship that forced many women into prostitution. By the end of 1941, conditions became so desperate that the entire population was at risk of starvation. Some Italian mothers interned by the British Army after Mussolini's forces surrendered similarly sold themselves to soldiers and truck drivers for cans of condensed milk for their babies.[65]

In light of these conditions, it is not surprising that venereal disease became a problem in East Africa. African soldiers had no difficulty attracting women in impoverished areas, and as more women became infected with the disease, they in turn transmitted it to other soldiers. Arguably, the colonial army was itself the primary vector of venereal disease during the war. This is borne out in the statistics on wartime infection rates. From June 1940 to May 1941, only 5,461 askaris in the East Africa Command received treatment for VD, but from August 1941 to January 1942, the number mushroomed to almost 15,000 recorded cases. This represented a loss of manpower equal to an entire division of soldiers or, as the EAC's Director of Medical Services put it, a total of 18,035,000 man hours lost to the "devotion to Venus." By the first quarter of 1944, the EAC had a VD infection rate of 471.8 per 1,000 men (up from 59.34 per 1,000 in 1941), and military authorities designated the control of VD a tactical priority.[66]

The colonial forces had difficulty arresting the spread of VD during wartime because it was virtually impossible to maintain the social isolation of so many rank-and-file askaris. In Ethiopia, Lieutenant Colonel Michael Blundell was so frustrated with the women who beset his battalion that he rounded them up, stripped them naked, and abandoned them twenty miles from the nearest town. In Addis Ababa, women crawled through barbed wire fencing to get into military camps, and at Gondar, an officer likened them to rapacious crows. A few near-mutinies occurred when askaris forcefully resisted attempts to deny them access to these women, which reinforced the EAC's bias that the innate sex drive of African soldiers made abstinence impractical.[67]

Military authorities therefore tried instead to control women who had sexual relations with servicemen. The EAC pressured the East African governments to force civilian women to undergo medical treatment by enacting legislation similar to the Contagious Diseases Acts in Victorian Britain. Pre-war Kenyan Public Health Ordinances empowered the Governor to order the examination of any person suspected of infection and were used in 1935 to compel women living near the 3 KAR lines in Meru to submit to medical inspections.[68] The East African territories broadened the wartime powers of the civil police to detain women found "loitering" in townships or near military camps. Medical officers required patients to describe the conditions under which they were infected, including the name, race, and address of the woman involved. If they were married but infected by another woman, they also had to provide their wife's name and address so she too could be treated.[69]

Women living near major military installations at Nanyuki, Kenya, and Jinja, Uganda, were a particular problem. In 1943, medical officials found that eighty-six percent of the 398 African women examined in Nanyuki township were infected.[70] Military authorities therefore established their own VD clinics and tried to coerce women to accept treatment. The East Africa Command had de facto authority over African areas surrounding large cantonments, and women who refused to submit to monthly medical exams had their residence permits revoked and, in many cases, their huts pulled down. In defending these draconian measures, one high-ranking military officer argued that "there are times when the sanctity of the civil individual's rights cannot be allowed to militate against military interests."[71]

Yet the EAC was often frustrated by the East African governments' refusal to adopt more drastic measures to control VD. Many civil officials were uncomfortable with the extra-legal powers embodied in these regulations and refused to give Military Police blanket authority to arrest suspected prostitutes. T. A. Austin, Nyasaland's Director of Medical Services, particularly disliked the provision which required a patient to name the source of his infection:

> [It is] an incredible piece of legislation, suggestive of the Gestapo. . . . It is likely to accomplish little other than to drive the native prostitute from the town where she has been plying her trade, back to her village in the Reserve, beyond the reach of an order issued either by a medical practitioner or magistrate. This may be what the Military Authorities hope to achieve.[72]

Austin was not far from the mark. Forced examinations did little to lower the incidence of VD infection and were primarily intended to evict "troublesome" women. In 1943, the EAC's Senior Medical Officer in Uganda acknowledged:

> The scheme is officially an effort to improve VD treatment of Africans, but in practice it is an effort to control prostitution. . . . Infected women will be cleared out unless they go into hospital for treatment. . . . My reason for pressing the scheme was more to discourage the arrival of these people . . . by making life as disagreeable as possible for them, rather than a belief in the prophylactic value of the medical examination.[73]

Prostitutes responded to these inspection programs in a variety of ways. In the Kenyan townships of Kitale and Kisumu, such women welcomed the VD treatment centers and even offered to help pay their rent.[74] Most African women, however, resisted mandatory medical exams. In Nanyuki, Somali and other Muslim women locked themselves in their houses to avoid the inspections. Non-Muslim women often bribed Muslim men to pretend to be their husbands because British authorities were generally unwilling to antagonize the Islamic community by breaking into houses. In other cases, Nanyuki prostitutes tricked askaris into sleeping with them by using a rented medical inspection certificate to prove they were free of VD. Conversely, some women in Nanyuki valued medical treatment and demanded that the government crack down on these illegal tactics.[75] While they resented the army's intrusion into their personal lives, they had a personal stake in improving the overall health of the African military community.

Nevertheless, many prostitutes evaded the East Africa Command's inspection and treatment programs. The military could only employ coercive methods against soldiers' women in military cantonments like Nanyuki and Jinja. In the rest of East Africa, colonial governments refused to allow the army to inspect African women unless they were formally convicted of prostitution. Furthermore, coercive measures were feasible only in British colonial territory. In the Middle East and Asia, it was politically embarrassing to force non-British subjects to accept involuntary exams. As a result, many senior officers advocated the creation of regulated military brothels to ensure women who had sex with soldiers were subjected to regular inspections by military doctors. Prevailing moral standards in Great Britain prevented the open adoption of the French institution of official army brothels (*Bordels Mobiles de Campagne*). The British Army adopted a laissez-faire approach toward military prostitution, allowing field officers a free hand to deal with their units' VD problems.

Sanctioned military brothels were actually not uncommon during the Second World War. Venereal disease was not a specifically African problem, and most imperial troops had access to medically approved prostitutes in the Middle East and Asia. Civil opposition, however, ruled out officially approved brothels for askaris in British East Africa. Prostitutes in Nairobi operated out of private houses, and the Nanyuki cantonment supported informal brothels in schools, the Public Works Department lines, a European hotel, and a cemetery.[76] Some officers worried women in these unofficial brothels avoided inspections, but most viewed them as an unfortunate necessity. The military establishment did not formally endorse these arrangements, but public awareness of the brothels led to frequent rumors that the army intended to conscript African women for immoral purposes.[77]

Official military brothels were only practical when the colonial forces served outside British East Africa. In Ethiopia, the alarming rate of VD infection among askaris was the primary factor in their creation. Field brothels were usually begun by junior officers, staffed by Ethiopian women, and inspected by British medical personnel. In 1942, the Deputy Director of Medical Services for 12 (African) Division defended them on the grounds of medical utility:

> Where unit brothels exist in this area the inspection of the women and the supervision of the hygiene conditions are accepted as a medical liability, even at the expense of offending certain susceptibilities. . . . Absolute continence in the young African far removed from his home and natural surroundings is not as easy to inculcate as many, from ignorance of belief, would make out, and it is surely better to offer him a mistress who has been under medical supervision than to trust to the doubtful efficiency of preventive ablution to save him from the inevitable [consequences] of clandestine appointments with Ethiopian harlots.[78]

When a Free French West African unit joined the East Africa Command for the siege of Djibouti, British authorities agreed to provide them with prostitutes. It is hard to tell if Ethiopian women were willing participants in these ventures, but at least one attempt to set up a unit brothel failed because the women in question preferred the more lucrative company of Italian truck drivers to African soldiers.[79]

In the Middle East, brothels sprang up near leave camps frequented by the African Auxiliary Pioneer Corps. A few KAR battalions also set up informal unit brothels in Madagascar.[80] In Southeast Asia, conversely, many askaris found women through Indian pimps, but African veterans also claim British officers were their main suppliers of prostitutes. One ex-serviceman recalled how medical officers in Burma brought them "very brown, elegant and beautiful ladies" and apportioned them by giving each woman the regimental number of the man with whom she was to have intercourse.[81]

An additional advantage of sanctioned prostitution was that it intensified the social isolation of the African soldiery by giving military authorities a measure of control over their conjugal relations. During the Mau Mau insurrection, where medical concerns paralleled fears of political contamination, this isolation was a tactical necessity. Kikuyu women lured askaris into compromising positions to buy or steal weapons, and army investigators found that much of the ammunition captured from Mau Mau guerrillas came from the KAR. A secret army circular blamed the problem on the separation of African soldiers from their wives: "By and large, police and tribal police have their women with them whereas the soldier askari is a grass widower, and therefore more likely to sell [ammunition] to prostitutes." The report suggested that the best means of controlling the flow of ammunition to the Mau Mau was to establish army brothels, although it acknowledged that "obviously this baldly stated suggestion would have to be camouflaged in some way."[82]

When military brothels were established, prevailing British moral standards forced such arrangements to be made at the unit level and were rarely discussed in official military channels. The informal nature of sanctioned prostitution meant ranking officers and government officials could deny its existence. In 1945, Sir Geoffrey Northcote, the Principal Information Officer for the EAC, emphatically declared:

> [There is] no truth in the belief, which is occasionally expressed and may be fairly widely held, that the Army Authorities tolerate prostitution provided that the men concerned are protected from infection with venereal diseases; on the contrary, . . . all arguments appealing to the moral and social instincts and principles of African soldiers [are] frequently and forcibly put to them.[83]

A vocal minority in the colonial military establishment strongly opposed military brothels, and moralistic senior officers often overruled the efforts of their more pragmatic subordinates. The army's willingness to sanction sexual relations with women outside the bounds of Christian marriage was especially problematic for military chaplains. In 1941 the Deputy Assistant Chaplain General warned:

> It would not only hinder but gravely imperil our influence in the Army, if we were to refer in condemnatory terms at Divine Services to the arrangements that are made in the Army for controlling the incidence of VD. . . . On the other hand, while we may not offer such criticism publicly, we must be on our guard lest our tacit acceptance of authoritative rulings be regarded as a condonation of what cannot be other than grave sin.[84]

Many mission leaders believed the army's "brothel habit" undermined their teachings by encouraging excessive promiscuity among African soldiers.[85]

Other more pragmatic military officers doubted the utility of organized military prostitution. Brigadier Robert Lees, the Consultant Venereologist for the Middle East forces, pointed out that frequent medical inspections did not lower the infection rates for women in military brothels.[86] Many army doctors believed propaganda and prophylactic measures were the best protection against VD. All askaris returning from leave had to visit an "Early Treatment Room" where an African Nursing Orderly distributed "Preventative Packets" containing wool impregnated with soft soap for washing the genital area and a tube of antiseptic ointment consisting of calomel and one-tenth percent mercury cyanide for insertion into the urethra. Some military authorities considered the Early Treatment Rooms unworkable, but medical officers countered: "If you can train an African to lubricate and use a bren gun you can also teach him how to lubricate and use his own."[87] African veterans protested that they were rarely issued condoms; British officers, however, claimed their men refused to use them. This may have been due to the extreme age of the EAC's condoms, which were inferior models captured from the Italians in Ethiopia.[88]

While some British officers believed African soldiers were unwilling and unable to refrain from sex, African veterans, in turn, often disapproved of military prostitutes. Many were devout Christians or Muslims who considered casual sex immoral. As a Muslim veteran recalled: "When the officers brought us women I shunned them because of my religion." Other servicemen disliked sanctioned military prostitution because it reduced their relations with women to base physical contact. They wanted to choose their own partners and detested the army's Early Treatment Rooms. Thus, African soldiers' sexual attitudes do not appear to have been much different from other imperial troops; some askaris went to great lengths to find sexual gratification, but others remained abstinent because of their personal convictions.[89]

The EAC also encouraged chiefs and headmen to advise askaris to abstain from sex while away from home. Chief Kasina wa Ndoo sent a message to Kamba soldiers warning: "[I]f you get a disease of this nature and degenerate in the way that happens or you become impotent, whose is the loss? The loss is yours and ours. Be patient then, wait for your leave and when you return home your need can be met."[90] Many African religious and community leaders were offended by the army's depiction of African soldiers as sexually incontinent and opposed the immorality of sanctioned prostitution. In 1944, a delegation of Nyasaland chiefs wrote to their government to protest the army's policy of creating "whores' camps" near army bases: "[T]his does no profitable work more than encouraging the spread of VD, though from the officers' point of view it looks as a help to keeping their Askaris in good order."[91]

Civil officials also worried that sanctioned prostitution undermined the racial hierarchy of colonial society by encouraging sexual relations between non-African women and askaris serving overseas. British officers in Southeast Asia were alarmed to find askaris with "prurient picture magazines" showing non-African women and introduced a special pin-up series featuring clothed African women in *Heshima*, a magazine published for African soldiers.[92] Intelligence officials also warned that censored letters written by African soldiers serving overseas revealed they considered Middle Eastern and Asian prostitutes to be "white." A Ganda driver in Ceylon wrote to a friend: "We are having enjoyment with white ladies. We pay 7 ¹/₂ rupees to have a go with them." In the Middle East, a Kamba Corporal added: "There is no difference between black and white here. We go to the bar together, among white girls, who much prefer us to them. They long to be with us all the time and although we used to fear them at home, we are playing with them here. They cost sh5."[93] Egyptian entrepreneurs nurtured and exploited these misconceptions. For a fee, they would provide a light-skinned woman to pose for pictures with askaris.[94]

Many African soldiers saw no reason why they should not be allowed to have relations with European women. In one case, a Ugandan Storeman sent to Britain with an East African detachment to repatriate AAPC prisoners of war had an affair with an English woman. Askaris representing the KAR at King George VI's coronation in 1937 and the London Victory Parade in 1946 had relations with British prostitutes. These soldiers embarrassed colonial officials by bragging about their exploits when they returned home, which inflamed the Kenyan settler community. Commentators in the local press during the war warned sexual contacts with "white women" overseas would lead askaris to have "unwholesome ideas" about European women in East Africa. Military authorities therefore took steps to isolate askaris from such "unsuitable" British women when another contingent of East Africans represented the KAR at the coronation of Queen Elizabeth II in 1953.[95]

ABSENT HUSBANDS IN PEACE AND WAR

Most African soldiers endeavored to keep track of developments in their home regions while they were in the army. They worried about the health and welfare of their families because, like most African labor migrants, they had strong economic interests in rural society. Military wives took care of askaris' immediate domestic needs, but what was often a short-term relationship did not provide security for their old age. The East African governments' long-standing opposition to tax exemptions and pensions forced servicemen to invest their earnings in land and cattle. African soldiers therefore had a vested interest in using their privileged status in the army to influence rural affairs. Conversely, as members of extended families, askaris had extensive social obligations, and soldiers' relatives often exploited their absence to appropriate part of their earnings and benefits. These conflicts reflected the inherent tensions in the KAR's policy of treating African soldiers as though they were the monogamous heads of nuclear families.

Military authorities tried to protect African soldiers' interests while they were away in the army. Whenever KAR battalions were mobilized, junior British officers assumed responsibility for the domestic problems of their men. During the Second World War, they held "*shauri* parades" to hear soldiers' problems, and as one officer put it: "The resolution of these domestic affairs was vital for morale; a worried askari was unlikely to be an efficient soldier."[96] Illiteracy made it difficult for soldiers to correspond with their families, so British officers wrote directly to district officers with their men's domestic problems. This system was strained to the limit during the war, when over 300,000 askaris served in the East African forces. Civil officials complained they spent too much time on soldiers' affairs, and in 1944, the District Commissioner of Machakos estimated that only one-quarter of the cases he investigated constituted genuine hardship. This attitude led to friction between civil and military officials, and an officer with 71 KAR candidly admitted: "I worked up quite a hate against DCs in those days, and felt they might have taken more trouble to tell us whether letters had been received and family remittances paid."[97]

The East Africa Command therefore developed alternative avenues of communication to defuse tensions and improve morale by keeping askaris in better touch with their rural homes. The army published newsletters that reported on weather, crops, markets, community meetings, and local gossip. These were written in Swahili or vernacular languages for educated troops and in English for officers to read to illiterate askaris.[98] The EAC also beamed regular radio news broadcasts to East Africans in the Middle East, and during Mau Mau, 4 KAR showed its askaris films of their families in Uganda. The East Africa Command also encouraged family members to broadcast greetings to their relatives in the army and for a while also allowed soldiers

to send messages in return. Civil officials discontinued the practice, however, after Nyasalanders stationed in Nairobi made a broadcast that "soundly
rated" their chiefs for allowing soldiers' wives to commit adultery.[99]

While these forms of mass communication gave askaris a glimpse of the
goings-on in their home areas, they were of little use in addressing specific
problems of individual soldiers. Both military and civil authorities therefore
urged soldiers and their families to correspond whenever possible. During
the Second World War, military authorities established a free letter system in
which a family member or soldier wrote a message on one-half of a special
form, and the recipient used the other half to respond. The EAC discontinued the practice after the war but reestablished the program in 1951, when it
sent East Africans to Malaya and Egypt.

These free letter schemes only worked if both the askari and his relatives were literate. In 1944, General Platt pleaded with the East African
governments to do more to get soldiers' wives to correspond with their
husbands: "A great deal of the Askaris' trouble over mails boils down to
the fact that many Bibis [wives] cannot, or do not, write. The more Bibis
who can be encouraged or helped to write to their soldiers, the better for
the soldier overseas."[100] Few families understood the free letter scheme,
and the message forms often arrived too dirty or tattered for the response
section to be returned. Many wives and relatives could not master the
intricacies of the colonial postal system; their letters contained vague
addresses like *mpakani* (at the front) and "Keya" (KAR). The Post Office
also returned many letters because of insufficient postage, and the East
African Political Liaison Officer estimated three-quarters of all letters sent
to soldiers overseas failed to arrive at all. In many areas, District Officers
hired professional scribes to write and translate letters for illiterate military families, and European missionaries performed the same service for
relatives of Christian soldiers.[101]

As with soldiers the world over, askaris wanted regular reports from home
to confirm that their wives were remaining faithful. In some Tanganyikan
districts, a rash of murders occurred when returning askaris learned of their
wives' adulterous behavior. A District Officer in Bukoba observed:

> There was a general belief among Bahaya who joined the Army that the
> King's uniform conferred immunity against the ordinary processes of law,
> and that a soldier who killed the wife who had betrayed him would be safe
> from punishment thanks to the protection of King George. . . . Any clem-
> ency towards crimes of this kind would have put many soldiers' wives in
> danger, because fidelity to absent husbands was not widely practised.[102]

African soldiers often found it difficult to maintain stable relations with
women who did not live in the barracks. The army's patriarchal institutions

of authority rarely extended beyond camp gates, and women forced by their relatives to marry soldiers against their will took advantage of their husbands' absence to take up with other men of their own choosing. This was a particular problem in Kenya's Nyanza Province, where bride wealth policies and the institution of wife inheritance often compelled young women to marry older men. In most cases, askaris could only respond to their wives' infidelity by suing for the return of bride wealth, and district officers complained they spent too much time keeping track of these divorce proceedings.[103]

African soldiers who were not serving overseas could qualify for compassionate leave. Most civil officials pushed for a liberal leave policy during the Second World War, but the East Africa Command would only release men who had suffered the death of a close relative. Military authorities insisted cases involving property disputes or adultery could be handled by a man's District Commissioner or an appointed African representative. The EAC refused to grant compassionate leave for marital and legal matters until the 1950s, and even then an applicant had to produce a letter from his District Officer testifying that his presence was required under "native law and custom."[104]

Askaris who could not get compassionate leave put a great deal of pressure on the army and the East African governments to do something about adulterous wives. During the Second World War, a Corporal complained to the Kenyan government that another man was courting his wife: "On our engagement the Provincial Commissioner strictly spoke to us how no one can take neither your wife nor your cattle. [Were] the Provincial Commissioner's speeches only mere [talk] or . . . [has] the Government ordered that all the men who did not come to the Army can take soldiers' women?"[105] Askaris believed any man caught seducing the wife of a soldier should be conscripted into the army, but the civil administration could do little to force wayward women to remain faithful to their husbands. In Nyanza Province, where runaway wives were a particular problem, colonial officials ordered chiefs to prosecute adulterers for violating "native custom." Similarly, Uganda's Karamoja District Native Council passed a non-binding resolution making adultery with a soldier's wife punishable by a fine of £150 or six years in jail.[106]

The inability of the colonial administration to deal with such domestic problems understandably undermined the morale of the African soldiery. Askaris who received troubling news from home were prone to disciplinary problems if denied leave. Officers therefore pushed district administrators to deal more forcefully with unfaithful wives, and civil officials complained that the military expected too much from African "law and custom." In one particularly difficult case during the Second World War, the commander of a medical detachment insisted officials in North Kavirondo District compel a woman to remain married to an askari who had "inherited" her from his dead father. The Commissioner of Nyanza Province summed up the military's case this way:

> An askari has caused a great deal of trouble over the award of . . . [an African] Tribunal that he should inherit a certain woman as a wife, but that the woman refuses him and lives in her father's home. On investigation it appears that the award was in fact made to his brother and it was this man whom the woman refused. In order to get military influence to assist, the askari has represented himself as the injured party and I have a request from his Company Commander that I shall see the award is carried out— i.e. that I shall make the woman live with this askari as his wife. The implications stagger the imagination.[107]

In most instances, askaris needed compassionate leave to sort out their domestic problems, which was rarely possible in frontline combat units. The best advice district officers could offer men on active service was to have their relatives sue for the return of bride wealth payments.

Conversely, faithful spouses of African soldiers also suffered considerable hardship while their husbands were on active duty. Askaris complained that chiefs extorted money from their wives and used their judicial powers to force them off their land.[108] The greatest problem facing military women, however, was supporting themselves financially in their husbands' absence. In 1940, the Annual Report for the Rift Valley Province noted: "As amongst the Nandi the men and not the women do the tilling of the soil, the herding of the stock and generally the heaviest toils, the departure of so many young men had social reactions which might not at first be appreciated; wives and children and in some cases aged parents were left without an able-bodied male to look after them."[109] In keeping with established migrant labor practices, the KAR adopted a policy in the 1920s of encouraging askaris to send home a portion of their pay through their District Commissioners.

Soldiers' families often depended on these remittances. In 1939, 1,056 askaris of the KAR's Northern Brigade (made up of the Kenyan and Ugandan KAR battalions) sent home a total of 13,379 shillings each month. Table 5.1. shows thirty-nine percent sent family remittances to a brother, and thirty-two percent, to a wife. Wives' remittances averaged 14.8 shillings per month, as compared to the remittances sent to brothers, which averaged only 11.6 shillings monthly. These figures indicate that young, unmarried men tended to send relatively small remittances to a brother as an investment, but married askaris sent more money home to support their families.[110] Wives used remittances to pay taxes, buy food and livestock, purchase plows, and hire workers to help on their farms. Remittances helped military families survive the drought and food shortages of the Second World War, and military offi-

Table 5.1

Monthly Family Remittance Payments by the Askaris of the Northern Brigade, October 1939 (Total payments = 13,349 shillings to 1,056 recipients)

Type of Recipient	Number of Recipients	Percentage of Total Recipients	Average Payment (in shillings)
Brother	413	39.1	11.6
Father	213	20.2	12.0
Mother	65	6.2	11.9
Son	13	1.2	10.9
Wife	338	32.0	14.8
Other Relatives	14	1.3	10.1
Average Remittance (in shillings)			11.9

Source: Annexure to Northern Brigade Order No. 276, 13 October 1939, KNA, MD 4/5/118/9a.

cials estimated serving East African soldiers sent home a total of over £1 million by 1944.[111]

Although the remittance system worked reasonably well during peacetime, it became cumbersome and inefficient during World War II. The book-keeping system that the military used to transfer money to district officers was unwieldy and complicated, and few askaris or their families either understood or trusted it. Rumors circulated throughout Nyanza Province that family remittances were actually "blood money" for dead soldiers. Moreover, the army delayed or lost many payments because wartime officers with little personal knowledge of African cultures misspelled the names or addresses of their askaris' relatives.[112] Sometimes support payments were stolen by impostors posing as soldiers' relatives. This was a particular problem in Nyanza Province, where the Provincial Commissioner observed: "Askaris are very concerned that the person whom they nominate and whose relationship they state, should get the money; others are often ready to appropriate it; on the present safari in one case an uncle, a bogus wife, and the mother all presented themselves for a remittance which the askari had in fact made to his father who happened to be sick at home."[113] Civil officials usually relied on traditional authorities to confirm the identity of soldiers' relatives, but some chiefs and African clerks also conspired to steal family payments. Military officials found such incidents particularly troublesome because askaris accused the army of misappropriating their money when remittances were mislaid or stolen.

Much of the controversy over military payments stemmed from conflict within extended African families over how the money should be spent. Since the army encouraged African soldiers to name a father or brother to look after their domestic interests, wives and children of askaris often suffered when male relatives appropriated remittances for their own purposes. Many askaris, however, saw remittances as investments instead of family support payments and ordered their representatives to buy cattle or bury the money in the ground.[114] Askaris also sent payments to European missionaries because they did not trust their families, and many Nyasalanders, who were experienced labor migrants, opened bank accounts to protect their remittances. Ex-servicemen invariably became extremely upset when they returned home to find that their kinsmen had spent their investments. In Kenya's Central and Nyanza Provinces, the end of World War II sparked a flurry of court cases where veterans sued relatives for the return of their wartime savings.[115]

Thus, even though the army required askaris to send money home, many soldiers' wives became increasingly destitute as the war progressed. Their desperate plight embarrassed the colonial governments, and missionary leaders lobbied the army to pay a special separation allowance directly to wives of serving soldiers. Archdeacon Owen argued: "In England wives of men serving with the Forces have various organizations to which they can apply in their troubles. Something of a kind is needed here, for there can be no doubt that some people take advantage of the absence of the husband to trouble the wives."[116] The Kenyan government, motivated by fears of "detribalization," rejected these proposals because they believed family remittances disrupted rural society by allowing women to avoid agricultural labor. In Kenya, the newsletter for Central Kavirondo District urged askaris to exercise greater control over how their wives spent the money they sent home.

> It is very noticeable traveling along the roads these days that only the older women work in the shambas. The younger women and girls are to be found in the dukas, the trading centres and walking in groups along the roads or by the rivers or crowded in markets. These girls are finding life very easy with all the money they are sent by their soldier husbands or relations. They think that they need not cultivate their shambas very energetically as they can always buy food.[117]

These concerns were most certainly overstated, and the deteriorating status of military wives forced the Kenyan government to offer some protection by temporarily freezing most legal cases brought against them during the war.[118]

When wives and children returned to the barracks after the Second World War, the family support problem lessened. The East Africa Command retained a revamped remittance system to ensure the care of families who did not live in the lines. Civil officials in Kenya and Uganda opposed this decision, asserting that the remittance system was a destabilizing influence, arguing that most askaris viewed remittances as investments rather than family support payments. European employers similarly complained that family allotments were inflationary and dried up the African labor supply by freeing soldiers' relatives from having to work.[119] Nyasaland and Tanganyika, however, blocked the proposal and supported the East Africa Command's assertion that soldiers on active duty had a right to send money home. In the 1950s, askaris serving in Egypt and Malaya made regular family support payments, and by the end of the decade, African soldiers were allowed to designate up to fifty percent of their pay as a family remittance.[120]

Similarly, the treatment of the dependents of deceased African soldiers also changed over time. In the early KAR, military authorities assumed there was no need to pay pensions or death benefits to widows and orphans because they would be cared for by their extended families. In some East African societies, widows were even "inherited" by one of their husband's male relatives. The families of men who died in the KAR received a cash payment, but this was seen as "blood money" rather than an acknowledgment of governmental responsibility for supporting the dependents of deceased servicemen. In World War I, the colonial governments paid relatives of deceased askaris 150 rupees (roughly 113 shillings), and during the Second World War, military families received a death gratuity of 600 shillings.[121]

As a whole, most rural African families were generally satisfied with these relatively generous payments, but problems arose over which member or members of an askari's family should actually receive his death gratuity and personal possessions. During the First World War, the military considered a "Pagan" soldier's heir to be his oldest male relative. The 1932 KAR Ordinances allowed askaris to make a will. If a man died intestate, however, his death benefits were paid to "any claimant showing herself or himself to the satisfaction of the Governor to be the widow of the deceased or to be the child or any near relative of the deceased, according to the rules of kinship of the tribe to which the deceased belonged."[122] Colonial administrators insisted that askaris follow "tribal law and custom" in designating an heir, but the army allowed soldiers to dispose of their estates as they saw fit. As a result, it was not unusual for two different relatives to lay claim to the death gratuity.[123]

While various ethnic groups had their own customary laws governing inheritance, these disputes usually pitted an askari's widow against his oldest male relatives. Colonial officials insisted the problem had to be resolved by African tribunals, which usually ruled in favor of the heir designated under "tribal law." These bodies rarely ruled in favor of a widow, and as a result, many military women were left destitute by the deaths of their husbands. This was especially true for Muslim and Christian wives, who could not be inherited by male relatives under "tribal law." In such cases, civil officials grudgingly acknowledged that these women were entitled to their husband's death gratuity. In practice, however, most eligible widows were not aware they could apply for the benefits.[124]

The desperate state of many military women during the Second World War reignited debate over the need for widows' pensions. In 1944, the Kenyan government convened an Ad Hoc Committee on African Pensions to consider the matter. The Chief Native Commissioner opposed such payments on the grounds they would lead to a "breakdown of tribal and communal responsibilities." Rev. Leonard Beecher, the unofficial Legislative Council Representative for African Interests, responded that pensions were necessary because over sixty percent of East African soldiers were Christian, which meant their wives could not be inherited. Beecher's case was persuasive, and in spite of opposition from settler representatives in the Legislative Council, the Committee ruled that a wife could take her death gratuity as a pension if she were her husband's sole heir and beneficiary. In polygynous families, only the senior wife was eligible for the death gratuity, which would then presumably be shared among her juniors.[125] In spite of these reforms, few widows could survive on their small pensions once they were too old for agricultural labor. They lost their benefits if they remarried, and many had to turn to illicit enterprises like bootlegging and brothel keeping. Most African veterans believed the East African governments had a moral obligation to support these women and continued to press for more generous death benefits for widows and orphans throughout the post-war era.[126]

Children of deceased askaris were usually cared for adequately by their extended families, but these relatives rarely had the means to send them to school. During the Second World War, serving askaris pressed the army to take responsibility for military orphans. Nothing was done until after the war, when most of the East African governments established "War Memorial Funds" to build military monuments and provide scholarships for war orphans. Kenya's Nyanza Province War Memorial Committee decided it did not have the resources for a scholarship fund and instead allocated £1,144 to the construction of "visible memorials" in each district, a move that disgusted African veterans. In comparison, the governments of Uganda and Nyasaland devoted a substantial portion of their Memorial Funds to educate war orphans.[127]

In Kenya, the African Section of the British Legion assumed primary responsibility for educating the children of men killed in the war. The Legion's funding was limited, but it did provide for the primary education of all children who lost a father during the conflict. In 1947, an estimated 2,410 children (including girls) were eligible for five shillings in school fees for four years of primary school, which came to a total of £3,615. Yet the Legion only funded a small handful of children with "exceptional potential" to advance to secondary school.[128] There are no complete records of how many orphans took advantage of the scholarship program, but it appears many eligible children were left out. In 1948, Kitui District's Civil Reabsorption Officer estimated 162 Kamba askaris died during the war, of which 58 left a total of 126 children (68 boys and 58 girls). Of this group, only 53 boys and 24 girls applied for scholarships. The rest could not be found, were already in school, or working, or in the case of girls, remained at home at their mothers' insistence.[129]

Many war orphans disputed the Legion's refusal to offer scholarships for secondary education. They argued, with some justification, that their fathers would have paid for their continued education if they had survived. Under the colonial education system in Kenya, only a small percentage of African pupils advanced from primary to secondary school. Although these decisions were based primarily on academic merit, a number of qualified orphans had to leave secondary school because the British Legion would not pay their school fees. Students who received substandard scores on their primary school exams also lobbied civil and military officials to help them win a place in secondary school. As was the case with African soldiers, they attempted to use their military connections to improve their status in colonial society.[130]

The colonial army's domestic policies helped produce a disciplined African soldiery by offering tangible benefits to all of the parties comprising the regimental family of the King's African Rifles. Military service provided askaris with an alternative access to women, which improved their quality of life, enhanced their social status, and allowed them to sire children. Military women, in turn, gained access to the wealth and patronage of the army and achieved an added measure of security in colonial society. These arrangements also produced substantial benefits for the colonial military. The army strengthened the social isolation of the African soldiery by regulating askaris' conjugal relations. Military families reduced African servicemen's exposure to disease and unsuitable political ideas and provided the KAR with future soldiers and low-cost domestic labor.

Nevertheless, military families also embodied the inherent tensions and contradictions of the colonial army. African soldiers resisted the KAR's insistence on limiting their choice of partners, and their efforts to circumvent these restrictions led to disciplinary problems. Military women found that their association with the army undercut their personal freedom and left them vulnerable to a patriarchal system of authority. Moreover, the colonial military's attempt to co-opt African families led to social disruption in the East African countryside. Askaris gained access to women without having to defer to their elders but also had to negotiate new relationships with kinsmen who claimed a portion of their earnings. Thus, military service reordered domestic relations in martial societies and tended to destabilize prevailing institutions of civil authority.

NOTES

[1] Jane Parpart, *Labor and Capital on the African Copperbelt*, (Philadelphia: Temple University Press, 1983), p. 35.

[2] Visit to Ceylon, by EAPLO, 31 March 1943, KNA, MD 4/5/65/180a.

[3] GRO 1458, "Convictions by Court Martial," 20 April 1941, KNA, MD 4/5/117/II/101; Psychiatric Report, 1 (EA) General Hospital, October–December 1943, PRO, WO 222/1827; Interview, #137.

[4] Great Britain, *Standing Orders of the 6th Battalion the King's African Rifles*, (n.p., 1930); Williams, Mss.Afr.s.1715/300.

[5] AAG EAC to CSNY, 28 April 1944, MNA, PCS 1/18/6/35; EAC, GRO, No. 200, 12 October 1942, KNA, DEF 15/51/150d.

[6] GHQ MELF to GOC EAC, 1949, KNA, DEF 1/39/230/a/1–14.

[7] GOC EAC to WO, 2 January 1947, KNA, DEF 1/39/210/a/1.

[8] QHR, 2 KAR, 30 September 1946, PRO, WO 269/98.

[9] Recruiting Depot Lecture on "Food," May 1943, KNA, DEF 15/65/5a.

[10] DC Nandi to O/C "B" Company 7 KAR, 10 March 1955, KNA, DC KAPT 1/12/36/215; Swann, RHL, Mss.Afr.s.1715/268; QHR, EAC Medical Branch, 31 December 1946, PRO, WO 269/38; Lieutenant Colonial H.P.L. Glass, RHL, Mss.Afr.s.1715/105; Cree, RHL, Mss.Afr.s.1715/57.

[11] Roger Norman Buckley, *Slaves in Red Coats: The British West India Regiments, 1795–1815*, (New Haven, CT: Yale University Press, 1979), pp. 125–26; J. Malcom Thompson, "Colonial Policy and the Family Life of Black Troops in French West Africa, 1817–1904," *International Journal of African Historical Studies*, v. 23, (1990), p. 438.

[12] C. A. Sykes, *Service and Sport on the Tropical Nile*, (London: John Murray, 1903), p. 97.

[13] KAR Recruiting Poster, c. 1952, MNA, 1DCZA 1/20/26; Luise White, "Separating the Men from the Boys: Constructions of Gender, Sexuality, and Terrorism in Central Kenya, 1939–1959," *International Journal of African Historical Studies*, v. 23, (1990), pp. 1–25; Interviews, #10, #21, #58, #60.

[14] Memorandum by PC NZA, 27 September 1939, KNA, PC NZA/2/3/21/57; Interviews, #86, #93.

[15] EAC Conference Minutes, 7 May 1946, PRO, WO 169/24305; Recruitment of African Other Ranks, 28 May 1951, KNA, DC TAMB/1/9/18/80.

[16] Gavin Kitching, "Proto-Industrialization and Demographic Change," *Journal of African History*, v. 24 (1983), pp. 229–31.

[17] Extracts from African Mail, May 1945, KNA, DEF 10/64/36; Eugene Schleh, "The Post-War Careers of Ex-Servicemen in Ghana and Uganda," *Journal of Modern African Studies*, v. 6, (1968), p. 209; Bildad Kaggia, *The Roots of Freedom, 1921–1963*, (Nairobi: EA Publishing House, 1975), pp. 56–59.

[18] DC Tambach to Adjutant KAR Depot, 21 January 1930, KNA, DC TAMB/1/9/1; Interview, #146.

[19] DC Tambach to O/C 5 KAR, 11 March 1953, KNA, DC TAMB 2/13/2/24; DC Samburu to PC RVP, 5 May 1954, KNA, PC NKU 2/21/5/65b.

[20] Great Britain, *Standing Orders of the 6th Battalion,* para. 158.

[21] Cree, RHL, Mss.Afr.s.1715/57; Interview, #151.

[22] Service Records of Clerk John Kumbanga (n7022) and Wadi Nyalugwe (n7153), MNA, S1/105/34/133; O/C "A" Company 3 KAR to DC Nandi, 28 April 1955, KNA, DC KAPT 1/12/37/77; Interview, #12.

[23] Borradaile, KNA, MSS 78/1; Glanville, KNA, MSS 78/4.

[24] EAC Release Instruction #41, 2 October 1945, KNA, DEF 10/19/5; DC Marsabit to O/C NFP, 18 August 1943, KNA, DEF 13/182/1a.

[25] 3 KAR Circular, "Certificate of Marriage," 16 June 1959, KNA, DC KAPT/2/16/1/74.

[26] Interview, #9.

[27] Interviews, #2, #30, #57.

[28] Interview, #25.

[29] DC Tambach to O/C "A" Company 5 KAR, 9 August 1938, KNA, DC TAMB/1/9/1.

[30] Interview, #153; O/C "A" Company to DC Tambach, 6 October 1938, KNA, DC TAMB 1/9/1; Bowie, RHL, Mss.Afr.s.1715/24a.

[31] S. H. La Fontaine to Kenyan Director of Education, n.d., KNA, ED 2/17321/121.

[32] EAC Welfare Committee, 25 May 1951, KNA, DEF 6/61/61/9.

[33] Comments on Inspector General's Report, 1934, PRO, CO 820/17/6; Deputy Chief of Staff EAC to Minister for Defence Kenya, 7 February 1955, PRO, WO 276/163.

[34] DMS to Kenyan Member for Health, 18 January 1954, KNA, BY 4/205/255; Brigadier D. H. Nott, RHL, Mss.Afr.S.1715/202; AHR, 3 KAR, 1962–1963, PRO, WO 305/1650.

[35] Uganda Protectorate, *Standing Orders of the 4th Battalion, the King's African Rifles*, (Entebbe: Government Printer, 1934), Section 72; Great Britain, *Standing Orders of the 6th Battalion*, para 161; D.N.W. Irven, "KAR Subaltern," *The Gunner*. v. 65–66, (April–May 1976), p. 20.

[36] Many askaris believed Idi Amin's mother used sorcery to murder her former lover, a Corporal in 4 KAR. Edgar George Lardner, *Soldiering and Sport in Uganda, 1909–1910*, (London: Walter Scott, 1912); Lord Cranworth, *A Colony in the Making, Or Sport and Profit in British East Africa*, (London: Macmillan and Co., 1912), p. 209; David Martin, *General Amin*, (London: Faber and Faber, 1974), p. 27; Interview, #41.

[37] O/C "A" Company 3 KAR to DC Tambach, 3 September 1938, KNA, DC TAMB/1/9/1.

[38] CO Southern Bde to CST, 11 January 1934, PRO, CO 820/17/8.

[39] Interviews, #123, #124, #126, #127, #128.

[40] Dimoline to WO, 2 January 1947, KNA, DEF 1/39/210/a/1.

[41] IGR 2 KAR, 1930, PRO, CO 820/10/9; Great Britain, *Standing Orders of the 6th Battalion*, para. 161.

[42] Broomfield, RHL, Mss.Afr.s.1715/31; Army Welfare in the EAC, 10 May 1951, DEF 6/61/61/7; KAR Troop (45) Zomba, MNA, 17–SA 1/42; Lieutenant Colonel J.E.D. Watson, RHL, Mss.Afr.s.1715/288; Interviews, #25, #126.

[43] AHR, 4 KAR, 1961–1962, PRO, WO 305/1002; Chavasse, RHL, Mss.Afr.s.1715/141; Iain Grahame, *Jambo Effendi, Seven Years with the KAR*, (London: J. A. Allen, 1966), p. 43.

[44] Coles, RHL, Mss.Afr.s.1715/48; O/C 7 KAR to RVP DCs, 14 January 1957, KNA, PC NKU/2/21/8/183a.

[45] 4 KAR, QHR, 25 October 1946, PRO, WO 269/111; EAC Education Officer to Kenya Director of Education, 11 February 1948, KNA, ED 2/17321/21.

[46] The Lord St. Helens, KNA, MSS 78/3; AR, 4 KAR, 1926, PRO, CO 820/2/2.

[47] Director of Army Education to EAC, 22 May 1947, KNA, ED 2/17321/7c; Conference of EA Directors of Education, June 1947, KNA, ED 2/17321/3; Interview, #139.

[48] EAC Peace Time Order of Battle, 14 June 1948, PRO, WO 269/8; EA Defence Working Committee, 19 April 1955, KNA, DEF 6/61/133.

[49] Brochure, "Junior Leader Company—KAR," n.d., CPK Archives; Great Britain, *Annual Report on the Colony and Protectorate of Kenya for the Year 1959,* (London: HM Stationery Office, 1960); *Journal of the King's African Rifles,* v. 1, (December 1958).

[50] Great Britain, *Annual Report on the Colony and Protectorate of Kenya for the Year 1958,* (London: HM Stationery Office, 1959); DC Nandi to Headmasters Intermediate Schools, 14 May 1959, KNA, DC KAPT 1/12/45/53; EAC Circular, "Enlistment into the KAR of Persons Under 18 Years of Age," 31 July 1959, KNA, DC KAPT 1/12/45/69; Interview, #145.

[51] Aide-de-Camp Government House to DC Central NZA, 28 May 1959, KNA, DC KSM 1/22/25/88; Safari Report by ASBL ExO, 6 August 1959, KNA, OPE 1/7/78/1.

[52] Lieutenant N. St. Leger Moore to Major A. E. Majende, Colonial Office, 10 September 1958, PRO, CO 986/592.

[53] Chief Staff's Conference, 6 March 1957, PRO, WO 276/20; Interview, #145.

[54] Junior Private Meshack Abuonji to DC Central NZA, 5 May 1963, KNA, DC KSM 1/22/2/24; O/C JLC to Regional Government Authorities, 26 November 1963, KNA, DC GRSSA 2/20/4/77; Swann, RHL, Mss.Afr.s.1715/268; Interview, #24.

[55] Hubert Moyse-Bartlett, *The King's African Rifles,* (Aldershot: Gale & Polden, 1956), p. 29.

[56] QHR, 2 KAR, 12 April 1948, PRO, WO 269/100.

[57] Interview, #91.

[58] GOC Ceylon Army Command to Under Secretary of State WO, 12 October 1943, PRO, WO 106/4500; 5 (EA) FSS, Security Report, 3 June 1945, PRO, WO 172/9544; Visit to EA Troops in SE Asia, June 1945, KNA, by EALPO, KNA, DEF 15/12/80a.

[59] CnC India to Secretary of State for War, 5 November 1945, LHC, DP/IX/3; Kenya Commissioner of Police to CSK, 27 August 1945, KNA, MD 4/2/29/I/199; Robert Foran, *Kenya Police, 1887–1960,* (London: Robert Hale Limited, 1962), pp. 124–31.

[60] Morale of British Indian and Colonial Troops Southeast Asia, February–April 1945, PRO, WO 203/2045.

[61] Chief Chikumbu to PC Southern Province, Summer 1945, MNA, S41 1/23/5/63b.

[62] Inspector General to Nyasaland Governor, 2 April 1931, MNA, S2 11/30/23; Major J. W. Kaye to O/C SCC, 28 July 1931, MNA, S2 11/30/28.

[63] Interviews, #33, #54, #72, #134.

[64] EAC Committee for Combating VD, KNA, BY 13/91/21; QR, DADMS West Sub-Area, April–June 1944, PRO, WO 222/1815; QR, SMO Uganda, October–December 1944, PRO, WO 222/1824.

[65] Visit to Eritrea by Advisor in Venereology, 25 October–5 November 1941, PRO, WO 222/1302; John H. Nunneley, *Tales from the King's African Rifles,* (London: Askari Books, 1998), p. 13; Interview, #148.

[66] Consultant in Syphilology to the EAF to DMS, 14 November 1941, KNA, BY 13/91; Lecture by DMS Central Area, 1942, PRO, WO 222/1809; EAC Standing Committee for Combating VD, 3 March 1944, KNA, BY 13/91/19a; Committee for Combating VD, May 1944, KNA, BY 13/91/21.

[67] Michael Blundell, *A Love Affair with the Sun,* (Nairobi: General Printers, 1994), p. 75; Interview, #134.

[68] MO Meru Civil Hospital to DMS Kenya, 16 December 1935, KNA, MOH 2/456/23.

[69] QR SMO Uganda, October–December 1944, PRO, WO 222/1824; Tanganyikan "The Defence (Amendment Compulsory Treatment of Venereal Diseases) Regulations, 1944," MNA, S40/1/8/4/35a; Kenyan "The Defence (Compulsory Treatment of Venereal Diseases) Regulations, 1944," MNA, S40/1/8/4/41a; EAC VD Questionnaire, Appendix A to MRO No. 7 of 1944, KNA, DC KSM 1/29/7/160.

[70] Meeting at "A" Branch EAC, 14 September 1943, PRO, WO 169/13956.

[71] Central Province Military IR, December 1942, KNA, PC CP/13/1/1/9; QR, SMO Uganda, October–December 1943, PRO, WO 222/1824; ADMS Central Area to DMS EAC, 8 January 1942, KNA, BY 13/91/5a.

[72] DMS to CSNY, 22 September 1944, MNA, S40 1/8/4.

[73] QR, SMO Uganda, October–December 1943; January–March 1944, PRO, WO 222/1824.

[74] VD Memorandum No. 5, 19 June 1944, KNA, DC KSM/1/29/19/27; PC Nyanza to CSK, 7 October 1944, KNA, PC NZA/2/14/39.

[75] Captain Gibson to ADMS, 11 December 1942, Nursing Sister Roche to DC Nyeri, 13 February 1943, PRO, WO 222/1809.

[76] Cynthia Enloe, *Does Khaki Become You?: The Militarization of Women's Lives* (London: South End Press, 1983), pp. 26–29; Luise White, *The Comforts of Home: Prostitution in Colonial Nairobi*, (Chicago: University of Chicago Press, 1990); PRO, WO 169/13956; QMR Kenanda Sub-Area, January–March 1945, PRO, WO 222/1817.

[77] Husit O. Hosena to Driver P. Enduwaudi Vikumu Owangi, KNA, DEF 15/29/135.

[78] QR, DDMS 12 (A) Division, December 1942, PRO, WO 222/1808; Young, RHL, Mss.Afr.s.1715/309; Interview, #152.

[79] Matters Concerning 4 Bn de Marche, 15 September 1941, IWM, 83/21/1, Birkbeck Papers; Interview, #148.

[80] Report by Buganda Resident, 15 March 1943, KNA, MD 4/5/137/144a; Report for 4th Quarter 1943 by Consultant Venereologist, PRO, WO 222/1302; Swain, Mss.Afr.s.1715/265.

[81] 5 (EA) FSS, Security Report, 26 September 1945, PRO, WO 172/9544; Interviews, #63, #67, #81, #103.

[82] Waruhiu Itote, *"Mau Mau" General*, (Nairobi: EA Publishing House, 1967), p. 101; EAC Arms and Ammunition Reports, 4 May 1955, RHL, Mss.Afr.s. 1580/3/102.

[83] Chair, Conference on VD to CSK, 3 May 1945, KNA, BY 13/181/3a.

[84] DACG to all Chaplains (Except RC), 25 December 1941, CPK Archives.

[85] J. H. Duncan to Secretary CCK, 10 July 1944, CPK Archives.

[86] Report for 4th Quarter 1943 by Consultant Venereologist Lees, PRO, WO 222/1302.

[87] Lecture by ADMS Central Area EAC, 1942, PRO, WO 222/1809. See also Methods of Prevention of Venereal Diseases, 14 April 1942, PRO, WO 222/1302.

[88] Ethiopia Campaign, Hygiene and Principal Diseases, PRO, WO 222/1806; Visit of EAC Venereologist to Mogadishu, 20 July 1949, PRO, WO 269/41; Mans, RHL, Mss.Afr.s.1715/178; Interview, #90.

[89] Interviews, #64, #78.

[90] Kasina to African Other Ranks, 30 March 1943, MNA, M2/5/56/89.

[91] Report by Native Authority Mbelwa, 14 December 1944, MNA, S41/1/23/4/53.

[92] Visit to EA Troops in SE Asia, June 1945, by EAPLO, KNA, DEF 15/12/80a.

[93] Censorship Summary, EA Personnel, May–July 1943, KNA, MD 4/5/116/3; See also Censorship Summary, 11 (EA) Division, June–July 1943, KNA, MD 4/5/116/4.

[94] Diary of Buganda Resident, February 1943, KNA, MD 4/5/137/144c.

[95] Kaggia, *The Roots of Freedom*, pp. 44–45; Bowie, RHL, Mss.Afr.s.1715/24a; A. J. Knott, "East Africa and the Returning Askari; The Effect of Their War Service," *Quarterly Review*, v. 285 (January 1947), p.101; Interview, #148.

[96] John S. Harrison, Unpublished Memoirs, p. 12.

[97] Darlington, RHL, Mss.Afr.s.1715/62; See also Machakos District AR, 1944, KNA, DC MKS 1/1/28.

[98] Tour in EA Territories, by EALPO, 18 December 1944, KNA, DEF 15/12/57a; DC Samburu to O/C 3 KAR, 25 July 1952, KNA, PC NKU 2/21/5/51.

[99] KIO Report, 1942, KNA, CS 2/7/45/10; Political Intelligence Bulletin, No. 1, 1944, MNA, S34/1/4/1; Nott, RHL, Mss.Afr.s.1715/202.

[100] GOC EAC to East African Governors, 16 February 1944, MNA, S41/1/1/13/1.

[101] T.F.C. Bewes to Baptized Kikuyu Soldiers, 17 March 1942, CPK Archives; Tour by EAC Assistant Public Relations Officer, December 1943, KNA, MD 4/5/71/II/89; Tour by EAPLO, 18 December 1944, KNA, DEF 15/12/57a; Tanganyika Territory, *Annual Report of the Provincial Commissioners*, 1943, (Dar Es Salaam: Government Printer, 1944).

[102] E. K. Lumley, *Forgotten Mandate: A British District Officer in Tanganyika*, (Hamden CT: Archon Books, 1976), pp. 158–59; See also O/C 53 Light Battery to DC Central Kavirondo, August 1941, KNA, DC KSM 1/22/26/231; Zomba-Liwonde District AR, 1943, MNA, S11/3/1/93.

[103] Shauris of Private Otieno s/o Omoth (kml 22915) and Lance Corporal Wandera s/o Hayango (kml 17599), KNA, DEF 15/26/31; Corporal Harold Ndege to DC Zomba, 6 October 1955, MNA, 1DCZA/1/20/4.

[104] GRO, No. 200, 12 October 1942, KNA, DEF 15/51/150d; GRO 140, "Compassionate Leave—African Other Ranks in Malaya or Egypt," 13 July 1954, KNA, MD 4/5/83/IV/22/1; 70 Bde Circular, "Compassionate Leave," 10 April 1962, KNA, DC KMG 2/17/8/8.

[105] Corporal Hzron Ang'iro s/o Akoo to PC NZA, 7 August 1941, KNA, PC NZA 3/18/21/31.

[106] DC North Kavirondo to PC NZA, 2 September 1942, KNA, DC KSM 1/22/87/197; CSK to CSEAG, 5 October 1943, KNA, MD 4/5/151/90; Uganda Protectorate, *Annual Report for 1939–46*, (Entebbe: Government Printer, 1949).

[107] PC NZA to CSK, 21 February 1944, KNA, DEF 15/118/70.

[108] Report by Native Authority Mwase, December 1944, MNA, S41 1/23/4/53b; Corporal James Oyoya to DC North NZA, 16 July 1954, KNA, DC KMG 2/17/1/236.

[109] RVP AR, 1940, KNA, MAA 2/3/11/II/1a.

[110] Annexure to Northern Brigade Order No. 276, 13 October 1939, KNA, MD 4/5/118/9a.

[111] DC Tambach to Paymaster Northern Bde, 13 April 1932, KNA, DC TAMB 1/9/1; Savings and Remittances by African Soldiers, 18 March 1944, KNA, MD 4/5/72/33a.

[112] Brigadier C. N. Bednall to CSEAG, 23 March 1944, KNA, MD 4/5/72/41a; Central Kavirondo Tour by Provincial Welfare Officer, June 1944, KNA, DC KSM 1/22/149/8; Interview, #63.

[113] PC NZA to CSK, 19 July 1944, KNA, MD 4/5/71/II/182.

[114] DC Nandi to PC RVP, 2 October 1943, KNA, DC NKU 2/29/2/317; Interview, 133a.

[115] Dresser Wambua wa Ndunda, EAAMC, to DC Machakos, 23 November 1943, KNA, DC MKS/2/16/2; Report by Native Authority Mwase, December 1944, MNA, S41/

1/23/4/53b; Guchu Wamweya to DC Fort Hall, 27 June 1956, KNA, DC FH 3/12/21/351.

[116] Archdeacon Owen to DC Central Kavirondo, 3 September 1943, KNA, PC NZA 2/3/85/29.

[117] Central Kavirondo Newsletter No. 16, November 1944, KNA, DC KSM 1/28/58/161.

[118] CSEAG to CSK, 18 February 1944, KNA, MD 4/5/71/II/102; PC NZA to DCs, 9 September 1943, KNA, PC NZA 2/3/85.

[119] PC Northern Province Uganda to CSU, 1 September 1947, KNA, MD 4/5/71/III/124; Central Province IR, November 1941, KNA, MAA 2/3/16/III/26; Kenyan PCs Meeting, 13–14 November 1943, KNA, MD 4/5/72/14.

[120] CSNY to CSEAG, 17 February 1948, KNA, MD 4/5/71/III/149; Meeting at EAC HQ on FRs, 20 January 1949, KNA, MD 4/5/71/III/194; EALF Standing Orders, Section II/VIII, "Pay Services and Accounting Procedure," 1957, KNA, DEF 13/470.

[121] Adjutant 4 KAR to PC Mombasa, 6 June 1918, KNA, PC CST 1/1/234/35; HM Forces Pension Ordinance 1942, KNA, AG 5/2823.

[122] Kenya KAR Ordinance 1932, Sections 97–99, 103; Military Commissioner for Labor to DADML, 23 October 1917, KNA, PC CST 1/17/114/748.

[123] Minute by Nyanza Province DCs, May 1944, KNA, DEF 15/26/25a; EAC to CSK, 25 July 1944, KNA, DEF 15/26/33.

[124] Minute by Kenyan CNC, 18 December 1918, KNA, AG 5/1356/18a; Union of Sudanese to Colonial Secretary, 14 October 1940, PRO, CO 822/106/14.

[125] Meetings of the Ad Hoc Committee on African Pensions, May–June 1944, KNA, AG 5/2823.

[126] HM Forces Pensions and Gratuities (African Military Personnel) Regulations 1948, KNA, AG 5/2823/88b; 2nd Conference of the Nyasaland African Congress, 16–19 October 1945, MNA, S41/1/5/3/78a; Safari Report by ASBL ExO, 6 August 1959, KNA, OPE 1/7/78/1.

[127] Kenyan Secretariat Circular, "Kenya War Memorial Fund," 18 March 1947, KNA, PC NGO 1/15/5/9; GOC's Conference, Government House Entebbe, 29 January 1947, PRO, WO 276/75.

[128] Executive Meeting of the ASBL, 30 July 1947, KNA, DEF 10/24/76; Senior Education Officer to DCs, 25 June 1948, KNA, DC KTI 3/6/104/13; Kenyan Secretariat Circular, "War Memorial Fund of Kenya," 29 January 1950, KNA, PC NGO 1/15/5.

[129] CRO Kitui to Kenya Director of Education, 2 January 1948, KNA, DC KTI 3/6/104/9.

[130] Secretary ASBL to DC North NZA, 21 October 1953, KNA, DC KMG 1/4/14/37; Maithya Murya to DC Kitui, 19 November 1958, KNA, DC KTI 3/6/104/77.

6

DISCIPLINE AND RESISTANCE

African soldiers often challenged their subordinate status in the King's African Rifles and, by extension, in colonial society as a whole. This resistance shows up in the historical record as a broad spectrum of disciplinary problems ranging from minor violations of standing orders and regulations to a few mass strikes by entire units during the Second World War. While a certain degree of indiscipline is common to all armies, acts of resistance in the KAR show how askaris attempted to redefine the terms of their service. More significantly, colonial officials worried these incidents undermined the illusion of superiority that enabled a small handful of British officers to lead a body of politically marginal African soldiers.

Contrary to colonial stereotypes, Africans did not join the King's African Rifles to serve the British Empire or "Kingi Georgi." Most askaris enlisted because military service was the most lucrative form of unskilled wage labor in colonial East Africa. Most African soldiers thought of soldiering as prestigious work that entitled them to special consideration from the army and, consequently, the colonial state. As we have seen in previous chapters, they sought to use their status to win better pay and benefits from the army and greater privileges in colonial society. In practice, however, acts of resistance in the East African forces were usually tied to specific complaints over pay, benefits, and working conditions, and askaris usually articulated their demands in terms of labor issues. In recalling their grievances against the colonial army, most African ex-servicemen speak of being unable to negotiate the terms of their service. While the military establishment was often willing to revise African working conditions to improve discipline, the colonial governments insisted that the African soldiery could not be treated substantially better than the general population. Fearing military service would create a privileged class of "detribalized" askaris that would undermine the institutions of indirect rule, civil officials restricted the army's ability to address the grievances of the African rank-and-file.

Chronologically speaking, overt acts of resistance were rarely a problem in peacetime when the demands of colonial soldiering were relatively light and British officers found it relatively easy to maintain control over the small professional KAR battalions. Moreover, the prestige and perquisites of peacetime military service muted African soldiers' dissatisfaction with their subordinate status. On active service (particularly during the Second World War) however, African servicemen expected much greater compensation and objected to their inferior treatment in comparison to other imperial troops. This discontent led to increased disciplinary problems and illustrates the problems that colonial officials faced in trying to prevent African military service from disrupting the racial hierarchy of colonial society.

THE NATURE OF AFRICAN RESISTANCE

Unfortunately it is impossible to determine the full extent of African resistance in the colonial forces. Official records make only passing reference to serious disciplinary lapses. As a result, interviews with former officers and askaris are the only effective method of uncovering acts of day-to-day resistance. This limitation, in turn, means there is very little information on African resistance in the early KAR. We do know that Sudanese askaris in the Uganda Rifles mutinied in 1897 over irregular pay and unreasonable working conditions, and in 1913, the KAR Inspector General warned that African soldiers on Kenya's northern frontier were on the verge of rebellion over similar problems. There are no recorded incidents of serious unrest among African servicemen during the First World War, although Geoffrey Hodges's Carrier Corps informants described a company of askaris in 4 KAR beating an unpopular British Sergeant Major to death.[1] It is quite possible that these sorts of problems were not uncommon, but confirmation is difficult as there are few surviving veterans from this period.

Day-to-day discipline was not a significant problem in the peacetime KAR. Aside from arduous frontier patrols in northern Kenya, military service in the inter-war era was relatively undemanding, and askaris rarely saw combat. Martial recruiting policies weeded out ethnic groups with serious political grievances, and distinctions of rank between British officers and African soldiers disguised the racial inequality inherent in the colonial military. The KAR was a popular employer, and troublemakers were easily replaced. Askaris with complaints about their terms of service either deserted (which was relatively easy) or resorted to covert insubordination and petty crime. These are tactics commonly employed by rank-and-file soldiers of all nationalities, and KAR officers believed the "hard cases" they preferred to enlist were "naturally" inclined to break the rules.

The most serious acts of African resistance in the colonial military took place during the Second World War. The sheer size of the East African forces made it difficult to monitor constantly the activities of all askaris. Wartime manpower needs weakened recruiting safeguards and brought large numbers of men deemed unsuitable for peacetime service into the army. It was also harder to maintain favorable conditions of service when the colonial forces were on active duty. Askaris were separated from their homes and families for long periods of time with little opportunity for leave. Combat was unpleasant and dangerous and, unlike peacetime service, differed substantially from civilian forms of migrant labor. Few askaris were willing to die for "Kingi Georgi," and many became disillusioned after discovering other British imperial soldiers received considerably better pay and benefits. Since all combat soldiers stood an equal chance of dying, askaris wanted compensation commensurate with their risks. Their inferior terms of service exposed the racial inequality in the colonial army, and African soldiers responded by deserting in large numbers. East African units on foreign service experienced a rise in overt insubordination, strikes, and violent attacks on officers.

While serious acts of resistance occurred in every major army during the Second World War, these incidents are significant because they raised questions about the reliability of the African soldiery. Mutinies are always politically embarrassing, but colonial authorities had an added incentive to suppress reports of unrest in the East African forces. The Indian Mutiny drove home the danger of relying on politically marginal soldiers, and British officials were plagued by a subconscious fear that KAR askaris might turn their guns on their masters. Metropolitan British servicemen broke the rules, attacked their officers, and engaged in collective protests, but aside from minor concerns about socialist influences on lower-class soldiers, few officials believed these incidents might lead to a violent challenge to the British government. The East African governments, on the other hand, worried military unrest would undermine settler confidence in the KAR (which was never high to begin with) and, more importantly, would show Africans that the colonial regime was vulnerable.

Yet there is no evidence that any act of resistance by African soldiers had overtly political inspirations. Chapter 4 has shown how askaris used their status to challenge specific colonial policies, but there are no documented cases of serving African soldiers conspiring to overthrow British rule. No KAR battalion was ever formally disarmed in the entire sixty-two-year history of the Regiment. Effective military discipline played an important role, but for the most part, African soldiers were more concerned with issues relating to pay and working conditions than political sovereignty. While racial discrimination in the army led them to question the legitimacy of colonialism, they tended to seek redress within the system. Their strikes and protests were intended to force colonial authorities to grant them the full rights of British soldiers.

INSTRUMENTS OF CONTROL

During peacetime, British officers relied primarily on regulations and informal unit traditions to control African soldiers. As in most modern armies, British officers usually remained aloof from the problems of day-to-day discipline. KAR battalions had a Provost section to handle serious incidents, and during the Second World War, the East Africa Corps of Military Police kept track of African soldiers on leave. Yet discipline in the colonial army was never as strict or rigid as the official histories suggest. In peacetime rural Africa, young British officers in remote outposts commanded platoons of armed men who did not speak English. In such cases, officers relied heavily on bluff and trusted African NCOs to maintain discipline. While their word was absolute in matters relating to political reliability, the limited number of British personnel in each battalion forced them to be very selective about when to exercise their authority over secondary issues. As was the case with the KAR's family polices discussed in Chapter 5, attempts to intervene too extensively into the personal lives of askaris increased the number of petty infractions requiring punishment, which in turn undermined military effectiveness by increasing African discontent. Officers often gave way on minor issues that did not directly affect overall discipline or military readiness.

Thus, African soldiers exerted a strong, but indirect, influence on disciplinary policy. Yet the collision of the army's standards of conduct with African cultural values invariably led to regulatory violations requiring punishment. Military discipline was intended to restructure an askari's lifestyle and behavior, and as one of the Colonial Office's military staff officers observed:

> The code of conduct expected in the British Army is, in essentials, that to which the man has been accustomed from his very birth. His ideas of right and wrong are the national ideas transmitted from generation to generation. The Army discipline tightens the restrictions but does not impose a new code of ethics. Now the African soldier, taken from his tribe, has not the same view of what is right and wrong. Things that are, in his natural state, perfectly moral and right, become under an alien code, wrong; and, vice versa. . . . [H]e may well suffer pains and penalties in his early service which are necessary in order to teach him to adopt the new code and cast away his own.[2]

The KAR's disciplinary regulations were inspired by the nineteenth-century Victorian Army and were based on an official manual of regulations published by the Colonial Office, battalion standing orders, and KAR Ordinances based on the British Army Act. Yet these codes were incomplete and contradictory because each East African territory enacted its own separate KAR Ordinance. The Colonial Office guaranteed their basic consistency, but reform was difficult because each individual government had to approve every change. While the Ordinances were amended occasionally, they were revised only twice: once in 1932 (1933 in some territories) and again in 1958. As a result, discipline in the KAR was often based on antiquated and irrelevant regulations.

Nevertheless, it is possible to set out the basic framework of East African military discipline. Offenses in the KAR fell into two broad categories: serious crimes tried by court-martial and minor infractions dealt with summarily by unit commanders. Court-martials could award capital punishment for murder, rape, treason, mutiny, looting, desertion, or cowardice under fire. Askaris convicted of desertion, insubordination, sleeping at their post, or "disgraceful conduct" were usually discharged or imprisoned at hard labor. One of the most serious non-capital offenses an African soldier could commit was to sell or lose his rifle. Anxious to keep instruments of lethal force out of the hands of African civilians, British officers required askaris to account for their weapons and ammunition at all times. A man convicted of losing a rifle received up to six months' imprisonment at hard labor, and the crime for selling a weapon was two years' imprisonment. Drunkenness, failure to obey orders, and selling non-lethal equipment were lesser court-martial offenses, usually punished by fines and short-term imprisonment.[3]

Commanding officers inflicted summary punishments for violations of minor regulations dealing with punctuality, deference, and standards of hygiene. Sentences varied from imprisonment to fines to punishment drills to extra duties. Formal summary punishment was particularly difficult in remote rural areas, and officers often invented creative "field punishments" for askaris who broke minor rules. In the 1930s, a group of miscreants in Kenya's arid Northern Frontier Province were ordered into the midday sun to dig up a termite hill until they found the queen termite. Then, in what was most likely a display of dominance, their officer ate the queen. In another case, an African Pioneer in the Suez Canal Zone in the 1950s experienced the penalty for failing to observe military time: "I returned late to the barracks without a pass . . . [and so] they threw me naked into a room filled with icy water."[4]

The British Army banned corporal punishment in 1881, but flogging was common in the colonial army until the end of the Second World War. The retention of this Victorian tradition was due partially to institutional inertia but also reflected a widely held bias in colonial military circles that it took harsh measures to turn "primitive" Africans into trained soldiers. Recruits in the early KAR were routinely beaten for training mistakes, and KAR Ordinances allowed up to twenty lashes to be added to any kind of disciplinary sentence.[5] Sir Francis De Guingand offered the following account of a flogging in 1 KAR in the 1920s:

The prisoner would be marched in, and then be stripped. He would then be told to lie down on the floor on his stomach with his legs together and his arms placed under his head. A policeman would be stationed on either side of the prone figure, one holding his feet together and the other his shoulders. A damp rag would be placed over the man's buttocks and the Provost Sergeant would then draw his rattan cane and station himself on one side, opposite the askari's bottom and about a yard or so distant. The object of the wet rag was to prevent the skin being cut. On the order of the Adjutant or Orderly Officer, the lashing would commence, and the 4- or 5- foot cane would be slowly lifted and brought down with a horrible-sounding swish unerringly on the rag. . . . At the end of the ordeal the askari would be ordered to stand to attention and salute. . . . The whole thing was distasteful, but one accepted it as a necessary method of enforcing discipline with these rather primitive people.[6]

Mounting pressure from missionaries and other humanitarian groups forced the Colonial Office to order an unofficial moratorium on summary corporal punishment in 1932, but political opposition from the settler community kept it in the KAR Ordinances.[7]

While this informal ban stood throughout 1930s, during World War II, the military establishment asked the Colonial Office to return the power of summary corporal punishment to field commanders. In 1940, the East Africa Command's Judge Advocate General argued flogging was necessary to transform "several thousand raw African recruits into disciplined soldiers in the field in the shortest time possible." While many younger British officers were repulsed by corporal punishment, a significant number of senior field officers believed it was needed to deal with serious incidents of insubordination.[8] Their request was politically indefensible in wartime Britain, however, and the Colonial Secretary (with the full support of the War Office) ruled out summary corporal punishment.

The announcement by HM Government in this war that coloured British subjects are equally eligible in respect of enlistment and commissions carried with it the inference that coloured British subjects would receive equal consideration in matters of military discipline. A close watch is being kept by certain organizations for any evidence that colour discrimination is being maintained. An extension of powers to inflict flogging on African soldiers will be represented as a breach of this assurance with consequential embarrassment to HM Government.[9]

Nevertheless, many officers ignored this official prohibition and continued to use corporal punishment informally. Colonial military service gave field commanders a great deal of autonomy. In the Northern Rhodesia Regiment, an offender had the choice of a formal charge recorded on his conduct sheet (jeopardizing his chances of receiving a gratuity) or visiting the African Company Sergeant Major for "six of the best." In the latter case, there was no official record of his transgression.[10] Corporal punishment also continued to be used in training, in direct violation of standing orders and regulations. Young Signals trainees convicted of "misdemeanors" were ordered to ask their Regimental Sergeant Major for a beating, and Ugandan recruits in the AAPC complained that men died from the floggings. An askari wrote to his family: "I have already begun to repent [joining the army], it is true our European has nearly killed all of us. . . . A man is beaten daily like an ox."[11]

Moreover, court-martials retained the power to award corporal punishment for serious offenses. In 1943, a controversy erupted in Kenya when missionary leaders objected to the public floggings at Nairobi military bases. Jomo Kenyatta raised the issue in *Kenya: The Land of Conflict*, and in 1944, an embarrassed Colonial Secretary had to explain to the British Parliament why African soldiers were the only imperial troops who were still flogged.[12] Nevertheless, corporal punishment remained a legal punishment until 1946 because colonial military authorities successfully argued that it was still needed to control African solders.[13] Furthermore, a few officers in the post-war army continued to beat their soldiers in spite of the official ban. In 1948, a metropolitan officer assigned to the East Africa Construction Force at MacKinnon Road was sickened by how often local European officers (known as the "Kenya Cowboys") resorted to flogging.[14]

African reactions to military discipline were mixed. Most servicemen were suitably intimidated by the scale of punishment in the peacetime KAR, but like rank-and-file servicemen the world over, they exercised a soldier's time-honored right to circumvent unpopular regulations. Problems arose, however, when discipline was perceived as racial discrimination. The supporters of corporal punishment maintained that askaris did not resent flogging but accepted it as a "man's punishment." African veterans unequivocally dismissed this claim and despised the practice as degrading and humiliating. As one former askari maintained: "Being beaten was an insult. [It] was against our custom and . . . beneath our dignity."[15]

Contrary to official claims that corporal punishment was used for serious crimes, askaris complained many officers used it vindictively. In the early KAR, a soldier was flogged for startling an officer's horse with a brisk salute, and during the Second World War, a man received twelve lashes for pushing a cook into a small kitchen fire. Thus, it was not unusual for askaris to resist corporal punishment violently. A man sentenced to be flogged for sleeping at his post in Burma held his officers at bay with a grenade. Muslim soldiers refused adamantly to submit to corporal punishment, and in 2/3 KAR, a Somali askari committed suicide after being beaten. As a result, Somalis were usually fined instead of flogged, which indicates that African opposition could influence military policy if enough askaris resisted openly a particularly distasteful form of discipline.[16]

The outmoded forms of discipline practiced in the early KAR were of little use in controlling African soldiers recruited during the Second World War. Corporal punishment was politically unacceptable, and British officers had to motivate African servicemen by convincing them it was in their best interests to follow the rules. Moreover, colonial military authorities needed to secure the cooperation of tens of thousands of highly trained African combat soldiers. They therefore took steps to improve African morale and detect early signs of unrest. As the East African Political Liaison Officer (EAPLO), S. H. Fazan, a former Kenyan Provincial Commissioner, warned African soldiers that he was the eyes and ears of their home governments and threatened to report disciplinary problems to their district officers and chiefs. He also listened to the domestic problems of rank-and-file askaris and acted as their advocate in East Africa.[17]

To complement Fazan's activities, the East Africa Command also established a sophisticated propaganda network to motivate African soldiers and encourage proper behavior. Civilian newspapers like *Baraza* in Kenya and *Nkani za Nyasaland* carried detailed reports on the war in Swahili and Chinyanja. The Kenyan Director of Civil Intelligence criticized *Baraza* for publishing letters from African soldiers complaining about conditions in the army, but this made the paper very popular with askaris. A soldier with 6 KAR in Ethiopia wrote: "And now all our faces turn bright whenever news comes from our behind in a paper called 'Baraza.' All those who do not know how to read are being told what is in the Gazette by the other soldiers."[18]

In order to gain greater control over what askaris read, the EAC also published its own newspapers. These included *Habari Zetu* in Ethiopia, *Heshima* and *Ulema* (in Chewa) in Southeast Asia, and *Askari* and *Jambo* in East Africa. *Kwetu Kenya* brought local news to Kenyan askaris in the Middle East and the Indian Ocean "Islands Area." These newspapers reinforced military discipline by acting as a sounding board for askari discontent. *Askari* ran a special feature where soldiers wrote to an "Askari Mzee" (elder soldier) for advice. Their letters were passed to military intelligence officers for investigation, and army newspapers published articles that refuted complaints deemed serious by military authorities.[19]

Similarly, the EAC also censored soldiers' mail. Intelligence officers monitored African correspondence for issues relating to disciplinary problems in the army or political unrest in East Africa. Although the military promised askaris that their letters were censored only to ensure they did not disclose military information unintentionally, the EAC sent censorship reports to territorial governments and unit commanders. In 1941, a Ugandan AAPC askari at Nanyuki, Kenya, wrote to tell his family that he planned to desert. The

EAC's Deputy Censor alerted the man's officers in Nanyuki and recommended the Commissioner of Uganda's Eastern Province ascertain if the letter had caused "disaffection or despondency" in the civilian population.[20] In another case, military censors intercepted a letter from a Luo askari in Ceylon urging his friends to rebel against chiefs who allowed the Kenyan government to appropriate African lands. In response, Fazan interviewed the soldier in question, and the Nyanza Provincial Commissioner was notified when the man received home leave. African soldiers were aware of these policies, however, and developed innovative ways of defeating the censors. They learned to forge censors' stamps, and Pioneers in the Middle East used biblical references to tell their families where they were stationed.[21]

Military authorities also used more sophisticated methods to motivate African servicemen. In 1942, the East Africa Command created a Mobile Propaganda Unit to improve African morale and raise the prestige of military service. It consisted of twenty-eight handpicked askaris, including the youngest Sergeant Major in the EAC (age twenty-two), an East Africa Army Service Corps Sergeant from a seminary in Northern Rhodesia, a driver who was a former "bar boy" in the Belgian Congo, an African Petty Officer from the Tanganyika Naval Volunteer Force, a Nyasaland "star gymnast" recruited from the Rand Mines, an Ngoni "tommy gun expert" who was an ex-house boy, and a fifteen-year-old bugler who enlisted in the KAR at the age of seven. A typical performance by the unit included gymnastic exhibitions "of a spectacular nature," demonstrations of mine detection and unarmed combat, ceremonial drill, and pyrotechnic live-fire displays. African specialists also gave talks on the East Africa Command's technical units, and an African Education Instructor explained British war aims.[22] These performances created a favorable impression of the colonial army, which helped improve the morale and discipline of askaris by increasing their social prestige at home.

The East Africa Army Education Corps also had an important disciplinary role. African Education Instructors taught courses in "co-operation and toleration" to improve race relations and conducted mock trials, which charged Hitler with the German abuse of conquered territories. They made Britain's war aims more comprehensible to illiterate askaris and offered advice on how to deal with the army's complex regulations.[23] Yet education in the colonial forces was a double-edged sword. While it was an innovative method of controlling African soldiers, it also provided an effective means of articulating their grievances. Askaris often learned of their unequal terms of service from European newspapers. In Ceylon, senior commanders blamed disciplinary problems in 11 Division on the influence of the EAAEC:

> No one would question for a moment the ultimate wisdom of [the army's] educational campaign, but there is no doubt that [askaris] remain children at heart and are finding it difficult to digest their newly acquired knowl-

Figure 6.1 Propaganda instruction for East Africa Army Education Instructors, Jeanes School (Command School of Education), Kenya, World War II. Note that the students are mapping the fighting in the Soviet Union. Courtesy of the Trustees of the Imperial War Museum, London (K4952). Reprinted with permission.

edge. Many of them, in turn, have rather lost their heads and are inclined to be unduly touchy and take an exaggerated view of their newly acquired dignity.[24]

Many officers believed education was incompatible with military discipline, and the metropolitan Royal Army Education Corps (RAEC) acquired a reputation for being a "nursery for socialism." Traditionalists in the British Army grumbled that the RAEC's only "battle honor" was the defeat of the Conservative Party in the 1945 elections. Education courses in the colonial forces never covered overtly political topics, but the Command Education Library in Nairobi gave African soldiers free access to books—like Karl Marx's *Das Kapital*—that had been banned by the East African governments.[25]

Military officials therefore tried to recruit politically reliable men for the EAAEC. Even Fazan, who was generally in favor of army education, had misgivings about the influence of Education Instructors.

Even in so simple a matter as explaining to the class how their pay-book balances are kept or how remittances are made, the questions frequently carry an implication that there is fraud somewhere. If the Education NCOs get these questions on duty, those which they get off duty are probably still more pointed and, as the most educated Africans around, they are certain to be asked all sorts of posers about the war, about civil policy at home and about post-war conditions. Their character must be such as to resist the temptation of showing off; they must be adept at turning aside awkward questions; their loyalty must be beyond question and an example to others.[26]

To address these concerns, the East Africa Command went to great length to ensure that African Education Instructors were subject to military discipline. They received combat training, and the motto of the EAAEC was "first a man, secondly a soldier, thirdly an education instructor." In Southeast Asia, EAAEC personnel were not allowed to conduct classes, and many were posted to the intelligence sections of rifle companies.[27] In spite of these precautions, African education personnel had a huge amount of influence in the East African forces. Some teachers were sacked for engaging in "political agitation," and Kamba veterans credit Paul Ngei, an instructor who taught Swahili to British officers, with initiating them into politics.[28]

As elements of the African soldiery grew more politically aware, the East Africa Command developed sophisticated intelligence systems to monitor their activities. During the Second World War, L.S.B. Leakey directed a network of Kenyan "Voluntary Native Intelligence Agents" who listened to askaris in bars and public places while they were home on leave.[29] In Southeast Asia, the 5th (East African) Field Security Section (FSS) monitored African soldiers in 11 Division. The unit was composed of twenty-eight askaris under the direction of British intelligence officers. African members of 5 FSS posed as rank-and-file askaris to infiltrate a company of striking engineers and circulated through the East African Leave Camp at Ranchi, India, to gather information on unsanctioned prostitution and the sexual assault of a female European missionary.[30]

The East Africa Command disbanded 5 FSS at the end of the war but created a new 277 FSS in 1947 to detect "subversive activity directed at African troops." The unit's African NCOs conducted security checks and assisted civil intelligence officers in monitoring "subversive" organizations. Most significantly, they had official permission to wear civilian clothing while conducting their investigations.[31] Although 277 FSS was probably quite active during the Mau Mau Emergency, the extent of their operations cannot be known because military intelligence records from this period are unavailable.

In 1957, the East African Land Forces Organization disbanded 277 FSS as an economy measure. One year later, however, most of the African intelligence personnel were rehired for a special civilian Counter Intelligence Unit under the command of an officer from the Kenyan Special Branch. Africans of the Counter Intelligence Unit, wearing the uniforms of 92 Motor Transport Company and 1 Signal Squadron, again mingled with rank-and-file askaris to check for signs of dissent. Between January 1960 and March 1962, they carried out 470 security checks, thirty-nine security surveys of KAR battalions, and seven "special counter intelligence and security investigations" and cooperated with two special investigations by the Kenya Police.[32] It is impossible to determine if the Counter Intelligence Unit uncovered legitimate security threats because the results of their investigations have not been released by the British government. Nevertheless, the unit provided psychological reassurance to anxious colonial authorities who worried about unrest in the KAR during the final years of British rule.

GRIEVANCES OF THE RANK-AND-FILE

Many African veterans of the Second World War vividly recall their shock and anger at realizing how little they were paid in comparison to other British imperial soldiers. At the insistence of the colonial governments, the pay of the East African Auxiliary Pioneer Corps companies in the Middle East was set only slightly higher than civilian labor rates in East Africa. East Africans received an average of eight shillings a month less than Pioneers from West and South Africa, despite doing exactly the same work. Few askaris were satisfied with the civil authorities' explanation that they were paid twice as much as unskilled civilians back home. In 1943, the men of a Motor Transport Company in the Levant passed a petition to Fazan demanding the same pay as Europeans and Indians.

> [If] a soldier is in a foreign country or say, far from his land, his affairs and mode of living are entirely different from those of a native soldier. If he was getting twenty shillings in his native land, he should get forty shillings in a foreign country to meet the difficulties created by his being far from [home]. . . . If one offers himself to become his Majesty's soldier and agrees to his Government that he is prepared to meet his death if necessary, is it right that this man should be treated like a slave?[33]

The disparity between African and European pay was even greater in Southeast Asia. The East African governments paid askaris serving overseas a two-shilling "Expatriation Allowance," but rank-and-file British soldiers received a "War Service Increment," a "Japanese Campaign Allowance," and a "Far

East Allowance," all of which amounted to a fifty percent increase in their wages. Most askaris believed, with considerable justification, that they deserved the same bonuses. As a result, army chaplains and visiting chiefs warned that discriminatory pay rates could lead to serious unrest in the East African units.[34]

Military officials did not have the authority to unilaterally raise African wages without the consent of the colonial governments but tried to at least create the appearance of an equitable pay scale. They granted the East African Pioneers KAR pay levels, and Pioneers from the West African and South African High Commission Territory companies were required to send home larger family remittances. By 1943, all Africans received the same wages in the Middle East, but East African Privates sent home ten shillings per month, whereas their peers remitted forty-five shillings. Military authorities in Southeast Asia also raised the East African Expatriation Allowance to fifteen shillings in March 1945.[35] They realized that it was politically embarrassing and even dangerous to make blatant racial distinctions in pay for men facing the same risks and wearing the same uniform.

African anger over racial discrimination during the war covered virtually every aspect of military service. Askaris complained Europeans and Indians received better rations and uniforms, and men in KAR garrison battalions realized that even Italian POWs lived better than they did. African soldiers protested the army's refusal to commission African officers and questioned why African Americans were allowed to volunteer for the air force while they could not. Other soldiers noticed that press reports extolling Britain's victories in Ethiopia and North Africa made little mention of East Africans. A Kikuyu soldier asked: "We all know that after the 1914 War, when a white soldier was blinded he was looked after, whereas when a native soldier was blinded he was left to starve. Is it going to be the same after this war?"[36]

As a result, many askaris developed a profound distrust of the colonial military. Uneducated askaris had a great deal of difficulty making sense of the army's complex bureaucracy, and many of the strikes in African units during the war were due to misunderstandings and rumors. For example, it was common practice to fingerprint British soldiers to allow for easy identification of casualties, but in the KAR, a fingerprint took the place of a signature on an illiterate askari's attestation form. African soldiers in Ceylon therefore suspected the army was trying to trick them into enlisting for a longer term of service by fingerprinting their entire hand. British officers were reluctant to explain the real purpose of the fingerprinting because they did not want to give the impression they expected their men to become casualties.[37] Thus, even when military authorities established policies that were in the best interests of African soldiers, askaris often perceived them as further examples of deceit and discrimination.

The army's restrictive leave policies further compounded the problem. As with civilian labor migrants, askaris retained strong ties to their rural homes because the civil authorities' policy of "retribalization" prevented them from settling in urban areas. While this strategy had the advantage of transferring the cost of supporting aged soldiers to rural society, it undermined military efficiency because askaris expected to return home more often than European troops. Infrequent leave increased the social isolation of African soldiers, but morale fell precipitously when men became concerned about the security of their land, herds, and families. Moreover, African servicemen also needed regular leave to attend circumcision, marriage, and burial ceremonies. Although askaris considered themselves a privileged class of government servants, they expected the same rights as civil labor migrants and did not accept the argument that irregular family contacts were part of their job. As one veteran recalled: "It was a great hardship to be away from home for so long. . . . I could not find a wife in the army and I was worried that my uncle would take my land."[38]

Africans were largely denied leave during the First World War. It was out of the question for conscripted carriers, and the poor transportation system in German East Africa made it impractical to release frontline KAR askaris. Furthermore, when the KAR introduced an experimental leave plan in the summer of 1918, large numbers of soldiers deserted.[39] During the inter-war era the situation improved only slightly. Askaris received three months of leave after completing a three-year term of service, but many soldiers considered this much too long to be away from home. This dissatisfaction contributed to recruiting problems in Nyasaland, where civil labor migrants routinely received annual home leave.[40]

Long-serving professional askaris learned to adapt to infrequent home visits in the peacetime KAR, but problems arose during the Second World War, when the expanded recruiting program enlisted Africans who were far less willing to be away from home for long periods of time. Conversely, many wartime officers had little knowledge of East African society and could not understand why Africans should get leave when the privilege was denied to British soldiers. They believed askaris needed constant military discipline to prevent them from forgetting their training. Thus, African leave periods during the war were shortened from three months to fourteen days, and only five percent of a unit could be on leave at one time.[41] Most African servicemen considered two weeks insufficient time to attend to their personal affairs, particularly those involving marital and legal matters. In Kenya's Rift Valley Province, young Nandi askaris needed far more time to complete the circumcision ceremonies that marked their formal transition to manhood.

Yet colonial military authorities initially rejected appeals for extended leave on the grounds the war effort came before the personal needs of African soldiers. Their refusal led to high desertion rates, which eventually forced the East Africa Command to allow askaris serving in East Africa the choice of twenty days of leave per year or forty days every two years.[42] This was a substantial improvement but applied only to units under the direct control of the EAC; askaris serving overseas often received no leave at all. The inadequate and often non-existent leave programs for East Africans in the Middle East and Southeast Asia were a significant cause of soldiers' strikes and protests. As a result, the EAC generally allowed African soldiers twenty-eight days of home leave every year in the post-war era.[43] Insufficient leave was one of the most volatile problems in the KAR, and military authorities learned it was often better to accommodate African demands surreptitiously rather than to attempt to force askaris to endure a protracted absence from home.

INDIVIDUAL RESISTANCE

The privileged status of African soldiers, coupled with the army's internal security measures, limited the ability of askaris to organize themselves collectively to express their grievances. Yet as Bill Freund has pointed out in the case of civilian African workers, individual acts of labor resistance can take many forms, including theft, drug and alcohol abuse, sabotage, and desertion.[44] African soldiers were certainly less respectful than commonly portrayed in official histories. African veterans recall mocking officers with imitations and unflattering nicknames. An officer with an exceptionally long neck was "Captain *Twiga*" (Giraffe), whereas another grumpy officer was *Kunguru* (a carrion crow).[45] Most officers appear to have been relatively oblivious to this lack of deference. Those who were aware of it either ignored it or accepted it as good-natured teasing, which it sometimes was. Gerald Hanley observed:

> The mimicry of Nyasas is something to see and hear. At night, when you lie in your blanket, you will hear a familiar sound. It is the sound of a voice, and there may be laughter accompanying it. After a time you realise it is a perfect imitation of your own voice, and you are able to listen to yourself, or the nearest approach possible. . . . The irascible type of officer is imitated with great glee, and you have to laugh, for mixed in the general impression of the officer's rage is the waggish humour of the Nyasa. There is no harm in this.[46]

Yet African soldiers could also be openly defiant, and interviews and KAR disciplinary records reveal many incidents of insubordination over discipline and working conditions. As one veteran explained: "I was demoted to Private . . . because I [challenged] an officer who tried to discipline me for not using the urinals." Lacking a satisfactory means of negotiating their terms of

service, several veterans became defiant when given unreasonable assignments: "I was in the guard house for two months because I threatened to
shoot Sergant Ogolla [after] he ordered me to work the day and night shifts
... with no chance to rest."[47] In other cases, however, askaris psychologically unequipped to cope with excessive abuse committed suicide when subjected to racial taunts by British personnel. During the Second World War, a
few hanged themselves or took their lives with their own rifles. The East
Africa Command did not keep detailed statistics on suicide, and it is therefore impossible to determine if askaris were more likely to take their own
lives than other imperial troops, but medical officers in the Middle East believed they were.[48]

Crime was another common expression of African dissatisfaction. Askaris
unhappy with their wages found innovative ways to wring more money out
of the army. A common tactic was to forge military documents and pay books
to get more money and extra leave. This usually took the form of crude attempts to add zeros and move decimal places, but during the Second World
War, African soldiers and their civilian accomplices made off with thousands
of shillings. They stole pre-signed forms and skillfully altered documents to
invent fictitious units and British commanders. Most commonly a soldier or
a civilian in military uniform presented district officers with forged or stolen
pay books and Last Pay Certificates. In Kenya's Central Province, a man
posing as a KAR Sergeant Major conned civil officials in Kiambu and Fort
Hall out of 8,800 shillings. Military authorities tried to discourage forgery
by using fingerprints for identification and warned askaris that fraud would
be detected because the East Africa Command kept their master pay records
in a special ledger in Nairobi.[49]

Many askaris augmented their pay by selling parts of their uniforms
and equipment. Under civil law, it was illegal for non-soldiers to possess
such accoutrements, and the civil police searched African settlements
regularly to confiscate military material. Uniforms had considerable value
in rural East Africa, and askaris could easily sell parts of their kit for
more money than the fines the army would impose for the lost items.
Contraband uniforms allowed civilians to masquerade as soldiers, and
military greatcoats were very useful in the cool East African highlands.
In December 1943, a sweep through Kenya's Nyeri District seized 305
greatcoats, 442 blankets, 163 pairs of boots, forty-eight shirts, forty-seven
hats, forty-three pairs of socks, twenty-seven jerseys, twelve pairs of
puttees, ten pairs of trousers, ten belts, nine water bottles, eight pairs of
shorts, and five haversacks. Many civilians bought army clothing from
soldiers without knowing it was illegal, and the Kenyan government even
allowed European merchants to sell surplus military material in the "native reserves."[50] Military policemen inspected askaris on leave for unauthorized goods, and African soldiers resented the embarrassment of being

searched in front of their families. Most believed they had legitimately purchased the equipment by paying the army's fines.[51]

While the military's strict control of weaponry usually made it difficult and dangerous for African soldiers to lose their rifles, askaris found ways to surreptitiously sell their ammunition. This was a particularly serious problem at the EAC's Command Ammunition Depot at Gilgil, Kenya. In the late 1940s, audits discovered a shortfall of over 280,000 rounds of rifle ammunition, while over 11,000 rounds of ammunition disappeared from 4 KAR's base at Jinja, Uganda, during the same period. Almost 30,000 rounds of the stolen Kenyan ammunition were recovered in the Kikuyu Reserves, and a great deal of the remaining bullets probably found their way into the hands of the Mau Mau guerrillas in the early 1950s.[52]

Desertion was only a minor problem in the peacetime KAR because most African soldiers were volunteers and had accepted grudgingly long-term separation from their rural homes. Domestic hardship was less of an issue as well, because, as discussed in Chapter 5, askaris were able to move their families into the barracks. During the inter-war period, most KAR battalions reported desertion rates of less than one percent of total strength, and in many years, there were no desertions at all.[53] Desertion increased substantially during the Second World War, when many askaris were conscripted and overseas service made home leave difficult. In 1944, the East Africa Command reported a total of 11,921 deserters, and by 1945, the number rose to over 14,000.[54] This was an enormous loss of manpower at a time when the EAC desperately needed replacements for the East African forces in Burma. Therefore military authorities put pressure on civil officials to round up the missing askaris. British officers attributed these problems to "war weariness," but high desertion rates were due primarily to African soldiers' unwillingness to incur the hardship of serving overseas. As one veteran put it: "My parents never wanted me to be an askari. . . . I never would have volunteered had I known they would make me go to *ng'ambo* [abroad, or literally, the farther side of a body of water]."[55]

When desertion was impossible, askaris invented physical and mental afflictions to secure a medical discharge. During the Second World War, there was a substantial increase in non-combat-related hospital admissions, and military censors intercepted letters from African soldiers admitting to faking injuries because they were tired of army life.[56] Servicemen's mental records reveal cases of delusions, facial ticks, and partial paralysis, which seemed to manifest themselves only in the presence of Europeans. The number of such cases peaked in 1944 and then dropped off markedly in the summer of 1945, when it became apparent that the war would soon be over.[57] Soldiers of all nationalities used similar tactics to secure medical discharges, but unlike other wartime armies, there were few reported incidents of Africans using self-inflicted wounds to escape the army.

African soldiers also concocted fictitious domestic problems to qualify for compassionate leave. Military censors often intercepted letters from servicemen asking relatives to invent family emergencies. A Nyasaland askari wrote to his mother:

> I am tired of being a soldier, and I want you to carry out a plan for me. . . . Go to the District Commissioner at the Boma and say to him, "My children are all dead, there remains only one and he is a soldier, and we are left with girls only. What shall I do?" These words will bring me luck. Do not be afraid, do this quickly; I am very tired indeed. Try this plan my relatives.[58]

Nyasalanders also purchased special medicines and charms that were believed to force civilian labor migrants to return home. In other cases, unmarried African soldiers invented destitute wives or pretended healthy family members had suddenly fallen ill. Soldiers also played on the ignorance of British officers by concocting phony "rituals" that required their presence. One man claimed "tribal obligations" required him to cut the grass on his brother's grave.[59]

Askaris fortunate enough to receive leave often refused to report to their units until they concluded their domestic affairs. A soldier might delay his return to rebuild his hut, plow his fields, or bring a matter before an African Tribunal. As one former askari recalled: "The army never understood that we had our own lives. . . . If a man didn't look after his own affairs, no one else would." In the Kamba Reserves, Leakey's intelligence agents found servicemen stayed to impregnate their wives or to enjoy their popularity with young women if they were single.[60] The army termed these men "absentees" instead of deserters on the grounds they eventually intended to return to their units. Military authorities were reluctant to charge a soldier with desertion because it required formal disciplinary action, usually resulting in the askari's imprisonment and discharge. Absenteeism was a much less serious offense, and a convicted serviceman returned to duty after serving a relatively minor sentence.

Nevertheless, colonial officials often resorted to draconian tactics to round up deserters as the EAC's civil ban on recruiting created a severe manpower shortage in the final years of the war. With the tacit acquiescence of the East Africa Command, some units used flogging to punish absentees. African chiefs seized the cattle of deserters, and the EAC stopped the family remittance payments of any askari who overstayed his leave.[61] Askaris, in turn, used a variety of tactics to thwart civil and military efforts to return them to the army. They fled across territorial borders into other British territories or, in the case of Nyasalanders, into Portuguese East Africa. Many Kenyan deserters found refuge on European farms where settlers were not overly concerned with the backgrounds of their agricultural laborers. African soldiers resented the army's excessive force in arresting absentees, and in Nyasaland, askaris spread rumors that military policemen kidnapped people to extract their blood and brains to make quinine.[62] Deserters in Kenya occasionally banded together to battle the police and rescue comrades from civil jails. In Kitui District, many absentees become *shifta* (armed bandits) and the District Commissioner of Elgeyo-Marakwet complained his "tribal policemen" were afraid to confront renegade askaris. Many servicemen believed they had every right to withdraw from an unfair system: "I ran away after I feel asleep on guard for a second time. . . . If I had stayed [they] would have killed me." Some deserters even tried to recover back pay and service gratuities once the war was over.[63]

In the colonial army itself, British authorities suppressed most accounts of overt and violent African resistance because they threatened the cornerstones of military discipline in the East African forces: European status and prestige. The KAR's tiny British officer corps believed its authority over the African soldiery depended on the illusion of its superiority and invincibility. In their eyes, African soldiers were reliable only if they were convinced it was futile to defy military authority.

Nevertheless, court-martial records reveal it was not unusual for Africans to be disciplined for striking an officer. Many recall fighting with British officers over incidents ranging from refusal to go overseas to dealing with a drunk officer while on guard duty. One ex-serviceman beat an abusive Lieutenant: "He bullied me and challenged me to fight . . . but I was never [punished] because he chose to make the fight." Another veteran threatened a Captain with a grenade after the officer, concerned with the safety of the unit, smacked a cigarette from his mouth on a jungle patrol in Burma.[64] These incidents were not necessarily motivated directly by racial animosity. Since the day-to-day imposition of military discipline usually fell to African NCOs, they often bore the brunt of soldiers' grievances. African veterans fought NCOs who mistreated them, and one ex-serviceman "disciplined" a Somali Sergeant for discriminating against Africans. Another veteran recalls that he "properly beat Sergeant Musau for his abusiveness . . . until the [Regimental Sergeant Major] stepped in to rescue him." Ex-servicemen who served in Malaya recall how an unpopular Meru Regimental Police Sergeant in 3 KAR was murdered by askaris who set him on fire while he was passed out in a drunken stupor.[65]

Most fatal assaults on officers took place during the Second World War. Short of treason, the murder of a superior officer is the most serious crime a soldier can commit, and violent attacks were rarely reported in the press or official histories. African veterans, however, claim such incidents were quite common, particularly overseas. As one former askari maintained: "We had a particularly cruel Lieutenant [whom] we beat and kicked . . . until he was dead." In Ceylon, an African military policeman (the only askaris to carry live ammunition regularly) "laboring under a sense of grievance" murdered his commander and wounded two British NCOs.[66] These attacks continued in Southeast Asia, where certain African soldiers responded violently to grievances over racial discrimination and the tensions of combat. In some cases, askaris charged with relatively minor disciplinary offenses attacked British personnel. An officer with 1 Northern Rhodesia Regiment was murdered in the mess, and askaris from 5 KAR left live grenades in the tents of unpopular officers and African NCOs.[67] On the whole, court-martial records reveal that thirty-eight East Africans in Southeast Asia were tried for "violence to a superior" between August 1944 and October 1945.[68]

The murder of British officers under the cover of combat (known as "fragging" by American soldiers in the Vietnam War) is even more difficult to document. Official military histories make no mention of such incidents, and many former British officers are uncomfortable discussing them. Some African veterans, on the other hand, readily tell detailed stories about killing unpopular or cowardly officers in the heat of battle. A number of ex-servicemen assert that the Burmese town of Kalewa was captured by an all-black unit: "We killed all the Boers [incompetent officers] except the Quartermaster who wasn't as bad. . . . [W]e were led by our own officers when we took Kalewa." By their account, British officers did not paint themselves black to avoid Japanese snipers but to protect themselves from being killed by African soldiers. African veterans describe raising a black flag along with the Union Jack after the battle for Kalewa and claim to have been decorated by an American general named "Box," who promised they would never again be led by white officers. "Box" was actually a nickname for the British commander of 11 Division, Major General C. C. Fowkes. His transformation into an American most likely reflects the widespread hope among askaris that Americans (particularly African Americans) would rescue them from colonial rule. As for the consequences of their actions, another veteran recalls that "we worried that [the British] would take their revenge when we returned home. . . . [W]e wouldn't board the ships until [we] received word our friends had arrived safely."[69]

While a great deal of this account was clearly inaccurate because many of the officers who fought in the battle for Kalewa survive to this day, there are elements of truth in these African stories of resistance. In 1942, an East African brigade in Eritrea struck to protest the order to deploy overseas, and a battalion commander received the following anonymous note from his soldiers: "If we go to war again we ourselves will shoot you. This is no lie. . . .

We know that you are all completely bad and, if God so wills it, we hope the enemy defeat you."[70] In Burma, an African soldier confessed to the murder of a British NCO originally believed killed by the Japanese, and in one of the most infamous incidents of "fragging" in Southeast Asia, a Nyasaland askari killed or wounded most of the British leadership of "D" Company, 13 KAR with a well-placed grenade.[71] Censorship reports of letters written by British personnel in the SEAC reveal they were well aware of such incidents, and by the end of 1944, intelligence officers warned of increasing racial friction in the East African forces. In a letter intercepted by military censors, a British NCO wrote: "These wogs don't help cheer one up much, as today we have buried one of the lads owing to his head having been smashed by one of them. . . . He will have his firing party very shortly which is a little consolation for us."[72] Similarly, when the Maasai Education Instructor who led the protests against substandard uniforms in Malaya (see Chapter 4) was threatened with a court-martial, "the Samburu askaris of the battalion promised me they would take care of any officers who gave me trouble on the next jungle patrol."[73]

While the evidence for serious unrest in the colonial military is compelling, on the whole, these were relatively infrequent occurrences. It is difficult to determine the extent to which accounts of violent resistance have been inflated over time. Allowing for the official suppression of reports on these assaults, if even a fraction of the stories were true, the British officer corps in Southeast Asia would have been decimated. Moreover, the majority of African veterans of the Burma Campaign make no mention of attacking their officers and are proud of their stoic endurance of difficult jungle fighting. In modern East Africa, stories of shooting an officer enhance the nationalist credentials of former colonial soldiers. Yet most convicted murderers were executed by African firing squads. While some officers feared askaris would not shoot a fellow African, there was never a recorded case of a soldier refusing to serve on an execution detail.[74]

Nevertheless, the small handful of violent assaults in the colonial military are significant. Contrary to official histories, they demonstrate that individual African soldiers were willing and able to use force to contest military discipline. The assaults created a crisis of confidence in colonial military circles, and British officers preferred to interpret such incidents as aberrations. Official reports described murderers as mentally unbalanced or under the influence of alcohol or *bhang* (cannabis).[75] Yet violent soldiers were also often described as "laboring under a sense of grievance," and these incidents should be seen primarily as an extreme extension of the passive forms of protest used by African soldiers. There are few satisfactory explanations for why an individual resorts to violence, but in this case, the violent acts committed by African soldiers appear to have, at least in part, constituted a rejection of racial inequality in the colonial military.

COLLECTIVE PROTESTS DURING THE
SECOND WORLD WAR, 1939–1945

African soldiers resorted to collective action to protest pay and working conditions but rarely articulated their grievances in an overtly political manner. Yet most collective protests stemmed ultimately from anger over the subordinate position of Africans in colonial society. By opposing discriminatory treatment, African soldiers mounted an indirect assault on the East African color bar. Their collective protests were tangible expressions of anti-colonial resistance by men who lacked the means to challenge the colonial regime directly. Military authorities, on the other hand, rarely acknowledged that collective resistance had political undertones. They used terms like "collective insubordination" and "strikes" to describe organized protests by rank-and-file Africans, which allowed a measure of flexibility in confronting large-scale resistance. A handful of insubordinate askaris were easily court-martialed for mutiny, but it would have been impractical and politically embarrassing to charge an entire battalion with the same crime. In these cases, it was easier to label a non-violent collective protest by a large number of African soldiers as "collective insubordination." By implying askaris had not openly defied military authority, officers could compromise surreptitiously on non-political matters not directly affecting the overall reliability of the colonial forces.

The most serious incidents of collective resistance took place during the Second World War, when the size of the East African forces did not permit a high degree of control over African soldiers. Such protests were rare during peacetime because the relatively privileged status of the African soldiery obscured the subordinate status of Africans in colonial society. Moreover, collective action required a degree of coordination that was largely impossible when the size of the peacetime KAR allowed officers to keep a closer watch on their men. Any askaris attempting to organize full-scale protests would have been easily discovered and individual ringleaders prosecuted as mutineers. Therefore during peacetime, African servicemen relied on individual resistance to circumvent unpopular rules and protest inequitable working conditions. Yet conventional strikes were also difficult during wartime. African servicemen tended to distrust fellow soldiers from different territories and ethnic groups, and men in combat and specialist units looked down on military laborers. As a result, collective protests were usually spontaneous actions in which common grievances temporarily transcended barriers dividing the African soldiery.

There were no organized armed uprisings by African servicemen in the KAR. The largest and most openly defiant act of non-violent collective resistance by combat askaris in the Second World War took place after the liberation of Ethiopia. In February 1942, an entire East African infantry brigade at Massawa, Eritrea, refused to board ships for Ceylon. Most of the men of 25 Brigade (composed of 2/3, 2/4, and 3/4 KAR) had served for more than two years without leave. They took General Platt's statement that they would have "a short rest before more campaigning" as a promise they would be allowed to return home. Illiterate askaris had lost touch with their families and were troubled by rumors of adulterous behavior by their wives. In 2/3 KAR, many young Nandi soldiers needed to undergo circumcision ceremonies. These soldiers understood that an overseas assignment would postpone indefinitely their chances for home leave. Platt was aware of these problems, but the War Office turned down his request for embarkation leave for the Brigade. Nevertheless, the East Africa Command unwisely allowed British officers to fly to Nairobi for a brief rest, and most of the Brigade's African soldiers considered this privilege hypocritical and unjust.[76]

Hubert Moyse-Bartlett, the official historian of the KAR, has claimed askaris accepted overseas service "philosophically." In reality, civil intelligence officers were greatly concerned about the "discontented state" of African soldiers after the end of the Ethiopian Campaign. On 29 January 1942, an anonymous letter left in the orderly room of 2/3 KAR protested the planned deployment of the battalion to Ceylon:

> The Government want to send us to a war a long way away which has nothing to do with us as our war is over. Now our pay is very small, only 28 shillings. You will realize that it is extremely small for a distant land like that. You appear to think that we black men are like dogs but all of us (black and white) are subjects of God. We cannot refuse to obey your orders, and if you force us we will go, but we will surrender ourselves when we meet the enemy because here our existence is like that of a prisoner.[77]

These tensions came to a head on 15 February 1942 when the askaris of 25 Brigade refused to go overseas to fight the "Bwanas' war." They insisted they were promised leave at the end of the fighting with the Italians and had not been warned they would ever have to leave Africa. While the original tone of their protest was respectful, discipline faltered when it became apparent that British officers could do little to end the strike. Soldiers broke out of camp to look for women and drink in nearby Eritrean towns, and a football match intended to defuse tensions between officers and men in 2/4 KAR was attended by only six askaris. Incidents of overt insubordination increased, and there were a few minor assaults on officers.[78]

The askaris of 25 Brigade succeeded in their protest because they were protected by their numbers. It was impossible to arrest several thousand soldiers, and attempts to disarm the Brigade would have been a propaganda disaster. Colonial military authorities had no choice but to grant leave. As an officer with 3/4 KAR put it: "I submit leave parties MUST continue, the old slogan 'leave is a privilege and not a right' means nothing to the African, especially as a large number of officers went on leave soon after we arrived at this station."[79] In March 1942, the Brigade began to send leave parties to East Africa. Askaris insisted on going by truck on the long overland route to Kenya because they feared transport ships might take them to Asia. As one veteran recalled: "Once a ship is at sea, who knows where it will go." Yet although the army gave in to the soldiers' demands, military intelligence officers still went to considerable lengths to identify the leaders of the strike. Reports indicated that protests began in the Kenyan 2/3 KAR, but military authorities determined the "ringleaders" of the protest were Ganda and Kikuyu askaris in transport units. Many of these soldiers were surreptitiously court-martialed after the majority of the Brigade received leave, and at least one man was flogged.[80]

The scope and effectiveness of 25 Brigade's collective protest unnerved British officials. While the official history of the KAR makes only passing reference to the strike, the colonial military establishment worried news of the incident would undermine the reliability of all East African soldiers. One of the staff officers in the Colonial Office minuted: "This is indeed a tragedy, and it is hard to see what can be done to lessen the harm. The news will fly round East Africa and African morale, both military and civilian, will be badly shaken." He even raised the possibility of firing Platt to provide African soldiers with a "scapegoat."[81] The Kenyan government was equally perturbed and feared the strike might lead to civil unrest in the "native reserves." Civil officials therefore demanded "drastic" punishment for the "ringleaders." They suppressed all reports of the incident and warned askaris not to discuss the matter on leave. District officers also made arrangements to "discredit [the strikers] before their fellow tribesmen."[82]

In reality, however, there were few long-term consequences of the strike. To be sure, the intensity of the rhetoric used by a few African soldiers did have political overtones. A Luo askari in 2/3 KAR declared:

> You Europeans say you help us. But do you? It is us black men who help you. We have not got an Empire to defend. You have. But if the Italians had come into Kenya they would not have done any harm to us natives or our property.[83]

Nevertheless, the strike was primarily a labor protest against unfair working conditions and came to a swift conclusion once African soldiers received leave. The surreptitious court-martial of the ringleaders removed the men who had articulated collective grievances in political terms. District officers in Kenya monitored carefully the activities of askaris home on leave and concluded the incident would quickly be forgotten, as none of the men continued to "nurse a grievance." Moreover, few soldiers from the Brigade deserted, and British officers noticed an overall improvement in morale and discipline after their men returned.[84] Of the Brigade's three battalions, 3/4 KAR was eventually sent to Burma as part of 11 Division.

Colonial military authorities tried to take these lessons to heart. In 1943, General Platt successfully lobbied the War Office to reallocate shipping space to allow askaris training in Ceylon to have leave before going to Southeast Asia. The East Africa Command ordered officers to avoid making any statement that could be construed as a promise of leave and did its best to standardize European and African leave policies.[85] Yet logistical problems made it next to impossible for askaris to receive home leave once they were in India and Burma. Space on return shipping from Southeast Asia was extremely scarce, and even a slow trickle of askaris would have left unacceptable manpower gaps in their units. Rotating entire battalions between East Africa and Southeast Asia was a possibility, but the EAC had devoted so much of its manpower and resources to raising an entire East African Division that it did not have enough battle-ready units for such an exchange.[86] Imperial manpower shortages in Asia ruled out the wholesale withdrawal of the East African forces; therefore, African soldiers had little prospect of going home until Japan surrendered.

Increased surveillance of African soldiers ensured there were no further collective protests on the scale of 25 Brigade's strike, but askaris grew more sensitive to inequitable terms of service the longer they remained overseas. The East African forces performed well in Burma in the summer of 1944, but most incidents of unrest and violence toward officers occurred later in the year, when askaris realized there was little prospect of a quick return home. Many soldiers lacked an accurate understanding of the objectives of the Burma Campaign and believed that the capture of Kalewa would mark the end of their role in the fighting. When this did not happen, discipline broke down. The East African specialist units, composed largely of better-educated askaris, were particularly prone to "collective insubordination." In January 1945, thirty Luo askaris in 54 Field Company were arrested for breaking a comrade out of jail. In another case, the entire 2004 Stretcher Bearer Company was disarmed and demoted to military laborers after an angry mob of soldiers surrounded their officers' mess to protest the death of a fellow askari who had hanged himself in detention.[87] Friction over military discipline sparked most of these incidents, but they also reflected East African soldiers' growing impatience with service in Southeast Asia.

Yet there was little individual unit commanders could do to get their men leave. African soldiers were eligible for local furlough, but few had any interest in the military leave camps in India. They feared local leave would count as home leave, and officers worried their men would be "got at" in the camps by subversives and malcontents from other units. A senior staff officer with 11 Division warned that leave issues were at the root of the unit's problems and summed up the attitude of the unit's African soldiers this way:

The majority do not expect to be sent back yet, though all would like it, but they do want some definite statement telling them how much longer they are to go on serving in a strange and unpleasant land far from their homes and families, in making war against a fierce and competent foe under an ever-changing series of officers and BNCOs [British non-commissioned officers] whom they do not know, and do not know them.[88]

General Sir William Slim, the commander of the 14th Army, warned the Southeast Asia Command that the effectiveness of 11 Division depended on a comprehensive leave plan for African soldiers. As a result, the SEAC granted home leave to 500 askaris in March 1945, with drafts of two thousand men to follow every two months. The plan called for disbanding entire battalions to create replacements for the missing men because substitute units from East Africa would not be ready until late 1945. Thus, despite logistical constraints, military authorities eventually had to accede to African demands for home leave. While collective protests in Southeast Asia were not as organized or coordinated as the strike by 25 Brigade, the end result was the same: African soldiers gained redress by banding together to protest unfair terms of service.[89]

Military laborers were even more prone to collective protests. While askaris in frontline units complained of poor treatment in comparison to Indian and European soldiers, askaris in the East African Pioneer Battalions, East Africa Military Labour Service, and the African Auxiliary Pioneer Corps also resented their inferior status as workers. Chapter 3 has shown how military laborers received low pay and substandard benefits and were often belittled by combat soldiers. Many also complained unarmed status made them less appealing to women. Labor askaris demanded the same privileges accorded to frontline soldiers and were especially intolerant of terms of service which reinforced their lesser status.

The 1st (EA) Pioneer Battalion's strike at Garba Tulla in northern Kenya was inspired by grievances over the unit's mission and lack of prestige. In recruiting the battalion, S. H. Fazan, then the Provincial Commissioner of Nyanza Province, promised Luo askaris they would receive full military training. Both military and civil officials, however, treated them as a "dressed up Public Works Department gang." As Michael Blundell, who took command of the battalion after the strike, noted: "[T]hey had been poorly equipped though in a forward area, many had no rifles, they were under establishment in officers, who treated them as labourers and not soldiers, and worst of all they were distinguished from combatant troops by a ridiculous sort of porkpie hat with a flap down the back."[90]

When the Pioneers were asked to retake their oath of enlistment to conform to the Military Units Ordinance in late 1939, Sudanese NCOs spread rumors the Pioneers were being tricked into accepting even harsher working conditions. On 30 December 1939, five hundred men refused to undertake any further road construction work. Although the protest was generally peaceful, the army called in Nyasalanders from 1 KAR armed with ax handles to put down the strike. Seventy Pioneers were hospitalized with head injuries, and two subsequently died.[91] The three Sudanese NCOs accused of instigating the unrest deserted before it broke out, but the army court-martialed four askaris as "ringleaders" of the mutiny. Kenyan officials responsible for raising and training the Pioneers were embarrassed by the incident and acknowledged the strike was an inevitable result of running the unit "on the cheap." As a result, the East Africa Command reorganized the Pioneer Battalions as frontline formations complete with KAR uniforms and pay.[92]

Nevertheless, the colonial military failed to apply the lessons learned at Garba Tulla to other labor units, and unrest in the East African Pioneer Battalions previewed the problems that plagued the AAPC companies in the Middle East. In spite of the EAC's official policy that only volunteers would serve outside East Africa, many AAPC askaris were actually conscripts. In November 1942, the men of 1845 Company refused to board a ship in Mombasa after watching a propaganda film about the threat of German submarines. Two-thirds of the unit eventually embarked, but the remaining men refused to surrender their arms and were fired on by British troops. One askari was killed, two were wounded, and eight of the survivors were court-martialed for mutiny.[93]

Problems persisted once the East African AAPC companies arrived in the Middle East. They had little military training but were assigned to provide frontline military labor for the British Eighth Army in the North African desert. Discipline broke down in units caught in the British mass withdrawal from Libya in 1942. The men of 1821 Company mutinied during the retreat from Tobruk and accused their commander of being "too brave" by altering the map to keep them in Libya.[94] Most Pioneers received less than twenty shillings per month for facing the Germans and were taunted by other imperial troops about their low pay. Moreover, like combat askaris in Southeast Asia, the East African Pioneers' morale plummeted because they were ineligible for home leave. Many men had volunteered for the AAPC from the East Africa Military Labour Service and had therefore already gone eighteen months without leave. Yet the War Office once again had insufficient shipping to send drafts of African soldiers home on a regular basis.[95]

As a result, East African Pioneers also resorted to collective protests to draw attention to their grievances. In some companies, soldiers drafted eloquent petitions appealing for better treatment. Luo askaris in 1860 General Transport Company staged a limited strike in March 1944 to protest their low pay in comparison to British drivers. Interestingly, they appointed their own African officers and continued to fulfill their transport duties. In other cases, however, African soldiers wrote anonymous messages threatening their commanders. In 1827 Company, they enclosed bullets with their letters and even burned officers' tents.[96] Although no AAPC officers were ever murdered, askaris in 1809, 1819, and 1822 Companies were court-martialed for beating their commanders. East African colonial officials were extremely embarrassed by these incidents and blamed them on the capricious behavior of poor-quality British officers. When Bildad Kaggia's company broke into their armory and beat their commander after he withheld their regular ration of cigarettes and beer, the men were not disciplined. An investigation by the Group Commandant found the company commander had indeed been embezzling unit funds.[97]

The East African AAPC companies acquired a reputation with senior officers in the Middle East for being prone to "blow-ups." As the Buganda Resident put it: "It appears that they may be behaving extremely well and then suddenly there will be mass disobedience without any warning of the likelihood of such an event occurring."[98] Colonial officials in East Africa were stung by these criticisms and worried the negative reputation of Pioneers would reflect poorly on their administrative competency. They therefore encouraged military authorities to take whatever steps were necessary to improve morale and discipline in the East African companies. By the end of 1942, most East African units were transferred from the North African desert to Egypt and the Levant for less arduous garrison duties. AAPC askaris finally received KAR rates of pay, and in 1944, the word "Auxiliary" was dropped from the unit's official title. More important, new transportation routes along the Nile River allowed 900 men to go on leave every month.[99] African soldiers were generally mollified by these changes, and the incidence of collective unrest decreased markedly toward the end of the war.

POLITICS, 1938–1963

Collective resistance in the army was rarely inspired by larger political issues in colonial East Africa; only the most educated askaris were overtly nationalistic. Most rank-and-file askaris were concerned primarily with local issues relating to grazing and land tenure in their home areas. The earliest, and perhaps most successful, intervention of African soldiers into domestic politics came in 1938, when Kamba askaris joined the opposition to the Kenyan government's mandatory destocking program in Machakos District. Kamba soldiers usually invested their wages in cattle, and the colonial administration's attempt to cull their herds amounted to the confiscation of a large portion of their savings. According to one former askari, the destocking campaign "turned Ukambani into a place of torment and deprivation." Other veterans recall raising funds to support protesters camped in Nairobi, and operating telephones for the Ukamba Members Association (UMA).[100] Colonial officials were alarmed at the prospect of alienating a martial race that supplied over twenty percent of all African soldiers in the Kenyan KAR battalions. Moreover, the reputation of Kamba askaris as "loyal servants of the Crown" won them public sympathy in Great Britain, which forced the Kenyan Governor to suspend the destocking campaign.[101]

During the Second World War, African servicemen similarly resisted the activities of the Livestock Control Board, which requisitioned African cattle for the army at substandard prices. Askaris believed their herds were unfairly targeted because they were not at home to speak for themselves and insisted army recruiters had promised their cattle would be spared if they enlisted. One man even demanded his discharge, arguing the government's seizure of his property constituted his contribution to the war effort.[102] Most British officers supported these appeals and lobbied district officers to exempt African soldiers' herds from the meat levy, but civil officials were entirely unsympathetic. The District Commissioner for Elgeyo-Marakwet District responded that "it was just too bad" if askaris did not get full market value for their cattle.[103] This attitude angered many African soldiers, but there was little they could do to oppose the Control Board while they were away from home. Moreover, the generally sympathetic tone adopted by most British officers prevented their bitterness from sparking collective protests.

Matters were different in 1955, however, when the Kenyan Government ordered mandatory auctions to reduce the cattle in Kitui District. Led by a pair of Warrant Officer Platoon Commanders, Kamba askaris in 3 KAR again protested that their herds were unfairly singled out for culling. Military authorities were sympathetic to these complaints because of the need to secure the cooperation of Kamba soldiers during counterinsurgency operations against the Mau Mau. The battalion commander of 3 KAR appealed directly to the Kitui District Commissioner to allow his men to sell their cattle on the open market. The threat of a Kamba flirtation with the Mau Mau made colonial administrators far more understanding than they had been during the war. District officers took the leaders of the protest on a tour of soil reconditioning projects in the district to convince them of the need for mandatory cattle auctions. More significantly, all Kitui askaris received a yearlong exemption from forced culling.[104]

In the final years of British colonial rule, African soldiers also used their influence to challenge the Kenyan government's policies on the distribution of Crown Land and ex-settler estates to Africans. By encouraging land consolidation, colonial officials tried to create a class of prosperous African farmers who would adopt progressive agricultural practices and act as a pro-government force in the new "multi-racial" Kenya. In 1961, they established a "Land Development and Settlement Board" to make loans to help "yeoman farmers" purchase land from departing settlers.[105] As absentee farmers, askaris were ineligible to receive a share of these new lands. The Deputy Secretary of Agriculture spoke for the Kenyan government when he declared:

Service in the KAR is considered to be a full and satisfactory career in
exactly the same way as service in any government department. Such government servants should consider themselves fortunate to have such satisfactory careers when so many others have not. When they retire they cannot expect to receive in peace-time preferential treatment over the less
fortunate.[106]

African soldiers rejected these distinctions and lobbied their officers to be
included in the land redistribution program. Their protests grew so vocifer-
ous that colonial authorities worried their dissatisfaction might undermine
the reliability of the KAR. Sir Patrick Renison, the Kenyan Governor, appealed to the Colonial Secretary for funds to extend the settlement scheme
from the Central Highlands to the Kamba and Kalenjin areas.

You know that these two tribes provide more than half of the present
strength of the Kenya Police and KAR, and if we cannot demonstrate to
them that the Government is determined to try and solve their land claims
there is a definite possibility that they may turn sour on us. In our very
difficult position in trying to preserve law and order, upon which really the
whole future of Kenya depends, any large scale defection by these tribes
could be a major disaster.[107]

These fears led the Land Development and Settlement Board to accept applications from serving soldiers and appoint military representatives to the land
selection boards to look after askaris' interests.[108]

There are very few documented cases of askaris using their military skills
to directly challenge British colonial rule in East Africa. Under normal conditions the army's system of regimenting and rewarding African soldiers fore-
stalled armed uprisings. Yet conditions were hardly normal during the Mau
Mau Emergency in Kenya, where for the first time since the early pacification campaigns, askaris were asked to undertake major operations against a
civilian African population. Along with units of the regular British Army, the
all-European Kenya Regiment, and the Kenya Police Reserve, the KAR conducted extensive counterinsurgency operations against the Mau Mau rebels.
Askaris patrolled the forests of the Central Highlands in small units to engage and kill Kikuyu guerrillas. Unfortunately, it is extremely difficult to
determine the true extent to which African soldiers sympathized with the
Mau Mau. While no KAR battalion was ever withdrawn from the fighting
for unreliability, tenets of popular Kenyan nationalism hold that askaris actively aided and abetted the guerrillas.

Many of these stories can be traced to the memoirs of Waruhiu Itote, who
served as a Corporal with 36 KAR in Burma and was "General China," commander of Mau Mau forces operating in the Mount Kenya area. In his book

"Mau Mau" General, Itote maintained that many Kamba, Meru, Embu, and Luo askaris took Mau Mau oaths. He also claimed African soldiers passed weapons and ammunition to his men and protected guerrillas from British troops. Some of Itote's stories border on the incredible. He describes being entertained with food and beer in a KAR sergeants' mess and claimed that askaris who served with him in Burma nursed his wounds after he was shot by a British officer.[109] The official Mau Mau records, which remain sealed in Britain and Kenya, may well confirm Itote's testimony, but at this point, it is difficult to verify his claims. Itote was considered a traitor by some Mau Mau partisans in post-colonial Kenya because he eventually surrendered to the British. He may therefore have had a vested interest in emphasizing his personal accomplishments and the nationalist credentials of all African soldiers. Many Kenyan writers have accepted Itote's book as fact, but British historians like Anthony Clayton believe he overstated the extent of fraternization between guerrillas and askaris.[110]

A number of African veterans who served in the early 1950s, however, support Itote's assertions. They recall warning Mau Mau fighters away from ambushes and purposely missing guerrillas during fire fights. An askari with 92 Motor Transport Company wrote threatening letters to the Governor and assaulted an officer of the Kenya Police Reserve who ordered him to drag the corpse of a dead guerrilla from behind a truck. "I punched him and threatened him with a pistol until he gave into the black bull." Veterans who served with 3 KAR in Malaya and Kenya attribute their sympathy for the Mau Mau to their awareness of anti-colonial struggles in Asia. An African Education Instructor attached to the battalion recalled that "they never kept us in one place for more than three weeks because the askaris would warn the guerillas about [pending] ambushes." These stories are entirely at odds with the recollections of former British officers, who insist emphatically they had no reason to doubt the loyalty of African servicemen.[111]

Conflicting accounts of the allegiances of African soldiers illustrate the problem of relying exclusively on oral testimony to study an event as complex and controversial as the Mau Mau. Fortunately, however, the few official documents from that era that are available offer some helpful clues. While no mention is made of combat soldiers actually joining the Mau Mau, 5 KAR court-martialed three Kikuyu officers' servants in 1952 for oath taking. In another case, the personal papers of a British officer reveal that one of his men was questioned for firing only four shots from his submachine gun at an escaping guerrilla.[112] Many former Mau Mau fighters describe purchasing rifles and ammunition from askaris, and court-martial records of African soldiers confirm this claim. The implications of this evidence, however, should not be overstated. In 1955, the East Africa Command's "Arms and Ammunition Investigation Unit" found only six percent of all rifles and nine percent of all ammunition recovered from the guerrillas came from military sources, including units of the regular British Army.[113]

One of the primary reasons so few askaris appear to have sided openly with the guerrillas was that military authorities went to considerable lengths to deepen the social isolation of the African soldiery during the conflict. Any askari even suspected of taking a Mau Mau oath was immediately discharged, even if there was insufficient evidence for a court-martial. All Kikuyu soldiers were screened by military intelligence officers, and those allowed to remain in the army were denied home leave for the duration of the Emergency. The few askaris who did receive compassionate leave had to report to the Kenyan Special Branch when they reached home.[114] The reliability of Kikuyu soldiers was never a serious concern for military authorities because they constituted only a small percentage of the Kenyan KAR battalions. The real fear was that askaris from other ethnic groups would be swayed by the Mau Mau. The Kamba were considered the most vulnerable of Kenya's martial races because of their close ethnic and cultural ties to the Kikuyu. In 1954, a special report on the Mau Mau in Kenya warned: "In view of the fact that the Kamba contribute a large percentage of African Security Force personnel, Mau Mau penetration of the tribe is particularly serious." As a result, Kamba chiefs visited KAR battalions to assess the mood of askaris, and chiefs in Kitui District barred Kamba soldiers from marrying Kikuyu wives.[115]

Moreover, colonial authorities took extra steps to ensure that ongoing African grievances over pay and terms of service did not undermine the reliability of the KAR. The Kenyan government temporarily amended its KAR Ordinances to count each year a man served against the Mau Mau as three to six years for the purposes of calculating his service gratuity. In addition, it temporarily raised the standard death benefit for men killed in counterinsurgency operations from 600 to 2,400 shillings.[116] These measures appear to have been largely successful in securing the tacit cooperation of most African soldiers. This was especially true for askaris from non-Bantu-speaking ethnic groups with fewer cultural links with the Kikuyu. Even Itote admits that most Kalenjin, Somali, and Turkana soldiers remained unequivocally hostile to the guerrillas. Numerous Kalenjin and Luo Warrant Officer Platoon Commanders were decorated for leading patrols that killed and captured Mau Mau guerrillas. Moreover, there were also cases where askaris, particularly from the Ugandan 4 KAR, were charged with torturing and murdering Kikuyu civilians.[117]

Clearly African soldiers were divided in their response to the Mau Mau. A small but significant segment of the African soldiery were passive supporters of the guerrillas, but the majority of African soldiers appear to have followed orders to suppress the rebellion. Yet the relative reliability of KAR askaris during the Mau Mau should not be taken as an affirmation of their support for British rule. The KAR's martial recruiting policies and unique military culture, discussed in Chapters 3 and 4, alienated rank-and-file soldiers from the Kikuyu population and made it difficult for askaris to identify with the guerrillas. This was especially the case for Kalenjin soldiers, who were disturbed by the movement of Kikuyu squatters on to European farms in the central Rift Valley and tended to perceive the Mau Mau as a hegemonic Kikuyu movement. Thus, reports of direct askari participation in the rebellion appear to have been somewhat overemphasized both by African ex-servicemen and those Kenyan historians who interpret the Mau Mau Emergency as a nationalist anti-colonial struggle.

The first overt signs of political activity by KAR askaris came in the late 1950s after the British government's constitutional reforms allowed East Africans greater participation in the political process. In an effort to give "responsible" middle-class Africans a stake in the government, the British extended the franchise to a small segment of African society that met specific age, education, and property requirements. Once unofficial African representatives were elected to the various colonial legislatures, the army's lack of African officers and racially discriminatory terms of service became legitimate political issues. When legislation to enact new KAR Ordinances under the East African Land Forces Organization was introduced in 1957, newly elected African politicians in all three East African territories took the opportunity to attack the organization and mission of the KAR. These new politicians did not object to the existence of the Regiment; rather, they asserted that the colonial army should be run to benefit the African population that paid for it. In the Tanganyikan Legislative Council, Rashidi Kawawa declared:

> All [African soldiers are] illiterate people of just small ranks. That is not very pleasing to us; we would like to see that the Army is ours, it belongs to this country, and we can only have that feeling by seeing that everyone of us have equal opportunities in the Army and we should see that if there is any slight sign of discrimination it should be stopped at once.[118]

As African politicians raised these issues during their campaigns, military authorities became concerned that the politicization of the KAR would undermine the reliability of the African soldiery. Intelligence officers warned that "nationalist agitators" were working to spread disaffection among African servicemen. The Kenyan government accused popular politicians like Tom Mboya of championing soldiers' rights to seize power after the British left East Africa.[119] During the 1957 elections, military authorities rushed through a ban on political activity by askaris (the KAR Ordinances did not even mention politics) after receiving requests from African candidates to deliver speeches in military camps. The army allowed African soldiers to attend political rallies as spectators as long as they didn't speak or collect funds. Yet askaris found to be too close to a specific party or politician were

discharged quietly, which was usually sufficient to keep most African soldiers from exercising their political rights. Many veterans who served in the
late 1950s and early 1960s felt they had to discuss their political and economic grievances "in low tones." In the words of one veteran: "Politics was
dangerous . . . to a military career, . . . [especially] when work was so hard
to find."[120]

Nevertheless, internal security records reveal at least some African soldiers had ties to suspect political organizations. In 1956, five African NCOs
at the Kahawa Depot in Nairobi raised funds for the Nairobi District African
Congress. In Nyasaland, an African Colour Sergeant belonging to the Malawi
Congress Party (MCP) led his men in the party's "Kwacha" cheer after a
soccer game. Similar incidents occurred in Northern Rhodesia. Intelligence
officers uncovered an attempt by members of the Zambia African National
Congress to "penetrate" the barracks of the Northern Rhodesia Regiment and
monitored the close personal ties of an African Warrant Officer to one of the
Congress leaders.[121]

Senior British officers were disturbed by these events, but there is little
evidence that African politicians had much influence on the African soldiery.
The majority of askaris remained outside the political process. While a number of African soldiers in Nyasaland sympathized with the Malawi Congress
Party, they did not hinder the mass arrest of MCP leaders in 1959. On one
level, their hesitancy can be attributed to distrust of the non-martial origins
of African politicians. In most cases, however, it appears that the apolitical
nature of the African soldiery was due largely to their social isolation. They
had infrequent contact with their home areas and had no chance to interact
with political leaders. Military authorities also made it clear that politics could
lead to immediate discharge at a time when African unemployment was on
the rise. Thus, when African political parties were legalized during the closing years of the colonial era, many askaris began to refer to the KAR as their
political party, assuming it was the only organization that would protect their
interests.[122]

African resistance in the King's African Rifles was ultimately a product
of the contradictory nature of the colonial system. The security of British
rule in East Africa depended upon the creation of a reliable African soldiery.
Yet Africans did not join the KAR to serve "Kingi Georgi"; they enlisted in
large numbers because military service paid more than any other form of
unskilled labor during the colonial era. African soldiers expected a high level
of material compensation in return for their toleration of military discipline,
and their dissatisfaction with inequitable and racially discriminatory terms
of service had the potential to lead to serious unrest. Yet military officers had
only a limited capacity to address African grievances because civil officials
feared that the creation of a class of privileged "detribalized" askaris would

destabilize colonial society. As a result, discipline in the KAR depended on the army's ability to accommodate the African soldiery within the framework of indirect rule.

Clearly, the boundaries of military service in colonial East Africa were never fixed. In resisting discipline in the King's African Rifles, askaris sought to redefine their terms of service and, by extension, challenge their subordinate status as Africans in colonial society. While African soldiers took pride in their martial prowess, they mainly thought of themselves as workers and usually expressed their grievances in terms of labor issues. Askaris did not conceive of their protests as being political in nature and never articulated their resistance in explicitly political or nationalistic terms. Nevertheless, by challenging the racial hierarchy of colonial society, they were implicitly challenging the legitimacy of the colonial state.

NOTES

[1] Hubert Moyse-Bartlett, *The King's African Rifles*, (Aldershot: Gale & Polden, 1956), p. 72; Tour of IG KAR, March 1913, NAM, 8201–42; Geoffrey Hodges, *The Carrier Corps: Military Labor in the East African Campaign, 1914–1918*, (Westport: Greenwood Press, 1986), p. 158.

[2] Lieutenant Colonel S. J. Cole, Colonial Office, to Captain V. R. Booth, War Office, 20 December 1932, PRO, CO 820/13/10.

[3] Kenyan 1932 KAR Ordinance, Sections 6, 7, 9–11, 13, 16, 19, 20, 25, 29, 40, 51, 52; GRO 2886, "Court Martial Sentences," 23 November 1942, KNA, MD 4/5/117/III/67; EALF Standing Orders, Section XXXIV, "Miscellaneous," 1957, KNA, DEF 13/470.

[4] Interview, #110; see also Kenyan 1932 KAR Ordinance, Section 46; The Lord St. Helens, KNA, MSS 78/3.

[5] David Killingray, "The 'Rod of Empire'": The Debate over Corporal Punishment in the British African Colonial Force, 1888–1946," *Journal of African History*, v. 35, (1994), p. 205; 1932 Kenyan KAR Ordinance, Sections 44, 46; Great Britain, *Standing Orders of the 6th Battalion King's African Rifles,* (n.p., 1930), para. 276; Interviews, #39, #41.

[6] Francis De Guingand, *African Assignment*, (London: Hodder and Stoughton, 1953), p. 27.

[7] The Earl of Lytton (Noel Anthony), *The Desert and the Green*, (London: MacDonald, 1957), pp. 239–41; Kenya Governor's Deputy to Colonial Secretary, 9 March 1931, PRO, CO 820/10/2; *Bulwayo Chronicle*, 23 November 1938, LHC, DP/VI/3.

[8] JAG EAF to Kenyan Attorney General, 2 July 1940, KNA, DEF 6/10/29a; CSEAG to Colonial Secretary, 12 November 1940, KNA, DEF 6/10/83c.

[9] Colonial Secretary to Kenyan Governor, 28 September 1940, KNA, DEF 6/10/83b; Minute by S. J. Cole, 4 September 1940, PRO, CO 820/41/18; War Office to Under Colonial Secretary, 24 January 1941, PRO, CO 820/46/4.

[10] Interview, #150.

[11] Uganda Military Censor, Letters from 1821 Company, 21 November 1941, KNA, DEF 15/38/24a; see also P. G. Goodeve-Docker, RHL, Mss.Afr.s.1715/110.

[12] CNC to Kenya Governor, 30 September 1943, KNA, MD/4/5/54/19; CSEAG to Colonial Secretary, 30 June 1944, PRO, CO 820/52/8; CSEAG to Colonial Secretary, 1

July 1944, KNA, MD 4/5/54/85a; Jomo Kenyatta, *Kenya: The Land of Conflict*, (Manchester: International African Service Bureau, 1944), p. 20.

[13] Colonial Secretary to East African Governments, 5 June 1946, KNA/DEF/6/12/22; Kenyan KAR Ordinance Amendment #3, 18 December 1946, KNA, DEF 6/12/63.

[14] I. G. Thomas, RHL, Mss.Afr.s.1715/271a.

[15] Interview, #95; see also Lieutenant Colonel G. G. Robson, RHL, Mss.Afr.s.1715/231.

[16] Report by Native Authority Kandewere, December 1944, MNA, S41/1/23/4/49b; Catt, RHL, Mss.Afr.s.1715/55; John H. Nunneley, *Tales from the King's African Rifles*, (London: Askari Books, 1998); Lytton, *The Desert and the Green*, p. 122.

[17] Welfare and Morale of African Units, by CSEAG, 16 August 1943, PRO, CO 820/55/3; Visit to EA Troops in ME, August 1944, by EALPO, KNA, DEF, 15/12/45a; EA Troops in SE Asia, 30 June 1945, KNA, DEF 15/12/80a.

[18] Kenneth Gandar Dower, *Abyssinian Patchwork*, (London: Fred Muller, 1949), pp. 39–40; see also Managing Director *East African Standard* to CSK, 20 December 1939, KNA, MAA 2/5/41/II/74

[19] Nyasaland Governor to Colonial Secretary, HoW, 23 July 1940, MNA, S33/2/1/1/40; Civil Director of Demobilization to PC NZA, 29 June 1945, KNA, PC NZA 2/2/89/3; Kenya Information Office AR, 1945, KNA, CS 2/7/45/416; Interview, #90.

[20] Civil Recruiting Depot Lecture on "Askari Letters," May 1943, KNA, DEF 15/65/5a; Uganda Military Censor's Report, Samusani Uniyi, 1821 Company, to family members in Busoga, KNA, DEF/15/38/24a; Deputy Censor's Remarks, KNA, DEF 15/38/24b.

[21] PC NZA to CNC, 6 May 1943, KNA, DEF 15/12/66; General Staff Intelligence Officer to 11 Division SEAC, 1 December 1945, KNA, DC MKS 1/10b/17/1.

[22] A. B. Dickson, "Studies in Wartime Organization: Mobile Propaganda Unit, East Africa Command," *African Affairs*, v. 44, (1945), pp. 10–12; Program of the Mobile Propaganda Unit's Kenya Tour, 1944–1945, KNA, GH 4/451/122; A. B. Dickson, "Draft Programme for Mobile Information Units," April 1945, KNA, CS 1/10/44/167a.

[23] Education in the Colonies: VII Army Education, 31 July 1944, IWM, K.15189; T. H. Hawkins and L.J.F. Brimble, *Adult Education: The Record of the British Army*, (London: Macmillan & Co., 1947), pp. 255–57; William Platt, "The East African Soldier," *National Review*, v. 126, (January 1946), p. 47; Interview, #145.

[24] 11 Division Progress Report, No. 4, October 1943, PRO, WO 172/3985.

[25] Interviews, #35,#133, #139.

[26] EA Troops in SE Asia, by EAPLO, July 1944, KNA, DEF 15/12/1a.

[27] Platt, "The East African Soldier," p. 47; Use of Education Instructors, 8 January 1944, PRO, WO 172/6484.

[28] 3/4 KAR Fortnightly Progress Report, 19 December 1942, PRO, WO 169/7028; EA Troops in SE Asia, by EAPLO, July 1944, KNA, DEF 15/12/1a; Interviews, #35, #51.

[29] Report by L.S.B. Leakey, 1 June 1942, KNA, DEF 15/51/105a; L.S.B. Leakey, *By the Evidence: Memoirs, 1932–1951*, (New York: Harcourt Brace Jovanovich, 1974), p. 114.

[30] EAC Intelligence Conference Minutes, 1944, PRO, WO 276/531; 5 FSS, Weekly Security Reports, September 1945, PRO, WO 172/9544.

[31] EAC "G" Branch, QHR, 31 March 1947, PRO, WO 269/3; Instructions for O/C 277 Field Security Section, 25 April 1947, PRO, WO 269/4.

[32] Chief of Staff EAC to Kenyan Defence Ministry, 6 September 1958, KNA, LF 1/57/5; Historical Report, Counter-Intelligence Unit, January 1960–March 1962, PRO, WO 276/374.

[33] Petition of Motor Transport Company, 14 February 1943, KNA, MD 4/5/137/144e; EALPO to CSK, 27 April 1943, KNA, MD 4/5/137/150a.

[34] CO Minute by A. R. Thomas, 8 January 1943, PRO, CO 820/48/29; Memorandum by Section A, Kenyan Secretariat, 27 October 1944, KNA, DEF 1/39/151; Askari Questions for Under Colonial Secretary, March 1945, PRO, CO 820/55/11; Report by 15 African Chiefs on SEAC Tour, 8 September 1945, MNA, S41/1/23/5/72a; Cree, RHL, Mss.Afr.s.1715/57.

[35] CSEAG to CSK, 1 May 1942, KNA, DEF 15/38/76; Report by A. H. Cox, Buganda Resident, 15 March 1943, KNA/MD/4/5/137/144a; Colonial Secretary to EA Governments, 16 March 1945, KNA, DEF 1/39/166a.

[36] EAC Circular, "Subversive Talk," 8 October 1942, KNA, CS 1/10/44/72a; see also,Visit to Madagascar, June 1943, by EAPLO, 27 July 1943, KNA, MD 4/5/65/227a; Native Authority Chikumba's Visit to Nairobi, December 1944, MNA, S41/1/23/4/49a.

[37] Gregory, RHL, Mss.Afr.s.1715/119.

[38] Interview, #11; see also #59, #87.

[39] DADML to PC Mombasa, 9 July 1918, KNA, PC CST 1/13/124/23.

[40] IGR, 1 KAR, 1928, PRO, CO 820/6/1; Great Britain, *Standing Orders of the 6th Battalion*, para. 166; Kenyan 1932 KAR Ordinance, Section 76.

[41] GRO 900, "Leave—African Ranks," 4 September 1940, KNA, MD 4/5/117/II/59; EAC to CSK, 7 July 1942, KNA, DEF 15/51/80; Interview, #150.

[42] AAG EAC to CSK, 7 March 1942, KNA, DEF 15/51/31; DC Nandi to PC RVP, 23 April 1942, KNA, DC NKU 2/29/2/7; CNC to Kenyan PCs, 15 October 1942, KNA, DEF 15/51/139; William Platt, "Studies in Wartime Organization: (6) East Africa Command," *African Affairs*, v. 45, (1946), p. 28.

[43] EALF Standing Orders, Section I/V, "Leave," 1957, KNA, DEF 13/470; EAC–DCs Conference, 13 May 198, KNA, PC NKU 2/21/5/166; Interviews, #33, #146.

[44] Bill Freund, *The African Worker*, (Cambridge: Cambridge University Press, 1988), p. 59.

[45] Interviews #18, #91.

[46] Gerald Hanley, *Monsoon Victory*, (London: Collins, 1946), p. 124; History of 4/4 KAR, RHL, Mss.Afr.s. 1823.

[47] Interview, #67; see also Interviews #1a, #65, #103, #154.

[48] Brigade Order, 10 November 1939, KNA, MD 4/5/118/15; Formation of East African Pioneers, PRO, WO 253/7; Native Authority Chikumba's Visit to Nairobi, December 1944, MNA, S41/1/23/4/49a.

[49] EAC Circular, "Last Pay Certificates Lost or Stolen," 11 April 1946, KNA, PC CA 12/26/20; Kenyan Secretariat Circular, "Theft of Certain Negotiable Army Last Pay Certificates: Warning to Withhold Payment," 23 May 1946, KNA, PC NZA 2/3/70/121; EAC Pay Master to CSK, 31 March 1947, KNA, MD 4/5/141/241; DC Nandi to O/C 3 KAR, 17 June 1954, KNA, DC KAPT 1/12/6/18.

[50] Central Province IR, July 1941, KNA, MAA 2/3/16/III/17; PC Central Province to DCs, 5 October 1942, KNA, DC NYI 2/10/6/11; DC Nyeri to DAPM, NFD Sub-Area, 21 October 1943, KNA, DC NYI 2/10/6/31.

[51] GRO 2160, "Discipline—Kit and Equipment," 2 February 1942, KNA, MD 4/5/117/III/26; Rev. G. K. James, 96 Group AAPC to DC Nyeri, 18 November 1943, KNA, DC NYI 2/10/6/40–1.

[52] CAD, QHR, 31 December 1947, PRO, WO 269/85; Kenya Colony Intelligence Review, 15 October 1949, PRO, CO 537/4715.

[53] Annual Unit Returns, 1927–1938, PRO, CO 820.

[54] Absentees Kenya and Uganda Tribes, 26 June 1942, KNA, DEF 15/51/76a; Absentees by District and Provinces, 1 December 1944, KNA, MD 4/5/72/196/aii; African Manpower Conference, 6 March 1945, KNA, DEF 15/29/118a; Interviews, #35, #108.

[55] Interview, #62; see also, Signaler R. Alex Nyallapah, Nanyuki, to W. M. Nyallapah, Zomba, 29 September 1943, MNA, S45/3/2/2; Interview, #91.

[56] O/C Medical Division, 1 GH, October–December 1942, PRO/WO/222/1827; Victor Chintengato Evans Arthur, 4 May 1944, MNA, S45/3/2/2; Interview, #90.

[57] Psychiatric Report, 1 GH, July–September 1943, PRO, WO 222/1827; EAC Military Records to DC Central Kavirondo, 16 March 1944, KNA, DC KSM 1/22/52/17; ADMS to DMS (Civil), 6 October 1955, KNA, BY 1/218/168.

[58] Private Suwedi Ngomba, D Company 1/1 KAR, to Mother, 14 February 1942, MNA, S45/3/2/2; see also Uganda Military Censor's Report, November 1941, KNA, DEF 15/38/24a.

[59] Driver John Garason, 8 KAR, to Garason Unjitia Zomba, 1942, MNA, S45/3/2/2; Meeting at Jeanes School, EAC; DWOs, 1 February 1949, KNA, DEF 1/80/25/2; DC Nandi to O/C A Company 5 KAR, 19 May 1954, KNA, DC KAPT 1/12/34/28; Interview, #18.

[60] Report by L.S.B. Leakey on Kamba Absentees, 1 June 1942, KNA, DEF 15/51/105a; DC KTI to PC Central Province, 5 June 1942, KNA, DEF 15/51/58a; Interviews, #6, #11b, #87.

[61] CSEAG to CSK, 15 January 1945, KNA, DEF 15/52/165; African Manpower Conference, 6 March 1945, KNA, DEF 15/29/118a; GRO 4843.

[62] For detailed consideration of these kinds of rumors, see Luise White, "Cars Out of Place: Vampires, Technology and Labor in East and Central Africa," *Representations*, v. 43, (1993), pp. 27–50; DC South Kavirondo to PC NZA, 10 February 1941, KNA, PC NZA 2/3/40; CQMS R.A. Bishop to HQ Rhoasa Sub-Area, 21 July 1945, MNA, S41/1/2/1/18; DC Nandi to O/C Police Station Moiben, 23 September 1953, KNA, DC KAPT 1/12/16/62.

[63] Political Intelligence Bulletin, No. 4, 1943, MNA, S34/1/4/1; Central Province IR, September 1944, KNA, MAA 2/3/16/IV/22; Machakos District IR, April 1945, KNA, DC MKS 1/2/1/1/8; Central Kavirondo IR, by CRO, February 1947, KNA, DC KSM 1/1/22; Safari Report by ASBL ExO, 28 December 1959, KNA, OPE 1/7/93/1; Interview, #62; see also #24, #87.

[64] 11 Division, GRO No. 104, "Court-Martials," 18 December 1944, PRO, WO 172/6485; Interviews, #26, #36, #91, #111.

[65] Crown vs. Private Tonya wa Munyanga, 3 KAR, 21 September 1935, KNA, AG 5/2457; Interviews, #5, #35, #108.

[66] 11 (EA) Division Progress Report No. 8, April–May 1944, PRO, WO 172/6484; 11 Division GRO, No. 80, "Court Martial of Private Kitagwa, EACMP," 7 July 1944, PRO, WO 172/6485; Riley-Smith, RHL, Mss.Afr.s.1715/228; Interviews, #12, #137, #142, #143.

[67] 5 FSS, War Diary, 2 September 1944, PRO, WO 172/6585; Lieutenant Colonel M. W. Biggs to O/C 11 (EA) Division, 3 January 1945, M. W. Biggs, Private Papers; EA Troops in SE Asia, by EAPLO, 30 June 1945, KNA, DEF 15/12/80a; Interviews, #143, #147.

[68] By comparison, the Royal West African Frontier Force tried only ten soldiers for the same crime, whereas the much larger British and Indian Armies conducted just twenty-

five and thirty-two court-martials, respectively, for the same offense during the same period. Court Martial Cases, SEAC, August 1944–October 1945, PRO, WO 203/2045&2268.

[69] Interview, #81; see also Interviews, #20, #58; George Shepperson, "America Through Africa and Asia." *Journal of American Studies*, v. 14, (1980), pp. 45–66.

[70] Anonymous Letter to CO 2/4 KAR, February 1942, PRO, WO 169/6965.

[71] 5 FSS, War Diary, 27 October 1944, PRO, WO 172/6585; Biggs to O/C 11 (EA) Division, 3 January 1945, M. W. Biggs, Private Papers; EA Troops in SE Asia, by EALPO, 30 June 1945, KNA, DEF 15/12/80a; Interview, #137.

[72] Ceylon Army Command Censor to O/C 28 Brigade, 4 October 1944, LHC, DP IX/2; see also, 5 FSS, War Diary, 5 December 1944, PRO, WO 172/6585.

[73] Interview, #35.

[74] Gregory, RHL, Mss.Afr.s.1715/119; Interview, #137.

[75] GRO 1610, "Bhang (Cannabis Sativa)," 30 June 1941, KNA, MD 4/5/117/II/101; Bowie, RHL, Mss.Afr.s.1715/24a; Interview, #142.

[76] Platt to Sir Ronald Adam, WO, 16 February 1942, PRO, CO 968/11/7; Report by Major Trimmer, 2/3 KAR, February 1942, PRO, WO 169/6965; PC Central Province to DC Kitui, 14 March 1942, KNA, VP 1/4/31; Haigh, RHL, Mss.Afr.s.1715/122; Interview, #141.

[77] O/C 2/3 KAR to HQ 25 Brigade, 17 February 1942, PRO, WO 169/6965; see also Ministry of Information to Kenya Governor, 14 February 1942, KNA, CNC 10/64; Moyse-Bartlett, *The King's African Rifles*, p. 580.

[78] The African Leave Situation, by O/C 25 Brigade, February 1942, PRO, WO 169/6965; 2/3 KAR War Diary, February 1942, PRO, WO 169/7031; Report of Lieutenant E. H. Risley, 2/3 KAR, 18 February 1942, PRO, WO 169/6965; Report by O/C 2/4 KAR, February 1942, PRO, WO 169/6965.

[79] Report by Captain G. J. Pink, 3/4 KAR, 16 February 1942, PRO, WO 169/7028; see also, Message by Major General C. C. Fowkes, O/C 12 Division, February 1942, PRO, WO 169/7028; Kenya Governor to Colonial Secretary, 30 April 1942, PRO, CO 968/11/7.

[80] Morale Report of 3/4 KAR, 17 February 1942, PRO, WO 169/702; Destinations of 25 Brigade Leave Convoy, March 1942, KNA, VP 1/4/28; Haigh, RHL, Mss.Afr.s.1715/122; Interview, #51.

[81] CO Minute by Lieutenant Colonel W. Rolleston, 20 February 1942, PRO, CO 968/11/7.

[82] PC Central Province to CNC, 6 March 1942, KNA, VP 1/4/29; see also, Kenya Governor to Colonial Secretary, 30 April 1942, PRO, CO 968/11/7; Haigh, RHL, Mss.Afr.s.1715/122.

[83] Yeldham to HQ 25 Brigade, 17 February 1942, PRO, WO 169/6965.

[84] DC Kitui to PC Central Province, 20 March 1942, KNA, VP 1/4/35; Monthly Report 3/4 KAR, 2 April 1942, PRO, WO 169/7028; 3/4 KAR Security Report, 4 June 1942, PRO, WO 169/7028.

[85] GOC EAC to WO, 23 March 1943, PRO, WO 106/4499; Meeting, General Platt and Sir George Gater, 26 August 1943, PRO, CO 820/55/3; EA Troops in SEAC: Interim Report, by EAPLO, 9 June 1945, KNA, DEF 15/12/67.

[86] WO to SACSEA, 30 October 1944, PRO, CO 820/55/13; GOC EAC to WO, 9 November 1944, PRO, CO 820/55/13.

[87] Unfortunately it is not possible to determine if West African units experienced similar problems. Eighteen West Africans were court-martialed for mutiny between Au-

gust 1944 and October 1945, but the official history of the Royal West African Frontier Forces makes no mention of these incidents. Court Martial Cases, SEAC, August 1944–October 1945, PRO, WO 203/2045 & 2268; HQ 11 Division to 14 Army HQ, 13 February 1945, PRO, WO/203/46; EA Troops in SE Asia, by EALPO, 30 June 1945, KNA, DEF 15/12/80a; A. Haywood and F.A.S. Clarke, *The History of the Royal West African Frontier Force*, (Aldershot: Gale and Polden, 1969).

[88] Biggs to O/C 11 (EA) Division, 3 January 1945, M. W. Biggs, Private Papers.

[89] Incidents of collective protest were not limited to African units. In January 1942, British military personnel destined for the Middle and Far East struck in Durban, South Africa, and refused direct orders to board their troopship. In 1946, a battalion of the elite British Parachute Regiment stationed in Malaya struck to protest poor living conditions in their camp. Slim to HQ ALFSEA, 1 February 1945, PRO, WO 203/1794; CnC's Conference on EA and WA Forces, 1 March 1945, PRO, WO 203/474; CSEAG to CSK, 17 March 1945, KNA, MD 4/5/142/1; General Sir Richard O'Conner to GOC EAC, 18 June 1946, LHC, DP/X/5; G. R. Rubin, *Durban 1942: A British Troopship Revolt*, (Rio Grande, OH: Hambledon Press, 1992).

[90] S. H. Fazan, "The Pioneer Corps," 27 September 1939, KNA, PC NZA 2/3/21/57; Michael Blundell, *A Love Affair with the Sun*, (Nairobi: General Printers, 1994), p. 48.

[91] GOC EAC to War Office, 8 January 1940, PRO, CO/820/43/11; Kenya Governor to Colonial Secretary, 31 May 1940, PRO, CO 820/43/11.

[92] CO Minute by Whitfield, 11 January 1940, PRO, CO 820/43/11; DC North Kavirondo to DC Central Kavirondo, 18 January 1940, KNA, DC KSM 1/22/81; Blundell, *A Love Affair with the Sun*, pp. 50–55.

[93] Chief Censor Uganda to CSK, 26 June 1940, KNA, DEF 9/4/41a; Morale in the EAC, 31 December 1942, PRO, WO 169/13956.

[94] Diary of A. H. Cox, February 1943, KNA, MD 4/5/137/144c.I.

[95] EA Troops in Egypt & Libya, by EAPLO, 28 May 1942, KNA, MD 4/5/65/17; African Manpower Conference, 30 September 1942, KNA, MD 4/5/140/156; CSEAG to CSK, 11 December 1942, KNA, MD 4/5/137/126; Report by AAG 11, MEF, 12 August 1943, KNA, DEF 15/38/90a.

[96] O/C 1808 Garrison Company to PC NZA, 7 February 1944, KNA, PC NZA/2/3/21/120; EA Troops in the Middle East, by EAPLO, August 1944, KNA, DEF 15/12/45a.

[97] Diary A. H. Cox, February 1943, KNA, MD 4/5/137/144c; Bildad Kaggia, *The Roots of Freedom, 1921–1963*, (Nairobi: EA Publishing House, 1975), pp. 33–36.

[98] CSEAG to CSK, 11 December 1942, KNA, MD 4/5/137/126; Report by Buganda Resident A. H. Cox, 15 March 1943, KNA, MD 4/5/137/144a.

[99] African Manpower Conference, 30 September 1942, KNA, MD 4/5/140/156; CSEAG to CSK, 7 October 1942, KNA, MD 4/5/67/14; Army Order No. 116 of 1944, KNA, DEF 15/38/98a; Minute by CNC, 14 October 1944, KNA, DEF 15/12/47.

[100] Interviews, #26, #51, #88.

[101] Many Kamba soldiers continued to support the Ukamba Members Association. In 1942, Kamba chiefs and senior NCOs warned that some Kamba askaris in 3 KAR had "political propensities" and had remained in contact with detained leaders of the UMA. Visit of Wakamba Chiefs to Gilgil, 3 September 1942, KNA, DEF 15/60/8a; J. R. Newman, *The Ukamba Members Association*, (Nairobi: Transafrica Publishers, 1974), p. 33; J. Forbes Munro, *Colonial Rule and the Kamba: Social Change in the Kenya Highlands 1889–1939*, (Oxford: Clarendon Press, 1975), p. 233.

[102] Kenyan Secretariat Circular, "Requisitioning of Meat Supplies," 13 February 1942, KNA, DC KAPT 1/24/5/127; Nandi AR, 1942, KNA, MAA 2/3/11/III/5f; PC NZA to

CSK, 15 January 1943, KNA, MWAR 3VET/49/1; CSEAG to CSK, 1 November 1943, KNA, DEF 15/118/44a.

[103] EAC Morale Report on 24 KAR, 6 June 1944, KNA, DEF 15/118/53b; PC NZA to CSK, 15 January 1943, KNA, MWAR 3VET/49/1; DC Tambach to O/C "A" Company 5 KAR, 23 August 1944, KNA, DC TAMB 1/9/17/261.

[104] O/C 3 KAR to O/C 70 Brigade, 10 July 1956, KNA, DC KTI 2/7/5/19; O/C 3 KAR to DC Kitui, 19 April 1956, KNA, DC KTI 2/7/5/9; Southern Province AR, 1957, KNA, PC SP 1/1/1.

[105] "The Land Development and Settlement Board: How the Board Operates," 1 January 1961, KNA, BB 8/30; Interview, #134.

[106] Deputy Secretary of Agriculture to O/C 70 Brigade, 12 July 1961, KNA, DC MLE 2/12/2/235.

[107] Sir Patrick Renison to Colonial Secretary, 1 February 1961, PRO, CO, 822/2024.

[108] Executive Officer Land Development and Settlement Board to Brigadier Fitzalon Howard, 3 August 1961, KNA, DC MLE 2/12/2/235; DCs' Meeting at 70 Brigade HQ, 31 August 1962, KNA, PC NKU 2/21/4/132.

[109] Waruhiu Itote, *"Mau Mau" General*, (Nairobi: EA Publishing House, 1967), pp. 40, 85, 90, 105, 163.

[110] Paul Maina, *Six Mau Mau Generals*, (Nairobi: Gazelle Books, 1977), p. 77; Henry Kahinga Wachanga, *The Swords of Kirinyaga: The Fight for Land and Freedom*, edited by Robert Whittier, (Nairobi: Kenya Literature Bureau, 1991), p. 32; Anthony Clayton, *Counterinsurgency in Kenya: A Study of Military operations Against the Mau Mau, 1952–1960*, (Manhattan KS: Sunflower University Press, 1984), p. 20.

[111] Lieutenant Colonel P. A. Belton, RHL, Mss.Afr.s.1715/11; Major H. N. Clemas, RHL, Mss.Afr.s.1715/46; Glanville, KNA, MSS 78/4; Interviews, #35, #57.

[112] AHR, 5 KAR, 1952–1953, PRO, WO 305/259; Report on Operation Thunderbolt, 13 October 1954, NAM, 7712-40-1, Stockwell Papers.

[113] Brigade Commanders' Conference, 9 July 1954, PRO, WO 276/197; Third Report of Arms and Ammunition Investigation Unit, December 1955, PRO, CO 822/792; Akitui on Delegated Detention Orders, 13 January 1956, RHL, Mss.Afr.s.1469; Josiah Mwangi Kariuki, *Mau Mau Detainee*, (Oxford: Oxford University Press, 1963), p. 43.

[114] GRO 112, "Discharge of African Other Ranks," 31 May 1955, KNA, MD 4/5/83/IV/43/2; Kenya Intelligence Committee Minutes, 20 May 1953, PRO, WO 276/62; Inspector of Police Special Branch North NZA to DC North NZA, 27 July 1955, KNA, DC KMG 2/17/5/269.

[115] Infiltration of Mau Mau into Tribes Other Than Agikuyu, Kenya 1954, PRO, CO 822/780.

[116] EAC Military Pensions Branch to DCs, 3 May 1954, KNA, DC KAPT 1/12/42; EAC Circular "Akamba Marrying KEM Wives," 13 January 1956, KNA, DC MKS 2/16/5/364 & 393; Kenya Colony and Protectorate, *Emergency Regulations Made Under the Emergency Powers Order in Council 1939*, (Nairobi: Government Printer, 1953).

[117] Itote, *"Mau Mau" General*, p. 106; 5 KAR, AHR, 1952–1953, PRO, WO 305/259; 7 KAR, AHR, 1954–1955, PRO, WO 305/261; Major General (rtd) H.T.D. Hickman to Major General W.R.N. Hinde, 30 April 1953, RHL, Mss.Afr.s.1580/1/58; Nott, RHL, Mss.Afr.s.1715/202.

[118] Tanganyika Legislative Council Debates, December 1957, KNA, DEF 6/4/28/1.

[119] Kenyan Internal Security Working Committee, December 1960, PRO, CO 822/2024; Interview, #135.

[120] Memorandum by GOC EAC, "Political Activity of African Soldiers," 19 May 1956, KNA, WAR C 290; EAC to Kenyan Secretary of Defence, 4 June 1957, KNA, DEF 1/106/1; Interviews, #19, #32, #57.

[121] Intelligence Report, Nairobi District African Congress, June 1956, PRO, CO 822/847; SBIS, No. 8, 31 August 1956, PRO, CO 822/847; Commissioner of Police Nyasaland to Military Intelligence Officer Nyasaland, 26 February 1960, MNA, F 248/2076; O/C NR Area to Chief of Staff CAC, 6 February 1957, MNA, F 248/2072; Interview, #152.

[122] J. M. Lee, *African Armies and Civil Order*, (New York: Praeger, 1969), p. 34.

7

Ex-Servicemen

In spite of the best efforts of British officials, African military service had a significant impact on colonial society. Until recently, many historians and political scientists have argued that Africans learned politics in the army, and popular nationalist historiographies throughout East Africa assign former askaris a leading role in anti-colonial resistance movements. In reality, however, the African soldiery's primary influence on colonial society was economic and social. Rank-and-file askaris were divided by ethnicity, training, branch of service, and active combat, but on the whole, the average ex-serviceman was more experienced and wealthier than his civil counterpart.

With the encouragement of military authorities, askaris considered themselves superior to civilians. While most were relatively apolitical, they expected the army to continue to act as a source of patronage after their military careers were over. The East African governments categorically rejected this assumption. While military officers tended to believe that former askaris were due some form of consideration, civil officials worried generous benefits would create a privileged class of ex-servicemen incompatible with the institutions of indirect rule. Fearing "detribalized" veterans would become a counterweight to traditional authorities, colonial administrators strove to reintegrate ex-servicemen into rural African society with a minimum of social and political disruption.

"Retribalization" worked fairly well in peacetime, when only a small number of long-service askaris returned to civilian life each year. The Kenyan KAR battalions discharged an average of only 173 men annually between 1926 and 1938.[1] Most served at least nine years to earn a gratuity, and a significant number stayed in for the full eighteen-year term allowed under KAR Ordinances. As labor migrants, these professional soldiers tended to retain ties to rural society and had relatively modest ambitions. Long-service askaris with good conduct records retired as relatively wealthy men. If they wished to work, they found jobs easily as watchmen and agricultural overseers. They usually invested accumulated pay and service gratuities in wives and cattle or, in the case of veterans of the later KAR, in education and rural businesses. Furthermore, since most peacetime askaris came from societies that valued military service, they usually enjoyed a high degree of prestige. While ex-askaris felt their long service entitled them to more consideration, they lacked the means and opportunity to lobby for better treatment. If they challenged the government, they did so alone and exposed themselves to the full retaliatory force of the colonial legal system.

Wartime veterans had considerably more influence. The East African governments found it extremely difficult to control the tens of thousands of short-service askaris rapidly discharged after both world wars. These ex-servicemen, particularly those with overseas experience, received pay, food, clothing, and other benefits that were vastly superior to anything they had known in civilian life. They were more worldly than their peacetime counterparts and had considerably greater ambitions. Combat veterans expected generous rewards for risking their lives and, at the very least, wanted to maintain their higher standard of living after they were discharged. They also assumed a British victory would bring a greater degree of personal freedom and material prosperity to East Africa as a whole.

The East African governments did not have the inclination or resources to meet these expectations. Colonial authorities recalled the metropolitan government's problems with rebellious British ex-servicemen after the First World War.[2] African veterans of World War I were equally disgruntled but did not produce unrest on the scale experienced in Europe. In the 1940s, however, civil officials and settlers worried wartime African veterans had a much greater potential to turn against the colonial regime. Therefore, the colonial governments' main concern was to "reabsorb" African veterans without disrupting the fabric of colonial society.

Civil administrators calculated they only needed to provide jobs and vocational training to a small percentage of army tradesmen and senior NCOs; they expected rank-and-file askaris to return to rural society and fend for themselves. The vast majority of unskilled ex-servicemen were extremely dissatisfied with these reabsorption policies but lacked the means to oppose them collectively. Most of the educated and experienced veterans best suited to lead a soldiers' protest were co-opted by the colonial system. As a result, the collective political influence of African ex-servicemen was minimal. With the notable exception of Kikuyu veterans, former askaris were largely unrepresented in African nationalist movements.

THE FIRST EAST AFRICAN VETERANS, 1880–1939

As noted in Chapter 3, the bulk of the African soldiers in the early KAR were "Sudanese" Muslims recruited in northeast Africa. British officers considered them a single "tribe," but in reality, they had diverse ethnic backgrounds and were bound together by their Islamic faith and lifelong military vocation. Many were conscripted (or actually enslaved) as children by Afro-Arab military recruiters. As professional soldiers, they originally served the Egyptian Khedive or the Mahdi but readily transferred their allegiance to the British Crown when political fortunes in the region shifted. Sudanese soldiers tended to stay in the army for their entire adult lives, and when injury or old age finally ended their military careers, they found it very difficult to return to the societies into which they were born. The British relied heavily on Sudanese askaris during the subjugation of East Africa but made no plans for their demobilization. Believing all Africans belonged to a "tribe," colonial officials assumed former askaris would be supported by extended family networks. Those injured in combat received only a nominal disability pension. These policies not only absolved the colonial governments of responsibility for caring for aged or infirm ex-servicemen but also reduced the overall cost of the KAR.[3]

While the few locally enlisted askaris usually returned to their rural homes, the majority of Sudanese veterans had no place to go. In East Africa, they were technically "foreigners" with no "tribal homeland." As was common practice for military slaves in the Sudan, most settled in communities of ex-soldiers near KAR camps. In Kenya, the ex-soldiers' colonies in Machakos, Kiambu, Kakamega, and Mumias marked the primary caravan route to Uganda. Frederick Lugard specifically chose Eldama Ravine as a site for a fort because the area had good agricultural land for an ex-servicemen's settlement. This was one of the few communities to have official status.[4] Civil authorities originally paid little attention to soldiers' colonies because land was relatively plentiful at the time, and therefore only a handful of these settlements had official sanction.

Lacking title to their holdings, Sudanese veterans had no legal recourse when European settlers began to covet the land on which they had settled. In 1915, the East Africa Protectorate's Crown Lands Ordinance placed the ex-servicemen in a precarious position by restricting Africans to "native reserves." With no recognized historical claim to "tribal" land, the Sudanese became squatters. The government could evict them summarily at a moment's notice, which was the fate of the Sudanese colonies in Machakos and Kiambu.[5] Most displaced former askaris migrated to the Nairobi suburb of Kibera, creating a large ex-servicemen's community around the main barracks of 3 KAR. They founded a similar settlement near 4 KAR's original cantonment at Bombo, Uganda. Kibera and Bombo were military reserves in the years before the First World War, and veterans did not need civil permission to reside there. In Kibera, the army issued them informal "*shamba* passes" in place of land titles, but most Sudanese considered the settlement a "pension" granted in return for loyal service.[6]

As a result, Sudanese veterans tended to run afoul of civil officials. As "foreigners," they could not be administered under "tribal law." They had no "traditional authorities" to enforce colonial policy and collect taxes, and their settlements grew rapidly because they attracted large numbers of East African civilians who found this arrangement enticing. As the largest and most permanent veterans' community in Kenya, Kibera typi- fied the "Sudanese problem." Former askaris lived unmolested under the protection of the KAR until the late 1920s, when Kibera became a civil responsibility. Colonial officials hopped for a stable class of yeomen farm- ers on the model of demobilized Roman Legionaries, but instead many Sudanese became successful petty traders, butchers, and landlords by exploiting the extra-legal status of Kibera. They rented land to Kikuyu sharecroppers and rooms in their houses to local prostitutes and acquired a reputation for fencing stolen goods and brewing extremely potent boot- leg liquor, known as "Nubian Gin."[7]

By the early 1930s, the settler community had lost all patience with Kibera. The Kenyan Land Commission sanctioned the demolition of the settlement, but civil officials found it impossible to evict African ex-servicemen. The Ugandan government encountered much the same problem when they tried to transfer administrative responsibility for the Bombo enclave to the King- dom of Buganda.[8] Sudanese veterans claimed their land as their pension. They protested that since service to Britain had severed ties to their original homes, the British government had an obligation to look after them in their old age. So many former British officers, including Lugard, spoke out in their favor that it became politically embarrassing for the East African gov- ernments to brush aside their protests. The Ugandan government, therefore, recognized the Bombo Sudanese's land claims when their community was transferred to civil control.[9] The Kenyan government, however, refused to do the same in Kibera but still could not dislodge the Sudanese ex-service- men and their families.

Colonial administrators hoped unrealistically that the ex-soldiers' settle- ments would disappear when the original class of "detribalized" Sudanese veterans died out. They failed to recognize, however, that the ex-servicemen married local African women. The offspring of these unions identified them- selves as Muslim Sudanese and claimed the same rights and status due their fathers. Thus, one of the most lasting consequences of the army's early de- mobilization policies was the creation of what amounted to a new ethnic identity based, at least in part, on military service and Islam. By emphasiz- ing their martial origins as loyal imperial servants, the Sudanese thwarted government attempts to evict them.[10] Nevertheless, there was no room for these veterans in the system of indirect rule. To classify the Sudanese as a Kenyan "tribe" would have required colonial administrators to find them their own "native reserve;" granting them "non-native status" would have validated their claim to special privileges. The "Sudanese problem" therefore became a cautionary tale that had a profound effect on the later demobilization policies of the KAR. Colonial officials rejected African veterans' demands for increased benefits because they did not want to create more communities of "detribalized" veterans.

While the few hundred Sudanese veterans discharged each year from the early KAR did not greatly concern the colonial governments, the tens of thousands of askaris and carriers who served during the First World War were another matter. Most wartime soldiers were conscripted from local East African communities. They had little desire to fight in a war that did not concern them and endured terrible hardships during their service. Colonial officials feared their wartime experiences would alienate them from their "tribal communities," and worried demobilized soldiers and carriers would spread "Islamic fanaticism" and "Ethiopianism." The Governor of Nyasaland even worried about the possibility of an uprising by ex-askaris.[11]

Yet despite these concerns, the colonial governments' only tangible demobilization policy was to return African servicemen to civil life as rapidly and inexpensively as possible. After hostilities were concluded in November 1918, regional demobilization centers were soon swamped as the army disbanded units en masse. In the month of December 1918 alone, 4,000 ex-KAR askaris returned to the East Africa Protectorate (Kenya), and between April 1918 and March 1919, 73,057 carriers were demobilized in the territory.[12] These African servicemen received little more than transportation home.

Although army medical officers tried to retain sick and injured men for further treatment, in most cases, the army discharged African veterans with little regard for their physical or mental state. Askaris wounded on active service received limited disability pensions, but men discharged for disease were ineligible for similar compensation. In addition, as official non-combatants, most disabled carriers did not qualify for military benefits. A "Pension Assessment Board" determined a soldier's eligibility and could award a basic wound gratuity or a pension of up to one-third of their final pay. Wound gratuities ranged from 80 shillings for a Private to 200 shillings for a Native Officer. Disabled ex-servicemen also received a lifetime exemption from either the hut or the poll tax. Colonial administrators believed these limited benefits were sufficient because injured men would be cared for by their "tribal communities," but many disabled veterans were left destitute because their relatives could not support them.[13]

Even healthy ex-askaris suffered from the East African governments' inadequate demobilization plans. Lacking accurate wartime enlistment records, military authorities had difficulty paying out war bonuses (for combat askaris only), back pay, and long-service gratuities. Colonial officials promised full restitution but often lost track of discharged soldiers living in remote rural areas. Many ex-askaris also refused to collect their money because they feared it was a trick to conscript them for a new war. In 1922, colonial military authorities estimated that in Nyasaland alone some 2,439 KAR veterans were owed a total of £5,169 in back pay and war gratuities.[14] The East African governments proposed to turn over all unclaimed African benefits to "tribal welfare funds," but Winston Churchill, then the Colonial Secretary, ordered that all unclaimed funds be returned to the Imperial Treasury. Individual veterans could collect war gratuities until March 1928, and back pay and disability benefits until March 1931, but after that date, the East African governments could accept no further claims, no matter how legitimate.[15]

African veterans were understandably embittered by these developments. Even those fortunate enough to be paid in full had their savings wiped out by inflation caused by the introduction of paper currency in rural Africa in the early 1920s; some Asian merchants raised prices as much as fifty percent despite government warnings against profiteering.[16] Many ex-soldiers and their heirs also continued to petition colonial officials for their benefits long after the deadline had passed, arguing that they were not responsible for the government's failure to notify them that their money was available. Finally, African ex-servicemen insisted they were promised land and pensions during the war. Colonial officials adamantly denied this and blamed military officers for making unwarranted guarantees to their troops. Few veterans accepted these protestations and believed they had been cheated.[17]

While civil officials blamed these impoverished and rootless former soldiers for an increase in urban crime throughout East Africa, it is important not to overstate the political influence of African veterans of the First World War.[18] Among the better-educated Kikuyu and Luhya peoples of central and western Kenya, ex-carriers played a small role in nascent African political movements. A few future leaders of the Kikuyu Central Association (KCA) and the Young Kavirondo Association had been headmen in the Carrier Corps or the Kikuyu Mission Volunteers. Most of Geoffrey Hodges's informants in the Carrier Corps, however, told him they were too busy or sick to discuss politics during the war, and hardly any of the senior leaders of the KCA had military experience.[19] The few informal African ex-servicemen's organizations founded in the inter-war period were largely described by district officers as "friendly and loyal." Although there were some isolated cases of unrest among ex-servicemen, official worries about the disruptive influence of African soldiers were unfounded. In 1919, the District Commissioner for South Kavirondo reported: "It was feared that the influx of all these men coming here with new ideas after months and years of service in foreign parts, might make for unrest in the Reserve. I am glad to say, however, that with the exception of one or two minor cases of insubordination, no real trouble has resulted to date."[20]

Similarly, the war also failed to produce a significant level of "detribalization" among African servicemen. Unlike the Sudanese of the early KAR, the World War I askari was a locally recruited short-service soldier. To be sure, some veterans were alienated from their home communities by conversion to Islam or marriage to foreign women, but most wanted nothing more than to get home. The reabsorption process was aided by the relative prosperity of a small core of ex-servicemen. Responsible African NCOs became chiefs, and colonial governments reserved positions for veterans in the police and civil administration.[21] Ex-servicemen fortunate enough to receive back pay and war bonuses also gained status in rural African societies by investing their money in cattle. In northern Nyasaland, prosperous former askaris were known as the *Mahuni* (derived from Hun) and either replaced, or married into, local chiefly families.[22] The majority of the fifty-two Nandi World War I veterans interviewed by Lewis Greenstein also spent their savings on wives and cattle. Their reintegration into Nandi society was relatively easy, and few were interested in paid employment or maintaining the lifestyle they learned in the army. Kenyan ex-servicemen seeking to escape rural life used their wages to become landlords in Nairobi's African Locations. Restless veterans in Nyasaland traveled to southern Africa as labor migrants.[23]

A considerable number of ex-servicemen, however, fell into a life of poverty. Older men who lost touch with their families often became destitute once their discharge benefits were gone (if they received them at all). More significantly, many of the most impoverished ex-askaris also suffered from physical or mental disabilities incurred during military service. Some were entitled to small disability pensions but nevertheless failed to petition the Pension Assessment Board. Administrative headquarters throughout East Africa attracted infirm and mentally unbalanced veterans suffering from what was known as "war shock." Individual district officers often took pity on such men and tried to find funds to provide them with a modest living.[24] Yet their efforts were hampered by the East African governments' steadfast refusal to sanction any policy that might set a precedent for granting askaris service pensions.

In the absence of civil action, military authorities adopted a number of stopgap measures to care for destitute veterans. In 1930, they established an "Inspector General's Trust Fund" to provide assistance for veterans and their dependents "who owing to poverty are in need of pecuniary assistance." Although the Fund's goals were admirable, its modest endowment of £555 generated an annual income of only £27. This translated into a yearly grant of 120 shillings to just four ex-askaris.[25] In Nyasaland, the government used War Canteen profits and donations from the Red Cross and former British officers to build a KAR Memorial Home in Zomba. In addition to shelter, the Home provided twenty-five veteran residents with a small allowance to purchase food and clothing.[26] Unfortunately, these philanthropic measures were far too small to alleviate the suffering of most impoverished ex-servicemen. The exact number of African veterans who became destitute during the inter-war period is unclear, but it is safe to assume their number was far greater than the approximately thirty men served by the Inspector General's Fund and Nyasaland's KAR Memorial Home.

THE SECOND WORLD WAR, 1939–1945

Veterans of the Second World War were the largest and most influential class of African ex-servicemen. They were more educated and better trained than their predecessors and had substantially different goals and expectations than men who served during World War I or in the peacetime KAR. Over 300,000 thousand East Africans served in the Second World War, and more than 7,000 of them lost their lives. Many more were left sick and injured. Ideological blandishments about defending liberty did not mean much to men who were "protected persons" rather than citizens; rank-and-file askaris expected tangible rewards for their service to "Kingi Georgi" and his Empire.

Frank Furedi has convincingly argued that civil officials viewed the demobilization and resettlement of wartime African veterans as an economic issue because they were unwilling to make political concessions in the colonies.[27] Interviews with former askaris, however, reveal most ex-servicemen perceived the war's goals in social and economic terms. African soldiers in Southeast Asia knew Britain promised Indian nationalists full independence after the war, but only the most educated veterans anticipated an Allied victory would bring political change in East Africa. A pair of EAMLS askaris spoke for most rank-and-file Africans when they declared:

> There are hundreds of Askari who joined this War. These are fighting as Allies to overcome the enemy who wants to destroy the freedom of the world. These Africans are expecting liberty for which they have been fighting. This new life, of course, cannot be obtained without money, and money that is being received by one who is being employed. Their fighting will be of no use if, after the war, a man will be released to go to his village and sit idle without employment. This is contrary to what he is fighting for.[28]

Most ex-servicemen, particularly those who served overseas, had ambitious plans for their return to civilian life. They raised money for schools and hospitals in their villages and sought to become successful clerks, artisans and businessmen. As one veteran put it: "My hopes were not too high. . . . The war gave me many skills—I wanted a plot of land [and] the chance to use them."[29] Yet most ex-askaris had limited political goals. They wanted an end to oppressive colonial policies that curtailed their economic and personal freedom and expected to become leaders in their home communities by virtue of their experience.

Civil officials' reabsorption policies took little notice of these ambitions, and many veterans became angry and disillusioned when they realized there would be no "land fit for African heroes" (to modify a British phrase from the First World War) in colonial East Africa. The British and American Legions helped win comprehensive training and educational benefits for European veterans, but there was no one to speak for African soldiers.[30] While military authorities took considerable pride in the advanced training and intellectual development of African soldiers, colonial administrators were concerned the reintroduction of these sophisticated ex-servicemen into rural Africa would lead to serious social and political instability. Kenyan officials believed (largely incorrectly) that the Kikuyu Central Association and other nascent African political organizations were led by former askaris and carriers and feared World War II–era askaris were sufficiently prepared to adopt the radical tactics of British veterans of the First World War.[31] By 1942, the optimistic hope that the discipline and training of African soldiers might make them more inclined to support the government faded as reports of askari unrest filtered back from the Middle East and Southeast Asia.

Moreover, many Africans serving overseas had positive contacts with British soldiers, who fraternized with them as equals. Censored letters written by askaris in the Middle East described their satisfaction at living and working alongside Europeans, and some British soldiers with democratic sympathies even told Africans they had the right to rule themselves.[32] These experiences naturally led askaris to question the colonial color bar. Robert Kakembo mixed easily with white South Africans and metropolitan British troops but disdained the settlers he encountered in the army.

> [The] East African White . . . is always prejudiced. He thinks in the past. How much money were you getting before the war—six shillings was enough—why promote you? It is a waste of government money; and you always find vacancies in their units. All Africans are to him his personal servants, and they are always regarded as cow boys or shamba boys. . . . An East African White is never off duty, therefore whenever he goes about men must pay obeisance to the white man.[33]

While Kakembo's book was not published until 1947, the settler press was nevertheless full of ominous warnings about the dangerously subversive attitudes of African soldiers.

The Second World War also led askaris to question the privileged status of Asians and Arabs in colonial society. Africans had long resented the dominant position of Indian traders in the countryside. When East Africans arrived in India in 1944, this dislike grew into open contempt, as African servicemen observed the desperate condition of the Indian poor. Many askaris offended Hindu sensibilities by killing what they believed to be wild cattle and suspected Indian shopkeepers of trying to poison them with contaminated food and drink.[34] Similar problems developed in the Middle East, where a primary mission of the AAPC's garrison companies was to prevent local Arabs from stealing military supplies. This proved a difficult task, and one exasperated Ugandan serviceman complained that "the Arabs [are] a low type of people, probably the lowest in the world and they are the most treacherous, mischievous malignant and etc people in the world."[35]

Colonial officials defended the color bar on the premise that immigrant communities in East Africa were entitled to special status because they were more "civilized" than native-born Africans. Military service invalidated this falsehood by exposing African soldiers to lower-class Europeans, Asians, and Arabs. A morale report for the Southeast Asia Command quoted a group of askaris as saying: "It's funny to see that Indians in Africa are respected, whilst out here in their own country they are very poor, we even employ some of them to wash our clothes. When we return to Africa, there will be much trouble between us, because the Africans have learned a lot of their customs and ways of living."[36]

Askaris received further encouragement to reject colonial doctrines of African racial and cultural inferiority from African American servicemen. The handful of black U.S. troops stationed in Kenya created real problems for the colonial administration.[37] In spite of the efforts of civil officials to keep them isolated from the African population, African Americans had intimate contact with East African soldiers and civilians. Waruhiu Itote and Bildad Kaggia describe being urged by black Americans to demand fair treatment. Many askaris believed U.S. troops helped deserters escape to America, and in Nyasaland, rumors abounded that African American paratroopers would arrive to liberate the Protectorate from British rule.[38]

The East African soldiery's rising expectations and impatience with racial discrimination contributed to growing fears among metropolitan authorities about the potentially disruptive influence of colonial soldiers throughout the British Empire. In East Africa, a few returning askaris were caught smuggling weapons and explosives, and civil officials were unnerved by wartime reports of soldiers' strikes and assaults on British officers. Missionaries also worried the large numbers of servicemen baptized during the war would reject their authority by founding independent African churches. An article appearing in the *Times of London* in the summer of 1945 heightened anxieties by comparing "unsettled" askaris to the angry German veterans who helped bring the Nazis to power.[39] As

Figure 7.1 British fears about the social impact of military service on Africans during World War II. From *Jambo*, c. 1945, p. 116. Courtesy of Rhodes House Library, Oxford (Mss.Afr.s.1715/Box 18/295). Reprinted with permission.

a result, the Kenyan settlers demanded that the government assert control over these ex-servicemen. Few understood that their hostility toward the African soldiery threatened to bring to pass the very unrest they were trying to avoid.

Fears of subversive African veterans colored the colonial governments' demobilization plans. Their main goal was to return to the pre-war status quo. As the largest supplier of African troops, Kenya took the lead in developing reabsorption policies for the other East African territories.[40] In late 1942, the Kenyan government's Post-War Employment Committee divided African veterans into three groups: unskilled "tribal natives," semi-skilled "partially urbanized natives," and a small number of highly skilled "permanently urbanized natives." The vast majority of the African rank-and-file belonged to the first category. After hearing testimony from district officers and African civil servants, the Committee assumed the majority of former askaris, wanting nothing more than to return to the land, could be easily reabsorbed. Aside from encouraging soil conservation, the Committee concluded that nothing more needed to be done for this first group.[41] Their recommendation also had the virtue of being cheap and fostering political stability by confining former askaris to the countryside.

Most African tradesmen and army specialists fell into the latter categories. The Committee assumed "permanently urbanized" veterans would return to pre-war civilian jobs because they had been entirely dependent on wage labor in private life. It considered the much larger class of "partially urbanized" veterans to be the most serious threat. These askaris were primarily lower-level tradesmen recruited in the native reserves who received relatively high wages in the military and expected to find similarly lucrative positions after they were discharged. By the end of the war, the EAC listed 29,934 Kenyan askaris as specialists, which constituted roughly thirty percent of all Africans recruited in the Colony. Over sixty-three percent of these skilled soldiers were Luo, Luhya, or Kikuyu, the most educated and politically active ethnic groups in Kenya.[42]

European employers, however, had little regard for the expertise of ex-askaris. They believed army tradesmen learned simple tasks through drill and repetition and therefore lacked the qualifications for civilian positions requiring a higher degree of flexibility and personal initiative.[43] This reputation was largely undeserved; African tradesmen kept the modern East African forces functioning. Private employers and colonial officials appear to have been biased against them because they did not serve the apprenticeship required of civilian artisans. Nevertheless, colonial administrators worried semi-skilled veterans would erode "traditional" African society by swelling the growing ranks of the urban unemployed. Kenya's Chief Native Commissioner warned:

I do not fear detribalisation as much as I fear deruralisation. The men from the fighting ranks of the KAR are in the main yeomen who will return to the land. The iron has entered into the soul of the mechanic, and I doubt whether he will be content to live again the life of the agricultural peasant even if there was room for him on the land.[44]

Kenyan officials feared these embittered and rootless semi-skilled veterans would turn to crime or attach themselves to radical African politicians.[45]

To meet this challenge, the East African governments planned vocational training programs to bring the skills of army tradesmen up to civil standards. They reserved government jobs for army clerks, signallers, and medical orderlies and set aside positions as chiefs, headmen, and foremen for unskilled, but responsible, senior African NCOs. Most territories also created a Civil Reabsorption Board (CRB) to encourage private employers to hire these "re-trained" veterans.[46] Although many unskilled and semi-skilled veterans also wanted vocational training, the colonial governments opposed any policy that discouraged ex-servicemen from returning to agriculture. They gambled that it was only necessary to fund job placement and training programs for just a small minority of skilled ex-servicemen. Nyasaland was the only territory to deviate substantially from this policy. Officials there planned to train unskilled veterans to give them a reason to stay in the Protectorate instead of becoming labor migrants.[47]

Few colonial officials believed the successful reabsorption of rank-and-file askaris required substantial improvements in the quality of African rural life. The East African governments refused to expend their limited resources on ex-servicemen. The predominant view in every colonial territory was that it was dangerous to treat ex-askaris as a privileged class. The Kenya's Post-War Employment Committee declared: "[W]e have from the outset refused to view our problem merely as an ethical obligation to do right by a man who has fought for his country. For every man who enlisted there were many who were willing to enlist and who were debarred from enjoying terms of service in many cases more highly remunerative than that which they were impelled by circumstances to accept in civil life."[48] This view was even shared by some African politicians. Eliud Mathu, the unofficial representative for African interests in the Kenyan Legislative Council, told African soldiers: "I personally do not think that we should divide ourselves into sections of those who joined the military services and those who remained in the home front."[49]

At the end of the war, East African soldiers focused on returning to civilian life as quickly as possible. Like most men who served in the conflict, they had ambitious plans for their accumulated pay and bonuses and were anxious to learn how they would be rewarded for their service. They did not know, however, that the East African governments were largely unprepared for their return. Even though the Colonial Office had directed civil officials to begin planning for demobilization in 1943, the various colonial governments lacked a coordinated strategy. The result was an atmosphere of apathy and inertia. The East African Governors Conference did not appoint a Civil Director of Demobilization until May 1945, when Kenya's Principle Civil Dispersal Officer and Director of Training were finally authorized to formulate inter-territorial policy. These officials acknowledged they were unprepared for the end of the war, but the East Africa Command brushed aside Kenyan suggestions to delay the discharge of African soldiers until more detailed plans were in place.[50]

Colonial administrators protested they were not ready to cope with the sudden influx of returning veterans. Nevertheless, the growing restlessness among askaris in Southeast Asia and the unexpectedly sudden surrender of Japan dictated the rapid demobilization of the East African forces. The African Auxiliary Pioneer Corps and the East Africa Military Labour Service were disbanded en masse in the fall of 1945.[51] Some 25,200 more askaris were demobilized by the end of 1945, with a total of 170,809 released over the next six months. Roughly 6,000 African soldiers were discharged each week during the demobilization period, and by the end of 1947, only 275 Kenyans remained to be released.[52]

Soldiers marked for discharge were sent to Dispersal Centres, where they received back pay and an additional fifty-six days' "pay and ration allowance" in a Last Pay Certificate (LPC), redeemable at their District Commissioner's office. Unpaid family remittances and a war gratuity (4 to 6 shillings for each month of wartime service) were deposited in a Post Office Savings Bank (POSB) account. POSB accounts were intended to slow the rate of rural inflation by forcing veterans to stretch their savings through mandatory gradual withdrawals. The governments of Nyasaland and Northern Rhodesia opted out of the POSB scheme, believing that labor migration had given their soldiers a better understanding of how to handle their money.[53] In addition to these benefits, African soldiers received an extra 40 shillings to purchase civilian clothes and were allowed to keep up to 84 pounds of non-lethal military equipment. District Commissioners were told to expect to pay returning veterans an average of 350 shillings per man. This was a substantial sum in rural Africa but did not compare with what locally recruited Europeans received: a war gratuity of 10 to 55 shillings per month served, plus a clothing allowance of 600 shillings.[54]

Askaris awaiting demobilization at the Dispersal Centres were also given questionnaires asking them to list their previous civilian occupation, military specialty, army trade, tests and preferences for post-war jobs and training. The East African governments opposed the survey over concerns that veterans would interpret the inquiry as a promise of employment but had to accept the plan because African soldiers, fully aware European servicemen received the forms, insisted on equal treatment. The questionnaire promised the colonial governments would help find employment for soldiers with good military testimonials but also emphasized that since jobs were scarce, only army tradesmen were eligible for vocational training.[55]

The bitterness of many unskilled African ex-servicemen over their treatment by civil and military authorities increased once they finally returned home. Large numbers of rank-and-file veterans, particularly those living in Kenya, did not have enough land to guarantee a comfortable living and aspired to move into paid employment. Yet colonial officials geared training programs to just a small handful of skilled ex-servicemen. While many African veterans resented these restrictions, they could do little to oppose them. Resettlement policy polarized the ex-soldiers' community by ensuring that skilled and educated veterans, who had the greatest capacity to organize collective protests, could find lucrative jobs.

Kenya's Central Employment Bureau (CEB), along with similar labor exchanges in Uganda and Tanganyika, matched former army specialists with private employers and government departments. While all ex-servicemen were technically eligible to register with the CEB, most of the posted jobs required a high level of training (Tables 7.1 and 7.2). In the summer of 1946, over forty percent of the CEB's 720 job listings were for carpenters or masons. In comparison, over 12,000 Kenyan Africans trained as drivers during the war, but only two percent of the CEB's positions called for this specialty. Of the 17,120 ex-askaris registered with the CEB by the end of 1947, only 5,760 were ultimately placed in jobs. This group of successful applicants was almost entirely composed of skilled veterans. Civil officials had no illusions about the African employment picture in post-war Kenya and considered the CEB successful if it found work for just thirty percent of its clients.[56]

While the Kenyan CEB advertised positions for manual laborers, most unskilled ex-servicemen would not work for less than they had earned in the army (roughly thirty shillings per month). Unqualified former infantrymen applied for work as clerks and artisans, and over ninety percent of the 5,000 rank-and-file respondents completing demobilization questionnaires by October 1945 asked for jobs requiring special training. Men often forged their discharge documents to give themselves fictitious trade qualifications and exemplary military testimonials.[57] While reasonably lucrative positions as policemen, prison warders, customs agents, watchmen, and headmen required responsibility but no specific skills, there was limited demand for this class of African supervisory personnel. In Machakos District, civil officials attempted to find employment for unskilled Kamba ex-servicemen by creating a civil labor corps to work on soil conservation projects. Yet the Machakos Works Company, as the unit came to be known, was a total failure because few veterans would undertake manual labor under military discipline for just seventeen shillings a month.[58]

Table 7.1

African Ex-Servicemen Placed in Skilled Employment by Kenyan Central Employment Bureau, as of January 1948

Position	Registered Applicants	Successful Applicants	Percentage of Applicants Employed
Tailor	549	57	10.4
Teacher	256	57	22.3
Telephone Operator	266	36	13.5
Mason	349	183	52.4
Mechanic	962	211	21.9
Electrician	320	57	17.8
Fitter	454	58	12.8
Motor Driver	2,143	796	37.1
Clerk	1,100	362	32.9
Blacksmith	340	100	29.4
Carpenter	567	304	53.6
Total	7,306	2,221	30.4

Sources: Kenyan CEB Statements, December 1947–January 1948, KNA, DEF 10/9.

Many unskilled veterans who could not find suitable employment reenlisted in the post-war KAR where the East Africa Command welcomed back former askaris to reduce training costs. While most veterans initially rejected the idea of rejoining the army, large numbers of unemployed Kamba and Luo ex-servicemen reenlisted in the summer of 1946. By October, the Civil Reabsorption Officer (CRO) in Machakos estimated that ten percent of all Kamba World War II veterans had returned to the KAR. Furthermore, when recruiting for the East Africa Construction Force began in 1947, veterans of the Second World War comprised forty percent of the first draft of men. Yet the willingness of large numbers of ex-servicemen to reenlist did not mean they missed the army or were somehow unable to readjust to civilian life. Most veterans did not have enough land to support themselves and were unable to find a sufficiently lucrative civilian job. Given the choice between unskilled wage labor and a return to the army, they chose the army.[59]

Yet even skilled ex-servicemen had difficulty finding suitable work. Many European employers distrusted African veterans and preferred to hire former

Table 7.2
African Ex-Servicemen Placed in Unskilled Employment by Kenyan Central Employment Bureau, as of January 1948

Position	Registered Applicants	Successful Applicants	Percentage of Applicants Employed
Headman	328	89	27.1
Domestic Servant	1,598	483	30.2
Laborer	1,404	918	65.4
Kenya Policeman	334	96	28.7
Tribal Policeman	290	102	35.2
Prison Warder	173	31	17.9
Watchman	1,527	491	32.2
Customs Agent	166	1	0.6
Other Jobs	3,994	1,328	33.2
Total	9,814	3,539	36.1

Sources: Kenyan CEB Statements, December 1947–January 1948, KNA, DEF 10/9.

Italian POWs, who worked for relatively low wages. Some explicitly rejected Kikuyu or Luo veterans because of their alleged political inclinations.[60] More significantly, skilled ex-servicemen were also dissatisfied with civil wage levels. Ex-tradesmen routinely demanded 100 shillings per month. Yet the CEB's employment listings for the summer of 1946 offered African mechanics an average monthly wage of 30 shillings, as compared to the 55 to 150 shillings per month (based on rank) received during the war. Ex-servicemen rejected assertions that their skills were not up to civilian standards, and those who had adequate land often preferred to do nothing rather than take a low-paying or low-status job.[61]

Many unskilled Kenyan veterans hoped to qualify for high-paying jobs by enrolling in a vocational training program, but the colonial governments only accepted men who could demonstrate previous experience in a given trade. Civil officials rejected unskilled ex-servicemen out of hand because they believed the territorial economies of East Africa could only support a limited number of African clerks and artisans.[62] Moreover, none of the colonial governments had the resources or the inclination to fund a universal vocational training scheme. Plans for an inter-territorial training facility for highly skilled ex-servicemen (known as an "A Center") were scrapped soon after the war ended. Instead, qualified ex-tradesmen received training as carpenters, masons, mechanics, and electricians at "B Centers" in Kabete, Kenya, and Dar Es Salaam, Tanganyika. Uganda relied on six small regional craft schools to cover the same curriculum. Kenya was the only territory to have a "C Center" to provide clerical and administrative training but did accept students from Tanganyika. Patrick Williams, the Kenyan Director of Training, had hoped to create a network of ten small "D Centres" to teach unskilled veterans basic construction skills while they served as labor gangs on public works projects but only had the resources for a single experimental center.[63]

East African governments grudgingly provided funds for a few qualified ex-servicemen to continue their formal education because of the widespread knowledge that European veterans received scholarships for higher education. Makerere College offered a special "half course" in Arts and Sciences for African veterans, and fifty-seven ex-servicemen from Kenya, Uganda, and Tanganyika received bursaries for advanced study. Nyasaland was the only territory to allow men recruited directly from secondary school to resume their education. Here, civil officials felt an obligation to help askaris who passed up lucrative civilian careers for military service. They urged European mission schools to readmit their former students and provided a yearly allowance of 120 shillings for each ex-serviceman. Older Nyasaland veterans with the equivalent of a Standard III education attended a special government school.[64]

Nyasaland was also the only East African territory to offer vocational training to unskilled veterans. The Protectorate's long experience with labor migration reduced fears of "detribalization," and Nyasaland officials offered agricultural training to induce more men to stay home by making farming more profitable. They also hoped freely accessible vocational training would alleviate the Protectorate's chronic skilled labor shortage. Interested veterans could attend a regional artisan training program at Mpemba or join the vocational construction scheme building the new Polytechnic Institute at Blantyre. Rather than developing formal training centers, Nyasaland offered a range of courses in agricultural development, cobbling, shopkeeping, and tea production at small temporary schools scattered throughout the Protectorate. Yet although Nyasaland's programs could accommodate only a few hundred veterans each year, they were often under-enrolled because ex-askaris suspected the courses were a ruse to get them to reenlist.[65]

Vocational education was much more popular in Kenya because African veterans did not have the option of working in southern Africa, and by 1946, most training courses were over-subscribed. Only 98 of the 192 eligible men who applied for training in Fort Hall District were accepted, and in South Kavirondo, only 50 out of 400 applicants were successful.[66] This popularity was due in part to the promise by civil officials that there would be enough jobs for every graduate. Some did have difficulty finding suitable employment, but many used their training to establish prosperous rural businesses and workshops.[67]

As a result, these vocational programs divided African veterans along class lines. Kenyan officials claimed to have trained 4,000 veterans before the centers were transferred to civil use in 1948. If this figure is accurate (2,000 seems more realistic), only six percent of Kenyan veterans received some form of additional training.[68] This small class of skilled specialists often became quite prosperous. The vast majority of former combat soldiers, however, complained they had nothing to show for risking their lives, while men who served safely behind the lines in support units received all the benefits.[69] In 1947, Patrick Williams admitted candidly that his East African Training Directorate had little to offer the average ex-askari:

> It is indeed a tragedy that nothing in the way of training had been available for the excellent type, the ordinary infantryman, because it is his character and grit which are so badly needed in the Colony today. Training is confined, by force of circumstances, to producing a semi-skilled artisan of as high a standard possible, and in order to do so we had to take the already partially trained Army artisan. This has left out the footslogger.[70]

Disabled veterans of the Second World War were the segment of the African ex-servicemen's community most in need of resettlement aid. In 1943, the East Africa Command estimated that 270 sick or injured askaris were discharged every month (with only 170 due to combat), and in Nyasaland over seventy percent of all medical dischargees needed further treatment. Since the first concern of most infirm askaris was to get home as quickly as possible, they often refused physical rehabilitation therapy. Concerned untreated, severely disabled veterans would be a financial burden and political embarrassment, civil officials asked the army to delay the discharge of these askaris until they could be treated. The EAC rejected this request on the grounds military hospitals did not have the bed space to accommodate permanently disabled soldiers. Askaris suffering from tuberculosis were the only exception. Conversely, the West Africa Command accepted responsibility for rehabilitating all disabled West African soldiers.[71]

The East African governments did, however, liberalize their pension policies during the war. While World War I veterans had to prove their infirmity was due directly to combat, men who fought in the Second World War were eligible for pensions if their wounds or illnesses were in any way associated with military service. Under the East African Pension Ordinances of 1942, African soldiers received from one-third to one-quarter of their base pay as a monthly pension, depending on the degree of their disability. In addition to these monthly stipends, eligible soldiers also received a wound gratuity, based on rank and extent of disability, of 500 to 1,000 shillings. Men more than fifty percent disabled still qualified for a lifetime exemption from the hut or poll tax.[72] Yet many former Privates could not survive on the 5 to 10 shillings per month that constituted twenty-five to thirty-three percent of their army salaries. Conversely, all disabled local Europeans received the same size pension regardless of rank because the colonial governments wanted to avoid the creation of a class of poor whites in East Africa. Civil officials brushed off Colonial Office warnings that African pension levels were too low because they still assumed "tribal custom" would ensure pensioners would be cared for by their home communities.[73]

Disabled African veterans who wished to work were automatically eligible for vocational training and employment assistance, regardless of their military specialty. Blind ex-servicemen were offered special training at the Salvation Army's School for the Blind in Nairobi or a similar facility at Magwero, Northern Rhodesia.[74] African servicemen who lost a limb received a simple peg or rocker-based leg, but only double amputees and educated men "accustomed to wearing shoes" were issued the complex articulated legs given to European soldiers. Many disabled African servicemen considered this policy discriminatory. One man sat outside his hospital's orderly room and refused to move until he was given a mechanical leg or a large cash payment. By the end of the war, the colonial governments finally provided disabled African ex-servicemen with articulated legs as it became politically impossible to defend this policy. Unfortunately many amputees did not have the money to repair the complex mechanical limbs once they broke down.[75] Thus, despite the availability of rehabilitation therapy and vocational training, a substantial number of disabled veterans could not support themselves. Their pensions were too small to live on, and they faced serious hardship if they did not have friends and relatives to take them in. As one former askari complained: "I lost my leg in the [Middle East] . . . but have received nothing in return."[76]

On the whole, most African ex-servicemen's complaints stemmed from the colonial governments' insistence on treating them as ordinary civilians. Veterans insisted they were promised land, trading licenses, jobs, and service pensions and accused the British of tricking them into serving by making baseless guarantees. As one former askari charged: "We were told that . . . if we worked hard the *Serikali* [government] would reward us. . . . Every soldier knows this, [but] the officers now refuse to admit it."[77] Colonial officials adamantly denied ever promising such benefits. They blamed metropolitan officers, who had no knowledge of East Africa, for raising the expectations of their soldiers to improve morale and discipline. While this may have been true in isolated cases, most former British officers also deny making such guarantees.[78]

Most of these "unkept promises" probably had their origins in wartime propaganda, which tried to motivate African soldiers by praising their bravery and accomplishments. It was common practice in the British Army for senior commanders to issue laudatory "orders of the day" at the end of a successful campaign, congratulating rank-and-file soldiers for their heroic efforts. Civil officials engaged in similar practices. In 1942, Fazan, then the Nyanza Provincial Commissioner, recommended students at the Maseno Army Depot School receive lectures "which will tend to make them take pride in the performance of the East African Troops and their officers." Fazan later realized the consequences of this propaganda when he became the East African Political Liaison Officer. In 1945, he warned that unless askaris were convinced their service was necessary to defend East Africa from Axis aggression, the colonial governments would have "a quarter of a million ex-askaris with a vaguely disconnected feeling that they won the war for the Europeans and have not got their reward."[79] This was an accurate assessment. Many askaris took wartime propaganda praising their fighting abilities as a promise that they would receive commensurate compensation when the conflict was over.

Stories of unpaid "pensions" and government duplicity still circulate widely in modern East Africa. Yet these rumors are based on more than simple misunderstandings; many African veterans never received their back pay or war bonuses. Even though it was against the East Africa Command's official policy to release men without Last Pay Certificates, large groups of soldiers were often discharged prematurely to keep the demobilization process moving. Some bored askaris simply walked away from Dispersal Centres or were mistakenly declared deserters after receiving medical discharges. Unpaid ex-servicemen could always apply to District Commissioners for their benefits, but many did not understand how to do this and concluded they had been cheated. Civil officials in districts with large numbers of ex-servicemen found it extremely difficult to avoid bookkeeping errors while paying out tens of thousands of shillings in back pay and benefits. In Kenya's Central Kavirondo District alone, there was a £1,200 shortage in the Civil Reabsorption Officer's accounts for 1946.[80]

District officers were also hampered by inaccurate discharge rolls that confirmed the authenticity of Last Pay Certificates. This uncertainty allowed confidence men to claim military payments by impersonating ex-servicemen. Unscrupulous clerks robbed unsuspecting veterans by forging their signatures (often a smudged thumb print) in the district receipt books. They would then tell claimants the government had never sent their money.[81] Similar problems arose from the administration of the Post Office Savings Bank accounts. Askaris had long distrusted the complex POSB system and were troubled by frequent rumors that the colonial governments intended to confiscate their savings. These fears appeared to become real in 1946 when the Kenyan postal system failed to cope with over 60,000 new depositors.[82] Many men could not claim their account books because army clerks had improp-

erly recorded their names and "tribal particulars." Illiterate veterans were
also cheated by unofficial scribes who helped them fill out withdrawal forms.
Most former askaris wanted no part of the POSB system and stampeded rural Post Offices to withdraw their money. By 1947, over 34,000 of the 64,000
accounts opened for Kenyan askaris had been closed.[83] Yet by the end of the
demobilization period in 1948 colonial officials were holding over 640,000
shillings in unclaimed military payments, and district officers continued to
receive appeals from ex-servicemen for years after the official closing date
for submitting new claims in 1953 had passed.[84]

Many ex-servicemen were also angered by the colonial governments'
hypocritical insistence that they return to the land. While the majority of
unskilled Kenyan veterans genuinely wanted to be farmers, the native reserve system limited the number of men who could be reabsorbed into the
agricultural economy of the Colony. The powerful settler community refused
to surrender land in the "White Highlands," and the Kenyan government's
efforts to alleviate the problem through ambitious soil reconditioning programs were ineffective and extremely unpopular. Kamba and Kikuyu veterans refused to build terraces and grumbled that the campaign was a plot to
steal what little land they had left. As one veteran recalled: "I became interested in politics . . . after leaving the army because the [reconditioning cam-
paign] was a threat to us all."[85] Ex-servicemen had no interest in back-break-
ing labor reclaiming marginal land; they wanted direct land grants. A medical orderly wrote: "The settlers in Kenya have more fertile land than they
need. We wish our representatives would fight for us to get some of the unused land given back to us, instead of us crowding and pushing one another."[86]
Nandi askaris lobbied for the return of territory lost to the Soldier-Settlement
Scheme, and Marakwet veterans demanded to know why the British government couldn't give them land in Japan.[87]

Land was a less contentious issue in East African territories that lacked
African reserves. Yet many veterans, who hoped to engage in lucrative commodity production, expected land grants in fertile regions near major transportation routes. The Nyasaland African Congress called for the settlement
of ex-soldiers on unused Crown land, and Northern Rhodesian askaris insisted they were promised such land during the war.[88] While the governments of Nyasaland and Uganda were originally willing to consider land grants
for veterans, civil officials backed away from the plan because they feared
"detribalized" veterans would create another Kibera, which the Chief Secretary of Nyasaland described as "pestilential" and an "Alsatia of the worst
description." The Ugandan government eventually allotted ten square miles
of land to veterans in the Kingdom of Buganda. Southern Rhodesia had to
abandon a plan to make land grants to veterans of the Rhodesian African
Rifles because the Nyasaland government protested it could not make the
same promise to Nyasalanders serving with the RAR.[89]

Many African soldiers hoped to form cooperatives to fund schools, hospitals, and trading companies that would challenge local Asian merchants. Askaris in Southeast Asia and the Middle East took the lead because they saved large amounts of money while overseas. Membership dues and subscriptions ranged from 25 to 500 shillings, and the cooperatives were usually organized along ethnic lines, with names like the Mzimba KAR Society, the Kisii Ex-Soldiers Association, and the Luo Soldiers Union (of Tanganyika). Askaris with pastoral backgrounds rarely contributed to these organizations because they generally preferred to invest their earnings in cattle. Most cooperatives were established by men from regions where land hunger and grazing controls dictated a shift to non-agricultural forms of employment.

The most ambitious societies were founded by well-educated Ganda askaris. The founder of the Buganda Bewayo Society offered the following sales pitch to potential askari investors:

> In this company we want to put everything like the astonishing shops in which our men go [in the Middle East]. We want to bring motor cars, clothes, motor cycles and bigger repair shops than those of the Uganda Company. . . . We have skilled workers. . . . The only other thing we want is money. We want cinemas in the towns where bands will play such as we will be taught by the Americans. We want our banks and hotels and there are very many askaris who can do work of this kind. If we collected our money to the extent perhaps of 100,000 shillings I feel both the British Government and the Kabaka will help us to utilize all the money we want. The company will help many and your children will become rich.[90]

Robert Kakembo was president of a similar Ganda soldiers' cooperative known as the Kawonawo Trading Company. With branches in East Africa, the Middle East, and Southeast Asia, the company planned to market Ugandan produce internationally and employ 5,000 veterans in workshops, newspapers, and entertainment centers. Military authorities refused to recognize these organizations at the urging of civil officials, who feared they were fronts for subversive anti-colonial movements. Some British officers, however, still served as unofficial treasurers and bankers for their soldiers.[91]

Even before the war was over, commercially inclined askaris bombarded the East African governments with requests for economic assistance, trading licenses, and a swift end to wartime price controls and commodity shortages. In Kenya's Central Province, groups of Kikuyu (and some Kamba) veterans applied for permission to open hotels, pubs, coffee houses, mobile cinemas, taxi associations, bakeries, construction companies, soap factories, and tailor shops. The Central Province Commissioner estimated that by April 1946 over seventy-five percent of his 1,967 requests for African trade and commercial licenses had come from veterans.[92]

Kenyan administrators rejected most of these applications. Colonial economic policy tied the number of African merchants permitted to operate in a given area to the size of the general population, which usually produced a ratio of one trader for every 500 Africans. Civil officials argued most African businessmen did not have the resources or expertise to compete in an open market and therefore had to be protected from the threat of bankruptcy.[93] They were willing to favor African veterans only if they met the same high standards required of civilian applicants. Between August 1946 and May 1947, only 353 of the 5,115 ex-servicemen who applied for trading licenses in Kenya (excluding Rift Valley Province) were successful. In North Kavirondo District, the Nyanza Provincial Transport Licensing Board rejected seventy-six percent of veterans' applications it received during November 1946, even though many ex-servicemen met the minimum requirements for a license and had already spent as much as 10,000 shillings on vehicles to carry agricultural produce. As a result, their trading cooperatives had to hire trucks from Asian companies. The Board's rulings therefore sparked a sharp protest from the District's Civil Reabsorption Officer:

I cannot put too strongly my feelings that the activities of the Board have shown a flagrant disregard for the *promises* [italics added] that were made to ex-soldiers, many of whom have been "through" three or more boards and are still waiting. It is even more shocking when it is realized that, in the opinion of competent local authorities, there is a reasonable livelihood to be made by these Africans, who are not even being given the opportunity of competing with Indians and Europeans, whose buses appear to be daily on the increase.[94]

Even those veterans fortunate enough to receive a license were still hampered by restrictive regulations. Kenya's post-war shortage of building materials made it difficult for African merchants to comply with stringent building codes. Moreover, many transport companies could not hire veterans because their military driving licenses were invalid. African traders had difficulty acquiring retail stock and were allowed to purchase only a small fraction of the surplus military material allocated to European wholesalers. While some of these new entrepreneurs eventually prospered, many veterans went bankrupt, believing colonial officials had conspired to impoverish them through discriminatory trade policies.[95]

Many former askaris therefore concluded they could only win concessions from the East African governments through collective action. Yet their hopes of forming a unified African ex-servicemen's organization were dashed by the distinctions of ethnicity, education and training that divided the African soldiery. Veterans were usually interested primarily in local and regional issues, and in Kenya, their most common political demand was for representation on Local Native Councils. African nationalists had difficulty enlisting the support of ex-servicemen because few issues united former soldiers. The Kenya African Union (KAU) drew support from many Kikuyu and a few Kamba veterans but failed to draw ex-askaris from other ethnic groups.[96]

Ex-servicemen tended to found small, ethnically based veterans' organizations with limited local goals. Their membership was usually drawn from veterans of labor and specialist units, and few were established by combat askaris from martial races. Most groups depicted themselves as self-help societies and professed their loyalty to the British Crown to win government recognition. While anxious civil intelligence officers kept a careful watch on these unofficial organizations, most groups lacked the capacity to instigate significant political unrest. They were unfocused and tended to collapse soon after they were founded. In Kenya's Central Province, Kikuyu ex-servicemen founded a confusing array of ephemeral and loosely structured organizations with names like the Muranga District Ex-Soldiers Union, Nyeri District Ex-Soldiers African Friendly Association, and the Kikuyu Ex-Soldiers Education Union. Some collected money for overseas scholarships, war memorials, welfare centers, and aid for the relatives of deceased soldiers, but differed from cooperative societies by advancing a more explicitly political agenda. Kikuyu veterans' organizations opposed African taxation, the *kipande,* and government soil reconditioning programs. They also demanded increased African representation on the Legislative Council and the expulsion of Asians from the native reserves.[97]

Some groups like the Nyeri District Ex-Soldiers African Friendly Association boasted a thousand members and made a sincere effort to bring their development plans to fruition, but others collapsed because they were run by unscrupulous veterans. Few organizations lasted more than several months, and many disbanded when their members shifted support to the Kenyan African Union. In some areas, however, Kikuyu veterans' groups had an adversarial relationship with local KAU branches. Veteran leaders often viewed the politicians as competitors, and conversely, African nationalists tended to distrust the ex-servicemen's demands for preferential treatment. Some organizations also appear to have existed only in the minds of their founders. J. W. Gaithi, the self-professed General Secretary of the Kikuyu Organizers Provincial Ex-Soldiers Association, demanded that the Kenyan government provide him with a salary, office, and automobile in return for his cooperation in defusing potential strikes and organizing army recruiting safaris.[98]

Although Kamba ex-servicemen voiced strong opposition to the Kenyan government's destocking and soil reconditioning programs, unlike the Kikuyu, they did not form organizations to articulate their grievances in political terms. Some ex-askaris joined politically oriented independent African churches, and a few embittered Kamba veterans joined the KAU. As one veteran explained: "I wanted to be associated with all the enemies of the [Europeans]." A handful of educated askaris also founded small short-lived cooperative societies, but most unskilled Kamba veterans joined organizations based on their clan associations. The largest of these, known as the *Ikundo ya Mbaa Lili* (the Knot of the Bond of the Lili Clan), was open to all Kamba soldiers and was concerned primarily with raising money for education.[99]

In Uganda, Robert Kakembo's Kawonawo Group constituted a special problem for civil officials because it was much better organized than any of the Kenyan organizations. Kakembo's book, *An African Soldier Speaks*, laid out his plans for harnessing the skills and experience of former askaris in post-war Uganda. It eloquently articulated the aspirations of African veterans and was initially well received by the Colonial Office in March 1945, which was receptive to his call for an evolutionary transition to African rule under British tutelage. Three months later, the Colonial Office's attitude changed dramatically, as Ugandan officials warned the book would contribute to unrest in the Kingdom of Buganda and antagonize Kenyan settlers. Thus, *An African Soldier Speaks* was barred from general publication. The East Africa Command, however, printed 400 copies, with "Confidential: Not for Publication or Circulation" stamped on the cover to warn district officers about what to expect from educated African servicemen.[100] On the recommendation of the Colonial Office, the Ugandan government tried to co-opt Kakembo by offering him an appointment to the staff of the Register of Cooperative Societies in return for quitting the Kawonawo Group. He was threatened with an audit of his company's books and possible prosecution for fraud if he refused.[101]

The East African governments undercut unofficial African veterans' groups by refusing to recognize any other organization but the African Section of the British Legion (ASBL) as the official representative of ex-servicemen's interests. Similarly, Nyasaland ex-askaris were represented officially by an African Section of the British Empire Ex-Services League (BESL), the main European ex-servicemen's group in southern Africa. Initially, some civil administrators had worried that any veterans' organization would hinder reabsorption by encouraging former askaris to view themselves as a privileged class, but most realized it was necessary to create a counterweight to the unofficial groups. As one Kenyan official put it: "[S]erving askaris [are] now tending to form all sorts of societies among themselves, many of them trading or political or both. We wish to divert this tendency into safe channels by providing for the ex-askari an organisation which would compete successfully with the spontaneous societies now appearing."[102] The colonial governments therefore tried to convince ex-askaris to choose the African Section of the British Legion over one of the unofficial groups.

While Legion officials stressed membership would bring no specific privileges or rewards, they promised the organization would work for the "common good" and aid veterans in cases of "genuine need."[103] In strictly material terms, a veteran's five-shilling lifetime membership fee brought only a Legion identity card and badge. Veterans judged sufficiently destitute were eligible for small cash awards of no more than thirty shillings per month for up to three months. The ASBL also built small Legion Halls in major towns and native reserves with large veteran populations, which were touted as a place for ex-askaris to gather to eat, read a paper, listen to the radio, and play darts. The more active district branches also sponsored ex-servicemen's rallies, reunions, and shooting competitions.[104]

While the ASBL was genuinely concerned with the welfare of ex-servicemen, its primary mission was social control. District branches kept careful watch over their members, and the Legion published a monthly newsletter in Swahili and English to spread official propaganda. The ASBL's Bulletin had a circulation of 32,500 and contained information on demobilization benefits, training and employment options, wartime exploits of decorated veterans, agricultural news, and domestic advice for veterans' wives. Articles explained how the British people endured terrible suffering during the war to protect East Africans from enslavement by the Nazis. Veterans were warned that African nationalists were the agents of "new enemies" (i.e., Communists) similarly seeking to oppress them. One of the Bulletin's most popular features was a serialized parable about a wise hare known as "Bwana Sungua," who outwitted the lazy and deceitful animals who opposed "Chief Simba." Ex-servicemen were urged to model themselves on the self-reliant Bwana Sungua, instead of expecting the free education, excessive wages, and pensions demanded by the evil hyenas and feeble-minded donkeys who conspired against Chief Simba.[105]

Most African ex-servicemen, however, distrusted the Legion's predominantly European leadership. As a veteran of the EAAMC put it: "The British Legion [played] the role of white man's welfare, yet we all fought in the war."[106] The Kenyan ASBL claimed a membership of 19,000 ex-servicemen in 1947, which amounted to just one-quarter of all African veterans of the Second World War. The Legion listed 10,448 members in Tanganyika and 7,126 members in Uganda in the summer of 1946. By comparison, the Nyasaland BESL had a membership of only 1,384 at the same date. Many of the veterans interviewed for this study had not even heard of the ASBL, and only 39 of the 97 men who had were members.[107]

ASBL funds came from African membership dues, donations from former officers, government grants, and profits from canteens run by the Navy, Army, and Air Force Institutes (the equivalent of the American United Service Organization). Most of the Legion's resources went to administrative costs, Legion centers, and the Bulletin. Of the 376,000 shillings raised by the ASBL between September 1945 and May 1947, only 2,500 shillings were paid out in direct welfare grants to veterans. Thus, the ASBL was largely irrelevant to most veterans. Attendance at ex-soldiers' reunions dipped sharply in the late 1940s and many Legion Halls fell into disuse. By 1950, the Kenyan ASBL was nearly bankrupt and needed an annual grant of £2,500 from the government to continue operating.[108]

Despite these problems, the ASBL achieved its primary goals. As the only sanctioned organization for ex-servicemen, the Legion diluted African discontent and blocked the formation of unified unofficial ex-servicemen's groups. The unofficial organizations that survived were too small and poorly organized to pose a serious threat. With a narrow ethnic base, they could not compete with the African Section of the British Legion. Kakembo's organization was a force to be reckoned with, but it, too, was little more than a Ganda interest group. None of the unofficial organizations were able to exert enough pressure on the colonial governments to force them to alter their policies toward African veterans.

African ex-servicemen began to realize the implications of the East African governments' limited resettlement programs in the first quarter of 1946. Unskilled veterans became extremely angry when they realized that, apart from their war bonuses, they would have little more to show for their service. In Kenya, unsuccessful former askaris swelled the ranks of the urban poor and were arrested in Nairobi for burglary and receiving stolen property. These conditions were reproduced to varying degrees in Uganda and Tanganyika, with Nyasaland being the only territory not to have serious concerns about dissatisfied veterans.[109] The Kenyan government first became aware of the extent of the problem when the Labour Commissioner, E. M. Hyde-Clark, surveyed ex-servicemen to assess the resettlement process. He spoke with over 12,000 veterans in eight public meetings in Nyanza, Rift Valley, Central and Coast Provinces. What he found alarmed him:

> The position in the Native Areas has never been so serious. . . . No one should be under the impression that Reabsorption is proceeding smoothly, and that the ex-soldier is reverting once more into his pre-war civilian status. They will never quite be the same again.[110]

To mollify former askaris, Hyde-Clark called for more liberal trade licensing policies, the distribution of surplus military stores to veterans, an increase in the rural food supply, and expansion of the district administration to monitor African ex-servicemen more closely.

In effect, Hyde-Clark's suggestions amounted to a strategy of co-opting the most influential class of ex-askaris while keeping a close watch on the majority of rank-and-file veterans. Furedi has suggested that the failure of discharged African servicemen to instigate serious unrest indicates colonial authorities overreacted to the threat of demobilized African soldiers.[111] While there is considerable truth to this assertion, much of the stability of the ex-soldiers' community in East Africa was also due to the effectiveness of the post-war reabsorption policies. The Kenyan government employed former KAR officers as Civil Reabsorption Officers to supervise ex-askaris and help them readjust to civilian life. They were assisted by approximately fifty trust-worthy former African NCOs, termed African Reabsorption Assistants. The other East African territories relied on similar arrangements.[112] These reab-sorption officials strengthened civilian control over ex-servicemen by repro-ducing the army's military hierarchy at the local level. African Reabsorption Assistants were not popular, but as former NCOs, they commanded the re-spect of most veterans.

Ex-askaris with the capacity to organize rank-and-file veterans by articu-lating their grievances in political terms received substantial privileges and benefits. Yet this is not to say they became enthusiastic supporters of the government. Rather, civil officials simply ensured such leaders had a reason to work within the colonial system. In Uganda, nearly 600 veterans received low-level positions in the "native administration" of Northern Province alone. Nyasaland officials encouraged traditional authorities to name at least one former askari to their "council of elders." A handful of educated Kenyan ex-servicemen became African Assistant Administration Officers. Senior NCOs who lacked the skills and education to qualify for a training program re-placed older chiefs and elders on Local Native Councils in districts with large veteran populations. These appointments helped satisfy veterans' demands for political representation, and colonial officials viewed their experience and authority as valuable assets.[113] As a Kikuyu veteran explained:

> They made me a chief—they thought that because I had been with the Government, I could explain the *mzungus'* [Europeans] ways to the Afri-cans better. Because I did not argue with them, they thought that I would force people to follow them. But because I was a chief, I didn't do any of these evil things.[114]

Nevertheless, most ex-servicemen who became traditional authorities lived up to expectations, and became a relatively conservative force in rural com-munities.

The East African governments also made limited economic concessions to select ex-servicemen. Hyde-Clark's warnings prompted the Kenyan gov-ernment to relax its licensing policies. To allow more veterans to qualify for trading licenses, Kenya's Chief Secretary ordered Provincial Commissioners to adopt a more "optimistic" view of the economy in calculating the number of merchants their provinces could support. District Commissioners in areas with high veteran populations reserved one-quarter of all trading plots for ex-servicemen. In Kitui District, civil officials issued enough transport li-censes so that African truckers outnumbered Asians.[115] These more liberal licensing policies did not signal a fundamental change in the government's policy of discouraging unqualified veterans from becoming traders; colonial administrators sought primarily to foster the creation of a small, stable class of prosperous ex-servicemen.

Unskilled former askaris who did not qualify for further assistance usually lacked the means to take collective action. They were left with the choice of facing criminal prosecution for inciting unrest or making do with their demobilization benefits, if they were fortunate enough to receive them. Rank-and-file veterans could become wealthy if they had land and knew how to invest their savings in agriculture. A significant number of men genuinely desired to resume their former lives, which aided the reabsorption process significantly. Some turned down jobs or additional training because they had no wish to leave their farms ever again. As one former askari explained: "They offered me [a place in a training program] and a job in the tribal police, but I never wanted to work again. . . . I used my money to buy cows [and] for a second wife." When a Kikuyu veteran was asked what he planned to do with his military skills, he replied: "I shall put on my dirtiest old clothes and sit in shade and watch my wives work."[116]

For better or worse, most African veterans settled into civilian life by the beginning of 1947. While many were unable to realize their social and economic aspirations, the East African governments took their relative passivity to mean reabsorption was complete. Even Kenyan administrative officers stationed in areas where veteran discontent had been judged dangerously high one year earlier concurred. In Nyasaland, the WNLA gave explicit preference to ex-servicemen, and labor migration drew off the most dissatisfied and restless veterans. Most former Tanganyikan askaris also returned to the land, and Uganda's *Annual Report for 1948* stated: "The majority of the ex-askaris have quietly slipped back into the village life of a rural peasant without apparently having derived from their travels or experiences any desire for anything different."[117]

These relieved and optimistic reports were based largely on the failure of expected veteran unrest to materialize. Yet many unskilled ex-servicemen, who found it difficult to readjust to civilian life and did not qualify for vocational training, still believed they were betrayed. As one man put it: "We helped the Englishman win the war . . . but we were not equally rewarded for our service."[118] Colonial officials with firsthand knowledge of the veteran community worried about the long-term ramifications of these festering grievances. Kenya's Principal Civil Reabsorption Officer (PCRA) warned:

> We have so far kept the ex-soldier quiet, if not always happy, and we have prevented him from causing general dissatisfaction in the community. . . .
> We have, however, built up considerable bitterness amongst the rank-and-file of ex-soldiers by failing to provide them with any means, or even the

hope of such means, of maintaining or improving the standard of living to which they feel they are entitled. Some openly say that, if another war should eventuate, they will take good care to be in a non-combatant unit, as such men get the easier life during the war, and richer rewards after it. This bitterness is real, and no more talk will suffice to eradicate it.[119]

The East Africa Command shared these concerns and, throughout the late 1940s, listed alienated ex-servicemen as a potential internal security threat. Many African veterans never stopped believing they were abandoned by an ungrateful British government, which indirectly contributed to the growing anti-colonial sentiment throughout East Africa in the closing decades of British rule.

AFRICAN VETERANS IN POST-WAR SOCIETY, 1945–1963

The East African ex-servicemen's community in the post-war era was divided between wartime veterans and ex-askaris who served in the peacetime KAR. The former tended to dominate the latter by virtue of their greater numbers. While there were over 300,000 East African veterans of the Second World War, the post-war KAR was rarely larger than 10,000 askaris. Thus, only a few hundred men were discharged each year.[120] While World War II veterans were divided by training, class, and ethnicity, most shared the conviction that they were not sufficiently rewarded for their service. The East African governments devoted little attention to ex-servicemen's issues in the 1950s, but when they did, they focused on the potentially disruptive influence of the wartime veterans.

Better trained veterans of the post-war KAR were in many ways more influential than their wartime predecessors, but civil officials considered them less of a problem because they had fewer grievances. With the exception of the Malayan and Mau Mau campaigns (which produced relatively few casualties), these askaris saw little direct combat. While there were disciplinary problems in the late 1940s when KAR wages lagged behind inflation, military authorities were more committed to African welfare in the post-war era, and army wages, medical care, and training all improved substantially in the 1950s. Thus, African soldiers of this era were more prosperous than their predecessors and usually found it much easier to return to civilian life.

Moreover, the limited enfranchisement of Africans in the mid-1950s required the East African governments to revise their attitudes toward ex-askaris. District officers paid closer attention to the welfare of ex-servicemen because they believed contented and prosperous African veterans were a stabilizing influence in rural society. All askaris were eligible for service pensions by 1956, and the colonial governments opened discussions on raising disability pension levels. District Officers, unit commanders, and the British

Legion (the BESL in Nyasaland) worked together to find employment for former askaris, and in 1956, the Kenyan government finally gave preferential status to veterans applying for government jobs.[121] Thus, although veterans of the post-war KAR often lacked the breadth of experience of their wartime predecessors, it was much easier for them to retain their status after they were discharged.

The influence of individual veterans on colonial society was determined largely by their education, military skills, and individual initiative. Former specialists and senior NCOs were usually quite prosperous because they received considerable benefits and government assistance. Rank-and-file askaris who wisely invested their pay and service gratuities also did well. Veterans who lost their demobilization benefits through disciplinary action, official incompetence, carelessness, or plain bad luck were less fortunate. These men, along with the physically disabled and mentally ill, formed a sizable class of destitute former askaris. Yet they tended to disappear into the growing ranks of the civilian African poor and had a minimal influence on colonial society.

In 1951, the Civil Reabsorption Officer for Central Kavirondo estimated there were 1,000 such veterans in his District alone, but in 1956, the "War Pensions Branch" of the Kenyan Treasury officially listed only 1,700 African pensioners in the entire Colony. Men denied pensions had access to an African Pensions Appeal Tribunal, but in 1950, the Tribunal dismissed 2,392 of the 3,015 cases it reviewed. There were few additional sources of funding to help needy veterans. Military officials used private subscriptions and surplus money from disbanded wartime units to establish an East African Army Benevolent Fund to assist charities working for the welfare of ex-servicemen. The Fund did not, however, make direct grants to former askaris.[122] Moreover, many ex-servicemen fortunate enough to receive disability pensions could not live on them. Although the East African governments introduced new pension regulations in 1948, these did not apply to veterans of the Second World War. As one disabled man complained: "I explained to the DC that my pension didn't fit me, but he did not care." Penurious colonial officials kept cost-of-living increases to a minimum, and the base African pension in 1954 was still slightly less than nine shillings per month. By the late 1950s, the value of most pensions was wiped out by inflation.[123]

Yet former askaris rarely resorted to political action to express their grievances. The political influence of African ex-servicemen has been the most debated issue relating to the colonial military. Many historians have argued that ex-askaris learned nationalism in the army. They depict veterans of the Second World War as highly politicized, and the ex-servicemen's defiance of the colonial government has become a tenet of popular Kenyan nationalism. O.J.E. Shiroya has tried to reconcile this interpretation with the competing depiction of African soldiers as collaborators by arguing that askaris remained under the sway of British propaganda until they eventually experienced the hypocrisy of the colonial system. In Shiroya's view, enlightened servicemen became agents of political change when they shared their ideas with the civilian population.[124]

These interpretations are based largely on a number of debates that are not particularly relevant to East Africa. Furedi has pointed out correctly that nationalist historians tend to accept official British warnings about disruptive colonial soldiers as fact, even though demobilization produced few actual cases of unrest.[125] The most serious incident involving ex-servicemen in all of British Africa took place in the Gold Coast in 1948 and has been the topic of considerable debate among historians of West Africa, who disagree on whether the event was politically inspired.[126] Equally influential were political scientists in the 1960s who viewed African armies as instruments of "nation building" that encouraged soldiers to adopt territorial, instead of ethnic, loyalties.[127] Nationalist historians adapted these theoretical models to East Africa in the absence of specific studies of the African rank-and-file.

The fundamental problem with most of their conclusions is that former askaris were noticeably absent from East African nationalist movements. Considered wealthy and experienced in their home communities, they could not compete with better-educated African bureaucrats, businessmen, and civil servants at the territorial or national level. A few Tanganyikan ex-servicemen were founding members of the Tanganyikan African National Union, but the model of the highly politicized veteran fits only a small handful of men like Bildad Kaggia, Waruhiu Itote, and Paul Ngei. Moreover, for each of these radical leaders, there were men like Justus Kandet ole Tipis, Musa Amalemba, and Jonathan Nzioka, who served as comparatively moderate representatives in the Kenyan Legislative Council.

Only fifty-five of the Africans listed in *Who's Who in East Africa* between 1963 and 1965 described themselves as veterans of the colonial army. The majority of these prominent ex-servicemen were local politicians, union leaders, junior magistrates, or lower-level bureaucrats. As a rule, most had strong educational backgrounds before joining the army, and few appear to have advanced themselves solely on the basis of their military careers.[128] As the most educated and politically aware class of African soldiers, it is not surprising that Army Education Instructors were the most influential ex-servicemen. Paul Ngei was one of only two veterans to join Jomo Kenyatta in detention (Bildad Kaggia was the other) for Mau Mau offenses. Ngei was also the only former askari in the inner circle of Kenyatta's Kenyan African National Union (KANU). The more moderate Musa Amalemba and Jonathan Nzioka were also former Army Education Instructors. In Uganda, Robert Kakembo was a Saza chief, and another ex-Education Instructor became Idi Amin's Minister for Education. Other jobs held by former members of the EAAEC included administrative officer, journalist, headmaster, interpreter, and independent filmmaker.[129]

By comparison, the average African ex-serviceman was neither ignorant nor apolitical, and civil officials noted many veterans had a particularly strong grasp of current events. Most had little love for British rule but had little in common with the radical nationalists, who rarely took an interest in issues pertaining to ex-servicemen. Politics for most former askaris meant lobbying colonial governments to make good on "unkept promises." Their impatience led to a resurgence of unofficial veterans' organizations when civil officials relaxed restrictions on African associations in the 1950s. The African Section of the British Legion, which had to keep these groups in check, had become moribund, and attendance at the ASBL's parades and rallies plummeted. In Kenya, the only Legion Halls still operating were in Kitui, Maralal, and Mombasa. Most were taken over by African District Councils or were rented out to government departments.[130] The new unofficial organizations explicitly promised to improve the lot of rank-and-file ex-askaris, thereby diverting attention away from the new African political parties.

The most ambitious of the new Kenyan groups was J. S. Ogara's National Ex-Servicemen's Union of Kenya (NESUK). Ogara was a decorated Luo Regimental Sergeant Major and a veteran of the Second World War. He had a questionable reputation, however, and the Kenyan government deregistered his organization in 1955, when an audit of its account books turned up no trace of the thousands of shillings in membership fees collected from the NESUK's 369 members.[131] Yet Ogara was popular because he forcefully and effectively articulated the ex-servicemen's grievances. Over the course of the 1950s, he bombarded the Kenyan government with petitions for veteran tax exemptions, vocational training courses, hiring preferences, free education for their children, and reserved seats on Local Native Councils. More significantly, he promised to deliver the long-awaited war pensions. By 1959, the NESUK had effectively replaced the ASBL in Nyanza Province. Complacent Legion officials allowed Ogara to take over the Kisumu Legion Hall, and he petitioned the Legion unsuccessfully for a salary, house, and travel allowance. [132]

The NESUK's success spawned a host of imitators. Ogara's primary rival was another Luo ex-Sergeant Major named Alex Oloo (alias Magina Magina). Oloo originally called his organization the Kenya Ex-Servicemen's League but changed its name to the National Ex-Servicemen's Union to attract some of Ogara's followers. While the NESUK was based primarily in Nyanza Province, Oloo concentrated on the rest of Kenya. His nominal association with Tom Mboya caused civil intelligence officers to worry Mboya was using him to gain influence in the post-colonial army. Oloo's real agenda, however, was not much different from Ogara's; he eventually stole most of his followers' subscriptions. Ogara was never formally convicted of theft or fraud, but Oloo fled to Uganda after independence. In another case, the General Secretary of the North Nyanza Ex-Servicemen's Union disappeared with his group's receipt books and 3,385 shillings. These notorious cases of fraud and embezzlement only made the African ex-servicemen's community even more distrustful of leaders who claimed to speak for them, which also helps explain their limited political influence.[133]

Nevertheless, the popularity of unsanctioned veterans' groups forced British officials to form a new organization to replace the ASBL. In 1961, the East Africa Command assumed direct responsibility for the basic welfare of former askaris by sponsoring the King's African Rifles Old Comrades Association (KAR OCA).[134] The Association made onetime "benevolent grants" of 50 to 200 shillings to destitute ex-servicemen (or their widows and orphans). The KAR OCA was underfunded, and only veterans in particularly dire straits qualified for assistance. The grants were intended to purchase basic necessities but could occasionally be used for school fees.[135] Most Kenyan veterans did not accept this limited focus and flooded the Association with ambitious petitions for grants to invest in coffee trees, butcher shops, secondhand clothing stores, and overseas education. In one month, eight requests from a single district totaled 100,000 shillings, twice the KAR OCA's entire operating budget.[136] Having neither the inclination nor the ability to grant these petitions, the Old Comrades Association failed to draw members away from the unofficial veterans' organizations. Yet this was not a serious problem in the long run. Ogara and his competitors embarrassed British officials at an awkward moment when they were trying to cope with mainstream African nationalism, but they were never a serious political threat to the colonial regime.

The most effective way to measure the influence of African ex-servicemen is to compare their status in two separate, but culturally related, Kenyan communities. As the premier martial race in Kenya, the Kamba provided more soldiers to the post-war KAR than any other ethnic group. As noted in Chapter 3, an absence of lucrative opportunities for civilian employment in the Kamba Reserves made military service the most popular form of unpaid wage labor for young, unskilled Kamba men. The dominant position of Kamba askaris in the Kenyan KAR battalions forced the government to be sensitive to their interests, and the Kamba often used their reputation as reliable soldiers to oppose successfully unpopular destocking and soil conservation schemes. Most chiefs were veterans, and while they had minimal influence in national politics, almost every Kamba politician in the post-war era had some military experience. These factors made it relatively easy for Kamba veterans to return to private life. As one former askari explained: "The Kamba considered it an honor to be a soldier." Similarly, another veteran opined: "If all people would be like KAR soldiers, life will be very smooth for this nation. Too much politics has spoiled the people." Although they shared the same grievances over pensions and benefits with ex-servicemen from other ethnic groups, Kamba veterans had the consolation of being some of the most wealthy and respected members of Kamba society.[137]

Kikuyu veterans, on the other hand, faced a substantially different set of circumstances. The loss of large tracts of the Central Highlands to white settlement made the Kikuyu leading opponents of the colonial regime. As a rule, they were rarely interested in military service because they had far more profitable opportunities in commercial agriculture, education, and skilled labor. Classified as a non-martial race by military authorities, the Kikuyu were recruited in large numbers only during the Second World War. Thus, Kikuyu veterans found it much harder to return to civilian life than their Kamba counterparts. Since the Kikuyu were a non-martial race, civil officials ignored their grievances. Ex-askaris rarely became chiefs and lost seats on Local Native Councils to better-educated civilians. While Kikuyu ex-servicemen were extremely ambitious, they had difficulty getting trade licenses, and few European employers would hire them. Moreover, the growing land shortage in the Kikuyu Reserves made it difficult for them to return to agriculture. In the novel *Weep Not, Child*, Ngugi wa Thiong'o presents a classic model of the alienated and rootless Kikuyu veteran in the character of Boro, a young ex-askari who disdains his father, joins the Mau Mau and murders his Chief and District Commissioner.[138]

While the majority of Kamba veterans either rejoined the army or settled into civilian life by 1947, Kikuyu veterans remained the most angry and restless ex-servicemen in Kenya. Although the two Bantu-speaking communities had close cultural ties and frequently intermarried, the marked difference in their treatment of veterans was a reflection of the degree to which military service was valued in the two societies. Landless Kikuyu veterans who spent their savings had little choice but to join the ranks of Nairobi's urban unemployed. Many helped found the resistance movement that grew into the Mau Mau Emergency.

Mau Mau field commanders like Waruhiu Itote and Stanley Mathenge had combat experience and based the organization of their Mau Mau units on the KAR. Karigo Muchai served in the East Africa Army Service Corps, and Dedan Mugo Kimani was an army Hygiene Instructor. The illustrious Dedan Kimathi, however, appears to have spent just a few months as a sweeper (latrine orderly) in the East Africa Military Labour Corps. Kimathi ordered his followers to grind up elephant tusks to make gun powder. Very few Kikuyu veterans served in frontline infantry battalions (Itote was a Mess Corporal in 36 KAR), and it is likely the British Army would have had a much more difficult time in the Kenyan forests if a few Kalenjin or Kamba Warrant Officer Platoon Commanders had joined the Mau Mau.[139] While it is impossible to determine exactly how many former Kikuyu askaris were active or passive supporters of the Mau Mau, they were the only African veterans to use violence against the colonial regime. Yet this case does not prove nationalist arguments about the political influence of ex-servicemen. The Mau Mau was a predominantly Kikuyu movement, and with the exception of a few Kamba veterans, no other ex-askaris took part.

In conclusion, the political influence of East African veterans has been largely overstated. On the whole, most askaris sought to maintain their privileged social status after they left the army. They expected material rewards from the colonial governments and deference from their peers. Civil officials, on the other hand, were willing to grant ex-servicemen a relatively generous, one-time demobilization payment, but after that, they were largely on their own. They expected aged or disabled veterans to be cared for by "tribal communities," and district officers repeatedly reminded ex-servicemen they were entitled to no better treatment than the average African civilian. Ex-servicemen bitterly resented their treatment but lacked the means to express their grievances through political protests. Many were exploited by unscrupulous leaders of unofficial ex-servicemen's groups, which made veterans less likely to trust nationalist politicians. Yet the relative wealth and practical experience of prosperous ex-askaris also made them respected men in their home communities, with the extent of their influence based on education, military occupation, and service experience. Thus, veterans were much more likely to be agents of economic and social change rather than instigators of political unrest.

NOTES

[1] Annual Battalion Returns, 1927–1938, PRO, CO 820.

[2] These ex-servicemen also demanded war bonuses and jobs, and the British Home Office warned disgruntled veterans were vulnerable to exploitation by "socialist demagogues" and Bolshevik sympathizers. The British government therefore placed unofficial veterans' organizations under police surveillance. Stephen R. Ward, "Intelligence Surveillance of British Ex-Servicemen, 1918–1920," *Historical Journal*, v. 16, (1973), pp. 183–85; Stephen Ward, ed., *The War Generation: Veterans of the First World War*, (Port Washington, NY: Kennikat Press, 1975), pp. 20–27.

[3] Great Britain, Colonial Office, *Regulations for the King's African Rifles*, (London: Waterlow and Sons, 1908), para. 232.

[4] Hubert Moyse-Bartlett, *The King's African Rifles*, (Aldershot: Gale & Polden, 1956), p. 52; Douglas Johnson, "The Structure of a Legacy: Military Slavery in Northeast Africa," *Ethnohistory*, v. 36, (1989), p. 82; Interview, #40.

[5] Only the handful of semi-official settlements had any protection. The Sudanese at Eldama Ravine received "temporary occupation licenses," which gave them rent-free tenure to one-acre parcels of land. In 1925, the Kenyan government established a veterans' village at Mazeras in the Coast Province for Sudanese ex-servicemen who chose to leave Jubaland after the former Kenyan Province became part of Italian Somaliland. Report by J. W. Barth, J. Ainsworth, W. J. Monson, and O. F. Waktins, 3 July 1916, KNA, PC

CST 1/11/68; Agreement between Kenyan Land Officer & Sallam Abdalla of Yonte, KNA, PC CST 1/17/28; PC NZA to CSK, 6 April 1949, KNA, OPE 1/364/46.

[6] IGR, 4 KAR, 1927, PRO, CO 820/3/17; Major W. G. Edward to CNC, 6 March 1936, KNA, MAA, 2/1/3/I/28; "Memorandum by Ex-Soldiers of the KAR," 7 January 1933, in Kenya Land Commission, *Evidence, Volume I*, (Nairobi: Government Printer, 1933).

[7] Major A. W. Sutcliffe, DC Nairobi, to Commissioner of Lands, 13 September 1935, KNA, BN 46/6/32; Commissioner of Police to Kenyan Colonial Secretary, 28 May 1934, KNA, MAA 2/1/3/I/5; Memorandum by Sutcliffe, 6 April 1936, KNA, MAA 2/1/3/I/37a.

[8] Kenya Colony and Protectorate, *Report of the Kenya Land Commission*, (Nairobi: Government Printer, 1933); Holger Bernt Hansen, "Pre-Colonial Immigrants and Colonial Servants: The Nubians of Uganda Revisited," *African Affairs*, v. 90, (1991), p. 572.

[9] Hassanabia, Secretary Sudanese Union to Lord Lugard, 24 August 1940, PRO, CO 822/106/14; Union of Sudanese to Colonial Secretary, 14 October 1940, PRO, CO 822/106/14; Sudanese Association to Kenyan Governor, 14 May 1951, PRO, CO 822/820.

[10] David Clark, "Social Organization in Kibera, Nairobi," (M.A. thesis, Makerere University, n.d.), pp. 25–26; Interviews, #40, #42, #43.

[11] Nyasaland Governor to Colonial Secretary, 30 August 1919, MNA, S2/45/19; Lewis Greenstein, "Africans in a European War: The First World War in East Africa with Special Reference to the Nandi of Kenya," (Ph.D. dissertation, Indiana University, 1975), p. 175.

[12] EAP Secretariat Circular, no. 100, "Repatriation of KAR Askaris," 5 December 1918, KNA, PC CST 1/1/234/49; Medical Arrangements for Demobilization of the KAR, by KAR ADMS, 24 December 1918, KNA, PC CST 1/13/118/886; Anthony Clayton and Donald Savage, *Government and Labour in Kenya, 1895–1963*, (London: Frank Cass, 1974), p. 87.

[13] GRO no. 764, "Compensation," 14 September 1915, KNA, PC CST 1/13/135/185; PC Mombasa to CS EAP, 17 August 1916, KNA, PC CST 1/11/68/2; Pensions and Gratuities, Native Ranks, c. 1918, MNA, NSB 3/9/1.

[14] Adjutant 4 KAR to PC Mombasa, 6 June 1918, KNA, PC CST 1/1/234/35; CNC to PC Mombasa, 30 November 1918, KNA, PC CST 1/13/118/866; Military Labour Corps Certificate of Discharge, 1919, KNA, PC CST 1/13/118/899; Memorandum by Military Commissioner for Labour, 9 May 1918, KNA, AG 5/1356/10a; Resident Mlanje to CSNY, 13 September 1920, MNA, S1/1460/19/36; O/C 1 KAR to KAR Inspector General, 31 May 1922, MNA, S1/1472/22/2.

[15] Colonial Secretary to Kenya Governor, 1 February 1922, PRO, WO 32/4135; Kenyan Secretariat Circular, No. 54, "Unclaimed Wages Due to Members of the Native Carrier Corps," 5 November 1930, KNA, AG 5/1356/57; EA War Medals and Records Department to DC Nakuru, 9 July 1932, KNA, DC NKU 2/29/14/4.

[16] Charles Hordern, *Military Operations in East Africa, Volume I, August 1914–September 1916*, (London: HM Stationery Office, 1941), p. 574.

[17] Hare wa Nzaka to Kenyan Colonial Secretary, 5 August 1936, KNA, PC CA 12/3; Japhet Hare (s/o Hare Nzaka) to PC Coast, 9 July 1954, KNA, PC CA 12/28/92; Kenyan Colonial Secretary to Kenya Governor, 24 November 1926, KNA, PC CST 1/11/68; Diana Ellis, "The Nandi Protest of 1923 in the Context of African Resistance to Colonial Rule in Kenya," *Journal of African History*, v. 17, (1976), p. 563.

[18] Ukamba Province AR, 1918–1919, KNA, DC MKS 1/5/11; Geoffrey Hodges, *The Carrier Corps: Military Labor in the East African Campaign, 1914–1918*, (Westport CT: Greenwood Press, 1986), p. 98; John McCracken, "Coercion and Control in

Nyasaland: Aspects of the History of a Colonial Police Force," *Journal of African History,* v. 27, (1986), p. 134.

[19] Carl Rosberg and John Nottingham, *The Myth of "Mau Mau": Nationalism and Colonialism in Kenya,* (New York: Praeger; reprint, Nairobi: TransAfrica Press, 1985), pp. 27–32; F. D. Corfield, *Historical Survey of the Origins and Growth of Mau Mau,* (London: Her Majesty's Stationery Office, 1960), p. 17; Hodges, *The Carrer Corp,* pp. 151, 190.

[20] South Kavirondo District AR, 31 March 1919, KNA, DC KSI 1/2.

[21] O/C Central Records to Resident Blantyre, 2 April 1919, MNA, NSB 3/9/1/252; Notes on Mobilization by Nyasaland Police Commissioner, 1930, MNA, S2/11/29/90a; DC South Lumbwa to PC NZA, 5 January 1932, KNA, PC NZA 2/1/10/19.

[22] Melvin Page, ed., *Africa and the First World War,* (New York: St. Martin's Press, 1987), p. 18; Robert Benson Boeder, "Malawians Abroad: The History of Labor Migration from Malawi to Its Neighbors, 1890 to the Present," (Ph.D. dissertation, Michigan State University, 1974), p. 103.

[23] Lewis Greenstein, "The Impact of Military Service in World War I on Africans: The Nandi of Kenya," *Journal of Modern African Studies,* vol. 16, (1978), pp. 499–502; Ellis, "The Nandi Protest of 1923," p. 562; Luise White, *The Comforts of Home: Prostitution in Colonial Nairobi,* (Chicago: University of Chicago Press, 1990), p. 64.

[24] DC Kasama to Adjutant NRR, 18 April 1935, PRO, CO 820 19/7; Nyasaland Governor to Colonial Secretary, 22 June 1940, PRO, CO 820/42/4.

[25] Deed of Declaration of Trusts, 1930, PRO, CO 820/16/12; KAR Inspector General to O/Cs Northern & Southern Brigades, 24 October 1932, PRO, CO 820/16/12.

[26] Report on the KAR Memorial Home, 1925, MNA, S1/805/25; Inspection of the KAR Memorial Home by O/C Southern Brigade, 1934, MNA, NVR 1/4/3.

[27] Frank Furedi, *The New Ideology of Imperialism: Renewing the Moral Imperative,* (London: Pluto Press, 1994), p. 28.

[28] Corporal David Mubwanga and Corporal Daudi Mnubi, HQ 5 (EA) EAMLS, to "Askari Mzee" (Editor of *Askari),* 14 November 1944, KNA, DEF 10/64/6; see also, 3/4 KAR Security Report, 2 December 1942, PRO, WO 169/7028; North Kavirondo District AR, 1943, KNA, MAA 2/3/10/III/8a; "St. Boniface," SEAC, to Editor of *Askari,* n.d., MNA, S41/1/23/5/60a.

[29] Interviews, #6; see also, #16b.

[30] Graham Wootton, *The Official History of the British Legion,* (London: Macdonald & Evans, 1956); Davis Ross, *Preparing for Ulysses,* (New York: Columbia University Press, 1969).

[31] DC Fort Hall to CNC, 6 July 1946, KNA, MAA 2/7/6; Rosberg and Nottingham, *The Myth of "Mau Mau,"* p. 32.

[32] Censorship Summary, Mail by EA Personnel, May 1943, KNA, MD 4/5/116/2; Interview, #51.

[33] Robert Kakembo, *An African Soldier Speaks,* (London: Livingstone Press, 1947), pp. 14–15.

[34] Interview, #112.

[35] Censorship Summary, March–May 1943, KNA, MD 4/5/116/1.

[36] Morale of Allied Land Forces, SE Asia, May–July 1945, PRO, WO 203/2045.

[37] Civil officials found it difficult to enforce the color bar when on the average an African American Private received roughly sixty-eight shillings per week, as com-

pared to the fourteen shillings earned by British Privates. A black American Sergeant received twice the pay of a British Lieutenant. CSEAG to Colonial Secretary, 23 October 1943, PRO, CO 968/92/2; Graham Smith, *When Jim Crow Met John Bull: Black American Soldiers in World War II Britain*, (London: I. B. Tauris, 1987), p. 46; Interview, #137.

[38] Waruhiu Itote, *"Mau Mau" General*, (Nairobi: EA Publishing House, 1967), p. 11; Bildad Kaggia, *The Roots of Freedom, 1921–1963*, (Nairobi: EA Publishing House, 1975), pp. 26–27; Okete J. E. Shiroya, "The Impact of World War II on Kenya: The Role of Ex-Servicemen in Kenyan Nationalism," (Ph.D. dissertation, Michigan State University, 1968), p. 95; George Shepperson, "America Through Africa and Asia," *Journal of American Studies*, v. 14, (1980), p. 53.

[39] Extract from the *Times*, 21 August 1945, KNA, DEF 10/24/5a & b; Annual Letter 1945, by Peter Bostock, KNA, PBG 134/AD; Rev. M. G. Capon, CCK Secretary to DACG, 30 August 1945, "CCK Correspondence, 1945–48"; Furedi, *The New Ideology of Imperialism*, p. 30.

[40] African Manpower Conference, 7 May 1943, KNA, DEF 15/27/70a; East African Demobilization Conference, 16 November 1943, KNA, BY 49/17/22; *Uganda Standard*, "Demobilisation," 18 April 1945, PRO, CO 968/141/4.

[41] DC Nandi, to PC RVP, 20 August 1942, KNA, DC KAPT 1/12/29/2; DO Central Kavirondo to PC NZA, 22 August 1942, KNA, PC NZA 3/1/358/7; Testimony of J. M. Omino Before the Post-War Development Committee, 2 September 1942, KNA, DC KSM 1/1/174/13; Colony and Protectorate of Kenya, *Post-War Employment Committee Report and Report of the Sub-Committee on Post-War Employment of Africans*, (Nairobi: Government Printer, 1943).

[42] Kenyan Tradesmen by District, 1945, KNA, DEF 10/9; Plan for the CEB, July 1945, KNA, DEF 10/9/38a; Statistics on East African Service and Casualties, July 1947, KNA, DEF 10/43/93.

[43] David Easterbrook, "Kenya Askari in WWII and Their Demobilization with Special Reference to Machakos District," in *Three Aspects of the Colonial Crisis in Kenya*, Bismark Myrick, ed. (Syracuse, NY: Syracuse University, 1975), p. 35; R. Surridge, Kenya Secretariat to D. C. Watherston, CO, 20 January 1943, PRO, CO 820/47/6; Bowie, 22 KAR, 1940–47, , RHL, Mss.Afr.s.1715/24a.

[44] CNC HoR, December 1943, KNA, MAA 8/53/5.

[45] East African Demobilization Conference, 16 November 1943, KNA, BY 49/17/22; Colony and Protectorate of Kenya, *Post-War Employment Committee Report*.

[46] African Manpower Conference, Item II, 7 May 1943, PRO, CO 968/79/5; Proposals on Training—African, by Patrick Williams, 1944, KNA, MAA 8/146/8; Talk on the CRB to European Employers, 1945, KNA, DEF 10/51/9.

[47] Draft Ugandan Publication on Demobilisation, 1944, KNA, DEF 10/63/1; CRB Meeting Notes, 22 September 1944, KNA, MAA 8/146/4; Nyasaland Protectorate, Post-War Development Committee, Interim Report No. 7—Demobilisation, 2 August 1944, MNA, LB 8/2/3.

[48] Colony and Protectorate of Kenya, *Post-War Employment Committee Report*.

[49] "Mr. Mathu Answers Askaris' Questions," *East African Standard*, 20 October 1945, KNA, OP EST 1/7/11.

[50] Kenya Colony and Protectorate, *Progress Report on Demobilization*, (Nairobi: Government Printers, 1944), pp. 4–10; CSEAG Memorandum on Demobilisation, n.d., KNA, DEF 10/43/67; Sir Philip Mitchell, Kenya Governor, to Colonial Office, 9 April

1945, PRO, CO 968/141/5; Mitchell to Colonial Office, 19 April 1945, KNA, DEF 10/151/5c; East Africa Governors Conference, 3–4 May 1945, KNA, CS 2/2/6/22a.

[51] DC Kericho to PC NZA, 26 July 1945, KNA, PC NZA 2/3/70/58; Meeting of East African PCDOs, 20 August 1945, KNA, DEF 10/151/19a; The Reduction of the East African Forces, by EAC Demobilisation Branch, 22 August 1945, KNA, DEF 10/151/20a; EAC to PCDO, August 1945, KNA, DEF 10/151/18a; LCK to CSK, 3 October 1945, KNA, DEF 9/5/3.

[52] Military Releases, East Africa Command, 29 June 1946, KNA, DEF 10/19/30; Kenyan Report on Demobilisation and Reabsorption, August 1946–April 1947, KNA, DEF 1/130/15a/1; Kenyan Manpower Demobilization and Reabsorption Report for the Year 1947, KNA, DEF, 10 108/2c.

[53] War Gratuities to African Soldiers, 21 January 1944, KNA, PC NGO 1/15/4; CSEAG to CSK, 3 February 1945, KNA, MD 4/5/72/155; POSBs for African Ex-Servicemen, 11 May 1945, KNA, MD 4/5/72/219a; EA Directorate of Demobilization to CSNY, 15 September 1945, MNA, S41/1/5/3/78; Payment of War Gratuities, 30 November 1945, KNA, DC TANA 11/14/20.

[54] E. M. Hyde-Clark to CSEAG, 27 February 1945, KNA, DEF 10/43/75; "Release Benefits," *East African Standard*, 29 June 1945, KNA, MD 4/5/80/12a; Release of Africans, by PCDO, 11 September 1945, KNA, DC TAMB 1/9/14/21.

[55] Ugandan CRO to PCDO, 16 December 1944, KNA, DEM 25/56; CSNY to CSEAG, 13 October 1945, MNA, S41/1/1/3/35.

[56] Report on the Dar Es Salaam Labour Exchange, 26 October 1945, KNA, DEF 10/41/22; Kenyan Trades and Tradesmen, by District, 1945, KNA, DEF 10/9; CEB Reports May–July 1946, KNA, DEF 10/41; CEB Employment Statistics, October 1945–September 1946, KNA, DEF 10/41; Report on Demobilisation and Reabsorption, August 1946–April 1947, KNA, DEF 1/130/15a/1; CEB Registration Statement, December 1947–January 1948, KNA, DEF 10/9.

[57] PCDO to KIO, 24 April 1946, KNA, DEF 10/64/79; African CEB Bulletin, No. 2, July 1946, KNA, DEF 10/9; Minute by Kenyan Labour Officer, 24 August 1946, KNA, DEF 10/24/5; R. N. Edmundson, Kenya Farmer to Editor, *Kenya Weekly News*, 1 July 1946, KNA, MD 4/5/134/51a; Machakos District IR, October 1946, KNA, DC MKS 1/2/1/1/35.

[58] O/C Works Coy to LCK, 25 April 1946, KNA, DC MKS 3/90/50; Machakos Meeting on the Works Company, 3 June 1946, KNA, DC MKS 3/90/62.

[59] CSEAG to CSU, 7 May 1946, KNA, MD 4/5/134/32; MKS IR, October 1946, KNA, DC MKS 1/2/1/1/35; Demobilisation and Reabsorption, August 1946–April 1947, KNA, DEF 1/130/15a/1; East Africa News Review, 19 February 1948, KNA, MAA 8/102/26; Interview, #105.

[60] CEB Monthly Report, 5 June 1946, KNA, DEF 10/41/26; African CEB Bulletin, No. 2, July 1946, KNA, DEF 10/9.

[61] CDO South Kavirondo to CRB, 15 May 1946, KNA, DEF 10/22/59; CRB Meeting, 21 November 1946, KNA, DEF 10/41/34; CEB Listings, 1946, KNA, DEF 10/9.

[62] Minute by Kenyan Labour Officer, 24 August 1946, KNA, DEF 10/42/5; CRB Meeting, 14 May 1947, KNA, DEF 1/130/15a.

[63] Director of Training to CSEAG, 1944, KNA, DEF 10/43/67; East African Training Directorate AR, 1946, KNA, DEF 10/4/22; Training of Ex-Servicemen in East Africa, by Patrick Williams, 1 October 1948, KNA, MAA 7/481/19/1; Uganda Protectorate, *Annual Report for 1939–46*, (Entebbe: Government Printer, 1949); Great Britain, Colonial Of-

fice, *British Territories in East and Central Africa, 1945–1950*, (London: HM Stationary Office, 1950), p. 144.

⁶⁴ Kenya Education Department to PCDO, 21 August 1945, KNA, DEF 10/65/3; Principal Makerere College to Territorial Directors of Education, 17 January 1946, MNA, LB 8/2/2; LCN to CSNY, 12 October 1946, MNA, LB 8/2/9; Nyasaland Director of Education to Mission Educational Secretaries, 16 December 1946, MNA, 1DCZA 1/20/28; Progress Report—Ex-Servicemen's Training, 5 May 1947, KNA, DEF 1/130/15a/1.

⁶⁵ LCN to Inter-Territorial Director of Training, 15 May 1946, MNA, S41 1/1/3/76; To All Ex-Askari in Central & Northern Provinces, 21 March 1946, MNA, LB 8/2/3; Vacancies at Artisan Training Centre, 1 November 1946, MNA, NN 1/9/12/21; O/C Training Centre Likuni to Senior Agricultural Officer, 6 November 1946, MNA, NN 1/9/12/30.

⁶⁶ Absorption of African Artisans, Centre B, July 1946, KNA, DEF 10/4/20; Fort Hall District AR, 1946, KNA, PC CP 4/4/3; South Kavirondo District AR, 1946, KNA, MAA 2/3/10/IV/1ai.

⁶⁷ CEB Monthly Report, 4 April 1946, KNA, DEF 10/41/24; Director of Training to LCK, 22 July 1946, KNA, DEF 10/4/20; Kisumu District HoW, July–September 1947, KNA, PC NZA 2/3/61.

⁶⁸ Director of Training to CSK, 30 May 1947, KNA, MAA 2/1/49/138; Great Britain, Colonial Office, *British Territories in East and Central Africa, 1945–1950*, p. 144.

⁶⁹ Director of Manpower to PC Central Province, 16 January 1946, KNA, DEF 10/4/3; DC Tambach to PC RVP, 5 September 1946, KNA, DC TAMB 1/9/14/62; Machakos District AR, 1947, KNA, DC MKS 1/1/30.

⁷⁰ Report on Demobilisation and Reabsorption, August 1946–April 1947, KNA, DEF 1/130/15a/1.

⁷¹ Repatriation and Disabled Askaris, 27 September 1943, KNA, DEF 10/25/4a; War Pensions Officer to E. M. Hyde-Clark, 22 November 1943, KNA, DEF 10/25/8; EAC Circular, "African Rehabilitation," 9 June 1944, KNA, DEF 10/25/103; Memorandum on Rehabilitation, by Hyde-Clark, 17 April 1945, KNA, DEF 10/26/9; William Platt, "Studies in Wartime Organization: (6) East Africa Command," *African Affairs*, v. 45, (1946), p. 34.

⁷² Kenyan Native Poll Tax Ordinance, 1942, KNA, MAA 2/4/115/I/145; HM Forces Pension Ordinance, 1942, KNA AG/5/2823.

⁷³ East African Pensions Committee, 15 May 1942, KNA, MD 4/5/73/77a; CSK to PCs, 30 March 1943, KNA, DC KAPT 1/12/19/15; CO Minute by Formoy, 5 September 1946, PRO, CO 820/53/6.

⁷⁴ Training Blind Africans, 30 October 1943, KNA, CS 1/10/50/15b; Minute by Nyasaland DMS, 19 June 1945, MNA, S41/1/23/17; Kenyan Director of Manpower to Accountant General, 15 June 1946, KNA, DEF 10/26/3.

⁷⁵ Report on G.2722 Andala Kutoyi, by DMS EAC, 9 June 1942, KNA, MD 4/5/81/12a; Kenya Medical Department Report, 25 July 1944, KNA, DEM 18/I/131; PC Coast to PCRO, 15 August 1945, KNA, CA 12/26/10; Kenyan DMS to Accountant General, 3 April 1947, KNA, DEF 10/28/94b.

⁷⁶ Interviews, #63; see also, #82.

⁷⁷ Interview, #168; see also Ex-RSM E Mgoge Mgoge MBE to CSK, 24 July 1950, KNA, MAA 2/5/226/IV/277/1; Interviews, #10, 16b, #37, #61, #64, #78, #103.

⁷⁸ Nyasaland Governor to CSNY, 13 July 1942, MNA, S41/1/5/2; Memorandum to Standing Finance Committee on Manpower, Demobilisation and Training, by Hyde-Clark,

30 April 1946, KNA, DEF 1/130/1; PC NZA to Ex-RSM Mgoge, 2 August 1950, KNA, MAA 2/5/226IV/277; Interviews, #135, #142, #143, #147, #148, #150, #151, #154.

[79] S. H. Fazan, PC NZA, to Director of Education, 23 December 1942, KNA, DEF 15/55/11a; also see EA Troops in SEAC: Interim Report, by EAPLO, 31 December 1945, KNA, DEF 15/12/105a.

[80] PCDO to CSEAG, 15 August 1944, KNA, DEF 10/43/21; Assistant DC Mlanje to BESL, 12 January 1946, MNA, NSM 1/4/2/15; Progress Report on African Demobilization, 31 March 1946, RHL, Mss.Afr.s.1158/2; Kenyan CRB Minutes, 21 November 1946, KNA, DEF 10/41/34.

[81] DC Voi to CRO, 18 February 1947, KNA, CA 12/27/123; CRO Circular, "Unclaimed Emoluments—Ex-Askari or Dependents," 31 July 1947, KNA, DC LDR 2/18/11/17; DC Nandi to PC RVP, 28 June 1948, KNA, DC KAPT 1/12/61/7; Interview, #99.

[82] African Releases—Periodic Letters, Nos. 1–5, October 1945–January 1946, KNA, DEF 10/20/1–4; PCDO to Kenyan Postmaster General, 13 February 1946, KNA, MD 4/5/80/61a.

[83] Central Province IR, May 1946, KNA, MAA 2/3/16/IV/94; KIO to PCDO, 25 June 1946, KNA, DEF 10/64/80; NZA AR, 1946, KNA, MAA 2/3/10/IV/1; Ex-Servicemen's Training, 5 May 1947, KNA, DEF 1/130/15a/1.

[84] Memorandum on Manpower, Demobilisation and Re-absorption, KNA, DEF 1/130/48/I; Safari Report, by ASBL ExO, 2 December 1959, KNA, OPE 1/7/90/1; ExO KAR OCA to DC North Nyanza, 22 January 1962, KNA, DC KMG 1/11/3/114.

[85] Interview, #51; see also Kikuyu District Ex-Soldiers Association to Fort Hall Residents, 7 May 1946, KNA, DC MUR 3/1/11; Machakos District AR, 1946, KNA, DC MKS 1/1/30; Interviews, #6, #51.

[86] Lance Corporal Willie B. Muturu, Station Hospital Mogadishu, 22 January 1945, KNA, DEF 10/64/15.

[87] RVP AR, 1944, KNA, MAA 2/3/11/V/1a; Demobilization & Reabsorption IR, November 1946, KNA, DC TAMB 1/9/14/66.

[88] Visit to Madagascar, by EAPLO, 27 July 1943, KNA, MD 4/5/65/227a; Resolution of the Nyasaland African Congress, 19–22 December 1944, MNA, S41/1/1/3/9.

[89] Minute by Jaxon Barton, CSNY, 26 November 1941, MNA, S41/1/5/2; Barton to Nyasaland Governor, 26 August 1943, MNA, S41/1/5/2; RAR Newsletter, No. 47, 21 January 1946, MNA, LB 8/7/1; Eugene Schleh, "Post-Service Careers of African World War Two Veterans: British East and West Africa with Particular Reference to Uganda and Ghana," (Ph.D. Dissertation, Yale University, 1968), pp. 61 & 144.

[90] Extracts from African Mail, May 1945, KNA, DEF 10/64/36; see also George Kinnear, "Askaris Are Making Their Own Post-War Plans," *East African Standard*, 4 July 1945; 5 FSS, Security Report, 22 August 1945, PRO, WO 172/9544; African, Arab and Somali Associations, by Kenyan Director of Intelligence and Security, 24 July 1947, KNA, MAA 2/5/66/89/3.

[91] Robert Kakembo to Editor of *Gambuze*, c. 1945, PRO, CO 822/118/4; I.J.W. Crawford to CNC, 3 November 1945, KNA, CNC 10/68/65.

[92] Ex-Service Co-Operative Society to DCs Fort Hall; Nakuru, 24 January 1946, KNA, DC MUR 3/1/11; Minutes of Kikuyu Ex-Soldiers Company, Thika Branch, 27 February 1946, KNA, MUR 3/1/11; Fort Hall District AR, 1946, KNA, PC CP 4/4/3.

[93] CSK to Kenyan PCs, 14 March 1946, KNA, DEF 10/63/1a; Kenyan Secretariat Circular, No. 114, 1 October 1946, KNA, DEF 10/63/12a.

[94] CRO North Kavirondo to DMP, 28 December 1946, KNA, DEF 10/63/17; see also, Central Province IR, January 1946, KNA, MAA 2/1/49/24; Kenyan Trading Licenses

Issued, August 1946 to May 1947, KNA, DEF 10/39/221 & 226; DC North Kavirondo to PC NZA, 29 November 1946, KNA, DEF 10/63/16b.

[95] CSNY to Director of Public Works, 25 September 1945, MNA, PCS 1/18/3/54a; PC Central Province to DCs, 3 December 1946, KNA, MUR 3/1/11; Kenyan Secretariat Circular, No. 8, 18 January 1946, KNA, DEF 10/62/5; Machakos District AR, 1947, KNA, DC MKS 1/1/30; O.J.E. Shiroya, *Kenya and World War Two: African Soldiers in the European War*, (Nairobi: Kenya Literature Bureau, 1985), p. 114.

[96] John Njoroge to CNC, 29 June 1946, KNA, MAA 7/2/4; DC Tambach to PC RVP, 5 September 1946, KNA, DC TAMB 1/9/14/62; Nyeri District AR 1946, KNA, PC CP 4/4/3; Interviews, #12, #51, #64, #82, #90, #103.

[97] Muranga District Ex-Soldiers Union to DC Fort Hall, 12 February 1946, KNA, DC MUR 3/1/11/1; Nyeri District Ex-Soldiers African Friendly Association General Meeting, 10 March 1946, KNA, DC NYI 2/10/9/2; Kikuyu District Ex-Soldiers Association, by John Njoroge, 7 May 1946, KNA, DC MUR 3/1/11; Muranga District Ex-Soldiers Union to CSK, 6 October 1946, KNA, DC MUR 3/1/11; Superintendent of Police Central Province to Assistant Superintendents, 21 November 1946, KNA, DC MUR 2/11/16/15.

[98] Fort Hall District AR, 1946, KNA, PC CP 4/4/3; J. W. Gaithi to CSK, 5 January 1947, KNA, MAA 7/2/21.

[99] Registrar of Societies Machakos, KNA, DC MKS 4/6; CCK, African Churches Conference, January 1947, CPK Archives; Machakos District AR, 1948, KNA, DC MKS 1/1/30; Mary Teffen, Michael Mortimore, and Francis Gichuki, *More People Less Erosion: Environmental Recovery in Kenya*, (Chichester: John Wiley & Sons, 1994), p. 137; Interviews, #12, #51, #81, #82, #91, #103.

[100] Kakembo, *An African Soldier Speaks*; see also CO Minute by Creasy, 15 March 1945, PRO, CO 822/118/4; CO Minute, 6 June 1945, PRO, CO 822/118/4; PIO EAC to EA Governments, 22 October 1945, KNA, CS 1/10/50/79.

[101] Unfortunately there are no available records of Kakembo's decision. He never joined the Registrar's staff, but was a Saza Chief in the 1950s. Ugandan Governor to CO, 10 October 1945, PRO, CO 822/118/4; Eugene Schleh, "The Post-War Careers of Ex-Servicemen in Ghana and Uganda," *Journal of Modern African Studies,* v. 6 (1968), pp. 149, 152–60; Interview, #122a.

[102] R. Tatton Brown to CNC, 2 October 1945, KNA, DEF 10/24/5; see also Tanganyikan Secretariat Circular, "British Legion," 1 May 1945, KNA, OPE 1/7/17a.

[103] Demobilization Branch EAC, 15 October 1945, KNA, DEF 10/24/12; Kenyan Secretariat Circular, "African Section British Legion Appeal Fund," 21 January 1946, KNA, OPE 1/7/20; ASBL Bulletin, No. 3, 1946, KNA, PC NZA 3/1/372/53.

[104] Kenyan Secretariat Circular, "African Section British Legion," 24 April 1946, KNA, OPE 1/7/45; CSK to Kenyan DCs, n.d., KNA, DEF 10/24/44; ASBL Bulletin, No. 6, January 1947, KNA, PC NZA 3/1/372/68; Welfare—African, n.d., KNA, DEF 6/61/39.

[105] ASBL Bulletin, No. 8, March 1947, KNA, DEF 10/24; ASBL Bulletin, No. 18, January 1948, KNA, DC TAMB 3/12/3/43; ASBL Bulletin, No. 31, January 1949, KNA, BB 23/3/3; ASBL AR, 1949, KNA, DEF 6/61/32/3.

[106] Interview, #90.

[107] Welfare—African, 1947, KNA, DEF 6/61/32; ASBL Membership, 31 July 1946, KNA, DC TAMB 3/12/3/10.

[108] ASBL Funds Collected 1 September 1945–31 May 1947, KNA, DC TAMB 3/12/3/26; Machakos District AR, 1950, KNA, DC MKS 1/1/30; Secretary of ASBL to Kenyan Secretariat, 27 April 1950, KNA, DEF 6/61/10.

[109] Inspector of Police Kabete to Assistant Superintendent of Police, 31 January 1946, KNA, DEF 13/120/1a; Tanganyikan CID to Police HQ Dar Es Salaam, 30 September 1947, KNA, CS 1/12/12; Interview, #148.

[110] Memorandum to the Standing Finance Committee on Manpower, Demobilisation and Training by LCK E.M. Hyde-Clark, 30 April 1946, KNA, DEF 1/130/1.

[111] Furedi, *The New Ideology of Imperialism*, pp. 29–30.

[112] Post-War Training and Employment, 1945, MNA, LB 8/2/2; Hyde-Clark to CNC, 28 February 1946, KNA, MAA 2/1/49/1; Memorandum to the Standing Finance Committee, by Hyde-Clark, 30 April 1946, KNA, DEF 1/130/1.

[113] PC Southern Province to Nyasaland DCs, September 1945, MNA, S41/1/1/1/1a; Baringo District AR, 1945, KNA, MAA 2/3/11/VI/1b; Kitui District AR, 1946, KNA, DC KTI 1/1/5; Kericho District AR, 1946, KNA, MAA 2/3/10/IV/1aii; NZA AR, 1946, KNA, MAA 2/3/10/IV/1; Machakos District AR, 1947, KNA, DC MKS 1/1/30; North Mara District (Tanganyika) AR, 1948, RHL, Mss.Afr.s.1750; Uganda Protectorate, *Annual Report for 1939–46*.

[114] Interview, #89.

[115] CSK to PCs, 14 March 1946, KNA, DEF 10/63/1a; Central Province IR, August 1946, KNA, MAA 2/3/16/IV/98; Kitui District AR, 1946, KNA, DC KTI 1/1/5.

[116] Interviews, # 65 and 135; see also, Interviews, #25 and #104.

[117] Machakos District AR, 1946, KNA, DC MKS 1/1/30; Fort Hall District AR, 1946, KNA, PC CP 4/4/3; Uganda Protectorate, *Annual Report for 1948*, (Entebbe: Government Printer, 1950); John Iliffe, *A Modern History of Tanganyika*, (New York: Cambridge University Press, 1979), p. 377; Nyasaland Governor's Permit for WNLA, 2 January 1951, MNA, LB 10/4/7/1.

[118] Interview, #96.

[119] Report of the PCRO, 1947, KNA, DEF 1/130/15a/1.

[120] See Table A.1.

[121] Secretary BESL to Civil Employers, April 1957, MNA/PCN/1/3/6/22; Cabinet Office Secretary to Kenyan Solicitor General, 3 December 1957, KNA, AG 5/1530/109; PS for Defence to ASBL Secretary, 2 September 1959, KNA, DC TAMB 3/12/3/66; DC Central Nyanza District to O/Cs KAR Bns, 5 June 1961, KNA, DC HB 2/18/2/2.

[122] African Pension Branch to African Pensions Appeal Tribunal, 4 March 1951, KNA, TRS 4/1912/1101; CRO Central Kavirondo District to DWO, 13 November 1951, KNA, DC KSM 1/22/67/233; Kenyan Secretariat Circular, "East Africa Army Benevolent Fund," 3 June 1952, KNA, PC NKU 2/21/5/43; Kenya Colony and Protectorate, *The Calculation and Payment of War Pensions in Kenya, Report No. 14*, (Nairobi: Government Printer, 1956), pp. 3–4; Interviews, #63, #82.

[123] HM Forces Pensions and Gratuities (African Military Personnel) Regulations, 1948, KNA, AG 5/2823/88b; DC Fort Hall to Harrison Comba Kimoku, 11 March 1952, KNA, DC FH 3/12/21/32; EAC Pensions Branch to DC Meru, 1 February 1954, KNA, DC MRU 2/12/2/222; Interviews, #11a, #29, #151.

[124] Shiroya, "The Impact of World War II on Kenya," pp. 92–3; Shiroya, *Kenya and World War Two*, pp. 154–5; Tabitha Kanogo, *Dedan Kimathi, Makers of Kenya's History, No. 3*, (Nairobi: East African Education Publishers, 1992), p. 12; George Bennett, *Kenya: A Political History; The Colonial Period*, (London: Oxford University Press, 1963), p. 112.

[125] Furedi, *The New Ideology of Imperialism*, p. 19.

[126] Ronald Robinson, "Andrew Cohen and the Transfer of Power in Tropical Africa," in *Decolonisation and After*, edited by W. H. Morris and Georges Fischer, (London: Frank

Cass, 1980), p. 67; David Killingray, "Soldiers, Ex-Servicemen, and Politics in the Gold Coast, 1939–50," *Journal of Modern African Studies*, v. 21, (1983), p. 525; Adrienne Israel, "Ex-Servicemen at the Crossroads: Protest and Politics in Post-War Ghana," *Journal of Modern African Studies*, v. 30, (1992), p. 363.

[127] William Gutteridge, "The Place of the Armed Forces in Society in African States," *Race*, v. 4, (1962), p. 25.

[128] The *Who's Who* listings were not comprehensive, and some former askaris failed to mention their military careers. For example, Bildad Kaggia's entry makes no mention of his service in the AAPC during the Second World War.

[129] E.G. Wilson, ed., *Who's Who in East Africa*, (Nairobi: Marco Publishers, 1964); E. G. Wilson, ed., *Who's Who in East Africa*, (Nairobi: Marco Publishers, 1965); E.G. Wilson, ed., *Who's Who in East Africa*, (Nairobi: Marco Publishers, 1966); Interviews, #35, #146.

[130] Chair ASBL to Kenyan Finance Minister, 18 December 1957, KNA, OPE 1/7/69/1; A. F. Sagar, Defence Ministry, to PCs, 4 January 1960, KNA, PC NZA 4/20/26/9.

[131] J.S.P. Ogara to DC South Nyanza District, 16 June 1953, KNA, DP 1/92/10; Registrar of Societies to Ogara, 1 September 1955, KNA, DP 1/70/1.

[132] Ogara to PC NZA, 30 November 1950, KNA, PC NZA 3/1/314/18; Kenyan Ex-Servicemen to the British Parliamentary Commission, 18 January 1954, KNA, DP 1/92/27; Ogara to Kenya Governor, 21 March 1961, KNA, PC NZA 4/20/26/46.

[133] SBIS, Nos. 7 & 8, July–August 1960, PRO, CO 822/2058; Kenya Ex-Servicemen's Union Meeting, Taveta Branch, 6 July 1963, KNA, DO TAV 1/19/33/41; North Nyanza Ex-Servicemen's Union to Police Commissioner Western Region, 16 December 1964, KNA, DC KMG 2/17/19/74; Interviews, #1, #16, #56, #117.

[134] Kenyan Secretariat Circular, "KAR and EA Forces Old Comrades Association," 17 December 1960, KNA, DC TAMB 3/12/3/94; British Legion (Kenya) Executive Council Meeting, 23 February 1961, KNA, OPE 1/7/127/1.

[135] KAR OCA Executive Officer to DC NNZA, 28 March 1962, KNA, DC KMG 2/17/19/4; DC Taita to KAR OCA Executive Officer, 30 April 1963, KNA, DC TTA 3/10/2/166; Yakobo Njebeni to RGA Kakamega, 27 January 1964, KNA, DC KMG 2/17/19/30.

[136] EAC Circular, "KAR and EA Forces Old Comrades Association," 10 April 1962, KNA, PC NKU 2/21/4/122/1; KAR OCA to Kenyan PCs & DCs, 21 December 1962, KNA, DC KAPT 2/16/1/164; Limo arap Karya to KAR OCA, 22 March 1963, KNA, DC KAPT 2/16/1/172.

[137] Machakos Political Record Books, 1930–1938, KNA, DC MKS 4/9; The Story of My Life by Chief Kasina Ndoo, 1957, KNA, OPE 1/381/5; Interviews, #25, #93, #133, #133a.

[138] Record Book of Chiefs and Headmen, Fort Hall, 1937–1954, KNA, DC MUR 1/4/6; Monthly Report of the CEB, 5 June 1946, KNA, DEF 10/41/26; Ngugi wa Thiong'o, *Weep Not, Child*, (Oxford: Heinemann, 1989).

[139] Appreciation on Future Military Policy in Kenya, EAC, 1954, PRO, WO 216/863; Henry Kahinga Wachanga, *The Swords of Kirinyaga: The Fight for Land and Freedom*, (Nairobi: Kenya Literature Bureau, 1991), pp. 26, 42, 172; Rosberg and Nottingham, *The Myth of "Mau Mau,"* pp. 193–94; Itote, *"Mau Mau" General*; Karigo Muchai, *The Hard Core: The Story of Karigo Muchai*, (Richmond: L.S.M. Information Center, 1973), p. 14; Interview, #143.

8

EPILOGUE

The King's African Rifles was a product of the colonial system, and as such, the Regiment mirrored the larger contradictions of British rule in East Africa. Operating within an administrative system governed by fiscal austerity and indirect rule, the East African governments relied on askaris and other African intermediaries out of necessity. Yet as "protected persons" rather than citizens, African servicemen had little reason to love the colonial regime. British officials were often troubled by unreliable African chiefs, clerks, and policemen, but African soldiers were a special problem. As the colonial state's primary instrument of lethal force, the African soldiery required political surveillance, social isolation, and domestic supervision but, above all else, suitable incentives to accept military discipline. Yet just as the colonial state tried to promote economic development without destabilizing African society, the King's African Rifles sought to make military service appealing without creating a class of "detribalized" veterans. This was easier said than done, and there was considerable room for negotiation among the army, the state, and the African rank-and-file in defining the nature of colonial military service. African servicemen both consciously and unconsciously exploited these tensions to seek greater status. Thus, it is unproductive to debate whether they were loyal colonial servants, oppressed conscripts, or self-interested mercenaries. In choosing—or in the case of coerced recruits, accepting—a military career, they simply made logical choices within the context of the political economy of the times. In spite of the well-documented cases of resistance by African soldiers, the KAR was an effective instrument of colonial authority because the colonial regime kept askari discontent from reaching unmanageable proportions by walking a careful line between repression and accommodation.

This precarious balance was only possible because the autocratic colonial state, although limited in scope, had sufficient authority to restrict opportunities for African advancement. One of the best ways to understand this complex system is to explore how it broke down after the newly independent East African states inherited territorial KAR battalions as their national armies. Faced with the conflicting demands for representative democracy, political patronage, and economic development, the post-colonial governments struggled to maintain the delicate social and economic equilibrium that disciplined rank-and-file askaris under British rule.

As noted in Chapter 6, African servicemen often resented their inferior terms of service in comparison with other imperial troops. Their impatience grew in the early 1960s when their pay failed to keep pace with inflation because colonial officials were unwilling to saddle their successors with unwieldy military budgets. Under the new era of *uhuru* (freedom), askaris were full citizens of an African state and therefore expected substantial improvements in their pay, uniforms, housing, rations, and medical care. With the end of the color bar, African servicemen saw no reason why their most experienced comrades should not be commissioned. More significantly, they tended to attribute the most restrictive aspects of the colonial army's strict code of discipline to racial discrimination and therefore expected *uhuru* to bring a greater degree of personal freedom.[1]

These expectations were incompatible with conventional notions of military efficiency, and it was inevitable that the former colonial soldiery would be dissatisfied with their new leaders. Rank-and-file askaris had no clear concept of the financial and political problems that confronted the East African governments. The entire African population expected independence to bring an improved standard of living, and the young states had to weigh their military expenditures against civil demands for land, education, health care, and employment. In 1964, Kenya spent over £3 million on the military, or five percent of the national budget.[2] Many African politicians, however, inherited the colonial administrators' dislike of the armed forces, and had little inclination to increase military spending at the expense of social welfare programs. Tanganyika's Julius Nyerere believed initially that national armies were unnecessary in postcolonial Africa. Moreover, the new national governments retained most of the KAR's European officers on a provisional basis. Britain was willing to pay their salaries, and African leaders did not consider the ex-colonial soldiers sufficiently trustworthy. Thus, in spite of the many letters and petitions they received from askaris complaining about low pay and slow promotions, African politicians had neither the inclination nor the ability to meet their soldiers' expectations.[3]

To make matters worse, the changing political climate in post-colonial East Africa threatened the economic security African servicemen had previously enjoyed under British rule. Where colonial officials had gone to great lengths to keep the King's African Rifles apolitical, many African politicians viewed the new national armies as instruments of patronage and influence and planned to expand them without raising existing pay levels. In 1960, the Dalgeish Report estimated there were over 120,000 unemployed adult males in Kenya and worried that the new nation would be unable to find suitable work for the 100,000 students leaving school each year. By January 1964, the unemployment picture had become so serious that hundreds of men marched on Parliament to demand that the Minister of Labour find them jobs. The protesters declared they would work for as little as 30 shillings per month, a fraction of the lowest-ranking Private's monthly wage of 105 shillings.[4] In light of these tensions, it is easy to understand the intense political pressure to expand the armed forces. The Kenyan government planned to raise a fully equipped modern infantry brigade within a year of gaining independence. This required a minimum of 2,000 new recruits, and Africans on the special Cabinet Committee appointed to supervise the modernization of the KAR brushed aside British warnings that rapid expansion would leave the army "non-operational" and demoralized.[5]

There was some truth to these warnings. While soldiers from martial races assumed independence would bring increased opportunity, they did not expect it to lead to increased competition from better-educated non-martial ethnic groups. In responding to Oginga Odinga's legislative motion to eliminate ethnic recruiting quotas, E. N. Mwendwa, the Kamba representative for Kitui, responded: "There are only two important jobs which the Akamba have to do: one is to keep cattle; the other is to go into the Army. We are prepared to accept the Kikuyus and Luos as teachers, but we ask them to accept the Akamba and Kalenjin as Army people. We are going to defend them."[6] Mwendwa's statement not only reflected the degree to which military service influenced the ethnic identity of the Kamba; it also demonstrated that askaris were afraid that the shifting balance of political power would rob them of what little they already had. In light of these concerns it is not surprising that many soldiers began to refer to the KAR as their political party.[7]

Rank-and-file anxiety and dissatisfaction came to a head in the last week of January 1964 when African soldiers in Tanganyika, Uganda, and Kenya struck in rapid succession. Malawi was spared because its Chewa-speaking battalions were divorced from the East Africa Command in the 1950s. While these incidents of collective resistance have been labeled "mutinies" because they involved a degree of violence, they were essentially labor protests over low wages, slow promotions, unpopular terms of service, and the continued presence of British officers in what was now an African national army.

The colonial military establishment was shocked by the apparent disloyalty and unprofessionalism of its former askaris and blamed the strikes on a sinister, perhaps Communist-inspired, plot by unscrupulous African politicians to take control of the new East African armies. In reality, Jomo Kenyatta, the President of Kenya, was probably closer to the mark: "I think some silly fool heard of the situation in Zanzibar and perhaps those in Tanganyika thought they could do a little better. When Kenya heard about Tanganyika somebody got it into their minds that perhaps they could do a little better than Tanganyika."[8] In Tanganyika, the striking soldiers declared they had no political agenda and told reporters they were protesting low pay and bad working conditions. Informants who participated in the Kenyan mutiny also emphatically deny their actions were directed against the new state and portray themselves as patriots who challenged the continued presence of British officers.[9]

Askaris in Tanganyika, Uganda, and Kenya struck in rapid succession because their governments could not maintain the delicate balance that disciplined the African soldiery under British rule. The strikes should be viewed primarily as a final manifestation of the collective protests that occasionally flared up in the old KAR battalions. The mutineers did not attempt to seize power, nor did they declare their loyalty to a particular politician; for the most part, they sat on their weapons and demanded to renegotiate their terms of service. While British authorities had previously defused such incidents through a careful mix of repression and accommodation, the end of colonial rule raised expectations and created new opportunities for advancement. Military service was no longer the most lucrative form of unskilled labor in East Africa, and rank-and-file askaris decided spontaneously that collective action was necessary to protect their interests.

African veterans of the King's African Rifles also found themselves in an equally difficult position in the post-colonial era. After independence, the new nationalist governments assumed formal control over the various territorial branches of the British Legion. In Kenya, the King's African Rifles Old Comrades Association became the Kenya Armed Forces Old Comrades Association. The new Association was run by the Kenyan Army as a parastatal organization, and all former colonial soldiers received automatic memberships. While a representative of the metropolitan British Commonwealth Ex-Servicemen's League still makes regular visits to local branches of the Old Comrades Association, primary responsibility for veterans' affairs devolved to the Kenyan government, which felt little obligation to devote scarce resources to servants of the old colonial regime. Individual former officers and members of the London-based King's African Rifles Dinner Club still take an active interest in the welfare of former askaris, but their private contributions are not enough to alleviate the poverty of many destitute ex-ser-vicemen.[10]

As a result, many veterans of the King's African Rifles still look to London to make good on the "promises" they received in the army. J.S.P.O. Ogara threatened to take their case to the United Nations:

> Again it was the duty of the British Government to deal with their victims after the war was over. Instead the British Government pensioned the British families and forgot the African families with effect from that time, these neglected African families spelt poverty in every way, and as for this course, most of their children missed every chance in education and better standards of living.[11]

Other veterans sought to play upon British emotions by expressing continued loyalty to the old empire. In most cases, however, ex-servicemen demanded an accounting of British Legion and KAR OCA funds on the assumption that the new African government would find vast sums of money to distribute to deserving former askaris. There was, of course, no such financial windfall, contributing to the lasting sentiments of many veterans that they had been cheated by their former colonial employers. The self-appointed leaders of the ex-servicemen's community tried unsuccessfully to convince the Kenyan government that it had an obligation to make good on the commitments of the previous regime. Failing that, many continue to exploit poor and unsophisticated veterans by collecting dues and subscriptions for non-existent organizations that promised to convince the British government to deliver the long-awaited bonuses and pensions.[12]

NOTES

[1] Interviews, #7, #24, #56, #85.

[2] Area Handbook Series, *Area Handbook for Kenya*, (Washington, DC: U.S. Government Printing Office, 1967), p. 647.

[3] Approval of Sessional Paper No. 105, Kenya Legislative Debates, V. 74, 11 June 1957; W.B.L. Monson, CO, to Tanganyikan Governor, 3 March 1961, PRO, CO 968/724; Motion by Oginga Odinga, "KAR Commissioned Ranks: Africans," 13 December 1962, Kenya Legislative, V. 90; Petition from Soldiers, KAR Infantry Bde, n.d., KNA, GH 4/705/224.

[4] Note for Colonial Secretary, Unemployment in Kenya, October 1960, PRO, CO 822/2851; *Daily Nation*, 18 January 1964.

[5] Expansion of the KAR, 7 September 1963, KNA, WC CM 1/13/145; CAB (63) 145, Interim Report by the Cabinet Committee Appointed to Consider Kenya's Future Army, 14 September 1963, KNA, SH 4/24; Cabinet Minutes 4-7, 13 September 1963, KNA, SH 4/24.

[6] Motion by Oginga Odinga, KAR Commissioned Ranks: Africans, 13 December 1962, Kenya Legislative Debates, V. 90.

[7] J. M. Lee, *African Armies and Civil Order*, (New York: Praeger, 1969), p. 34.

[8] *East African Standard*, 8 February 1964.

[9] *East African Standard*, 21 January 1964; Interview, #4.

[10] Report of the Ex-Service Position in East Africa, October–November 1964, LHC, DP/XIV/F/10; Interviews, #56, #117

[11] Kenya Ex-Servicemen's Union to British High Commission, 27 October 1964, KNA, DC KMG 2/17/19/72.

[12] J.S.P.O. Ogara to DC NNZA, 8 August 1963, KNA DC KMG 2/17/19/9a; David Ilenye, ASBL, Machakos Branch, to GOC EAC, 27 November 1963, KNA, PC NKU 2/21/4/196; Interviews, #1, #64, #65.

APPENDIX A:
THE ORGANIZATION OF
THE KAR

The King's African Rifles was composed primarily of lightly armed infantry battalions nominally linked with the various East African territories. While the Northern Rhodesia Regiment, the Somaliland Camel Corps, and the (Southern) Rhodesian African Rifles were not officially part of the KAR, they were organized and administered in the same manner as East African military units. Colonial officials made frequent adjustments in the size and organization of the KAR and its allied Regiments. Table A.1. shows how the East African forces changed over time.

The early KAR was composed almost entirely of infantrymen and had no specialized support units. During the First World War, the Regiment expanded to twenty-two frontline combat battalions, supported by an East African artillery arm, transport service (not to be confused with the Carrier Corps), signal corps, medical department, intelligence wing, and military police detachment. The KAR shrank to its original size in the inter-war era and had no additional support units other than a Supply and Transport Corps.

The East African colonial forces became considerably larger and more complex during World War II. Additional support, technical, and labor units were raised during the war. With one exception, all of the new battalions were disbanded in 1946, but the East Africa Command retained elements of the East African specialist arms as cadre units for a reserve African division. These included: 156 (EA) Independent Heavy Artillery Battery, 303 Depot & Training Regiment, 54 Composite Field Squadron EAE, the East Africa Armoured Car Squadron, and a number of General Transport Companies.

Table A.1

Approximate Forces Levels in the East African Colonial Military, 1913–1960

Year	Enlisted Askaris
1913	2,440
1914	2,319
1915	3,885
1916	8,159
1917	23,325
1919	30,658
1920	5,740
1926	3,780
1928	3,580
1930	3,080
1931	2,974
1932	2,640
1933	2,380
1934	2,471
1938	4,114
1939	6,450
1940	25,000
1941	56,000
1942	141,600
1945	236,522
1947	13,263
1949	22,490
1957	4,563
1958	4,036
1959	4,386
1960	4,672

Source: PRO, WO/32/4127; KNA, LF/1/70/1; KNA, LF/1/27/17 & 27; KNA, MD/4/5/80/5a; KNA, DEF/15/29/88a; KNA, MD/4/5/140/170; Hubert Moyse-Bartlett, *The King's African Rifles*, (Aldershot: Gale & Polden, 1956); Great Britain, Colonial Office, *The British Territories in East and Central Africa, 1945–1950*, (London: HM Stationery Office, 1950); William Platt, "East African Forces in the War and Their Future," *Journal of the Royal United Services Institute*, (August 1948), pp. 403–13.

The East Africa Command gradually disbanded most of these cadre units over the next ten years as the mission of the KAR shifted from imperial to local defense. When the East African forces returned to local control in 1957 under the East African Land Forces Organization, the KAR reabsorbed the remaining specialist units. These included: No. 1 Signal Squadron, 92 and 93 Mechanical Transport Companies, 67 Animal Transport Troop, No. 1 Advanced Workshop Detachment, and the East African pool of chaplains and education instructors.

APPENDIX B: INTERVIEWS

As noted in the introduction, African informants were found by undergraduate research assistants who identified ex-askaris in their home areas between 1993 and 1996. Former British members of the KAR were either contacted by word of mouth or through the King's African Rifles Dinner Club. Additional useful material on European experiences in the colonial military is available from written testimonies of former officers collected in the Oxford Development Records Project (ODRP), the British Imperial War Museum, and the Kenyan National Archives. Finally, Derek Peterson shared some of his interviews with African veterans who joined African independent churches, and Dr. J. Forbes Munro generously provided access to material from interviews with Kamba ex-askaris collected for his *Colonial Rule and the Kamba: Social Change in the Kenya Highlands 1889–1939.*

Informants who provided material for the study are identified by a random number rather than by name to conceal the identity of a few former askaris and officers who provided sensitive information on ethnic tension, crime, and political unrest. In the case of British informants, some ex-officers with files in the Oxford Development Records Project were also interviewed directly for this study.

Table B.1
African Veterans

Number	Unit	Service Dates	Ethnic Group	Rank	Interview Date
1	1 &3 KAR	1948–55	Kamba	PTE	April 1994
1a	1 KAR	1952–59	Chewa	PTE	March 1995
2	11 KAR	1958–63	Kamba	PTE	November 1993
3	11 KAR	1939–55	Kamba	PTE	March 1994
4	11 KAR	1959–64	Kamba	SGT	May 1994
5	11 KAR	1940–63	Kamba	SGT	March 1994
6	11 KAR	1942–46	Kipsigis	PTE	February 1994
7	11 KAR	1958–64	Samburu	PTE	June 1994
8	11 KAR	1951–57	Samburu	CPL	June 1994
9	11 KAR	1951–60	Kamba	LCPL	December 1993
10	12 Bde	1939–45	Kamba	SGT	April 1994
11	12 KAR	1938–45	Kipsigis	PTE	February 1994
11a	13 KAR	1941–46	Yao	PTE	March 1995
12	16 KAR	1942–46	Kamba	PTE	March 1994
13	2 KAR	1942–45	Ngoni	PTE	April 1995
14	2 KAR, 1 NRR	1938–45	Sudanese	CPL	June 1994
15	2/3 KAR	1940–46	Kamba	CPL	March 1994
16	22 & 3 KAR	1942–96, 1950–96	Kamba	PTE	November 1993
16b	22 KAR	1942–45	Chewa	PTE	March 1945
17	23 KAR	1951–60	Kamba	CPL	November 1993
18	23 KAR	1951–57	Samburu	CPL	May 1994
19	3 & 11 KAR	1948–57	Turkana	CPL	May 1994
20	3 & 4 KAR	1940–46	Kamba	PTE	March 1994
21	3 & 4 KAR	1938–52	Kamba	SGT	February 1994
22	3 & 5 KAR	1948–55	Kamba	PTE	February 1994
23	3 KAR	1951–91	Kamba	CPL	December 1993
24	3 KAR	1945–68	Kamba	CPL	March 1994
25	3 KAR	1942–86	Kamba	General	March 1994
26	3 KAR	1929–45	Kamba	LCPL	April 1994

Table B.1 *(cont.)*

27	3 KAR	1958–85	Kamba	SGT	November 1993
28	3 KAR	1956–86	Kamba	SGT	November 1993
29	3 KAR	1959–80	Kamba	SGT	November 1993
30	3 KAR	1958–69	Kipsigis	PTE	February 1994
31	3 KAR	1949–56	Samburu	CPL	May 1994
32	3 KAR	1950–60	Samburu	CPL	May 1994
33	3 KAR	1948–54	Samburu	CPL	June 1994
34	3 KAR	1940–46	Samburu	CPL	June 1994
35	3 KAR, EAAEC	1950–56	Maasai	SSGT	April 1994
36	4 & 7 KAR	1940–46	Kamba	CPL	March 1994
37	4 KAR	1940–46	Kamba	CPL	February 1994
38	4 KAR	1939–46	Kamba	PTE	March 1994
39	4 KAR	1905–20	Luhya	CPL	April 1994
40	4 KAR	1913–18	Sudanese	CPL	March 1994
41	4 KAR	1904–21	Sudanese	CPL	April 1994
42	4 KAR	1913–18	Sudanese	PTE	March 1994
43	4 KAR	1901–03	Sudanese	PTE	March 1994
44	5 KAR	1941–47	Kamba	PTE	November 1993
45	5 KAR	1940–46	Kamba	PTE	March 1994
46	5 KAR	1954–59	Kipsigis	CPL	February 1994
47	5 KAR	1939–45	Sudanese	PTE	June 1994
48	5 KAR	1929–49	Sudanese	SGT	June 1994
49	5 KAR, EAA	1937–46	Kamba	SGT	March 1994
50	6 KAR	—	—	—	February 1993
51	7 & 3 KAR	1939–45	Kamba	CPL	April 1994
52	7 KAR	1947–55	Kamba	LCPL	February 1994
53	7 KAR	1940–46	Kamba	PTE	November 1993
54	7 KAR	1949–57	Nandi	PTE	March 1994
55	71 KAR	WWII	Somali	PTE	June 1994
56	91 GT Coy	1958–86	Kamba	WOII	April 1994
57	92 MT Coy	1952–57	Kamba	PTE	March 1994

Table B.1 *(cont.)*

58	AAPC	1939–49	Kamba	LCPL	February 1994
59	AAPC	1942–54	Kamba	PTE	March 1994
60	AAPC	1941–45	Kamba	PTE	March 1994
61	AAPC	1939–45	Kisii	CPL	March 1994
62	AAPC	1939–45	Kisii	CPL	March 1994
63	AAPC	1940–43	Kisii	CPL	March 1994
64	AAPC	1941–45	Kisii	CPL	March 1994
65	AAPC	1941–45	Kisii	LCPL	March 1994
66	AAPC	1940–44	Luhya	LCPL	April 1994
67	AAPC	1942–44	Luhya	PTE	April 1994
67a	AAPC	1941–45	Luhya	CPL	April 1994
68	AAPC	1940–45	Luhya	SGT	April 1994
69	AAPC	1940–45	Mbere	CPL	March 1994
70	AAPC	1940–45	Mbere	CPL	March 1994
71	AAPC	1940–45	Mbere	CPL	March 1994
72	AAPC	1940–45	Mbere	LCPL	March 1994
73	AAPC	1940–45	Mbere	PTE	March 1994
74	AAPC	1940–45	Mbere	PTE	March 1994
75	AAPC	1940–45	Mbere	PTE	March 1994
76	AAPC	1940–45	Mbere	PTE	March 1994
77	AAPC	1940–45	Mbere	PTE	March 1994
78	AAPC	1940–45	Nubian	LCPL	March 1994
79	EAA	1939–45	Bajun	LCPL	March 1994
80	EAA, Signals	1940–82	Kamba	SSGT	April 1994
81	EAAC	1939–46	Kamba	DVR I	March 1994
82	EAAC	1939–45	Kamba	PTE	April 1994
83	EAAMC	1942–46	Kamba	CPL	November 1993
84	EAAMC	1939–46	Kamba	CPL	February 1994
85	EAAMC	1953–56	Kamba	CPL	March 1994
86	EAAMC	1942–51	Kamba	PTE	February 1994
87	EAAMC	1914–19, 39–45	Kamba	PTE	February 1994

Table B.1 *(cont.)*

88	EAAMC	1936–55	Kamba	PTE	April 1994
89	EAAMC	WWII	Kikuyu	—	June 1994
90	EAAMC	1940–45	Taita	SSGT	June 1994
91	EAASC	1940–46	Kamba	CPL	March 1994
92	EAASC	1939–45	Kamba	CPL	April 1994
93	EAASC	1943–50	Kamba	LCPL	February 1994
94	EAASC	1940–46	Kamba	PTE	February 1994
95	EAASC	1940–52	Kamba	PTE	February 1994
96	EAASC	1942–46	Kamba	PTE	April 1994
97	EAASC	1942–48	Kamba	PTE	April 1994
98	EAASC	1939–51	Kamba	SGT	March 1994
99	EAASC	1940–45	Ngoni	DVR I	April 1995
100	EACF	1940–50	Kamba	LCPL	February 1994
101	EAE	1941–48, 56–58	Kamba	LCPL	February 1994
102	EAE	1940–42	Kamba	PTE	April 1994
103	EAE	1941–45	Kisii	CPL	March 1994
104	EAE	1939–45	Kisii	CSM	March 1994
105	EAE, EACF	1943–46, 48–50	Kamba	PTE	March 1994
106	EAMLS	1941–47	Kamba	CPL	February 1994
107	EAMLS (cook)	1939–50	Kamba	PTE	March 1994
108	EAOC	1954–60	Kamba	PTE	February 1994
109	EAPC	1945–59	Kamba	CPL	April 1994
110	EAPC	1950–54	Kamba	LCPL	November 1993
111	Signals	1941–46	Kamba	PTE	April 1994
112	Signals	1940–51	Kamba	SGT	April 1994
113	Snuff maker	1944–47	Kamba	PTE	February 1944
114	TT KAR	1939–40	Kamba	PTE	February 1994
115	—	1940–59	Kamba	CPL	February 1994
116	—	1948–50	Kamba	PTE	February 1994
117	—	—	Kamba	WOII	June 1994

Table B.2
Civilian Informants

Number	Related Unit	Related Dates	Ethnic Group	Relationship	Interview Date
118	5 KAR	1958–89	Kamba	Son	November 1993
119	1 KAR	1958–74	Kamba	Son	November 1993
120	—	WWII	Kamba	Son	November 1993
121	5 KAR	1935–48	Kamba	Son	December 1993
122	EAAMC	1914–29	Kamba	Son	November 1993
122a	7 KAR, EAAEC	1939–45	Ganda	Son	March 1996
123	—	1958–68	Kamba	Wife	December 1993
124	22 KAR	1940s–50s	Kamba	Wife	December 1993
125	7 KAR	1940–49	Kamba	Wife	December 1993
126	—	1948–54	Kamba	Wife	December 1993
127	5 KAR	1950s–60s	Kamba	Wife	December 1993
128	7 KAR	1940–46	Kamba	Wife	December 1993
129	23 KAR	1940s–1950s	Kamba	Wife	December 1993
130	Civilian	n/a	Ngoni	n/a	April 1995
131	Civilian	n/a	Ngoni	n/a	April 1995
132	Civilian	n/a	British	District Officer	January 1995
133	Civilian	n/a	Kamba	n/a	February 1994
133a	Civilian	n/a	Kamba	n/a	February 1994

Table B.3
Former KAR Officers

Number	Unit	Service Dates	Ethnic Group	Rank	Interview Date
134	1/6 KAR	1938–42	British	Captain	December 1994
135	11 Div, EAC	1938–46, 60–63	British	Brigadier	November 1994
136	11 KAR	1957–58	British	Lieutenant	October 1994
137	13 KAR	1942–46	British	Captain	November 1994
138	15 & 1/6 KAR	1942–47	British	Captain	March 1994
139	2 & 3 KAR, EAAEC	1950s	British	Major	June 1995
140	3 KAR	1956–58	British	Lieutenant	December 1993
141	3 KAR, 34 KAR	1939–45	British	Major	February 1994
142	34 KAR	WWII	British	Captain	February 95
143	36 KAR	WWII	British	Captain	October 1994
144	4 KAR	1956–57	British	Lieutenant	August 1994
145	4 KAR, JLC	1950s	British	Major	July 1995
146	5 KAR	1955–67	British	Major	May 1994
147	5 KAR	1940–45	British	Captain	December 1994
148	6 KAR, 1 TR	1940–45, 63–44	British	General	November 1994
149	EAA	1939–41	British	Lt Colonel	January 1994
150	NRR	1939–46	British	Captain	March 1994
151	NRR, 5 KAR	1934–72	British	Lt Colonel	January 1994
152	NRR, RAR 70 Bde	1937–61	British	Brigadier	December 1994

Table B.4
Written Deposits

Name	Unit	Service Dates	Rank
Belton, P. A.	5 KAR	1956–59	Lt Colonel
Bowie, D.F.T.	22 KAR	1940–47	—
Broomfield, C. F.	4 KAR, KR	1938–58	—
Chavasse, H.K.P.	4 KAR	1960–62	Lt Colonel
Clark, A. L. St. G. S.	5 KAR	1961–63	Lt Colonel
Clemas, H. N.	23 KAR	1951–54	Major
Coles, G.H.H.	4 KAR	1949–57	—
Catt, C. W.	Signals	1939–43	Staff Sergeant
Crawford, H. N.	11 KAR	1959–62	Lt Colonel
Cree, G. H.	6 KAR, 25 Bde	1931–45	Brigadier
Darlington, R. R.	71 KAR	1942–45	Captain
Davies, K. W.	SCC, 71 KAR	1942–44	Major
Durrant, G. R.	3 KAR	1956–57	Lt Colonel
Edwards, P. L.	46 KAR	1939–44	Captain
Flory, F.	23 & 6 KAR, 2 TR	1952–64	Major
Glass, H.P.L	2 KAR, 1 NRR	1937–53	Lt Colonel
Goode, G.H.W.	NRR, RAR, 70 Bde	1937–61	Brigadier
Goodeve-Docker, P. G.	Signals	1941–44	—
Green, P.W.P.	4 KAR	1954–60	Brigadier
Gregory, Rev J. E.	26 Bde	—	Chaplain
Haigh, E.G.W.	3, 2/3, 5/6 KAR	1939–45	—
Nunneley, J.	36 KAR	WWII	Captain
Howard, J. W.	5 KAR	1940–44	Major
Ivy, C. W.	11 KAR	1963–66	Lt Colonel
Jenkyns, H. L.	Signals	1941–5	—
Khanna, S. K.	3 KAR	1961–64	Major
King, T. R.	5 KAR	1939–46	Major
Lambert, B. J.	5 KAR	1959–62	—
Langford, P. E.	156 HAA Bty	1952–57	Lt Colonel
Leahy, T.	3, 5, 2 KAR	1936–41	Lt Colonel
Malyn, R. A.	44 KAR	1940–43	—
Mans, R.W.N.	6 KAR, 1 TR	1940–45, 1963–4	Major General

Table B.4 *(cont.)*

Martin, J.H.S.	96 Ind. Garrison Coy	1940–45	Colonel
Moore, E. A.	3 & 4 NRR	1940–44	—
Morgan, W. A.	91 GT Coy, 1 TP Coy	1958–65	Major
Mott, A. R.	1 & 2 KAR	1950–55	Major
Nott, D. H.	4 KAR	1952–54	Brigadier
O'Connell, T. D.	2 KAR	1954–57	Major
Peddie, J.C.T.	4 KAR	1956–59	Lt Colonel
Riley-Smith, W. H.	Rft Camp Ceylon	WW2	DAA&QMG
Robson, G. G.	1/6, 12, & 36 KAR	1938–45	Lt Colonel
Sampson, R. C.	1, 2, & 3 KAR, NRR	1940–56	—
Scott, M. B.	3 KAR	1955–59	—
Sheldon, R. H.	Signals	1943–45	—
Shields, J. G.	1 NRR	1940–46	—
Shirreff, D.	5 KAR	1940–45	Captain
Smale, J.	5 KAR	1949–52, 58–59	Major
Spanton, E.J.C.	3 & 6 KAR	1950–64	—
Stoneley, C. H.	Signals N Bde	1935–41	Brigadier
Swain, A. E.	34 KAR	1942–46	—
Swann, Sir A.	2/3 & 5/6 KAR	1940–44	—
Thomas, I. G.	EACF (RASC)	1947–52	—
Thompson, Sir P.	2/6 KAR	1954–46	Lt Colonel
Wallis, C. St. J.	4 KAR	1949–55	Major
Watson, J.E.D.	2, 1, & 4 KAR	1935–53	Lt Colonel
Watts, A. S.	EAAMC	1944–6	Major
Whitworth, G.B.	6 & 5 KAR	1941–51	Major
Williams, E.D.H.	EAAMC (RAMC)	1955–58	—
Williams, H.	1 & 13 KAR	1931–55	Colonel
Woodcock, J.	EAAC	1940–45	—
Young, G. K.	11 & 12 Divisions	1940–43	—
Bannister, D. J.	1 KAR	1936–41	Colonel
Barnes, P.	22, 27, 31 KAR	1942–45	Major

Source: Oxford Development Records Project, RHL, Mss.Afr.s.1715.

Table B.5
Transcripts of Interviews with British Officers

Number	Name	Unit	Service Dates	Rank
MSS/78/1	Borradaile, H. A.	4 KAR	1930s	Major General
MSS/78/2	Cockcraft, W.G.L.	4 KAR	1938–39	Captain
MSS/78/3	Lord St. Helens	5 KAR	1933–?	Lt Colonel
MSS/78/4	Glanville, R. C.	4 KAR, 6 KAR	1930s	Lt Colonel

Source: The Kenya National Archives.

APPENDIX C: CURRENCY AND COMPARATIVE VALUES

The rupee was the primary unit of currency in East Africa until 1921, when it was replaced by the East African shilling. Generally speaking, a rupee was worth 1.5 shillings, and all pre-1921 figures cited in this study have been converted into shillings for ease of comparison. The East African shilling was equal in value to the British shilling throughout the colonial era. One shilling totaled 100 cents, and there were 20 shillings in a pound. For purposes of comparison, in 1940, the British pound sterling was equal to approximately U.S. $4. Thus, 5 East African shillings were equal roughly to one U.S. dollar.[1]

These figures are of limited use in determining the actual value of military wages in rural East Africa. Nevertheless, it is possible to estimate the purchasing power of the monthly wage of a KAR Private's 28 shillings in the late 1930s and early 1940s. In the two Kamba districts that supplied almost one-quarter of all askaris to the Kenyan KAR in 1938, informants recall that a pound of ground maize meal cost approximately 0.5 shillings, whereas the average cow could be purchased for roughly 20 shillings. Kamba askaris sent home an average family remittance of 11.9 shillings per month, which should have been enough to support a small family if it lived unostentatiously. School fees, however, were another matter and generally ranged from 60 to 160 shillings per year for primary education.[2] In addition to these standard expenses, a civilian worker paid a hut or poll tax of 12 shillings per year (more if he had extra wives), plus a Local Native Council yearly rate of 1 to 2 shillings.[3] Askaris, on the other hand, enjoyed tax-exempt status for as long as they served in the military and therefore had a distinct advantage over their civilian counterparts.

NOTES

[1] John Iliffe, *A Modern History of Tanganyika*, (New York: Cambridge University Press, 1979), p. xiii; Anthony Clayton and Donald Savage, *Government and Labour in Kenya, 1895–1963*, (London: Frank Cass, 1974), p. xxiv; Walter Morton, *British Finance, 1930–1940*, (Madison: University of Wisconsin Press, 1943), p. 124.

[2] Annual Battalion Reports, 1938, PRO, CO 820; Annexure to Northern Bde Order No. 276, 13 October 1939, KNA, MD 4/5/1/118/9a.

[3] Clayton and Savage, *Government and Labour in Kenya,* p. 168.

SELECTED BIBLIOGRAPHY

OFFICIAL SOURCES

East Africa Command. *The Infantry of the East Africa Command, 1890–1944.* Nairobi: EA Standard, c. 1944.

East Africa Command. *Official Programme of Army Exhibition and Displays.* Nairobi: no publisher, 1944.

East Africa Command. *The Story of the East Africa Army Service Corps.* Nairobi: EA Standard, c. 1944.

East African Army Education Corps. *Kiswahili: A Kiswahili Instruction Book for the East African Command.* Entebbe: Government Printer, c. 1942.

Great Britain. *Standing Orders of the 1st (Nyasaland) Battalion, the King's African Rifles.* Zomba: Government Printer, 1927.

Great Britain. *Standing Orders of the 2nd (Nyasaland) Battalion, the King's African Rifles.* Nairobi: Uganda Railway Press, c. 1926.

Great Britain. *Standing Orders of the 6th Battalion, the King's African Rifles.* N.p., 1930.

Great Britain, Colonial Office. *Regulations for the King's African Rifles.* London: Waterlow and Sons, 1908.

Great Britain, Colonial Office. *Regulations for the King's African Rifles.* London: Waterlow and Sons, 1925.

Great Britain, General Staff. *Military Report and General Information Concerning Nyasaland.* London: HM Stationery Office, 1909.

Great Britain, Ministry of Information. *A Spear for Freedom.* Nottingham: HM Stationery Office, n.d.

Great Britain, War Office. *Notes on Land and Air Forces of the British Overseas Dominions, Colonies, Protectorates and Mandated Territories.* London: HM Stationery Office, 1922.

Great Britain, War Office. *Notes on Land and Air Forces of the British Overseas Dominions, Colonies, Protectorates and Mandated Territories.* London: HM Stationery Office, 1934.

Hordern, Charles. *Military Operations in East Africa, Volume I, August 1914–September 1916*. London: HM Stationery Office, 1941.

Kenya Colony and Protectorate. *Instructions to Civil Officers, Military Officers, RAF Officers, Police Officers and Local Defence Force Officers on the Use of Armed Force in Civil Disturbances*. Nairobi: Government Printers, c. 1936.

Kenya Colony and Protectorate. *Labour Department Annual Report 1946*. Nairobi: Government Printer, 1948.

Kenya Colony and Protectorate. *Progress Report on Demobilization*. Nairobi: Government Printer, 1944.

Kenya Colony and Protectorate. *Report of the Kenya Land Commission*. Nairobi: Government Printer, 1933.

Kenya Colony and Protectorate, Native Affairs Department. *Report on Native Affairs, 1939–1945*. London: HM Stationery Office, 1948.

Kenya Colony and Protectorate, Organizational Methods Unit. *The Calculation and Payment of War Pensions in Kenya, Report No. 14*. Nairobi: Government Printer, 1956.

Kenya Land Commission. *Evidence, Volume I*. Nairobi: Government Printer, 1933.

Kenya Land Commission. *Evidence, Volume II*. Nairobi: Government Printer, 1933.

Northern Rhodesia. *Standing Orders of 2nd Battalion, the Northern Rhodesia Regiment*. Lusaka: Government Printer, n.d.

Tanganyika Territory. *Annual Reports of the Provincial Commissioners, 1939–1945*. Dar Es Salaam: Government Printer, 1940–1946.

Uganda Protectorate. *Report of the Civil Reabsorption and Rehabilitation Committee*. Entebbe: Government Printer, 1945.

Uganda Protectorate. *Standing Orders of the 4th Battalion, the King's African Rifles*. Entebbe: Government Printer, 1934.

SEMI-OFFICIAL MILITARY HISTORIES AND MEMOIRS

Anonymous (Major P. F. Vowles). *The Eleventh (Kenya) Battalion, the King's African Rifles, 1941–1945*. Ranchi, India: Catholic Press, 1946.

Barber, D. H. *Africans in Khaki*. London: Edinburgh House Press, 1948.

Brelsford, W. V., ed. *Story of the Northern Rhodesia Regiment*. Lusaka: The Government Printer, 1954.

De Guingand, Francis. *African Assignment*. London: Hodder and Stoughton, 1953.

Dickson, A. B. "Studies in Wartime Organization: Mobile Propaganda Unit, East Africa Command." *African Affairs*, v. 44, (1945), pp. 9–18.

Doig, Andrew. "The Christian Church and Demobilization in Africa." *International Review of Missions*, v. 35, (1946), pp. 174–82.

Dower, Kenneth Gandar. *Askaris at War in Abyssinia*. Nairobi: East African Standard, n.d.

Dower, Kenneth Gandar. *The King's African Rifles in Madagascar*. Nairobi: East Africa Command, n.d.

Draffan, W. D., and Lewin, T.C.C. *A War Journal of the Fifth (Kenya) Battalion, the King's African Rifles*. N.p., c. 1946.

Gakaara wa Wanjau. *Mau Mau Author in Detention*. Translated by Ngugi wa Njoroge. Nairobi: Heinemann, 1988.

Gatheru, R. Mugo. *Child of Two Worlds*. London: Heinemann, 1966.

Grahame, Iain. *Amin and Uganda: A Personal Memoir*. London: Granada Press, 1980.

Grahame, Iain. *Jambo Effendi, Seven Years with the KAR*. London: J. A. Allen, 1966.

Hanley, Gerald. *Monsoon Victory*. London: Collins, 1946.

Hudson, E.V.H. "The East African Education Corps." *Army Education*, v. 25, (June 1951), pp. 76–80.

Irven, DNW. "KAR Subaltern." *The Gunner*, v. 65–66, (April–May 1976), n.p.

Itote, Waruhiu. *"Mau Mau" General*. Nairobi: EA Publishing House, 1967.

Kaggia, Bildad. *The Roots of Freedom, 1921–1963*. Nairobi: EA Publishing House, 1975.

Kakembo, Robert. *An African Soldier Speaks*. London: Livingstone Press, 1947.

Kariuki, Josiah Mwangi. *Mau Mau Detainee*. Oxford: Oxford University Press, 1963.

Kinnear, George. "Askaris Are Making Their Own Post-War Plans." *East African Standard*, 4 July 1945.

Knott, A. J. "East Africa and the Returning Askari; The Effect of Their War Service." *Quarterly Review*, v. 285, (January 1947), pp. 85–111.

Lardner, Edgar George. *Soldiering and Sport in Uganda, 1909–1910*. London: Walter Scott, 1912.

Lloyd-Jones, William. *Havash!* London: Arrowsmith, 1925.

Lloyd-Jones, William. *K.A.R.; Being an Unofficial Account of the Origin and Activities of the King's African Rifles*. London: Arrowsmith, 1926.

Lumley, E. K. *Forgotten Mandate: A British District Officer in Tanganyika*. Hamden, CT: Archon Books, 1976.

Lytton, Earl of (Noel Anthony). *The Desert and the Green*. London: MacDonald, 1957.

MacDonald, J.R.L. *Soldiering and Surveying in British East Africa*. London: Edward Arnold, 1897.

Meinertzhagen, Richard. *Army Diary, 1899–1926*. Edinburgh: Oliver & Boyd, 1960.

Meinertzhagen, Richard. *Kenya Diary 1902–1906*, Edinburgh: Oliver & Lloyd, 1957. Reprint, New York: Hippocrene Books, 1984.

Mitchell, Philip. *African Afterthoughts*. London: Hutchinson, 1954.

Montieth, Malcom. *Ceylon to the Chindwin, Burma 1944*. Lusaka: Government Printer, 1945.

Moyse-Bartlett, Hubert. *The King's African Rifles*. Aldershot: Gale & Polden, 1956.

Muchai, Karigo. *The Hard Core: The Story of Karigo Muchai*. Richmond: L.S.M. Information Center, 1973.

Newell, H. W. *Notes on Ki-Swahili as Spoken by the K.A.R.* N.p., 1930.

Nunneley, John H. *Tales from the King's African Rifles*. London: Askari Books, 1998.

Penwill, D. J. *Kamba Customary Law*. Nairobi: Kenya Literature Bureau, 1986.

Platt, William. "East African Forces in the War and Their Future." *Journal of the Royal United Services Institute*, (August 1948), pp. 403–13.

Platt, William. "The East African Soldier." *National Review*. v. 126, (January 1946), pp. 41–49.

Platt, William. "Studies in Wartime Organization: (6) East Africa Command." *African Affairs*, v. 45, (1946), n.p.

Ross, J. S. *First Third: History of the Third Battalion, King's African Rifles in Abyssinia, Somaliland and Eritrea*. N.p., n.d.

Sykes, C. A. *Service and Sport on the Tropical Nile*. London: John Murray, 1903.

Wachanga, Henry Kahinga. *The Swords of Kirinyaga: The Fight for Land and Freedom*. Edited by Robert Whittier. Nairobi: Kenya Literature Bureau, 1991.

Whitehead, E. F. "A Short History of Uganda Military Units Formed During World War II." *Uganda Journal*, v. 14, (1950), pp. 1–14.

Wilson, H. A. *A British Borderland: Service and Sport in Equatoria.* London: John Murray, 1913.

Worker, J. C. "With the 4th (Uganda) KAR in Abyssinia and Burma." *Uganda Journal,* v. 14, (March 1950), pp. 52–56.

SECONDARY SOURCES

Allen, Louis. *Burma: The Longest War.* London: J. M. Dent and Sons, 1986.

Barnett, D. L., and Njama, K. *Mau Mau from Within.* London: Macgibbon & Kee, 1966.

Berman, Bruce. *Control and Crisis in Colonial Kenya: The Dialectic of Domination.* Nairobi: EA Publishers, 1990.

Blundell, Michael. *A Love Affair with the Sun.* Nairobi: General Printers, 1994.

Boeder, R. B. *Silent Majority: A History of the Lomwe in Malawi.* Pretoria: Africa Institute of South Africa, 1984.

Boeder, Robert Benson. "Malawians Abroad: The History of Labor Migration from Malawi to Its Neighbors, 1890 to the Present." Ph.D. dissertation, Michigan State University, 1974.

Brereton, J. M. *The British Soldier: A Social History from 1661 to the Present Day.* London: Bodley Head, 1986.

Clark, David. "Social Organization in Kibera, Nairobi." M.A. Thesis, Makerere University, n.d.

Clayton, Anthony. *Communication for New Loyalties: African Soldier's Songs.* Athens: Ohio University Press, 1978.

Clayton, Anthony. *Counterinsurgency in Kenya: A Study of Military Operations Against the Mau Mau, 1952–1960.* Manhattan, KS: Sunflower University Press, 1984.

Clayton, Anthony. "Sport and African Soldiers: The Military Diffusion of Western Sport Throughout Sub-Saharan Africa." In *Sport in Africa,* edited by William Baker and J. A. Mangan. New York: Africana Publishing, 1987.

Clayton, Anthony, and Killingray, David. *Khaki and Blue: Military and Police in British Colonial Africa.* Athens: Ohio University Press, 1989.

Clayton, Anthony, and Savage, Donald. *Government and Labour in Kenya, 1895–1963.* London: Frank Cass, 1974.

Easterbrook, David. "Kenya Askari in WWI and Their Demobilization with Special Reference to Machakos District." In *Three Aspects of the Colonial Crisis in Kenya,* edited by Bismark Myrick. Syracuse, NY: Syracuse University Press, 1975.

Echenberg, Myron. *Colonial Conscripts: The* Tirailleurs Senegalais *in French West Africa, 1857–1960.* Portsmouth, NH: Heinemann, 1991.

Enloe, Cynthia. *Does Khaki Become You?: The Militarization of Women's Lives.* London: South End Press, 1983.

Enloe, Cynthia. *Ethnic Soldiers: State Security in a Divided Society.* Athens: University of Georgia Press, 1980.

Feld, Maury. *The Structure of Violence: Armed Forces as Social Systems.* Beverly Hills, CA: Sage Publications, 1977.

Greenstein, Lewis. "Africans in a European War: The First World War in East Africa with Special Reference to the Nandi of Kenya." Ph.D. dissertation, Indiana University, 1975.

Greenstein, Lewis. "The Impact of Military Service in World War I on Africans: The Nandi of Kenya." *Journal of Modern African Studies,* v. 16, (1978), pp. 495–507.

Gutteridge, William. "The Place of the Armed Forces in Society in African States." *Race*, v. 4, (1962), pp. 22–33.

Hansen, Holger Bernt. "Pre-Colonial Immigrants and Colonial Servants: The Nubians of Uganda Revisited." *African Affairs*, v. 90, (1991), pp. 559–80.

Hodges, Geoffrey. *The Carrier Corps: Military Labor in the East African Campaign, 1914–1918*. Westport, CT: Greenwood Press, 1986.

Johnson, Douglas. "The Structure of a Legacy: Military Slavery in Northeast Africa." *Ethnohistory*, v. 36, (1989), pp. 72–88.

Killingray, David. "Labour Exploitation for Military Campaigns in British Colonial Africa, 1870–1945." *Journal of Contemporary History*, v. 24, (1989), pp. 483–501.

Killingray, David. "The 'Rod of Empire': The Debate over Corporal Punishment in the British African Colonial Force, 1888–1946." *Journal of African History*, v. 35, (1994), pp. 201–16.

Killingray, David, and Rathbone, Richard, eds. *Africa and the Second World War*. New York: St. Martin's Press, 1986.

Kipkorir, B. E. *The Marakwet of Kenya: A Preliminary Study*. Nairobi: EA Literature Bureau, 1973.

Kirk-Greene, A.H.M. "Damnosa Hereditas: Ethnic Ranking and Martial Race Imperatives in Africa." *Ethnic and Racial Studies*, v. 3, (1980), pp. 393–411.

Kitching, Gavin. *Class and Economic Change in Kenya: The Making of an African Petite-Bourgeoisie*. New Haven, CT: Yale University Press, 1980.

Lee, J. M. *African Armies and Civil Order*. New York: Praeger, 1969.

Lunt, James. *Imperial Sunset: Frontier Soldiering in the 20th Century*. London: Macdonald Futura Publishers, 1981.

Lwanga-Lunyiigo, S. "Uganda and World War One." *Makerere Historical Journal*, v. 3, (1977), pp. 27–39.

McCracken, John. "Coercion and Control in Nyasaland: Aspects of the History of a Colonial Police Force." *Journal of African History*, v. 27, (1986), pp. 127–47.

Munro, J. Forbes. *Colonial Rule and the Kamba: Social Change in the Kenya Highlands 1889–1939*. Oxford: Clarendon Press, 1975.

Newman, J. R. *The Ukamba Members Association*. Nairobi: Transafrica Publishers, 1974.

Njoloma, James C. "The King's African Rifles and Colonial Development in Nyasaland (Malawi), 1890–1914." M.A. thesis, Chancellor College, University of Malawi, 1988.

Ogot, Bethwell A., ed. *War and Society in Africa: Ten Studies*. London: Frank Cass, 1972.

Omara-Otunnu, Amii. *Politics and the Military in Uganda, 1890–1985*. London: Macmillan Press, 1987.

Owen, Christopher. *The Rhodesian African Rifles*. London: Leo Cooper, 1970.

Page, Melvin, ed. *Africa and the First World War*. New York: St. Martin's Press, 1987.

Page, Melvin. "Malawians and the Great War: Oral History in Reconstructing Africa's Recent Past." *Oral History Review*, v. 8, (1980), pp. 49–61.

Page, Melvin. "The War of Thangata: Nyasaland and the East African Campaign, 1914–1918." *Journal of African Studies*, v. 19, (1978), pp. 87–100.

Ranger, Terence. *Dance and Society in Eastern Africa, 1890–1970*. London: Heinemann, 1975.

Rosberg, Carl, and Nottingham, John. *The Myth of "Mau Mau": Nationalism and Colonialism in Kenya*. New York: Praeger, 1966; reprint, Nairobi: TransAfrica Press, 1985.

Savage, Donald, and Munro, J. Forbes. "Carrier Corps Recruitment in the British East Africa Protectorate, 1914–1918." *Journal of African History*, v. 7, (1966), pp. 313–42.

Schleh, Eugene. "Post-Service Careers of African World War Two Veterans: British East and West Africa with Particular Reference to Uganda and Ghana." Ph.D. dissertation, Yale University, 1968.

Shepperson, George. "America Through Africa and Asia." *Journal of American Studies*, v. 14, (1980), pp. 45–66.

Shiroya, O.J.E. *Kenya and World War Two: African Soldiers in the European War*. Nairobi: Kenya Literature Bureau, 1985.

Shiroya, Okete J. E. "The Impact of World War II on Kenya: The Role of Ex-Servicemen in Kenyan Nationalism." Ph.D. dissertation, Michigan State University, 1968.

Spencer, Ian. "Settler Dominance, Agricultural Production and the Second World War in Kenya." *Journal of African History*, v. 21, (1984), pp. 497–514.

Spencer, Paul. *Nomads in Alliance: Symbiosis and Growth Among the Rendille and Samburu of Kenya*. London: Oxford University Press, 1973.

Spiers, Edward. *The Late Victorian Army, 1868–1902*. Manchester: Manchester University Press, 1992.

Teffen, Mary; Mortimore, Michael; and Gichuki, Francis. *More People Less Erosion: Environmental Recovery in Kenya*. Chichester: John Wiley & Sons, 1994.

Throe, David W. *Economic and Social Origins of Mau Mau*. Nairobi: Heinemann Kenya, 1988.

Trustram, Myna. *Women of the Regiment: Marriage and the Victorian Army*. Cambridge: Cambridge University Press, 1984.

White, Luise. *The Comforts of Home: Prostitution in Colonial Nairobi*. Chicago: University of Chicago Press, 1990.

White, Luise. "Separating the Men from the Boys: Constructions of Gender, Sexuality, and Terrorism in Central Kenya, 1939–1959." *International Journal of African Historical Studies*, v. 23, (1990), pp. 1–25.

INDEX

ABOUT THE AUTHOR

TIMOTHY H. PARSONS holds joint appointment as a Visiting Assistant Professor in the History Department and the African and Afro-American Studies Program at Washington University in St. Louis. Specializing in the social history of colonial Africa, he has conducted field research in both African military service and colonial education in Kenya, Malawi, and South Africa.

ISBN 0-325-00141-3

90000>

HARDCOVER BAR CODE